PERSPECTIVES ON THE STUDY OF SPEECH

Edited by

PETER D. EIMAS
Brown University

JOANNE L. MILLER
Northeastern University

LEA LAWRENCE ERLBAUM ASSOCIATES, PUBLISHERS
1981   Hillsdale, New Jersey

P95. P47

Lawrence Erlbaum Associates, Inc., Publishers
365 Broadway
Hillsdale, New Jersey 07642

Library of Congress Cataloging in Publication Data
Main entry under title:

Perspectives on the study of speech.

Bibliography: p.
Includes index.
1. Speech.   I. Eimas, Peter D.   II. Miller, Joanne L.
P95.P47   001.54′2   80-39499
ISBN 0-89859-052-3

Printed in the United States of America

Contents

Preface

The study of speech is an interdisciplinary endeavor that draws on the resources of many fields of science, from linguistics and psychology to ethology and engineering. It has, like many fields of study, experienced an unprecedented and, as yet, undiminished period of growth during the past several decades. The reasons for this growth are many and include the scientific Zeitgeist, the multidisciplinary nature of the science of speech, and, perhaps most importantly, the technological developments that permit the accurate and reliable assessments of empirical phenomena and tests of interesting and competing ideas. Certainly, the development and continuous refinement of instruments and techniques that could analyze and synthesize speech with great precision, as well as record and analyze the electrophysiological indicants of speech production, have yielded knowledge that otherwise would not be possible.

The acquisition of this knowledge has occurred in virtually all of the research areas that comprise the study of speech, although not always to the same extent. Indeed, in some aspects of research, progress has been so extensive and so rapid that it is difficult to believe that it has happened in the relatively short period of time since the early 1950s. During this period, we have learned, for example, much of what is known about the acoustic correlates of phonetic distinctions and their perception, the neuromuscular activity of speech production, and the inherent abilities that the human infant brings to the task of learning to perceive, produce, and understand the sounds of speech. We must note, however, that although we are willing to argue that the study of speech has met with notable success in recent times, we do not wish to imply that we are on the verge of achieving a comprehensive understanding of the processes and laws that govern speech. There is, as in all sciences, much that remains unknown.

In bringing this collection of original contributions together, we intended to convey to the reader some of the recent advances in the study of speech along with some of the current approaches to issues and controversies. It was also our intention to select topics and authors that together reflected the very pronounced diversity that has been and continues to be characteristic of the study of speech. This diversity is evident in the present collection of papers in the range of specific research topics, methodologies, and nature of the theoretical descriptions, and is even found in the academic backgrounds and departmental associations of our contributors, there being at least five different disciplines represented among the 14 authors. In part because of the diversity of the selections, we have included brief comments before each chapter that provide some background with respect to the issues and history of the discussion that follows. We hope that our remarks are sufficient to provide a frame of reference that readers will find helpful, especially those whose expertise is not in the study of speech.

We recognize, of course, that our choices of topics and authors are a part of our own values and biases regarding the importance and potential influence of our selections. There are omissions of areas of content and distinguished investigators, which will be apparent to our colleagues and which will draw their criticism, although, we suspect, not always with a single, collective voice. We can only apologize for these omissions, and hope that our selections prove to be helpful discussions of the contemporary study of speech.

Peter D. Eimas
Joanne L. Miller

PERSPECTIVES ON
THE STUDY OF SPEECH

1 The Search for Invariant Acoustic Correlates of Phonetic Features

Kenneth N. Stevens
Massachusetts Institute of Technology

Sheila E. Blumstein
Brown University

Editors' Comments

One of the major activities in the study of speech has been the search for the acoustic correlates of perceived phonetic distinctions. The history of this research can be viewed as a three-part story. In the initial period, investigators tended to assume that the waveform of speech contained acoustic properties that mapped onto phonetic structures in a relatively simple one-to-one manner. However, the empirical evidence proved to be just the opposite: invariant properties could not be found and in their stead investigators inevitably discovered complex mappings between the acoustic signal and the phonetic percept. Of course, the failure to find acoustic invariance should not be taken to mean that progress in describing the acoustic structure of speech was limited. Indeed, in many respects the search was quite successful as evidenced, for example, by our ability to produce rather intelligible synthetic speech.

In the middle period of the search for acoustic correlates, which extends to the present, researchers, virtually abandoning the assumption of acoustic invariance, continued to obtain evidence for a complex, context-conditioned relation between the acoustic signal and the perceived phonetic structure. However, there are also, at present, investigators who have argued that earlier failures to find invariance were essentially the result of incorrectly characterizing the acoustic information. They have resumed the search for invariance and, in so doing, have initiated the most recent phase of this work. The research of Stevens and Blumstein is one of the most extensive efforts along these lines. In their chapter, they describe their work to discover the invariant acoustic information for perceived distinctions in place of articulation and speculate on possible invariant cues for other phonetic distinctions. In addition, they discuss the significance of their findings for issues related to the development of speech perception and to the nature of processing models of speech.

1

INTRODUCTION

The nature of the speech perception process in man has been the topic of considerable research and discussion for the past 20 years. The research paradigms devised to study this process, as well as the theoretical approaches taken, have been rich and imaginative. To date, there are three competing theories of the speech perception process. The first and perhaps the most widely accepted argues that the perception of speech depends ultimately on the analysis of the continuous acoustic signal to yield discrete phonetic segments (Liberman, Cooper, Shankweiler, & Studdert-Kennedy, 1967). These segments themselves have an intrinsic organization and structure based on underlying features (Chomsky & Halle, 1968; Jakobson, Fant, & Halle, 1963). The relation between the acoustic signal and the phonetic percept is not a direct one. Rather, the perception of phonetic segments requires the extraction of context-dependent cues, which are interpreted phonetically in different ways depending on the nature of the context in which the phonetic segment appears. Such a theory requires an active perceptual mechanism in which identification of phonetic segments depends on some kind of special computation or look-up procedure (cf. Halle & Stevens, 1972; Liberman et al., 1967).

The second theory also proposes that perception depends on the analysis of the speech signal into discrete phonetic features. However, unlike the context-dependent theory, it is hypothesized that the properties of speech *can* be uniquely and invariantly specified from the acoustic signal itself (Blumstein & Stevens, 1979; Cole & Scott, 1974; Fant, 1960; Stevens & Blumstein, 1978) and that these properties are closely related to the distinctive features. The hypothesis is that the speech perception system responds in a distinctive way when a particular sound has these properties so that the process of decoding the sound into a representation in terms of distinctive features can be a fairly direct one. The role of context-dependent cues in the acoustic invariance theory is not denied but is rather considered to provide only alternative or secondary cues to the phonetic dimensions of speech, whereas the invariant properties provide the basic or primary cues. (The notion of primary and secondary cues is elaborated further in the following section.)

The third theory denies neither acoustic invariance nor contextual dependence and their relation to phonetic segments, but proposes that in ongoing speech it may be necessary to have recourse to the identification of acoustic patterns of larger units rather than to features and segments. As a result, word recognition may depend on the extraction of the entire acoustic pattern for a word or syllable as a gestalt without further analysis in terms of component features (Klatt, 1979).

In the past few years, we have focused our research on an examination of the second theory described above, the theory of acoustic invariance. It is the object of this chapter to elucidate this theory, discuss its theoretical and experimental bases, and consider the implications of these findings for a model of speech perception.

The theory of acoustic invariance is based on several major assumptions. The first, of course, is that acoustic invariance corresponding to a particular phonetic category or distinctive feature resides in the acoustic signal. Second, this invariance is not derivable from an analysis of individual components of the acoustic signal, as might be observed in particular regions of an intensity-frequency-time display or spectrogram of speech, but rather is provided by *integrated* acoustic properties that may encompass several of these components. These properties are sampled at particular points in time, often where there is a rapid change in the amplitude or in the spectrum. Thus, for example, although individual components of the acoustic signal, such as the burst, onset frequencies of particular formants, or directions of formant transitions, do not provide invariant cues to place of articulation in stop consonants (Cooper, Delattre, Liberman, Borst, & Gerstman, 1952; Delattre, Liberman, & Cooper, 1955; Schatz, 1954), the shape of the spectrum sampled over a particular time interval at the release of the consonant does seem to provide an invariant pattern (Blumstein & Stevens, 1979; Fant, 1960). The spectrum shape includes *all* the acoustic information within the first 20 msec or so at the release of the consonant and, in this sense, reflects an integrated acoustic property.

We make three further assumptions concerning the theory of acoustic invariance. The nature of these invariant properties and their relation to phonetic segments reflects: (1) the way in which the articulatory mechanism constrains the possible range of speech sounds (i.e., there is evidence that a limited set of articulatory configurations produces stable acoustic patterns [Stevens, 1972]); (2) the way in which the perceptual mechanism constrains the possible range of speech sounds (i.e., categorical perception studies have shown that the physical scale along which pairs of sounds differ is not the same as the scale used by the auditory system to judge differences between speech sounds [Liberman, Harris, Hoffman, & Griffith, 1957]); and (3) the way in which the set of classes of speech sounds based on underlying distinctive features are defined. These distinctive features provide the framework for the phonological grammar of the language system. That is, correspondences among speech sounds form natural classes, which in turn help to structure the nature of the linguistic grammar (Halle, 1972; Jakobson, Fant & Halle, 1963).

The theory of acoustic invariance has been elaborated most completely for place of articulation in stop consonants. Considerations from acoustic theory, analysis of acoustic characteristics of natural speech production, and the results of experiments investigating the perception of synthetic speech have contributed to the elaboration of the theory, and we review these findings in the following section. Nevertheless, a complete theory of speech requires that it can characterize *all* of the features found in natural language. In this chapter we do not attempt to discuss all of the properties that might be relevant to the formulation of a system of features. We do, however, attempt to go beyond the properties that characterize place of articulation for stop consonants, and we review some of the basic properties relevant to the consonant system in English.

THE NATURE OF SPEECH SOUNDS

Before discussing in detail the various acoustic properties of speech sounds and their perceptual correlates, we should first place boundaries on the characteristics of the sounds that we are considering. All speech sounds appear to have a particular kind of structure in both the temporal and spectral dimensions that distinguish them from nonspeech and musical sounds, and the studies we describe here are concerned primarily with the perception of sounds having this structure.

One common attribute of speech sounds is that the spectra are usually characterized by a series of rather narrow peaks. This property can be observed in the spectra in Fig. 1.1. Spectra of speech sounds are not flat or monotonically changing with frequency, but rather they tend to exhibit peaks and valleys, the spectral amplitude in the valleys being 10–30 dB below the amplitude of the spectrum at the peaks. One way of specifying the properties of such a spectrum is to say it contains several narrow peaks, but another way of describing the spectrum is to say it contains valleys or ''holes'' that are sufficiently deep in relation to the peaks. When this kind of spectral structure is weakened by reducing the amplitudes of the spectral peaks or by filling in the valleys of the spectrum, the speech-like nature of the sound is weakened or disappears (Remez, 1979).

A second universal attribute of speech is that the amplitude of the sound rises and falls. The rises and falls are associated with the syllabic structure, as shown in the example of Fig. 1.1. Peaks in amplitude occur during vowels when the vocal tract is maximally open, and minima in amplitude occur during consonants when the vocal tract is constricted. The amplitude maxima or minima normally occur at a rate of 3–4 per second.

A third broad property of speech sounds is that there are changes in the short-time spectrum of the sound. These variations occur as a consequence of movements of the spectral peaks and of changes in the relative amplitudes of the peaks. Often these spectral changes are quite rapid and occur over time intervals of a few milliseconds up to 40-odd milliseconds (as illustrated by the spectra sampled in the vicinity of the [b] release in Fig. 1.1), but sometimes the spectrum changes more slowly.

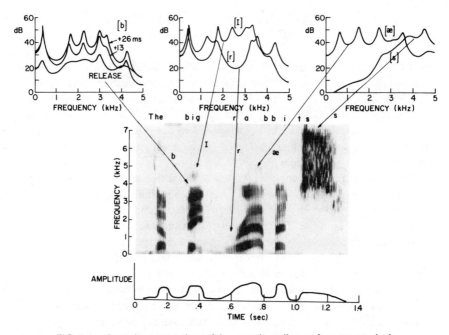

FIG. 1.1.   Several representations of the acoustic attributes of an utterance in the frequency and time domains. Middle: Spectrogram of the utterance "The big rabbits." Bottom: Variation of amplitude versus time during the utterance. Top: Spectra sampled at various points throughout the utterance as indicated. In the case of [b] at the left, three spectra are shown, and these are obtained by sampling at three points in time 13 msec apart. The spectra are computed for the preemphasized waveform, and are smoothed using a linear prediction procedure.

We suggest that these three attributes provide a set of constraints within which the detailed properties of individual speech sounds are described—an acoustic baseline or "posture," as it were. The implication is that the auditory system is predisposed toward extracting detailed properties from sound signals that have a frequency-time structure of this type. A signal with these three attributes provides the possibility for a wide variety of properties to which the auditory system can respond distinctively. That is, the auditory system may be predisposed to produce a variety of distinctive responses when the properties of the sound are characterized by change or by lack of constancy: changes in spectral amplitude over frequency at a fixed time, changes in amplitude over time, and changes in spectral peaks and valleys over time. As we proceed to discuss the acoustic properties and the perception of different phonetic classes, it will always be understood that we are restricting our consideration to sounds that have these general attributes.

INVARIANT PROPERTIES FOR
PLACE OF ARTICULATION

One of the phonetic dimensions along which consonants in all languages are classified is the place-of-articulation dimension, i.e., the location of the point of maximum consonantal constriction in the vocal tract. In most languages, at least three places of articulation can be distinguished: labial, alveolar, and velar. Within each of these classes, further subdivisions are made in many languages, and, in addition, some languages have consonants with constrictions in the uvular and pharyngeal regions.

The results of acoustic analyses have suggested that stop consonants can be characterized by integrated properties (Fant, 1960; Halle, Hughes, & Radley, 1957; Stevens, 1975). These properties reflect the configuration of acoustic events that occur at the release of a stop consonant—acoustic events that are a consequence of a particular place of articulation. It has been implied (Fant, 1960, 1973; Fischer-Jorgensen, 1954, 1972; Stevens, 1975) that the auditory system responds to these properties in an integrated manner rather than by processing each of a number of simpler properties and combining these at a later stage.

These issues have been examined more recently in a series of studies focusing on acoustic theory, acoustic analysis of natural speech, and perception of synthetic speech for stop and nasal consonants (Blumstein & Stevens, 1979, 1980; Stevens & Blumstein, 1978). We turn now to a review of this work.

Theoretical Considerations

The shape of the spectrum sampled at the release of a stop consonant for different burst frequencies and formant starting frequencies can be predicted from the theory of sound production in the vocal tract (Fant, 1960). This theoretical analysis can be used as a guide for examining the spectra at the onset for naturally produced syllables beginning with stop consonants and for interpreting the results of speech perception experiments. Thus, before discussing data from speech-production and speech-perception studies, we review briefly this theoretical background.

When the articulatory structures achieve a particular configuration, the acoustic cavities formed by these structures have certain natural frequencies or formants. These formants are manifested in the sound as spectral peaks at particular frequencies. When a constriction is made in the vocal tract in the oral cavity, the frequency of the first formant (F1) is always lower than it is for a vowel. On the average, the second and higher formants (F2, F3, etc.) occur at regular intervals in frequency, the average spacing between these higher formants being about 1 kHz for adult male speakers, and somewhat greater for adult female speakers and children. The spectrum envelope for a sound with the lowered F1 corresponding to a constricted vocal tract and with F2 and higher formants at their average frequencies is shown in the upper panel of Fig. 1.2. This envelope assumes that the acoustical excitation of the vocal tract arises from normal glottal vibration.

Depending on the position and shape of the constriction, however, the frequencies of the second and higher formants undergo displacements upward and downward relative to their average values. These shifts in the frequencies of the spectral peaks are accompanied by changes in the relative amplitudes of these peaks, such that the gross shape of the spectrum can be influenced by changes in the formant frequencies.

Shifting of F2, F3, and higher formants downward in frequency (while keeping F1 at the same frequency) causes a decrease in the amplitudes of the higher formant peaks in relation to the lower formants, as shown in the upper panel of Fig. 1.2. Such a downward shift in the formant frequencies occurs when a constriction is made at the lips, and hence this is the short-time spectrum that is to be expected at the onset of voicing for a labial consonant immediately after release of the constriction. The reduction of the amplitudes of the higher formant peaks arises from the fact that, as the frequency of a given formant Fn shifts downward, the spectral peaks arising from formants of higher frequencies ride vertically up and down, so to speak, on the "skirts" of the formant Fn. Thus a decrease in the frequency Fn causes a reduction of the amplitudes of the higher formant peaks (Fant, 1956; Stevens & House, 1961). On the other hand, shifting of F2, F3, and higher formants upward in frequency (while keeping F1 at the same frequency) causes an increase in the amplitudes of the higher formants (e.g., F4 and F5) in relation to the lower formants (e.g., F2), as shown in the same figure. Such a configuration of formants is expected for an alveolar consonant.

Similar shifts in the relative amplitudes of the higher formants, and hence changes in the gross shape of the spectrum for different places of articulation, will also occur in the spectrum sampled in the aspirated portion of the sound following the release of an aspirated voiceless consonant. The theoretical considerations are the same, except that the source of excitation for the vocal tract now consists of turbulence noise at the glottis, rather than glottal vibration, and, as a consequence, there is less spectral energy in the region of F1 and possibly F2. Furthermore, the spectrum in the low-frequency region (in the vicinity of F1) may be affected by acoustic coupling through the glottis to the trachea (Fant, Ishizaka, Lindquist, & Sundberg, 1972).

At the release of a syllable-initial alveolar voiced or voiceless consonant in English, a burst of turbulence noise (sometimes called frication noise) is generated at the constriction. This burst usually occurs just prior to the onset of voicing for initial voiced stops, and just prior to the onset of aspiration noise for voiceless stops. This noise source excites the higher vocal-tract resonances (usually F4 and F5 and higher) but produces only weak acoustic excitation of the lower formants (F2 and F3), resulting in a burst spectrum like that shown by the dashed line in the middle panel of Fig. 1.2. This burst spectrum contributes to the overall

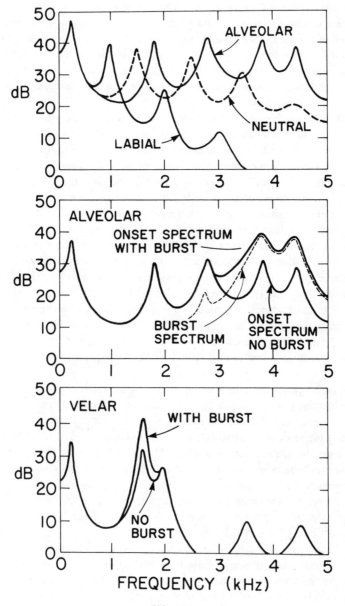

FIG. 1.2.

property of the gross shape of the spectrum sampled at the consonant release by accentuating the amplitudes of the high-frequency peaks in relation to the lower peaks. The solid line in the figure shows the spectrum for a voiced alveolar stop consonant sampled at the onset to encompass both the burst and the initial 10 or so msec at voicing onset. Note that the burst enhances the greater energy in the higher frequencies (F4 and F5).

For the labial consonant, the spectrum of the burst is relatively flat, because the frication noise source at the lips tends to excite all of the formants about equally. The burst is, however, relatively weak, and its influence on the overall spectrum shape at the onset of the consonant is probably relatively small. As a consequence of the burst, there could be a tendency toward a somewhat flatter onset spectrum than the theoretical labial spectrum without a burst, shown in the upper panel of Fig. 1.2.

Because the resonances of the cavities anterior and posterior to the point of constriction tend to be roughly equal in the production of velar consonants, the second and third formants are often relatively close together at onset. The acoustic consequence of the proximity of the two formants is to enhance the amplitudes of both spectral peaks in relation to the amplitudes of higher formants. The lower panel of Fig. 1.2 shows the theoretical spectrum envelope at the onset of a voiced velar stop. As the noise burst at the release of a velar stop consonant excites the resonance of the vocal-tract cavity anterior to the constriction, it is usually continuous with either the second or third formant of the following vowel (depending on whether it is a back or front vowel). Thus the spectrum of the burst has a relatively narrow peak in the vicinity of the proximate second and third formants at the onset of voicing. The presence of this burst then enhances the spectral energy concentration in the mid-frequency region. The lower portion of Fig. 1.2 shows the theoretical spectra at onset for a voiced velar stop with and without burst. As in the case of the labial and alveolar consonants, it is expected that the onset spectrum for a voiceless aspirated velar consonant in natural speech will be similar to the spectrum shown in this figure, except that the spectral peak

FIG. 1.2. (*Opposite page*) Top: The dashed line represents the theoretical spectrum obtained with a voice source and with a low first-formant frequency and the second and higher formants located at the neutral positions of 1500, 2500, 3500, and 4500 Hz. Also shown are theoretical spectra for formant locations corresponding to an alveolar consonant (upward shifts of F2, F3, and F4) and a labial consonant (downward shifts of F2 and higher formants. Middle: The spectrum for voice-source excitation of formants corresponding to an alveolar consonant is shown (from the upper panel), together with a theoretical spectrum for a noise burst at the release of an alveolar consonant (dashed line), and a composite spectrum obtained with both sources. Bottom: The theoretical spectrum for voice-source excitation of formants corresponding to a velar consonant is shown, together with the modified spectrum when a noise burst is present. (Adapted from Stevens & Blumstein, 1978.)

corresponding to F1 will be missing, because the aspiration noise source has little energy at low frequencies.

On the basis of these theoretical considerations, then, we observe that the gross spectrum shapes sampled at consonant release are quite different for alveolar, labial, and velar stop consonants. For alveolars, there is spectral energy over a wide frequency range, but the spectrum rises with increasing frequency. In the case of the labials, there is also a diffuse spread of spectral energy, but the gross shape is flat or falling. Velars, on the other hand, are characterized by a prominent spectral peak or spectral compactness in the mid-frequency range.

The theoretical spectra for the various places of articulation for voiced stop consonants in the absence of bursts should be similar to the spectra sampled at the release of nasal consonants with the same place of articulation. Nasal consonants are normally produced with glottal excitation, and the formant frequencies at the release of a nasal consonant with a given place of articulation should be similar to the frequencies at the release of a stop consonant with the same place of articulation. In fact, these theoretical spectrum shapes should be obtained at the release or implosion of any constricted vocal-tract configuration corresponding to the labial, alveolar, and velar places of articulation, including voiced and voiceless stop consonants, nasals, and fricatives.

As long as the relative positions of the formants remain roughly the same, the absolute frequencies of the formants in Fig 1.2 may shift up or down without affecting the gross shapes of the theoretical spectra discussed in the foregoing. These formant shifts at consonantal release would be expected when a given stop is followed by different vowel environments. These theoretical notions suggest that the gross shape of the short-term spectrum sampled at the consonantal release provides invariant acoustic properties for the various places of articulation for stop, nasal, and fricative consonants, and further, these properties for each of the places of articulation occur independently of the vowel context of the given consonant.

The hypothesis that invariant properties can be derived from sampling the spectrum at onset applies as well to the spectrum sampled at the offset or at the instant of vocal-tract closure in a vowel–consonant syllable. The formant frequencies at this instant of time approach target values appropriate to the consonantal place of articulation, and consequently the spectrum shape should be similar to the theoretically derived spectra illustrated in Fig. 1.2 provided that glottal excitation of the vocal tract continues up to the point of consonantal closure. Further, if a final stop consonant is released, the spectrum sampled at the release should show characteristics similar to those of the burst previously described, and consequently these spectra should have the appropriate gross shapes corresponding to the different places of articulation. Thus a perceptual mechanism that samples spectra at onsets and at offsets in terms of attributes of their gross shape could, in principle, classify similarly both syllable-initial and syllable-final consonants.

Evidence From Acoustical Measurements

Given the foregoing theoretical considerations, it would be expected that acoustical measurements of short-term spectra in natural speech would reveal distinctive shapes for the various places of articulation. The results of several studies investigating the spectrum of the burst in isolation (Halle, Hughes, & Radley, 1957; Zue, 1976) and of the initial few tens of milliseconds following consonantal release (Fant, 1960; Jakobson et al., 1963; Searle, Jacobson, & Kimberley, 1979) have suggested that distinctive patterns for place of articulation can be derived from a short-time spectral analysis. These patterns can be seen in the examples of spectra for several naturally produced voiced and voiceless stop consonants shown in Fig. 1.3—in particular, the gross spectrum shape is diffuse-rising for alveolar consonants, diffuse-falling or flat for labial consonants, and compact for velar consonants. These spectra were obtained by using a window length of 26 msec beginning at the consonantal release and were derived by means of a 14-pole linear prediction algorithm, which preemphasized the higher frequencies (Blumstein & Stevens, 1979; Stevens & Blumstein, 1978). The 26-msec window encompasses different portions of the voiced and voiceless stop consonants. For voiced stops, the time window includes the burst as well as some portion of voicing onset (e.g., [b]) or only the burst (e.g., [g]). For voiceless stops, the window includes the initial frication burst and a portion of the aspiration.

Although the obtained spectral shapes for these few samples of natural speech utterances are qualitatively similar to the theoretically derived spectra, it is necessary to determine the extent to which such correspondences exist in a wide variety of utterances produced by different speakers and in different vowel contexts. That is, do invariant acoustic properties reside in natural speech utterances, and if so, are these properties context-independent? In order to address this question, it was necessary to develop a more quantitative measure of the gross spectral shapes corresponding to each place of articulation. To this end, a series of templates was developed in an attempt to reflect each of the spectral properties—diffuse-rising, diffuse-falling or flat, and compact. The configurations of these templates were determined in part from theoretical considerations and in part from an examination of a limited set of consonant-vowel utterances consisting of the initial consonants [b d g] in the environments of the vowels [i e a o u] produced by two male speakers.

The three templates are shown on the three panels on the left side of Fig. 1.4. The panels on the right side of the figure illustrate the application of the templates to spectra that fit and to those that fail to fit the templates. In general, these templates specify ranges of acceptable relative amplitudes of peaks in the spectra at consonantal onsets and offsets. Specific details concerning the procedures for fitting the spectra to the templates are given elsewhere (Blumstein & Stevens, 1979).

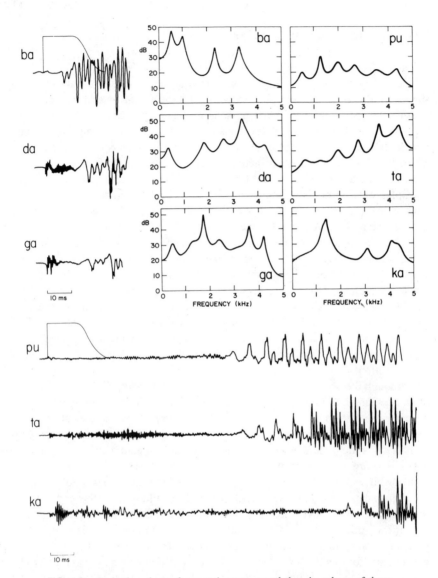

FIG. 1.3. Examples of waveforms and spectra sampled at the release of three voiced and three voiceless stop consonants as indicated. Superimposed on two of the waveforms is the time window (of width 26 msec) that is used for sampling the spectrum. Short-time spectra are determined for the first difference of the sampled waveform (sampled at 10 kHz) and are smoothed using a linear prediction algorithm; i.e., they represent all-pole spectra that provide a best fit to the calculated short-time spectra with preemphasis. (From Blumstein and Stevens, *Journal of the Acoustical Society of America*, 1979, *66,* 1001–1018. Copyright 1979 by the Acoustical Society of America. Reprinted by permission.)

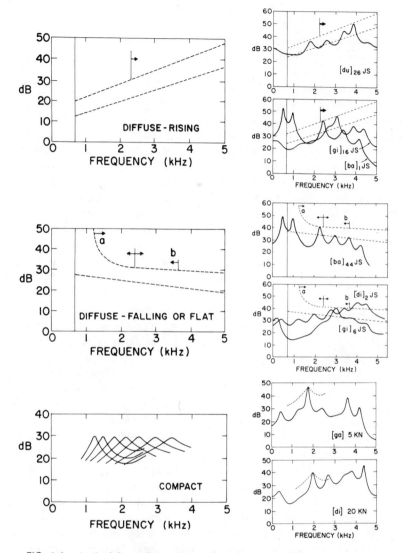

FIG. 1.4. At the left are shown the templates that are used to test whether a spectrum is diffuse-rising (top), diffuse-falling or flat (middle), or compact (bottom). For diffuse-rising template, the arrow indicates that a spectra peak above 2200 Hz is to be fitted to the upper reference line of the template. The vertical markers on the diffuse-falling template indicate regions where spectral peaks should occur (at least one in the range 1200–2400 Hz, and one in the range 2400–3600 Hz) within the reference lines if a spectrum is to match this template. For a spectrum to fit the compact template, a prominent mid-frequency spectral peak must fit entirely within one of the contours of the template. Two panels are shown to the right of each template. In each case, the upper panel shows a spectrum that fits the template, and the lower panel gives examples of spectra that do not fit the template.

13

The diffuse-rising template is represented by two reference lines about 10 dB apart. A spectrum is matched against the template by first adjusting its amplitude such that one peak is tangent to the upper reference line above 2200 Hz, and all other peaks are below that line. The overall requirement of a spectrum, if it is to fit this template, is that at least two spectral peaks minimally 500 Hz apart must lie within the reference lines (the diffuseness requirement), and that there is a general upward tilt of the spectrum with increasing frequency (the rising re-quirement). At least one peak of energy must fall above 2200 Hz and be higher in amplitude than a lower frequency peak. Thus, the template characterizes as belonging to a single class those spectra having a diffuse-rising spread of spectral energy with no one peak dominating the spectrum. The specific onset frequencies of the individual formants are, within limits, of no consequence. What is critical, however, is the gross shape of the onset spectrum. An example of a spectrum meeting the required characteristics is shown at the right of the diffuse-rising template in Fig. 1.4, superimposed on the template. Examples of spectra that do not have diffuse-rising characteristics are shown in the second panel from the top at the right of the figure. The spectrum of the [g] shows just one prominent peak, and thus does not satisfy the diffuseness requirement. Although the spectrum of [b] is diffuse, in that it contains energy spread over a range of frequencies, the spectral energy distribution is falling with increasing frequency, and thus does not fit within the template.

The property characteristic of labial consonants is diffuse-falling or diffuse-flat, and the template designed to fit these spectral shapes is shown in the middle panel of the left side of Fig. 1.4. A spectrum is matched against the template by adjusting its amplitude such that one peak is tangent to the upper reference line between 1200 and 3600 Hz, and all other peaks within the range are below that line. To fit the requirements of this template, a spectrum must have at least two spectral peaks a minimum of 500 Hz apart falling within the reference lines, one peak falling below 2400 Hz and the other peak falling within the range of 2400–3600 Hz. There is no condition on the amplitude of spectral peaks below 1200 Hz, but peaks above 3600 Hz must be below the upper reference line. An example of a spectrum of a labial consonant with the required characteristics is superimposed on the diffuse-falling template at the right of the figure. Examples of spectra with shapes that do not fit these characteristics are also shown. Al-though the [d] spectrum is diffuse, i.e., there are several peaks spread out in the frequency domain, the distribution of the spectrum is rising rather than either falling or flat; the [g] spectrum shows one prominent mid-frequency peak and thus is not diffuse.

The property that describes a velar consonant is the presence of a prominent spectral peak in the mid-frequency range. Two spectral peaks that are separated by 500 Hz or less are treated as comprising a single gross spectral peak. A peak is "prominent" if there are no other peaks nearby and if it is larger than adjacent peaks, so that the peak stands out, as it were, from the remainder of the spectrum. This is the sense in which the spectrum is compact. The template shown in the lower left panel of Fig. 1.4 attempts to capture this property. This template consists of an overlapping set of spectral peaks in the mid-frequency range (from 1200–3500 Hz). To meet the requirement for spectral compactness, a single peak in the spectrum of the sound must fit within a matching peak of the template. Further, there can be no other peak in the spectrum projecting through the reference line, nor can there be another peak of the same or greater magnitude falling below 1200 Hz or above 3500 Hz. An example of a spectrum that meets the requirements of the compact template is shown at the right of the compact template in Fig. 1.4. Note that the 1400 Hz peak of the spectrum is matched to a low-frequency peak on the template. Also shown at the right is an example of a spectrum that does not fit the compact template. A second peak (at 2500 Hz) juts through the major spectral peak of the template; further, there is an energy peak above 3500 Hz, which is higher in amplitude than the major mid-frequency peak.

Once the individual templates were developed and the particular fitting procedures were determined, a large number of natural speech utterances were collected in order to serve as a data base for determining the extent to which the spectra of initial and final voiced and voiceless stop consonants fit the hypothesized shapes. A total of six subjects, four male and two female, read a list of CV utterances containing five repetitions of each of the stop consonants [p t k b d g] in the context of the five vowels [i e ɑ o u], and a listing of VC utterances containing the same six stop consonants but preceded by the vowels [i ɛ æ ʌ u]. These 1800 utterances were tape-recorded in a sound-treated room and subsequently analyzed using the procedures for spectral analysis described earlier. Syllable-initial consonants were analyzed by the procedures shown in Fig. 1.3. For the syllable-final stop consonants, spectra were sampled at two points in the signal: at the point of consonantal closure at the end of the vowel, and at the onset of the burst that occurs at the consonantal release (if the final consonant is, in fact, released). In the measurement of the closure portion of the syllable, the peak of the spectral window was placed at the point of closure. For the release burst, the spectral measurements were analogous to those used for CV onsets with measurements made from the moment of burst release.

The spectra of the 1800 natural CV and VC utterances were individually tested against each template. A conservative strategy was adopted for assessing whether the spectral shapes were accepted or rejected by the particular template. In order to fit the template, the spectrum had to meet all the conditions specified for the template. If it did not fit for any reason, e.g., the shape was clearly wrong or the shape was correct but a peak failed to fit within the reference lines, then the spectrum was rejected. The design of the templates was such that it was possible for some spectra to fit more than one template. (See Blumstein & Stevens, 1979, for further discussion.)

Preliminary data were also obtained from about 110 alveolar and labial nasal consonants produced in consonant-vowel syllables by the same six speakers.

Spectra were sampled at the instant of consonant release, using a somewhat shorter time window than that shown in Fig. 1.3. Only the diffuse-rising and diffuse-falling templates were used in this study of the nasals.

The results of applying the three templates to all of these utterances are summarized in Table 1.1. Overall, about 83% of the initial stop consonants and about 77% of the initial nasals were correctly accepted by their respective templates. About 76% of the final-consonant bursts were also correctly accepted, but the spectra sampled at closure for alveolars and velars were rather poorly identified (31 and 52%, respectively). Initial stops and final bursts were generally correctly rejected by the templates (e.g., an alveolar stop was not accepted by the diffuse-falling or the compact templates). Final alveolars and velars, sampled at the closure, tended to have a diffuse-falling spectral shape. Initial alveolar nasals also tended (incorrectly) to fit the diffuse-falling template.

The principal conclusion from Table 1.1 (and from the details of the data from which Table 1.1 was derived) is that the templates effectively described the three types of spectra sampled at the release of stop consonants (including the release of final stop consonants) corresponding to the three different places of articulation. These spectrum shapes as defined by the templates are relatively independent of vowel context and of individual speaker characteristics. Further refine-

TABLE 1.1
Template-Matching Results for Initial and Final Stop Consonants
and for Initial Nasal Consonants[a]

	Diffuse-Rising Template	Diffuse-Falling Template	Compact Template
Initial alveolar stops	86	12	15
Final alveolars-closure	31	59	29
Final alveolars-burst	77	13	17
Initial labial stops	17	81	11
Final labials-closure	11	77	27
Final labials-burst	16	77	12
Initial velar stops	13	8	85
Final velars-closure	17	59	52
Final velars-burst	18	17	75
Initial alveolar nasals	72	67	
Initial labial nasals	10	81	

[a] The entries give the mean percentage of utterances of each consonant that were accepted by each template. Data for initial and final stop consonants are based on 300 utterances for each place of articulation (voiced and voiceless consonants, occurring in five vowel environments, and obtained from six speakers). Data for nasal consonants are preliminary, and are based on 55 utterances for each place of articulation.

ment of the analysis procedures and of the templates would undoubtedly improve the scores given in Table 1.1 for these aspects of the stop consonants.

There may be several reasons for the lack of success of the template-matching procedures for the closure of stop consonants and for initial alveolar nasals. In the case of the closure at offset, the spectral analyses obtained may reflect the fact that final consonants are often devoiced prior to closure. Consequently, the point of abrupt amplitude reduction at which the spectrum is sampled may occur several tens of msec before the closure (corresponding to the articulatory motion from the vowel to the target consonant) rather than at the actual closure itself. There are some perceptual data that are consistent with the observation that unreleased consonants often fail to show invariant acoustic properties. In particular, data from the perception of place of articulation in unreleased stop consonants indicate that identification is a good deal poorer than that obtained for final released stops, although the reported absolute level of identification varies across studies (Halle, Hughes, & Radley, 1957; Malecot, 1958; Wang, 1959).

In the case of both final consonants at closure and initial nasals, the point at which the spectrum is sampled is preceded by low-frequency energy—for the final stop consonant, it is the preceding vowel and for the initial nasal consonant, the nasal murmur. It may be that the spectral representation in the auditory system for a signal with an abrupt onset preceded by silence is different from the representation when the onset (or offset) is preceded by low-frequency spectral energy. The presence of this low-frequency energy may effectively reduce or mask the response of some neural units in the auditory system to the spectrum at the discontinuity, particularly the response to the low-frequency components of the spectrum. As a consequence, this spectral representation would show an attenuation of the low frequencies relative to the spectral representation of the onset when preceded by silence. The auditory representation of the spectra preceded by low-frequency energy would, then, tend to have a more sharply rising characteristic than the measured spectra and would presumably reflect better the diffuse-rising property of the alveolar template. Some support for this line of reasoning is provided by data on single-unit responses of the auditory nerve to stimuli with the acoustic characteristics of nasal-vowel syllables (Delgutte, 1980).

Evidence From Speech-Perception Studies

The acoustic data we have described in the foregoing section indicate that it is possible to find invariant acoustic properties that can be used to classify stop consonants according to place of articulation. It remains to be determined, however, whether these acoustic properties are utilized by a listener during the perception of these consonants. At least two approaches can be followed to gain an understanding of the acoustic information used by a listener when he is required to identify utterances containing stop consonants. One approach is to manipulate systematically the properties of the onset spectrum in a consonant-vowel syllable such that, in a series of stimuli, the spectrum changes gradually from a diffuse-falling shape through a diffuse-rising shape through a compact shape. Responses of listeners to this sequence of stimuli would then indicate the ranges of onset-spectrum shapes that give rise to labial, alveolar, and velar responses. A second approach is to strip away from the consonant-vowel stimuli all the information except the attributes that are postulated to provide the appropriate cues for place of articulation, and to determine whether the listeners can identify place of articulation from the sound that remains. This manipulation would involve removing the steady state vowel and portions of the formant transitions in the stimulus, leaving only the initial portion of the sound that contributes to the shape of the onset spectrum. Both of these approaches have been followed in a series of experiments aimed at uncovering the acoustic properties used by a listener in classifying place of articulation for stop consonants.

In the first study (Stevens & Blumstein, 1978), several series of stimuli consisting of stop consonants followed by vowels were synthesized. For each series, the vowel was the same and the starting frequency of the first formant was fixed, but the starting frequencies of the higher formants and the spectrum of an initial burst were manipulated to produce stimuli with a graded continuum of onset spectra. These stimuli were presented to listeners in random order, with a number of replications, and the listeners were instructed to identify the initial consonants as b, d, or g. For each stimulus sequence, three well-defined response regions were usually obtained, with rather sharp changes in the response functions in the vicinity of particular boundary stimuli.

Examples of onset spectra for stimuli that were identified unequivocally as [b], [d], and [g] in the series with the vowel [ɑ] are shown in Fig. 1.5 as spectra 1, 8, and 14, respectively. These spectra clearly have the gross properties of the type respectively described previously as diffuse-falling, diffuse-rising, and compact. Also shown in the figure are two spectra (5 and 10) for which the responses were equivocal. These spectrum shapes do not exhibit strongly any one of the properties defined by the templates in Fig. 1.4. Similar results were obtained with stimulus series containing other vowels.

These data provide support, then, for the notion that the process of identifying place of articulation in these syllables involves detection of the gross shape of the spectrum sampled at onset, and classifying the shape into one of the three broad categories: diffuse-falling, diffuse-rising, and compact.

In the second study (Blumstein & Stevens, 1980), listener responses were obtained to brief stimuli that reproduced acoustic events only in the initial portion of a consonant-vowel syllable. The aim was to determine whether acoustic information in this portion of the syllable was sufficient to give proper identification of consonant place of articulation.

The durations of the synthesized stimuli were in the range 10–46 msec, and the formants during this brief interval followed trajectories appropriate to

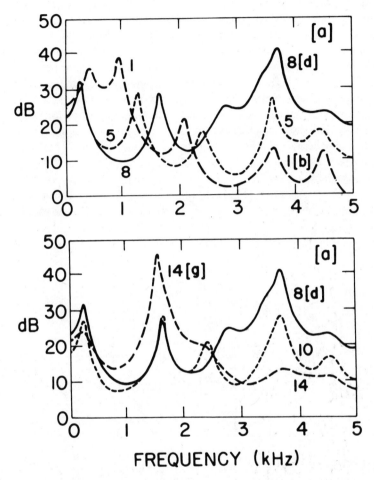

FIG. 1.5. Short-term spectra sampled at stop-consonant release for various stimuli used in identification tests. Each panel shows three spectra corresponding to three different items on a continuum of synthetic consonant-vowel stimuli ranging from [ba] to [da] (top) and [da] to [ga] (bottom). Two of the spectra (the solid line and the long-dashed line) represent stimuli in the middle of a phonetic category, for which the responses were close to 100% [b], [d], or [g], as indicated. The third spectrum in each panel (short-dashed line) represents a stimulus between phonetic categories, for which responses were equivocal. Spectra are calculated and smoothed in the manner described in connection with Fig. 1.3; i.e., they are spectra calculated using a linear prediction algorithm, with high-frequency preemphasis, and with a time window of 26 msec centered at onset. (Adapted from Stevens & Blumstein, 1978.)

consonant-vowel syllables beginning with [b], [d], or [g]. These trajectories moved toward target values corresponding to the three vowels [i, ɑ, u]. Various stimulus conditions were used, including stimuli both with and without bursts. An additional set of stimuli was produced by eliminating the movements of the second and higher formants, so that these formants remained at their frequency values at onset. Results averaged over the three vowel environments and over the straight- and moving-transition conditions are summarized in Fig. 1.6. The performance of listeners in the identification of place of articulation for these stimuli was always well above chance, even when the sounds were as short as 10 msec and when they contained no transitions of the second and higher formants. Thus the responses of the listeners tended to follow the pattern that would be expected if they were basing their identification on the gross shape of the spectrum sampled over the brief duration of the stimuli. However, lack of formant movements and the absence of a burst within this time interval did contribute to a reduction in

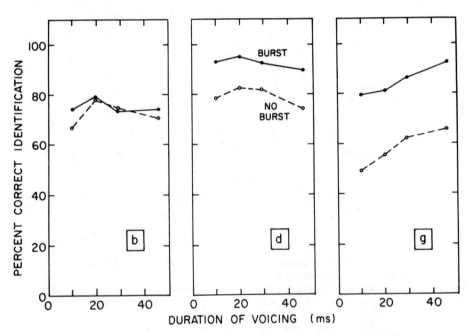

FIG. 1.6 Percent correct identification for synthetic consonant-vowel syllables with various durations of voicing as indicated on abscissa. The transitions are appropriate for the place of articulation labial (left), alveolar (middle), and velar (right). Data are shown for stimuli with bursts (solid lines) and without bursts (dashed lines). Data represent averages of responses to syllables with three different vowel contexts [i ɑ u]. (From Blumstein & Stevens, *Journal of the Acoustical Society of America*, 1980, *67*, 648–662. Copyright 1980 by the Acoustical Society of America. Reprinted by permission.)

the overall performance level. Further, there were a few stimuli (particularly velars before the vowel [i]) for which the identification responses were inconsistent. (See Blumstein & Stevens 1980, for further discussion.)

A further finding with these brief stimuli was that listeners were usually able to identify which of the three vowels [i ɑ u] the formant trajectories were moving toward, even for stimuli that were so short that they contained only one or two glottal pulses. Apparently, then, at least two kinds of information are packaged within these short stimuli and are accessible to a listener. The gross shape of the spectrum sampled over the initial portion of the stimulus (or perhaps over the entire stimulus duration for the very short stimuli) indicates the place of articulation of the consonant, based on whether it is diffuse-rising, diffuse-flat or falling, or compact. Other attributes of the spectrum, such as the frequencies of the spectral peaks sampled at the termination of the stimulus, are sufficient to enable the listener to determine the identity of the vowel.

In a final experiment with brief synthesized consonant-vowel sounds, several continua of stimuli were produced, spanning the range of acoustic characteristics (at onset) from [b] to [d] to [g] (Blumstein & Stevens, 1980). Three such continua were generated, with formant trajectories moving toward frequencies corresponding to the vowels [i], [ɑ], and [u]. Two stimulus durations (20 and 46 msec) were used. An additional set of stimulus continua was generated in which the second and higher formants remained at their frequency values at onset. Listener responses to these stimuli showed that the continua were for the most part divided into three categories with reasonably sharp boundaries, although there were a few exceptions. A general finding was that, when the spectrum sampled at stimulus onset was not a clear exemplar of one of the three gross shapes postulated for the three places of articulation, then the listeners utilized available information concerning the time course of the formant trajectories. Thus, for example, if the spectrum was diffuse but did not show either a rising or falling slope, then a listener would tend to identify the consonant as [b] if the second formant was rising and as [d] if it was falling.

The results of these experiments with brief stimuli excerpted from the onsets of synthesized consonant-vowel syllables support the hypothesis that information with regard to place of articulation for a voiced stop consonant resides in the initial 10–20 msec of a consonant-vowel syllable. The motions of the formants immediately following the consonantal release do not appear to contribute essential information regarding place of articulation, because elimination of the movements of the second and higher formants does not greatly modify the identification of consonantal place of articulation, given appropriate (i.e., unambiguous) onset spectra. The fact that consonant identification deteriorates only slightly when the initial noise burst is removed supports the hypothesis that both the burst and the attributes of the sound at voicing onset contribute to a more global acoustic property that is a cue for place of articulation for stop consonants.

These observations are consistent, then, with the view that the gross properties of the spectrum sampled over the initial 10–20 msec of a stop consonant provide invariant or primary cues to place of articulation. In this view, the transitions of the formants from the release of the consonant to the vowel provide the acoustic material that links the transient events at the onset to the slowly varying spectral characteristics of the vowel (Cole & Scott, 1974; Stevens & Blumstein, 1978). These transitions ensure that no further abrupt discontinuities in the spectrum occur following the initial transient at the release. Cues such as the directions of formant motions or frequencies of particular formants at consonantal release also provide information with regard to place of articulation. These cues are secondary in the sense that, for a particular consonantal place of articulation, they depend upon the vowel context. This use of secondary cues is most clearly seen when the primary attributes of the onset spectrum are equivocal, so that the spectrum does not demonstrate strong unambiguous properties such as compactness or diffuseness, or is neutral with respect to the distinction between a diffuse-rising or diffuse-falling shape.

INVARIANT PROPERTIES FOR
OTHER PHONETIC CATEGORIES

In the preceding section, we have discussed at some length the evidence indicating that invariant acoustic properties are associated with different places of articulation for stop and nasal consonants. The place-of-articulation dimension was considered in some detail in part because a considerable amount of data on the production and perception of place of articulation for consonants is available and in part because earlier studies concluded that the acoustic cues for different places of articulation show substantial dependence on context.

We now consider the acoustic properties and perceptual correlates of several other consonantal contrasts. The point of view in this discussion is that there are invariant acoustic properties associated with each of these phonetic categories as well as the place-of-articulation categories and that the auditory system is predisposed to detect or to respond selectively to these properties. Some of the material in this section is rather speculative, because data with regard to these phonetic categories are not as extensive as data on place of articulation. However, they provide preliminary evidence supporting the theory of acoustic invariance in speech, and they suggest avenues for future research on these issues.

The Consonant–Vowel Contrast

One of the basic contrasts in language is the contrast between consonants and vowels. From the point of view of articulation, a vowel is produced with a vocal tract that is relatively open, with no narrow constrictions along the length of the tract from just above the glottis to the lips. A consonant is generated with a narrow constriction at some point in the vocal tract. Acoustically, consonants and vowels are distinguished by the nature of the changes that occur in the acoustic spectrum. For consonants, the primary acoustic consequence of a narrow constriction in the vocal tract is the existence of a rapid change in the spectrum as the articulatory structures move toward or away from the constricted configuration (Stevens, 1971). The rapid spectrum changes are preceded and followed by regions in which the spectrum changes relatively slowly. One of these regions may be silence or a region of low acoustic energy (as in the case of stop consonants), but there may be appreciable energy in both regions (e.g., for fricative consonants or nasals). One possible source of the rapid spectrum change is the rapid rise of the first formant that always accompanies an increase in the size of the constriction. Spectral changes can also occur at higher frequencies as a consequence of changes in the source of noise in the vicinity of the constriction or changes in the frequencies of the higher formants. For vowels, the acoustic consequences of a relatively open vocal tract is a well-defined steady-state formant structure with relatively slow changes over time.

Segments that are produced with a narrow constriction along the midline of the vocal tract and exhibit rapid spectrum change are identified by the feature *consonantal*. Vowels and glides, which do not give rise to a rapid spectrum change, are *nonconsonantal*. The points in time where rapid spectrum changes occur in consonantal segments can be regarded as special events or landmarks in the signal, and it is suggested that the speech perception strategy used by listeners directs attention to attributes of the signal in the vicinity of these events.

The spectrogram in Fig. 1.7, which shows the sentence "Joe took father's shoe bench out," is marked to identify the locations of the events where rapid spectrum changes occur. A time window of width about 20 msec in the vicinity of these events would indicate regions where it is postulated that attributes of the speech signal are sampled. It is these regions and their respective time windows that define the domain for analysis of the acoustic events giving rise to phonetic features such as place of articulation, voicing, etc. In a sense, we are arguing that there are "regions of high information" to which the speech-processing system is directed during ongoing speech perception. These regions are joined to other regions where the spectrum changes are relatively slow. The regions between the slow and rapid spectrum changes constitute the so-called transitions, and these may vary in duration from a few tens of milliseconds to over 100 msec. Of course it is assumed that, in addition to being directed towards the events where rapid spectrum changes occur, the speech-processing system continuously monitors and decodes the signal in the regions between these events.

In Fig. 1.8 the contrast between a *consonantal* and a *nonconsonantal* segment is illustrated in terms of the rapidity with which the spectrum changes. In the case of the syllables [ba] and [sa] there are rather abrupt changes in the spectrum in the vicinity of the consonantal release, whereas for [wa] and [ʔa] the spectrum

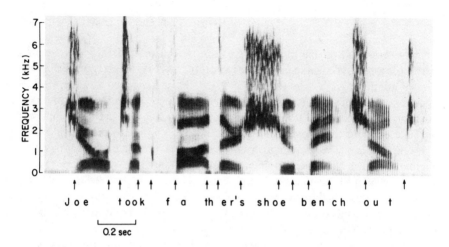

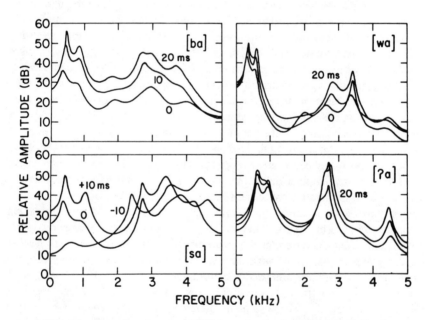

FIG. 1.7. Spectrogram of the sentence "Joe took father's shoe bench out." The arrows at the bottom indicate times where a rapid spectrum change occurs, corresponding to a consonantal event. It is hypothesized that certain phonetic features corresponding to place of articulation, voicing, etc., are signaled by the detailed acoustic properties in the vicinity of these consonantal events.

FIG. 1.8. Examples of spectra sampled at points in time in the speech signal where the spectrum is changing rapidly (in the vicinity of the consonantal release for [ba] and [sa], shown at the left), and at points where the spectrum is changing more slowly (at the point where the formants are moving most rapidly in [wa], and immediately following the glottal release in [ʔa]. In each panel, three spectra sampled at about 10-msec intervals are shown. The spectra are obtained by procedures described in connection with Fig. 1.3.

24

changes are relatively slow. There is an abrupt rise in amplitude at the release of the glottal stop, but the spectrum immediately following this abrupt rise changes very little.

The acoustic attributes that correlate with the identification of the feature *consonantal* have been examined in a series of speech perception experiments (Liberman, Delattre, Gerstman, & Cooper, 1956; Miller & Liberman, 1978). In these experiments, the rate of movement of the formants at the onset of a synthetic consonant-vowel syllable was manipulated to produce a series of stimuli ranging from those with rapidly moving formants to those with slowly moving formants. Listener responses to the consonant portion of the syllable were obtained. One of the stimulus continua was characterized by rising transitions of the formants, and encompassed a range corresponding to the consonants [b] and [w]. The results showed that fast transitions gave the response [b], which is consonantal, whereas slow transitions yielded the nonconsonantal response [w]. The boundary between these two classes occurred when the duration of the transitions was about 40 msec. The identification of stimuli with transition durations in the vicinity of 40 msec (i.e., stimuli for which the spectrum change is neither rapid nor slow) can be influenced by contextual factors (e.g., vowel duration, as reported by Miller & Liberman, 1978).

As is noted elsewhere in this chapter, the properties of the sound in the vicinity of these consonantal events are used to identify phonetic features of the consonant relating to place of articulation and voicing. The occurrence of a consonantal segment is indicated by the presence of some generalized kind of rapid spectrum change, without specification of the frequency regions or directions or other attributes of the change; certain other phonetic features of the consonant are signaled by the detailed properties of the signal in the vicinity of this rapid spectrum change. On the basis of neurophysiological and psychophysical experiments, evidence is emerging to indicate that components of the auditory system produce a specialized response when the stimulus is characterized by an abrupt onset or offset of amplitude in a particular frequency range, or by a rapidly changing spectrum (Delgutte, 1980; Kiang, 1975; Kiang, Watanabe, Thomas, & Clark, 1965) Thus, what we know about the response of the peripheral auditory system at the level of the auditory nerve and the cochlear nucleus is not inconsistent with the view that there is a specialized response to stimuli for which there are rapid spectral changes.

Continuant-Abrupt

There is a class of phonetic segments having the common acoustic property that the production of the segment produces an abrupt rise or fall in the amplitude of the sound, whether or not there is a rapid change in spectral shape. This class of *abrupt* (or stop) segments, includes the set [p t k b d g č ǰ m n ŋ ʔ]. All of these consonants except [ʔ] are a subset of the class of consonantal segments, i.e., they show an abrupt change in amplitude as well as a rapid spectrum change. (The glottal stop [ʔ]—a nonconsonantal segment—shows only an abrupt amplitude change without an accompanying rapid spectrum change, as shown in Fig. 1.8.) Abrupt consonants are produced by completely blocking the airstream at some point along the midline of the laryngeal and vocal-tract pathways. Consonantal segments, on the other hand, are produced by creating a complete or partial blockage of the airstream at a point in the vocal tract above the larynx. The closure for abrupt segments can occur at the glottis as well as above the glottis, i.e., a glottal stop is included in the class of abrupt consonants, whereas the constriction must be above the glottis for a consonantal segment. Immediately following the release of a glottal stop there is, in fact, not a rapid spectrum change.

The primary acoustic attribute that distinguishes abrupt from continuant segments is that abrupt segments show an abrupt rise in amplitude at the release (or an abrupt fall in amplitude at the implosion). The rise in amplitude occurs at all frequencies; that is, there is no frequency band for which the amplitude is greater before the release than after the release. This property seems to exist for the nasal consonants as well as for the stop consonants, because the spectrum for the nasal murmur is lower in amplitude than the spectrum immediately following the release at essentially all frequencies.

For a fricative consonant, that is, a continuant segment followed by a vowel, there may be a rather abrupt increase in amplitude over some part of the frequency range at the consonantal release, but there always appear to be other frequency regions in which the amplitude decreases, or at least does not increase, at this time. This aspect of fricative consonants can be seen in the example of Fig. 1.8, in which there is an amplitude increase at low frequencies but a decrease in some regions of the spectrum at high frequencies near the point where voicing begins. Furthermore, the amplitude increase at low frequencies is not as abrupt as that for a stop consonant.

Several experiments have examined the perceptual correlates of the feature *continuant*. These experiments have investigated listener responses to stimuli in which the abruptness of an onset or the silent interval preceding the onset were manipulated. These experiments provide an indication of the rate of increase of amplitude at the onset, and of the duration of the interval of low intensity prior to the onset, that are necessary to elicit a special response corresponding to an abrupt or stop consonant.

Experiments in which natural speech stimuli are manipulated in various ways have provided evidence that helps to define the acoustic property associated with the feature *continuant*. In one experiment, it was shown that the syllable [ša], for which the onset of the amplitude of the [š] is rather gradual, can be changed to [ča] by removing the initial part of the frication and by leaving an abrupt amplitude rise in the noise (Cutting & Rosner, 1974). The rise time at the perceptual boundary between responses of [š] and [č] was about 40 msec. In a second experiment, the word *slit* was generated, and the acoustic representation of the word was then manipulated by creating a gap of successively increasing duration between the end of the frication noise in [s] and the onset of voicing in [1] (Bastian, Delattre, & Liberman, 1959). When this duration of silence exceeded about 70 msec, the word was heard as *split*. Apparently, the onset of voicing in the [1] was sufficiently abrupt that a stop consonant was heard if the preceding silent interval was long enough. The suggestion is that about 70 msec of silence or of low amplitude is needed before an abrupt onset if the onset is to be heard as an abrupt consonant. In another class of experiments (Bailey & Summerfield, 1978; Repp, Liberman, Eccardt, & Pesetsky, 1978), the duration of a gap between a [s] or [š] and a following vowel or sonorant was manipulated, to determine the gap duration necessary to elicit the perception of a stop consonant between the fricative and the vowel. It was found that the duration required depended to some extent on the physical characteristics of the onset following the silent interval. If the onset exhibits more of the characteristics of a consonantal onset in terms of the degree of rapid spectrum change, it appears that it is a "stronger" onset, and thus requires less of a preceding silent interval.

Another experiment relevant to the perceptual correlates of the feature *abrupt* utilized nonspeech stimuli with onsets for which the rise time varied from a few msec to several tens of msec (Cutting & Rosner, 1974). These stimuli were categorized systematically by listeners: Those with rise times less than 40 msec sounded like "plucked" musical sounds, whereas those with longer rise times were identified as "bowed" sounds. Within each class, different stimuli along the continuum were essentially nondiscriminable by listeners; two stimuli with rise times of 30 and 50 msec (i. e., stimuli that were classified differently by the listeners) were easily discriminated. The implication of these results is that the auditory system is predisposed to categorize sounds with different rise times into two different classes—those with fast rise times and those with slow rise times. Such a predisposition could form the basis for the phonetic distinction between *abrupt* and *continuant* consonants.

Nasal–Nonnasal

Within the class of abrupt consonants, we can distinguish two categories—nasal and nonnasal. The nonnasal consonants are the stops [p t k b d g č ǰ]. The principal acoustic characteristic that distinguishes nasals from nonnasals is the presence or absence of an appreciable amount of energy within the closure interval, as shown in the spectrograms in Fig. 1.9. In nasal consonants, although the amplitude within this interval is lower than that in the adjacent vowel, it may only be a few dB lower at low frequencies (below about 300 Hz). There is also an appreciable amplitude in the spectrum of the nasal murmur in higher frequency regions. Some low-frequency energy may also be present in the spectrum sam-

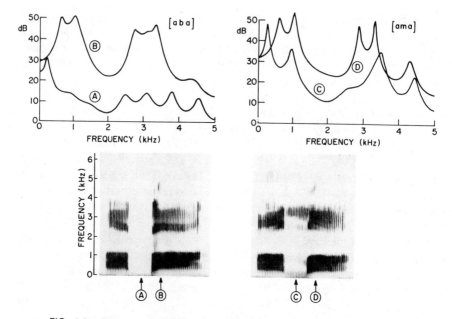

FIG. 1.9.   Bottom: Spectrograms of the utterances [ɑbɑ] and [ɑmɑ]. Top: Spectra sampled at points (as labeled) within the closure interval and in the following vowel. The figure illustrates the marked difference in relative amplitude at low frequencies for the voiced stop consonant (spectrum A) and the nasal consonant (spectrum C).

pled during the closure interval for an intervocalic voiced stop consonant. The amplitude in this low-frequency region is, however, considerably lower for voiced stops than for nasal consonants. This contrast is illustrated in Fig. 1.9, which shows the amplitude of the nasal murmur to be about 7 dB below that of the vowel.

The distinction between nasal and voiced stop consonants has been studied perceptually only in a limited way. Miller and Eimas (1977) constructed a continuum of stimuli that ranged from [b] to [m] and from [d] to [n] by effectively varying the duration of the nasal murmur. They found that if the onset of the nasal murmur preceded the consonantal release by more than 25 msec, a nasal consonant was heard, and otherwise the stimulus was perceived as beginning with a voiced stop consonant. Mandler (1976) generated oral-nasal continua by manipulating the amplitude of the nasal murmur relative to the vowel, and found that listener responses shifted from nasal to stop when this relative amplitude was in the range −8 to −15 dB. Further analysis of the stimuli used in these experiments is necessary before the nasal–nonnasal distinction can be interpreted in terms of some integrated acoustic property.

Voiced–Voiceless

There is a large number of languages that distinguish voiced from voiceless segments. Thus, for example, in English the consonants [p t k f s š] are voiceless, and are in opposition to the voiced consonants [b d g v z ž]. Voicing is indicated by the presence of low-frequency spectral energy or periodicity in the speech signal due to vibration of the vocal folds, whereas for voiceless sounds there is no such periodicity. In the case of nonconsonantal sounds (such as a vowel, or [h], or [w]), detection of voicing is relatively straightforward, and the presence or absence of low-frequency periodicity can be observed in the relatively steady-state or slowly varying time interval in the vicinity of the target configuration for the sound. For consonantal segments, acoustic data from a number of different languages suggest that the voiced feature can be identified by testing for the presence of low-frequency spectral energy or periodicity over a time interval of 20–30 msec in the vicinity of the acoustic discontinuity that precedes or follows the consonantal constriction interval (Lisker & Abramson, 1964). The time interval over which this test for periodicity is made usually extends to the left of the consonantal discontinuity for a consonant preceding a vowel (i.e., a test for prevoicing), or to the right of the consonantal implosion in the case of a syllable-final consonant (where left and right indicate times preceding and following the discontinuity).

This procedure of detecting voicelessness or voicedness is illustrated in Fig. 1.10 for contrasting stop consonants in Spanish and for fricatives in English. We observe that in the 20–30 msec prior to the rapid spectrum change near the release of the voiceless stop or the fricative, there is no low-frequency energy or periodicity in the sound, whereas low-frequency energy is present in the case of the voiced consonant.

Stop consonants in English are usually described as having a voiced–voiceless distinction, but the acoustic manifestations of this distinction differ from that previously described, particularly when the consonant occurs in prestressed position. For example, when a voiced stop consonant occurs in prestressed position, there is frequently no prevoicing, and low frequency periodicity does not begin until 0–20 msec *following* consonantal release.

In the case of a voiceless stop consonant in prestressed position in English, the consonant is aspirated, i.e., the vocal folds are in a spread configuration at the time the consonant is released, and the onset of low-frequency periodicity due to glottal vibration occurs 30 or more msec after the consonant release (Lisker & Abramson, 1964). In view of these characteristics, it may be appropriate to abandon the phonetic classification of voiced–voiceless for stop consonants in English, and rather to refer to the categories as unaspirated and aspirated, respectively, or to use terms such as tense and lax (cf. Jakobson et al., 1963).

The property that distinguishes an aspirated from an unaspirated stop consonant, then, is the absence of low-frequency periodicity in the 20-odd msec to the

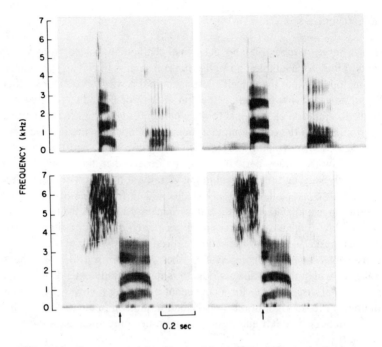

FIG. 1.10.   Spectrograms of words containing initial voiceless and voiced stop consonants in Spanish (*taco*, upper left, and *dato*, upper right) and initial voiceless and voiced fricative consonants in English (*sap*, lower left, and *zap*, lower right). The arrow below each spectrogram indicates the point in time at the consonantal release where the spectrum change is estimated to be most rapid. Low-frequency periodicity occurs immediately to the left of this boundary for voiced consonants but not for voiceless consonants.

right of the consonantal release. There are some languages that have both a voiced–voiceless and an aspirated–unaspirated contrast. Acoustic information concerning the voiced–voiceless contrast is carried by the presence or absence of low-frequency periodicity up to about 20 msec preceding the consonantal release, whereas the aspirated–unaspirated contrast is cued by detecting the presence or absence of low-frequency periodicity up to about 20 msec *following* the consonantal release.

Experiments on the perception of voiced and voiceless consonants tend to support the notion that the perceptual system uses the presence or absence of low-frequency spectral energy or periodicity as the basis for identification of the voicing feature. For the most part, these experiments have been restricted to the study of stop consonants in syllable-initial position. In these studies, series of stimuli were generated by systematically manipulating the relative time of the stop consonant release and the onset of low-frequency periodicity corresponding to vocal-fold vibration, and these stimuli were presented to listeners for identification as either voiced or voiceless consonants. In general, the results for Spanish listeners indicate that stimuli are heard as voiceless if there is no low-frequency periodicity immediately preceding the consonantal release and as voiced if there *is* low-frequency periodicity in this time interval (Williams, 1977). English listeners, on the other hand, hear an unaspirated stop consonant if low-frequency periodicity occurs within about 20 msec after consonantal release, and they hear an aspirated stop if there is no low-frequency periodicity within this time interval (Abramson & Lisker, 1970).

If we examine in somewhat greater detail the location of the boundary between the perception of voiced and voiceless consonants or between aspirated and unaspirated consonants while certain acoustic parameters in the vicinity of the stop-consonant release are manipulated, it becomes apparent that we need to define more precisely what we mean by the detection of low-frequency spectral energy or periodicity and the time interval within which this detection is to occur. One approach to the study of the acoustic correlates of the voiced–voiceless distinction for stop consonants in prestressed position is to define *voice-onset time* (VOT) as the time interval from the onset of the burst occurring at the consonantal release to the onset of the first glottal pulse, usually determined from visual observation of a spectrogram. In a number of experiments in which listener judgments were obtained to synthetic stimuli with various voice-onset times, it has been shown that the VOT corresponding to the phonetic boundary varies by a few msec depending on such factors as: (1) the frequency of the first formant at the onset of voicing (a low F1 starting frequency tends to shift the judgments in the direction of the voiced category [Stevens & Klatt, 1974]); (2) the fundamental frequency changes that occur immediately following voicing onset (a sharp drop in F_0 biases listener judgments toward the voiceless category [Haggard, Ambler, & Callow, 1970]); (3) the transitions of the second and higher formants and the spectral characteristics of the onset burst (stimuli with formant transitions and bursts appropriate for velar consonants tend to require longer VOTs to be heard as voiceless than do those for alveolars and labials [Abramson & Lisker, 1970]); and (4) the intensity of the aspiration noise relative to that of the vowel (stimuli with larger amplitude aspiration tend to be heard as voiceless [Repp, 1979]).

It has been suggested that each of these effects constitutes an additional independent cue for the perception of the voiced–voiceless distinction (Lisker, Liberman, Erickson, Dechovitz, & Mandler, 1977). An alternative view, however, is to regard each of these factors as contributing to an integrated acoustic property. As noted earlier, we postulate that the signal has the acoustic property corresponding to voicedness if there is low-frequency spectral energy or periodicity in the signal in a specified time window in the vicinity of the consonantal release. Detailed specification of this property requires that we define two events in time in the auditory representation of the signal: the time at which the consonantal release occurs, and the time at which the onset of low-frequency spectral energy or periodicity occurs.

Given the limited amount of data that are currently available on the response of the auditory system to transient onsets of various kinds, we can only speculate at present on the nature of the auditory representation of these onsets. For example, if the onset of the first formant (F1) is at a low frequency, the auditory system presumably detects the presence of relatively strong spectral energy at low frequencies, and a judgment of the onset of low-frequency periodicity can be made by examining the spectrum of the first glottal pulse. On the other hand, for an F1 onset at higher frequencies, the low-frequency energy (in the vicinity of the fundamental frequency) may not be detected in the first glottal pulse, and it may be necessary to wait until several glottal pulses have been generated before the presence of low-frequency periodicity can be detected on the basis of spectral energy above the frequency of the fundamental. Thus, a low starting frequency of F1 would be perceived as having an earlier onset of low-frequency periodicity, and consequently would be a positive cue for voicing.

Likewise, a rapidly falling F_0 at voicing onset would create a signal in which the first few glottal pulses are aperiodic, and the detection of low-frequency periodicity would then be delayed until the rate of F_0 change decreased after these initial glottal pulses. Consequently, a rapid initial fall in F_0 would create, in effect, a longer time from consonantal release to onset of low-frequency periodicity, and would tend to shift listener responses toward the voiceless category.

A more intense aspiration noise at the onset of a synthetic voiceless stop consonant could have the effect of producing a slightly earlier onset in the auditory representation than would a weaker aspiration noise, thus creating a longer time from consonantal onset to onset of low-frequency periodicity (Repp, 1979).

An explanation for the increased VOT associated with velar consonants relative to alveolars and labials is somewhat more speculative. A possible explanation is that for a velar there is a delay in the rising of F1 following the consonantal release (or at least F1 rises more slowly), and consequently, with F1 starting effectively at a lower frequency than it does with alveolars and labials, a longer VOT is needed to give a voiceless response, following the argument outlined previously.

The point of this discussion is that it may be possible to postulate an integrated property that classifies consonant segments as voiced or voiceless, independent of whether the segment is a fricative or a stop, and independent of the phonetic environment in which the segment occurs. If the integrated property is suitably defined in terms of detection of the presence or absence of low-frequency periodicity in specified regions of the signal, then several seemingly independent acoustic attributes can be regarded as contributing to the integrated property. It is recognized, however, that situations can be created, particularly with synthetic speech, in which a listener must utilize acoustic attributes that are not encompassed within this integrated property—attributes that might be labeled as secondary. Examples are the vowel shortening that precedes a word-final voiceless consonant (Denes, 1955; Klatt, 1973), the shorter duration of consonant closure for an intervocalic voiced consonant relative to a voiceless consonant, or the influence of the duration of the following vowel on the perception of voicing of an initial consonant (Summerfield, 1975). Close examination of natural speech indicates, however, that the primary property is usually present at the same time as these secondary cues.

DISCUSSION

We have attempted to show that for a number of phonetic categories it is possible to specify invariant acoustic correlates or properties that are usually independent of the phonetic context in which the segment appears. In particular, we have argued that invariant properties for the phonetic categories of language reside at various sampling points or regions in the acoustic waveform, and we have elaborated the theory of acoustic invariance most completely for place of articulation in stop consonants and nasals. However, given the analysis procedures and theoretical view discussed throughout this paper, we postulate acoustic invariance for other phonetic dimensions as well, including the features consonantal, continuant, nasal, and voicing. An hypothesis concerning the existence of these invariant properties implies that the auditory system is endowed with mechanisms that respond distinctively when a particular property is present in the acoustic stimulus. Property-detecting mechanisms of the type postulated here integrate a set of different acoustic attributes to yield an invariant or distinctive response in spite of the seeming variability of the individual attributes. We have reviewed some evidence in support of this characteristic of the auditory system.

Do these property-detecting mechanisms develop as a consequence of exposure to the sounds of speech, or are they an innate part of the infant's sound-reception system? We postulate that the mechanisms are innate and, further, that it is these kinds of mechanisms that are needed to get the speech-reception system started. When the infant is presented with speech in which particular phonetic segments occur in a variety of environments and which show considerable acoustic variability, these property-detecting mechanisms help the infant to organize the sounds into a relatively small set of classes in spite of this apparent variability. The property-detecting mechanisms of the type described here provide a framework upon which the speech/language system can be organized, and, we would argue, are critical to the acquisition of language. There is, in fact, evidence that infants are equipped with these property-detecting mechanisms and make use of them in perceiving speech and speechlike sounds as early as one month (Eimas, Siqueland, Jusczyk, & Vigorito, 1971). Two sounds with different physical attributes are not discriminated by infants if they lie within a phonetic category (as judged by adult listeners), but *are* discriminated if they lie in different phonetic classes.

We do not suggest, however, that invariant properties of the type described in this chapter are the *only* acoustic characteristics that an adult listener or even a child acquiring language uses to decode the speech signal into a phonetic representation. There are secondary, context-dependent cues that always accompany the primary properties, and it is hypothesized that these cues become utilized by the system through a process similar to that of incidental learning (Kemler, Shepp, & Foote, 1976; Shepp, Kemler, & Anderson, 1972). Having learned these secondary cues, a speaker–hearer can then utilize them in ongoing processing, particularly in situations where the primary properties are obscured by noise, or are missing, or distorted for some other reason. For example, the spectrum sampled at the onset of an initial alveolar stop consonant usually shows a diffuse-rising shape, but part of the fine structure of this spectrum shape is often a peak that lies in the frequency range 1600–1900 Hz, depending on the following vowel. This spectral peak corresponds to the starting frequency of the second formant. If high-frequency information is missing from the signal (due to noise or low-pass filtering, for example), then the diffuse-rising onset spectrum cannot be observed, and the listener must rely on the secondary cue, which is the frequency of the spectral peak corresponding to the second-formant starting frequency. This frequency must, however, be interpreted in terms of the vowel context of the consonant and, possibly, in terms of the second-formant range for a particular speaker. The ability of a listener to identify stop-consonant place of articulation based only on two-formant stimuli with appropriate initial transitions, with no higher frequency information, has been demonstrated by Cooper, et al. (1952). A number of examples of other secondary, context-dependent cues could be cited, corresponding to other phonetic dimensions.

We are arguing, then, that there is acoustic fine structure associated with the primary properties. This fine structure is available for use by the listener when it is needed to make a phonetic distinction. Variations in the acoustic details within a sound that has a given gross property could also enable a listener to make discriminations between sounds that lie within a phonetic category, if the listener can be trained to attend to this fine structure (Carney, Widin, & Viemeister, 1977).

The results of analysis of the stop-consonant stimuli using templates for different places of articulation shows that accuracy of identification falls somewhat short of 100%. In fluent speech, where all phonetic features are seldom represented unambiguously in the acoustic signal, the percentage of times that the features are identified correctly through property-detecting mechanisms may be even less. These levels of error in identification could be in part a consequence of the particular analysis procedures that were selected for examining the stop consonants. Adjustments and optimization of these procedures would undoubtedly increase the accuracy of identification, but would probably still leave some errors. Error-free identification based on primary properties is not, however, a rigid requirement, because, as we have just noted, secondary cues always accompany the primary properties. Thus, in situations where the primary properties yield equivocal identification, the secondary cues can be used to make the final identification. If an infant were equipped with primary property detectors, there might be a small proportion of utterances for which the primary invariant properties corresponding to the different phonetic categories would not be detected. If this percentage of utterances is sufficiently small, however, the infant would be able to identify the majority of speech sounds to which he or she is exposed, and consequently the ability to acquire language would not be greatly impeded. The utterances for which the primary properties are in evidence would provide the child with stimuli from which he or she could learn appropriate secondary cues that could ultimately be utilized in situations where the primary properties are not present. We cannot at this time, however, specify a minimum level of error in the detection of properties in speech that affect the acquisition of language skills.

The role of property-detecting mechanisms in setting up a phonological system must be distinguished, then, from the role of these mechanisms in ongoing adult speech perception. Property-detecting mechanisms play a crucial role in developing an internalized phonological system that is an essential part of the knowledge of a language user. Ongoing speech perception may, however, require recourse to secondary cues or stored templates for lexical items (Klatt, 1979) as well as to the property-detecting mechanisms. Nevertheless, acquisition of these speech-perception strategies depends on the prior ability to make phonetic classifications based on the detection of acoustically invariant and context-independent properties or features.

REFERENCES

Abramson, A., & Lisker, L. Discriminability along the voicing continuum: Cross-language tests. *Proceedings of the Sixth International Congress of Phonetic Sciences*. Prague: Academia, 1970.

Bailey, P. J., & Summerfield, Q. Some observations on the perception of [s] + stop clusters. *Haskins Laboratories, Status Report on Speech Research SR-53* (Vol. 2). New Haven, Connecticut, 1978, 25–60.

Bastian, J., Delattre, P., & Liberman, A. M. Silent interval as a cue for the distinction between stops and semivowels in medial position. *Journal of the Acoustical Society of America,* 1959, *31,* 1568(Abstract).

Blumstein, S. E., & Stevens, K. N. Acoustic invariance in speech production: Evidence from measurements of the spectral characteristics of stop consonants. *Journal of the Acoustical Society of America*, 1979, *66,* 1001–1018.

Blumstein, S. E., & Stevens, K. N. Perceptual invariance and onset spectra for stop consonants in different vowel environments. *Journal of the Acoustical Society of America,* 1980, *67,* 648–662.

Carney, A. E., Widin, G. P., & Viemeister, N. F. Noncategorical perception of stop consonants differing in VOT. *Journal of the Acoustical Society of America,* 1977, *62,* 961–970.

Chomsky, N., & Halle, M. *The sound pattern of English.* New York: Harper & Row, 1968.

Cole, R. A., & Scott, B. Towards a theory of speech perception. *Psychological Review,* 1974, *81,* 348–374.

Cooper, F. S., Delattre, P. C., Liberman, A. M., Borst, J. M., & Gerstman, L. J. Some experiments of the perception of synthetic speech sounds. *Journal of the Acoustical Society of America,* 1952, *24,* 597–606.

Cutting, J., & Rosner, B. Categories and boundaries in speech and music. *Perception & Psychophysics,* 1974, *16,* 564–570.

Delattre, P. C., Liberman, A. M. & Cooper, F. S. Acoustic loci and transitional cues for consonants. *Journal of the Acoustical Society of America,* 1955, *27,* 769–773.

Delgutte, B. Representation of speech-like sounds in the discharge patterns of auditory-nerve fibers. *Journal of the Acoustical Society of America,* 1980, *68,* 843–857.

Denes, P. Effect of duration on the perception of voicing. *Journal of the Acoustical Society of America,* 1955, *27,* 761–764.

Eimas, P. D., Siqueland, E. R., Jusczyk, P., & Vigorito, J. Speech perception in infants. *Science,* 1971, *171,* 303–306.

Fant, G. On the predictability of formant levels and spectrum envelopes from formant frequencies. In *For Roman Jakobson.* The Hague: Mouton, 1956.

Fant, G. *Acoustic theory of speech production.* The Hague: Mouton, 1960.

Fant, G. *Speech sound and features.* Cambridge, Mass.: MIT Press, 1973.

Fant, G., Ishizaka, K., Lindquist, J., & Sundberg, J. Subglottal formants. *Speech Transmission Laboratory QPSR* Royal Institute of Technology, Stockholm, 1972.

Fischer-Jorgensen, E. Acoustic analysis of stop consonants. *Miscellanea Phonetica,* 1954, *2,* 42–59.

Fischer-Jorgensen, E. Perceptual studies of Danish stop consonants. *Annual Report of the Institute of Phonetics,* University of Copenhagen, 1972, *6,* 75–168.

Haggard, M. P., Ambler, S., & Callow, M. Pitch as a voicing cue. *Journal of the Acoustical Society of America,* 1970, *47,* 613–617.

Halle, M. On the bases of phonology. In J. A. Fodor & J. J. Katz (Eds.), *The Structure of Language.* Englewood Cliffs, N.J.: Prentice-Hall, 1964.

Halle, M., Hughes, G. W., & Radley, J.-P. A. Acoustic properties of stop consonants. *Journal of the Acoustical Society of America,* 1957, *29,* 107–116.

Halle, M., & Stevens, K. N. Speech recognition: A model and a program for research. In J. A. Fodor & J. J. Katz (Eds.), *The Structure of Language.* Englewood Cliffs, N.J.: Prentice-Hall, 1964.

Jakobson, R., Fant, G., & Halle, M. *Preliminaries to speech analysis.* Cambridge, Mass.: MIT Press, 1963.

Kemler, D. G., Shepp, B. E., & Foote, K. E. The sources of developmental differences in children's incidental processing during discrimination trials. *Journal of Experimental Child Psychology,* 1976, *21,* 226–240.

Kiang, N. Y. -S. Stimulus representation in the discharge patterns of auditory neurons. In E. B. Eagles (Ed.), *The nervous system (Vol. 3): Human communication and its disorders.* New York: Raven Press, 1975.

Kiang, N. Y. -S., Watanabe, T., Thomas, E. C., & Clark, L. F. *Discharge patterns of single fibers in the cat's auditory nerve.* Cambridge, Mass.: MIT Press, 1965.

Klatt, D. H. Interaction between two factors that influence vowel duration. *Journal of the Acoustical Society of America,* 1973, *54,* 1102–1104.

Klatt, D. H. Speech perception: A model of acoustic-phonetic analysis and lexical access. *Journal of Phonetics,* 1979, *7,* 279–312.

Liberman, A. M., Cooper, F. S., Shankweiler, D. P., & Studdert-Kennedy, M. Perception of the speech code. *Psychological Review*, 1967, *74*, 431–461.

Liberman, A. M., Delattre, P. C., Gerstman, L. J., & Cooper, F. S. Tempo of frequency change as a cue for distinguishing classes of speech sounds. *Journal of Experimental Psychology*, 1956, *52*, 127–137.

Liberman, A. M., Harris, K. S., Hoffman, H. S., & Griffith, B. L. The discrimination of speech events within and across phonetic boundaries. *Journal of Experimental Psychology*, 1957, *54*, 358–368.

Lisker, L., & Abramson, A. A cross-language study of voicing in initial stops: Acoustical measurements. *Word*, 1964, *20*, 384–422.

Lisker, L., Liberman, A. M., Erickson, D. M., Dechovitz, D., & Mandler, R. On pushing the voice onset time (VOT) boundary about. *Language and Speech*, 1977, *20*, 209–216.

Malecot, A. The role of releases in the identification of released final stops. *Language*, 1958, *34*, 370–380.

Mandler, R. Categorical perception along an oral-nasal continuum. *Haskins Laboratories Status Report on Speech Research, SR-47*, 1976. New Haven, Connecticut.

Miller, J. L., & Eimas, P. D. Studies in the perception of place and manner of articulation: A comparison of the labial-alveolar and nasal-stop distinctions. *Journal of the Acoustical Society of America*, 1977, *61*, 835–845.

Miller, J. L., & Liberman, A. M. Some observations on how the perception of syllable-initial [b] versus [w] is affected by the remainder of the syllable. *Journal of the Acoustical Society of America*, 1978, *63*, Supplement No. 1, S21.

Remez, R. E. Adaptation of the category boundary between speech and nonspeech: A case against feature detectors. *Cognitive Psychology*, 1979, *11*, 38–57.

Repp, B. H. Perceptual trading relation between aspiration amplitude and VOT. *Journal of the Acoustical Society of America*, 1979, *65*, S8.

Repp, B. H., Liberman, A. M., Eccardt, T., & Pesetsky, D. Perceptual integration of acoustic cues for stop, fricative, and affricate manner. *Journal of Experimental Psychology: Human Perception and Performance*, 1978, *4*, 621–637.

Schatz, C. D. The role of context in the perception of stops. *Language*, 1954, *30*, 47–56.

Searle, C. L., Jacobson, J. Z., & Kimberly, G. Stop consonant discrimination based on human audition. *Journal of the Acoustical Society of America*, 1979, *65*, 799–809.

Shepp, B. E., Kemler, D. G., & Anderson, D. R. Selective attention and the breadth of learning: An extension of the one-look model. *Psychological Review*, 1972, *79*, 317–328.

Stevens, K. N. The role of rapid spectrum changes in the production and perception of speech. In *Form und substance* (Festschrift for Eli Fischer-Jorgensen). Copenhagen: Akademsk Forlag, 1971.

Stevens, K. N. The quantal nature of speech: Evidence from articulatory-acoustic data. In P. B. Denes & E. E. David, Jr. (Eds.), *Human communication: A unified view*. New York: McGraw-Hill, 1972.

Stevens, K. N. The potential role of property detectors in the perception of consonants. In G. Fant & M. A. A. Tatham (Eds.), *Auditory analysis and perception of speech*. London: Academic Press, 1975.

Stevens, K. N., & Blumstein, S. E. Invariant cues for place of articulation in stop consonants. *Journal of the Acoustical Society of America*, 1978, *64*, 1358–1368.

Stevens, K. N., & House, A. S. An acoustical theory of vowel production and some of its implications. *Journal of Speech and Hearing Research*, 1961, *4*, 303–320.

Stevens, K. N., & Klatt, D. H. Role of formant transitions in the voiced–voiceless distinction of stops. *Journal of the Acoustical Society of America*, 1974, *55*, 653–659.

Summerfield, A. Q. How a full account of segmental perception depends on prosody and vice versa.

In A. Cohen & S. G. Nooteboom (Eds.), *Structure and process in speech perception*. New York: Springer-Verlag, 1975.

Wang, W. S.-Y. Transition and release as perceptual cues for final plosives. *Journal of Speech and Hearing Research*, 1959, *3*, 66–73.

Williams, L. The voicing contrast in Spanish. *Journal of Phonetics*, 1977, *5*, 169–184.

Zue, V. W. *Acoustic characteristics of stop consonants: A controlled study*. Unpublished doctoral dissertation, Massachusetts Institute of Technology, 1976.

2 Effects of Speaking Rate on Segmental Distinctions

Joanne L. Miller
Northeastern University

Editors' Comments

As Stevens and Blumstein (Chapter 1, this volume) have ably demonstrated, the search for acoustic invariance underlying phonetic perception continues and, moreover, does so with realistic expectations of success. At least for one phonetic feature (place of articulation), it was possible to specify properties of the signal that remained constant across changes both in phonetic context and in speaker. There are, however, additional sources of potential variation in the speech waveform including, for example, the syntactic environment, the stress pattern, and the rate of speech. Only by taking into account all such factors will it ultimately be possible to determine whether invariant acoustic properties corresponding to perceived phonetic distinctions exist, or whether there is some context-conditioned variation. The theoretical consequence of the former is that the invariance for perception resides in the signal and presumably could be detected by relatively simple mechanisms. In the latter case, however, perceptual constancy must derive from the processing system, which would require that the mechanisms of perception be quite complex, perhaps even mediational in nature.

The effects of rate of speech present an interesting case in point. Although it was recognized quite early that variation in speaking rate may well be a source of considerable complexity, it was not until recently that systematic studies were undertaken to discover the consequences of changes in rate on the spectral and temporal properties of speech and the manner in which perceptual constancy is achieved. Miller has reviewed the available literature related to these issues and has presented some of her own findings. In addition, she has attempted to specify at least some of the complications that contextual variables, such as rate of speech, create for those who are concerned with modeling the perceptual system for speech.

INTRODUCTION

One of the most striking characteristics of speech is its variability; the particular acoustic energy pattern corresponding to a given consonant or vowel is not invariant, but changes systematically as a function of a number of factors. One of the primary sources of variability, and certainly the most thoroughly studied, is the phonetic context of the segment. That is to say, due to coarticulatory effects in speech production, the acoustic form of a segment is dependent on the identity of both the preceding and following phonetic segments[1] (cf. Liberman, Cooper, Shankweiler, & Studdert-Kennedy, 1967)[2]. In addition to the phonetic context, however, there are a number of other factors that also contribute to the systematic variation in the speech signal. These include, for example, the speaker (e.g., Peterson & Barney, 1952), the syntactic structure of the utterance (e.g., Cooper & Cooper, Chapter 9, this volume; Klatt, 1975; Oller, 1973), utterance length (e.g., Klatt, 1973, Lindblom & Rapp, 1973; Oller, 1973), the stress of the utterance (e.g., Klatt, 1975; Lindblom, 1963; Peterson & Lehiste, 1960), and rate of speech (see the following discussion.) Any complete theory of speech perception must include both a specification of the systematic variation inherent in the speech signal and a description of how the listener processes this variation to arrive at an invariant phonetic percept.

This chapter considers one factor that introduces variability into the speech signal; namely, changes in rate of speech, or speech tempo.[3] When a speaker changes his or her rate of speech, the number and duration of pauses in the

---

[1]Throughout this chapter, we refer to phonetic segments and acoustic segments. By phonetic segment we mean the perceived phonetic units of the language—the phones. The term acoustic segment refers to a stretch of speech that is defined solely in terms of acoustic properties. It is important to emphasize that the two types of segments are not isomorphic; that is, there is no one-to-one correspondence between acoustic segment and perceived phonetic segment. We should also point out that what constitutes an acoustic segment (and the location of boundaries between segments) is quite fuzzy, creating a serious measurement problem. For details of how the acoustic segments discussed in this chapter were defined, the reader is referred to the original papers.

[2]Although most of the work on speech perception has emphasized the context dependency of the acoustic information cueing a given phonetic segment, there have been a number of attempts to specify higher order invariant cues for particular phonetic distinctions. See, for example, Cole and Scott (1974), Delattre, Liberman, and Cooper (1955), and Stevens and Blumstein (Chapter 1, this volume).

[3]At the outset, it should be made clear that this chapter is limited in scope to the consequences— acoustic and perceptual—of changes in overall speaking rate and will not consider changes in so-called "local rate." That is, one of the major consequences of a change in speech tempo is variation in the duration of various acoustic segments; however, many other factors also cause such durational or "local rate" changes, including the syntactic structure, utterance length, etc. Only those durational changes due to an alteration in global speaking rate are reviewed here. Of course, a complete model of speech must necessarily include a specification of all factors influencing duration and a description of how they interact during the production and perception of speech (cf. Klatt, 1976).

utterance and the amount of time spent articulating is modified (Goldman-Eisler, 1968; Grosjean & Lane, Chapter 6, this volume). It is the latter of these factors, a change in articulation time, that is most critical for theories of segmental perception. This is because as a talker alters articulation time, certain spectral and temporal parameters of speech that are used by the listener as cues for phonetic segments are modified. We address two questions concerning these effects of speech rate, first for vowels and then for consonants: (1) what are the specific acoustic consequences of changes in rate of speech; (2) what is the evidence that listeners make perceptual adjustments for those changes?[4]

VOWELS

There are two primary ways in which changes in speech tempo potentially affect the production and perception of vowels. One concerns the spectral changes that are introduced by variation in rate and the other concerns changes in segment duration, which in and of itself can cue a number of vowel contrasts. Each of these is considered in turn.

Spectral Changes

The primary information specifying the identity of a vowel is assumed to be the value of the formant frequencies during the steady-state portion of the syllable or, if there is no steady-state portion (as in most naturally produced syllables), at the point of closest approximation to the "target" values associated with that vowel. Moreover, the lower two formants, F1 and F2, are thought to provide most of the necessary information to distinguish among the vowels of a language and, consequently, vowels are commonly represented as points in a "vowel space" defined by the values of F1 and F2. An example of a vowel space for a group of talkers is shown in Fig. 2.1.

If the formant values are to specify the intended vowel, two major problems arise. The first is that the absolute values of the formants, as well as their relative values, vary systematically from talker to talker, so that some sort of normalization for speaker differences must take place during perception (e.g., Joos, 1948;

---

[4]A closely related issue of considerable importance which, because of lack of space is not addressed in this chapter, is the way changes in speech tempo are accomplished by the speaker. Briefly, the available physiological and cineradiographic evidence suggests that, for both consonants and vowels, changes in speech tempo involve a complex reorganization of motor commands and movement patterns (e.g., Gay & Hirose, 1973; Gay & Ushijima, 1974; Gay, Ushijima, Hirose, & Cooper, 1974; Harris, 1974; Kuehn & Moll, 1976). A discussion of these findings, as well as a thorough consideration of various models of timing control in speech production, can be found in Fowler (1977).

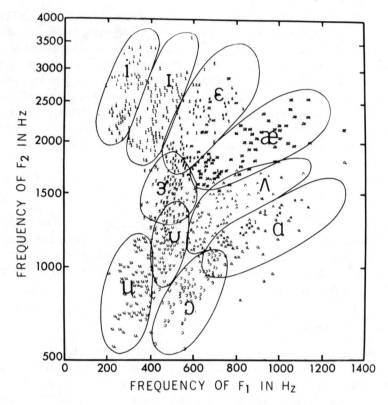

FIG. 2.1.   F1–F2 vowel space for various vowels spoken by 76 talkers. The data points are indicated by phonetic symbols and the loops enclose about 90% of the data points for each vowel category. (Adapted from Peterson & Barney, 1952. Copyright 1952 by the American Institute of Physics. Reprinted by permission.)

Ladefoged & Broadbent, 1957; Lieberman, 1973; but see Shankweiler, Strange & Verbrugge, 1977). The second problem is the phenomenon of vowel reduction. Vowel reduction refers to the tendency for the obtained formant frequencies of a vowel to fall short of the idealized target values for that vowel—those values that would be obtained if the vowel were produced in isolation—resulting in an overall shrinkage of the vowel space. Among the factors contributing to vowel reduction is the consonantal context of a vowel. Due to coarticulation, vowels embedded between consonants often fail to reach their targets, and are often assimilated toward the values of the surrounding consonants (e.g., Stevens & House, 1963). There is also evidence of vowel reduction in destressed speech (e.g., Lindblom, 1963; Tiffany, 1959) and in speech produced at a rapid rate of articulation (e.g., Lindblom, 1963). From the point of view of the listener, the occurrence of vowel reduction suggests the need to compensate not only for differences across speakers, but also for differences across utterances produced by the same talker.

Acoustic effects of Rate Variation. Before examining the evidence that listeners compensate for vowel reduction introduced by changes in speech rate, it is appropriate to consider whether vowel reduction does indeed occur at faster rates of speech. The classic research on this problem was conducted by Lindblom (1963), who studied the effect of a change in speech tempo, as well as stress, on eight Swedish vowels in three consonant-vowel-consonant (CVC) contexts. Stress was manipulated by putting the test syllable in different positions of various sentence frames, whereas speech tempo was manipulated by having the speaker repeat isolated test syllables at a number of repetition rates. For each syllable, Lindblom measured the duration of the syllable, the F1, F2, and F3 values at the onset and offset of the syllable, and the formant frequency values at the point in the syllable at which they reached their maxima or minima.

The results of the experiment were quite clear. As the duration of the syllable decreased, whether due to a change in stress or rate, there was an increasing tendency for the obtained formant frequency values to undershoot their targets. Thus, as the syllable (and hence, vowel nucleus) decreased in duration, the vowel became reduced, or more schwa-like in character. Furthermore, the two manipulations, that of stress and that of rate, had the same acoustic consequences. As Lindblom (1963) stated, "it is immaterial whether a given length of the vowel is produced chiefly by the tempo or degree of stress. Duration seems to be the main determinant of the reduction [p. 1780]." To account for the vowel undershoot at shorter syllable durations, Lindblom proposed that the pattern of neural commands to the articulators for a given vowel remains constant across changes in stress and rate (and consonantal context); however, due to physiological constraints, the vowel targets cannot be fully realized during fast speech, resulting in the obtained undershoot of target values.[5] Finally, it is important to point out that the existence of vowel reduction at faster rates of speech indicates that rate changes do not result in a simple compression and expansion of the speech signal, as originally proposed by Joos (1948), for that transformation would leave the formant frequency values unchanged.

In a study that focused exclusively on diphthongs, Gay (1968) also found evidence for target undershoot at faster rates of speech. The stimuli in this experiment consisted of instances of five diphthongs in various consonantal contexts spoken at three different rates of speech. For each diphthong, the overall glide duration and the onset and offset formant frequencies were measured. Although the effects of rate were somewhat different for various vowels, certain overall trends were observed. The total duration of the diphthong decreased as speech rate increased, but the rate of the glide remained constant. This was because although the onset frequencies did not change with rate, the offset frequencies did: The speaker did not attain the target values at the faster rates of speech. These findings, like those of Lindblom (1963), suggest that the main

---

[5]Stevens and House (1963) have proposed a very similar model to account for the vowel undershoot that arises from the influence of consonantal context on vowel production.

consequence of increased speaking rate is simply to cut off the gesture before the target is reached.

Although both the Lindblom and Gay studies show evidence of vowel reduction at faster rates of speech, more recent studies have failed to completely corroborate these findings. One such study, conducted by Verbrugge and Shankweiler (1977), examined the effects of speech tempo and stress on nine English vowels in a CVC context. Specifically, the stimuli for their study consisted of nine vowels in a [pVp] context, embedded in the carrier sentence: "I think it's the yellow [pVp]'s call." One speaker produced each of the nine sentences under four conditions: two levels of rate, fast and slow, crossed with two levels of stress, stress on the target syllable and stress on the word "yellow" (thereby leaving the target syllable destressed). Syllable duration and formant frequency values at the point of maximal syllable amplitude were determined for each syllable in each of the four sentence conditions.

As expected, variation in rate from slow to fast caused a decrease in average syllable duration (although, surprisingly, the stress manipulation did not affect duration in an orderly manner). However, quite unexpectedly, the formant frequency measurements showed only a slight trend toward a reduced vowel space for the fast compared to the slow vowels. It is of interest to note that although a change in rate had only a minimal effect on the formant frequency values of the vowel, the stress manipulation did produce a rather substantial effect, especially on F1.

In accord with the findings of Verbrugge and Shankweiler (1977), Gay (1978) has recently reported data that also call into question the extent of vowel reduction as a function of increased speaking rate. He studied the effects of changes in speech rate, as well as lexical stress, on the production of vowels in CV and CVCVC contexts. To obtain the variation in stress, he instructed subjects to stress either the first or second syllable of the CVCVC utterances. The rate variation was obtained by instructing subjects to produce the syllables (which were embedded in a carrier phrase) at normal and fast speaking rates.

As expected, variation in rate (and stress) systematically affected overall syllable duration, primarily by altering the durations of those acoustic segments corresponding to the vowel, rather than the consonant (cf. Gaitenby, 1965; Kozchevnikova & Chistovich, 1965). However, although a change in stress lead to a certain amount of vowel reduction, variation in rate did not systematically alter the obtained formant frequency values of the vowel. The stability of the obtained values across speech rates can be seen in Fig. 2.2, which presents the F1-F2 vowel space at fast and slow rates for the four talkers in the experiment.

On the basis of his findings, Gay concluded, contrary to Lindblom (1963), that changes in rate do result in a sort of horizontal compression of the speech waveform, as suggested by Joos (1948), although the compression is nonlinear. Furthermore, he noted that the different consequences of rate and stress suggest both that vowel reduction is not mediated simply through syllable duration, as

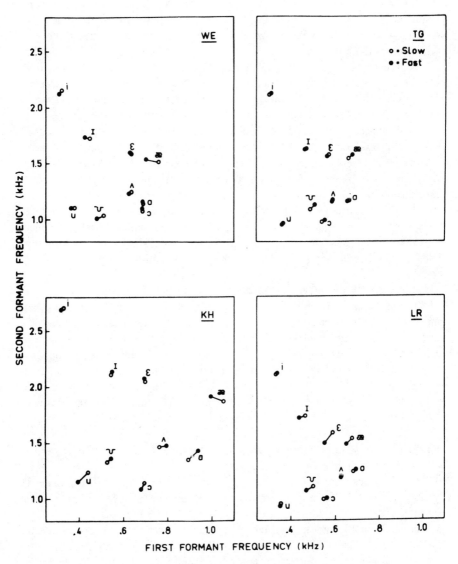

FIG. 2.2. F1–F2 vowel space for midpoint measurements for both speaking rates. (From Gay, 1978. Copyright 1978 by the American Insitute of Physics. Reprinted by permission.)

Lindblom (1963) suggested, and that variation in stress and rate are under control of different physiological mechanisms. Finally, he proposed that the decrease in syllable duration as a function of increased rate, coupled with the attainment of vowel targets, indicates that changes in rate involve the reorganization of neural commands to the articulators.

In summary, although increased rates of speech may sometimes result in a systematic deviation of the obtained formant values from their putative targets, such vowel reduction does not always occur at faster speaking rates. However, the numerous differences between the studies of Lindblom (1963) and Gay (1968), on the one hand, and those of Verbrugge and Shankweiler (1977) and Gay (1978), on the other hand, render it impossible to determine precisely which factors control when vowel reduction occurs and when vowel targets are attained. But it should be noted that if vowel reduction does indeed occur only under certain conditions as speech is speeded up, as the available evidence seems to suggest, then the listener has an even more complicated task: When interpreting any given formant frequency pattern as specifying a particular vowel, a listener must not only be sensitive to the rate of speech, but also the factors determining whether vowel reduction would be expected to occur in that context.

Perceptual Effects of Rate Variation.   As noted, the data of Lindblom (1963) and Gay (1968) indicate that increasing rate of speech may result in an undershoot of the vowel target formant frequencies. When this undershoot occurs, the listener must interpret the obtained formant values in relation to speech tempo if he or she is to perceive the intended vowel. Lindblom and Studdert-Kennedy (1967) found some initial support for this. Although the main concern of their study was the listener's adjustment for undershoot introduced by varying consonantal context, they also found that rate (and duration) of the formant transitions of a CVC syllable—presumably by specifying utterance rate—influenced the perception of the vowel in that syllable: For syllables with fast, as compared to slow, rates, more undershoot in the actual formant frequency values was tolerated for perceiving a given vowel.

There are also studies by Verbrugge and his colleagues (Verbrugge & Shankweiler, 1977; Verbrugge, Strange, Shankweiler, & Edman, 1976) that can be interpreted as providing evidence for perceptual compensation for vowel reduction. Actually, the initial interest of these investigators was not in rate of speech, per se, but in the extent to which listeners must normalize for speaker differences, and what information is used for such normalization. However, in the course of their research, it became apparent that even more important than speaker normalization is an adjustment for speech tempo. For example, in an early study, Verbrugge et al. (1976) tested the identification of nine vowels in a [pVp] context, spoken by a number of talkers, under three conditions of variation. In one condition, the test syllables were presented in the sentence context in which they were originally uttered ("the yellow [pVp]'s *chair* is red"). In a second condition, the test syllables were excised from the sentence and presented in isolation. Finally, in a third condition, these isolated syllables were preceded by a precursor sequence ([hi], [ha], [hu]) that was spoken by the same talker that produced the test syllable. Of particular interest to the investigators was whether the precursor sequence would increase performance level, as the normalization theory of Lieberman and his colleagues would predict (Lieberman, 1973; Lieberman, Crelin, & Klatt, 1972; cf. Joos, 1948).

The results of the study were quite revealing. First, vowels were identified significantly better when the syllable was presented in the original sentence frame than when presented in isolation and, moreover, the pattern of errors in the isolated condition suggested that this was due to a problem of speech rate and not one of insufficient information for talker normalization. Specifically, the error responses tended to be the reduced version of the intended vowel. That is to say, it was as if the listener were treating the isolated syllable not as the fast, de-stressed syllable that actually was spoken, but as a citation-form syllable. Con-sequently, because the formant frequencies were appropriate for a fast, de-stressed syllable, and not a citation-form syllable, the listener heard a reduced version of the vowel. For example, a syllable might be heard as [pip] when presented in the sentence context, but as [pIp] when presented in isolation (as can be seen in Fig. 2.1, [I] is a more central vowel than [i]—that is, it is toward the center of the vowel space).

The second interesting aspect of the results, closely related to the first, was that instead of aiding performance, the precursor string actually hindered it; vowel indentification was significantly poorer in the precursor condition than in the isolated vowel condition. This result can also be interpreted within a rate of speech framework. In particular, the authors proposed that the precursors specified a slow, citation-form rate of speech, whereas the syllables were actu-ally spoken in destressed syllable position. Again, support for this interpretation comes from the error responses: As before, the errors in the precursor condition were in the direction of more reduced vowels. Thus, instead of decreasing the ambiguity about speaker identity and thereby facilitating perception, the precur-sors actually specified the wrong rate of speech and, consequently, caused a diminution in performance. Taken together, both sets of findings indicate that the listener is sensitive to rate information and that he uses that information when judging vowel quality.

In an extension of their research, Verbrugge and Shankweiler (1977) at-tempted to separate the roles of stress and rate on the perception, and production, of vowels. As noted previously, variation in rate produced a systematic change in the duration of the test syllables but very little change in the spectral characteris-tics of the vowels, whereas stress changes lead to very little change in syllable duration but a more substantial change in the obtained formant frequency values. To determine the perceptual effects of stress and rate variation, the authors created five listening tests from the original sentences ("I think it's the yellow

[pVp]'s call''). In one, the syllables were kept in their original sentence frames; in the second, they were excised and presented in isolation; in the third, the test words were spliced into the sentence of opposite rate, but with the same stress; in the fourth, the test syllables were spliced into the sentence with the opposite stress, but the same rate; and fifth, the test words were spliced into sentences that differed both in rate and stress.

A number of important findings emerged from these perceptual tests. First, in accord with previous findings, the syllables were identified more accurately in a sentence context than in isolation and, moreover, the errors on the isolated syllables tended to be in the direction of reduced vowels. Second, the rate interchange affected performance in a complex manner: When the slow syllables were spliced into the fast sentences, no decrement in performance was obtained; however, when the fast syllables were spliced into the slow sentences, performance decreased. And, as expected, the errors were in the direction of hearing the vowels in reduced form (e.g., [pæp] was heard as [pɛp]). As the authors note, one possible explanation for this asymmetry is that the slow syllables contained sufficient information about rate to overcome any influence that the carrier sentence may have had, whereas the fast syllables did not and, consequently, the rate of the sentence partially determined the perception of vowel quality. However, the reason that the slow, but not the fast, syllables contained adequate rate information is left unresolved. Finally, for completeness, it should be noted that the stress interchange condition did not produce a decrement in vowel identification.

Taken together, the studies of Lindblom and Studdert-Kennedy (1967) and those of Verbrugge and his colleagues (Verbrugge et al., 1976; Verbrugge & Shankweiler, 1977) suggest that listeners use information about rate of speech when interpreting the obtained formant frequency values of a vowel, such that they compensate for any undershoot that may have been caused by increases in rate of articulation. However, as we discuss in some detail in the following section on temporal aspects of vowels, the findings of Verbrugge and his colleagues do permit an alternative interpretation. In particular, it is possible to argue that their listeners were not using information about speech tempo to compensate for vowel reduction—that is, spectral changes—but to normalize for the durational aspects of vowels. We should note that, to the extent this argument is valid, there remains only limited evidence of perceptual normalization for vowel reduction introduced by variation in speech tempo.

Temporal Changes

Vowels not only differ from each other in their relative formant frequency values, but also in their durations (e.g., Peterson & Lehiste, 1960; Stevens & House, 1963; Umeda, 1975). When factors such as consonantal context, stress, and tempo are neutralized, the vowels fall roughly into two categories, those with inherently short durations ([I], [ɛ], [ʊ], [ʌ]), and those with inherently long durations ([i], [æ], [a], [u], [ɔ]; cf. Peterson & Lehiste, 1960). Furthermore, a number of investigators have shown that listeners are sensitive to durational differences among vowels (e.g., Huggins, 1972a, 1972b; cf. Lehiste, 1970; Nooteboom, 1973) and that they use vowel duration as a cue for vowel quality, especially when trying to identify vowels that lie close together in the F1–F2 vowel space (e.g., Ainsworth, 1972, 1974; Bennett, 1968; Cohen, Slis, & 't Hart, 1963). In fact, not only can duration influence the perception of vowel quality, but a change in vowel quality can be specified solely by a change in vowel duration. For example, both Mermelstein, Liberman, and Fowler (1977), and Verbrugge and Isenberg (1978) generated a continuum of vowels ranging from a short vowel ([ɛ]) to a long vowel ([æ]) by manipulating only the duration of the formants, keeping the formant frequencies constant at values intermediate between those appropriate for [ɛ] and [æ].

Acoustic Effects of Rate Variation.   Not only do vowels differ from each other in duration, but the duration of any particular vowel varies with a number of factors, including speech tempo (e.g., Gay, 1978; cf. Gaitenby, 1965; Kozchevnikova & Chistovich, 1965; cf. Lindblom, 1963; Peterson & Lehiste, 1960; Port, 1976; Verbrugge & Shankweiler, 1977). Indeed, the most elastic part of a syllable is its vowel nucleus, so that most of the change in total utterance duration that occurs with rate actually takes place in the vocalic segment (e.g., Gay, 1978; Kozchevnikova & Chistovich, 1965).

Although it has been amply demonstrated that vowel duration, in general, varies with changes in speech tempo, the extent of variation for particular vowels, in particular contexts, remains to be fully specified. On the basis of available data, however, we can predict that the effect of rate on vowels will prove to be enormously complex. First, at least for some vowels, a change in speech rate alters not only the absolute durations of vowels, but also their relative durations: Port (1976) recently reported that an increase in speech rate reduced the duration of a long vowel ([i]) more than a short vowel ([I]), so that the absolute difference between the two vowels was reduced at the faster rate of speech. This finding raises the possibility that the cue value of vowel duration may itself change at different speech tempos. Second, the extent to which vowel duration changes with modification in articulation rate is not constant, but rather interacts with other aspects of speech. For example, Peterson and Lehiste (1960) showed that syllable duration (and, presumably, vowel duration) changed more with rate in an unstressed than in a stressed syllable. Such factors as utterance length, syntactic structure, and position in the word are also likely to affect the extent to which variation in speech tempo produces durational variation (cf. Klatt, 1976).

Perceptual Effects of Rate Variation.   Given that vowels vary in absolute duration at different rates of speech, it would clearly be advantageous for the listener not to judge a given duration as cueing a specific vowel independently of the rate of the utterance. One of the first series of studies to demonstrate perceptual normalization for rate was conducted by Ainsworth (1972, 1974). His stimuli were two-formant synthesized vowels (either in isolation or in a [hVd] context) that covered the F1–F2 vowel space and ranged in duration from 120 to 600 msec. In a first experiment (Ainsworth, 1972), he found, as expected, that vowel judgments varied as a function of duration: Physically longer vowels tended to be perceived as one of the inherently long vowels (e.g., [i] or [a]), whereas physically shorter vowels tended to be heard as one of the inherently short vowels (e.g., [I] or [ʌ]). In a subsequent study (Ainsworth, 1974), the role of speech rate was investigated by preceding the test vowels with a precursor sequence that contained three repetitions of a vowel of a given duration. Across precursors, the vowels ranged from 120 to 600 msec in 120 msec steps and within a single precursor the vowels were separated by a period of silence equal to the duration of the vowel. The major finding of the study was that, especially for test vowels of intermediate duration in an ambiguous region of the F1–F2 vowel space, the shorter precursor vowels biased perception toward longer vowels and the longer precursor vowels biased perception in the opposite direction, toward shorter vowels. Thus, a given vowel was judged differently depending on the duration of the precursor vowels.

As mentioned earlier, the studies of Verbrugge and his colleagues (Verbrugge et al., 1976; Verbrugge & Shankweiler, 1977), can also be interpreted as providing evidence for compensation for durational changes introduced by rate variation. As the reader will recall, Verbrugge found that if a rapidly articulated test syllable were presented for identification in the sentence in which it was originally produced, the intended vowel was identified (such as [pæp] or [pap]). However, when the test syllable was excised from the sentence and presented in isolation, preceded by citation-form precursor syllables, or spliced into a sentence uttered at a slower rate of speech, listeners tended to perceive a reduced version of the vowel (such as [pɛp] or [pʌp]). In their 1976 paper, Verbrugge et al. proposed that these errors were due to compensation for vowel reduction that may have occurred during the production of the test syllable. That is, when the test syllable was presented in the original sentence context, the listener adjusted for vowel target undershoot and correctly perceived the vowel. In the other test conditions, the context (or lack of context, in the case of the isolated syllables) misinformed the listener about the rate of speech by specifying a rate that was too slow. Consequently, the listener did not adjust for the undershoot, and perceived the reduced form of the vowel.

However, as we have indicated, there is another explanation for the error pattern, one that was implied in the discussion of the Verbrugge and Shankweiler (1977) paper. According to this explanation, the pattern of errors does not reflect the perception of reduced vowels for their unreduced counterparts, but the perception of short vowels for long vowels. Specifically, because the sentence context specified a relatively fast rate of speech, physically short vowels were heard (appropriately) as "long" vowels (e.g., [pap]). However, in the absence of the correct sentence context, and hence the proper specification of rate, a longer physical duration was required to hear a "long" vowel and, hence, the physically shorter (but actually "long") vowel was erroneously heard as a "short" vowel (e.g. [pʌp]).

Because many of the error responses were both a reduced version of the intended vowel and its "short" counterpart (such as [ʌ] for [a]), it is not possible to determine which explanation is correct—and, the listener may have been compensating both for changes in spectral parameters and changes in duration. It should be noted, however, that the acoustical measurements of the 1977 study are in accord with the duration-based explanation. Recall that an increase in speech rate did not lead to considerable vowel reduction, although it did produce substantial decreases in syllable duration. It is reasonable to suppose, then, that the listeners were adjusting to the duration changes when performing the perceptual tasks.

Finally, the experiments discussed in the foregoing showed that the context of a target syllable—the syllables surrounding it—affects the perception of the target vowel by specifying speech tempo and thereby influencing the interpretation of a given physical duration. However, it may not only be the context of a syllable that specifies rate, but also information contained in the target syllable itself. Briefly, Verbrugge and Isenberg (1978) have found some evidence that the duration of the transitions in a CVC syllable may reflect the articulation rate of the syllable (cf. Lindblom & Studdert-Kennedy, 1967) and, in turn, influence whether the vowel is perceived as long ([æ]) or short ([ɛ]).

Summary

There is little doubt that changes in speech tempo alter the temporal characteristics of the vowel nucleus of a syllable in predictable ways. Moreover, there is compelling evidence that listeners compensate for such changes when using duration to specify vowel identity. The story with regard to spectral changes due to rate is less clear cut. First, although vowel reduction probably occurs under some conditions, it does not seem to be a necessary consequence of speeded speech and, second, there is some question as to whether listeners are sensitive to the vowel undershoot that may be introduced by variation in tempo. Finally, we should point out that although it has been amply demonstrated that listeners adjust for speech tempo when perceiving vowels, the nature of the information that actually specifies tempo, and the process by which that information is used when making phonetic judgments has not been made explicit.

CONSONANTS

When a speaker alters the rate of speech he modifies not only acoustic properties cueing vowels, but also certain acoustic properties that signal consonantal distinctions. With few exceptions, the focus of attention has been on the way in which speech tempo affects temporal cues for consonants, presumably because of the widely held assumption that changes in tempo have very little effect on the spectral cues. Our discussion reflects this emphasis by being organized in terms of the temporal cues for various consonantal contrasts.

Single Versus Geminate Consonants

One of the earliest investigations of the role of speech tempo in the perception of consonants was conducted by Pickett and Decker (1960). It had been shown by Stetson (1951) that the duration of silence associated with an intervocalic stop consonant depends on whether the consonant is singular or repeated (geminate): Shorter durations correspond to a single consonant (as in "topic") whereas longer durations correspond to a double consonant (as in "top pick"). Pickett and Decker were interested in determining first, whether listeners could use silence duration to distinguish between single and double consonants and, if so, whether they would adjust for changes in speech rate.

To obtain test sentences, they asked speakers to produce the sentence "he was

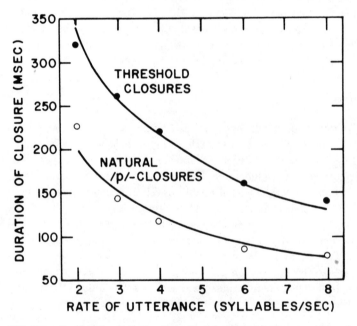

FIG. 2.3.   Showing the similarity of perceived threshold [p]-closure and natural [p]-closure. Threshold [p]-closure (top curve) is the duration of [p]-closure that is judged single-[p] 60% of the time. Natural [p]-closure (bottom curve) is the mean duration of [p]-closure for the two talkers, which occurred on the original test utterances. (Adapted from Pickett & Decker, 1960. Copyright 1960 by Kingston Press Services. Reprinted by permission.)

the topic of the year'' at five speaking rates. Using tape-splicing techniques, they then modified the silence duration of the word "topic" in each of the sentences so as to span a range of durations (50 to 800 msec across all five speaking rates). Subjects were asked to judge whether each of the modified sentences was "he was the topic of the year" or "he was the top pick of the year."

As expected, at shorter silence durations the single consonant was heard and, at longer durations, the double consonant. Most important, however, was that the duration at the crossover point between single and double consonant was not invariant: At faster rates of speech the boundary was at a shorter duration of silence and, at slower rates, at a longer duration. This result is shown schematically in the upper curve of Fig. 2.3, which plots the duration of silence (p-closure) that was judged a single [p] 60% of the time as a function of utterance rate. Clearly, there is an interaction between the duration of silence that cues a single versus double consonant and the tempo at which the utterance was produced. Note that because the variation in speech rate across sentences involved both the word "topic" and the remainder of the sentence, it is not possible to specify how much of the effect of rate was due to the tempo of the test word itself, and how much to the tempo of the rest of the sentence. Finally, the bottom curve of Fig. 2.3 shows the actual silence durations of the word "topic" in the original sentences produced at the various speaking rates. There is a clear relation between silence duration and speech rate: As rate increases, silence duration decreases. Moreover, this curve is remarkably similar to the upper curve in the figure, which presents the perceptual data. The parallel nature of the curves strongly suggests that the listener, in processing silence duration, employs just the appropriate compensation for the changes that actually occur during speech production as a result of changes in speech tempo.[6]

Although further studies of the single-geminate distinction in English have not been reported, Fujisaki, Nakamura, and Imoto (1975) have recently reported findings for Japanese that are highly relevant. Whereas segmental duration, per se, is not phonemic in English, it is in other languages, including Japanese. Thus, in Japanese, for a variety of consonants and vowels a change solely in the perceived duration of the segment can signify a change in meaning. Fujisaki et

---

[6]As well as cueing the distinction between a single and double consonant, silence can cue the distinction between the presence or absence of a consonant, as in "slit" versus "split" (Bastian, Eimas, & Liberman, 1961). Marcus (1978) recently investigated whether the amount of silence needed to hear the stop (instead of no consonant) depended on the utterance rate, as specified by the duration of the rest of the word. Surprisingly, word length (speech rate) did not affect the duration of silence at the [#] − [p] boundary. Whether this was due to a lack of sensitivity in the procedure used by Marcus, the insufficiency of the information supposedly specifying a change in rate, or to the fact that, for some unknown reason, the perception of silence as a cue for the presence of a consonant is not sensitive to rate, remains to be determined. In exploring these alternatives, it will be especially important to assess whether closure duration for a stop in this context actually changes as a function of variation in rate, as it does when it cues the distinction between a single and double consonant (see Fig. 2.3).

al. found that, for a voiceless fricative single versus geminate distinction (e.g., [isi]—a place-name—vs. [issi]—"a unit of area"), the absolute duration at which the percept changed from that of a single consonant to that of a double consonant varied as a function of the speaking rate of the utterance. Furthermore, this was true both when speaking rate was cued only by the vowel on either side of the consonant and when it was cued as well by the rate of a sentence context. Although perceptual normalization of this sort presumably occurs for consonants other than a voiceless fricative, this remains to be determined. Following the lead of Pickett and Decker (1960), it would be particularly instructive to examine the extent to which the various single and geminate consonants change in duration when produced at various rates of speech and to compare those values to the extent of perceptual compensation when using duration phonemically.

Voicing

One of the primary features that differentiates the consonants of a language is voicing. In English, consonants (in particular, stops, fricatives, and affricates) can take on one of two voicing values, voiced (e.g., [b], [d], [g], [z], [v]) and voiceless (e.g., [p], [t], [k], [s], [f]). Although it is appealing to suppose that there is one primary cue in the acoustic signal that specifies whether a given consonant is voiced or voiceless, the situation is vastly more complicated.

First, many of the primary cues for voicing seem to vary with the syllabic position of the consonant. For example, voice-onset-time (VOT), defined as the time between the release burst of the consonant and the onset of quasiperiodic energy, is a major cue for stop consonants in syllable-initial position (Lisker & Abramson, 1964, 1970), whereas closure duration is a primary voicing cue for intervocalic stop consonants (Lisker, 1957). In addition, an important cue for voicing in syllable-final position is the duration of the preceding vowel (e.g., Denes, 1955; Raphael, 1972; cf. House, 1961). Second, even for a consonant in a given syllabic position, numerous cues contribute to the specification of the voicing value. For example, it has been shown that the voicing value of a syllable-initial stop is cued not only by VOT, but also by such factors as characteristics of the first-formant transition after the onset of voicing (Lisker, 1975; Stevens & Klatt, 1974) and the fundamental frequency contour after voicing onset (Haggard, Ambler, & Callow, 1970). Similarly, there are numerous cues to the intervocalic voiced–voiceless distinction, including not only closure duration but also the intensity of the voicing buzz during closure and the duration of the preceding vowel (e.g., Lisker, 1978; Port, 1976). Thus, in order to accurately perceive the intended voicing value of a consonant, the listener must be sensitive to a variety of cues in the speech signal and able to integrate these cues to make a final judgment of voicing.

Inasmuch as many of the cues for voicing are temporal in nature, it might be expected that their production and perception are influenced by variation in speech tempo. And the limited, though rapidly growing, research on this issue suggests that this is indeed the case. To date, the relevant work has concentrated on two types of voicing contrasts: the voicing distinction, cued by VOT in syllable-initial position, and the intervocalic voicing distinction, cued primarily by the duration of closure and the preceding vowel.

Syllable-Initial Consonants.   In an extensive series of studies, Summerfield (1974, 1975a, 1975b, 1975c, 1975d, 1978; Summerfield & Haggard, 1972) has investigated the way in which changing speech tempo affects the production and perception of syllable-initial stop consonants that differ in voicing, cued by VOT. Although most of this research has focused on perceptual adjustments for changes in rate, for ease of explication the production data are reviewed first.

In a preliminary study (Summerfield, 1974), two speakers were asked to produce the sentence "the guard and the geese are eager to argue" at a slow, normal, and fast rate of speech. From spectrograms of each utterance, the VOT values of the [g] and [t] segments were measured. Although the data were quite variable, there was a tendency for the VOT value of the segments to decrease as rate of speech increased. Moreover, this was true both of the voiced ([g]) and voiceless ([t]) segments.

In a subsequent, more extensive study, Summerfield (1975a) asked six speakers to produce the sentence "why are you a C1V1 when you're a C2V2," where C was [b], [p], [g], or [k] and V was [i] or [a], at a normal, slow and fast rate of speech. Oscillograms of each utterance were made and the VOT values of C1 and C2 were measured. According to Summerfield, there was rarely an interruption in glottal pulsing (voicing) during the production of the consonant when it was voiced ([b] or [g]), yielding measured VOTs of zero msec. Consequently, only the measurements of the voiceless consonants ([p] and [k]), which had VOTs greater than zero msec, were reported in detail. (The reason that the VOT values of the voiced consonants were greater than zero msec in the preliminary study previously described, but not in this study, is not clear.) The voiceless stops were notably affected by changes in speech rate: As the rate of the utterance increased, measured by the duration of the sentence, there was a concomitant decrease in VOT value of 20 msec from the slow to the fast rate. Assuming that the VOT value of the voiced consonants remained constant (at zero msec), these results indicate, first, that fast speech results in decreased VOT values of the voiceless stops and, second, that the difference between the average VOT values of voiced and voiceless stops diminishes with increased speech rate. As the reader will recall, an analogous reduction was found for the contrast afforded by vowel duration as a cue for vowel identity (Port, 1976).[7]

---

[7]In a study investigating the influence of a variety of contextual variables on the VOT values of voiced and voiceless stops, Lisker and Abramson (1967) reported no change in VOT values across various speaking rates. However, this finding is difficult to interpret inasmuch as the authors do not report details of how rate of speech was measured, or the range of rates spanned.

In a number of experiments, Summerfield (1974, 1975b, 1975d, 1978; Summerfield & Haggard, 1972) has gone on to show that listeners use information about speech tempo when judging a particular VOT value signaling a voiced or voiceless stop. Specifically, by manipulating the speech rate of the utterance, the VOT value at the voiced–voiceless boundary between two cognates (e.g., [b] and [p]) can be shifted—toward lower VOT values as speech is speeded up and higher VOT values as speech is slowed down. This, of course, is the pattern of results one would expect if listeners were adjusting for the shortening of the VOT value of the voiceless (and possibly voiced) consonant that occurs as speech rate is increased.

Probably the most interesting aspect of Summerfield's work has been his attempt to specify more precisely which aspects of the "speech context" specify the speech tempo to which the listener adjusts. His studies fall roughly into two categories, those that manipulate the rate of the speech surrounding the target syllable and those that manipulate the characteristics of the target syllable itself.

Consider the first category of studies, in which the context of the syllable specifies speech rate. In an early experiment (Summerfield, 1975b), the precursor sentence "a bird in the hand is worth two in the . . ." was synthesized at a normal and fast rate of speech. The change in speech rate was accomplished by modifying the durations of the steady-state segments in the precursor string, that is, those acoustic segments roughly corresponding to the vowels. In addition, nine series of target CV syllables were synthesized, each series varying in VOT from a value appropriate for a voiced consonant to one appropriate for a voiceless consonant. The nine series consisted of three consonantal contrasts ([b–p], [d–t], [g–k]) paired with three vowels [a], [ɛ], [i]). For all nine series, as expected, the slower rate of speech yielded a higher boundary value than the faster rate of speech. Moreover, Summerfield (1975b) later found that the same general effect is obtained if the change in speech rate of the precursor is accomplished not by manipulating the steady-state segments of the utterance, but the transitional segments. Finally, Summerfield (1975d) has shown that as the rate of the precursor sentence is systematically altered from very slow to very fast, there is a systematic shift in the voiced–voiceless boundary of the target consonant ([g–k]) toward shorter VOT values, covering a total range of about 11 msec. This relation between precursor rate (duration) and the VOT value at the phonetic boundary is shown in Fig. 2.4. These data indicate that the perceptual system is making fine adjustments for changes in speech tempo when judging VOT, and not operating simply in terms of crude estimates of "fast" or "slow" speech.

In an additional series of experiments, Summerfield attempted to determine whether it is the rate of the entire precursor sequence that is important, or only those portions of the precursor that are close to the target syllable. In one study (Summerfield, 1975b), the speech tempo of the first and second halves of a precursor string were independently manipulated. It was found that only the rate of the second half of the sentence, which was less than a second long, influenced

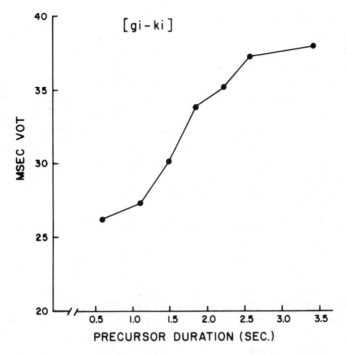

FIG. 2.4. Mean phoneme boundary position (msec of VOT) plotted against precursor duration. (Adapted from Summerfield, 1975d. Reprinted by permission.)

the voiced–voiceless judgment. However, in another study (Summerfield, 1978), in which the three thirds of a precursor string were independently manipulated, each of the three segments was found to have an effect on the voicing judgment of the target consonant. The weight of the influence was dependent, however, on the proximity to the target syllable, so that the last third of the sentence exerted the most influence on the boundary location and the first third exerted the least. Inasmuch as a speaker can readily change the rate of speech while uttering an entire sentence, it is reasonable that the listener gives most weight to the rate of those portions of the sentence closest to the information being judged.

There is also evidence that the continuity between the precursor sequence and the target syllable is an important determinant of the degree to which the listener compensates for the rate of the context. Summerfield (1975d), for example, found that as a silence gap between the precursor string and the target syllable was increased, there was a corresponding decrease in the effect of precursor rate on the voiced–voiceless judgment of the target consonant. Another way of altering the continuity between context and target is by changing certain relevant acoustic parameters of the precursor, relative to the target. In a study of this type, Souther and Diehl (1978) found that the effect of precursor rate on a voicing

judgment was substantially reduced if there was a sizeable difference in fundamental frequency (pitch) between the precusor sequence and the test syllable.
However, Summerfield (1975b) reported that a shift in the relative frequencies of
the formants between precursor and target, indicating a mismatch in vocal tract
characteristics (and hence speaker), caused no reduction in the normalization
effect for rate. The reason that a change in pitch, but not vocal tract characteristics, influences the effect of the precursor is somewhat puzzling in that a speaker
could easily change pitch, but not vocal tract characteristics. Finally, there is one
study suggesting that the rate of the precursor influences voicing judgments only
if the rate information is carried by speech: Changing the rate of a melody has no
effect on the voicing judgment of a target syllable (Summerfield, 1978).

Not only can the context surrounding a target syllable specify the rate of
speech, but so too can certain aspects of the target syllable itself. Because a
change in speech rate results in a substantial change in the duration of the vocalic
portion of a syllable, one potential source of information about rate is the duration of the syllable. Thus, it might be expected that listeners would interpret a
given VOT value in accordance with the duration of the vocalic segment of the
target syllable. Summerfield (1978; Summerfield & Haggard, 1972) has shown
this to be the case: As the vocalic segment of the syllable is lengthened, a longer
VOT value is needed to hear a voiceless, as opposed to a voiced, stop. Furthermore, this effect obtains whether the syllable is of the form CV (e.g., [bi–pi])
or CVC (e.g., [biz–piz]).[8]

The effect of syllable duration is complex, however, in that it is not actually
syllable duration itself that influences the location of the voiced–voiceless boundary. As previously stated, if the CV syllable is lengthened by extending the
steady-state segment, the boundary shifts toward a longer VOT value. However,
if the syllable is lengthened by adding a final fricative (for example, adding [z] to
a [bi–pi] series so as to create [biz–piz]), the boundary value actually shifts
toward a shorter VOT value (Summerfield, 1978). Presumably, the addition of
the fricative specifies a faster rate of speech, leading to the appropriate compensation by the listener; however, there is no independent evidence that the effect is
actually due to rate.[9]

---

[8]Ainsworth (1973) has reported a similar finding for a voicing distinction based on burst duration,
rather than VOT. Specifically, using synthetic syllables consisting of a noise burst of variable
duration followed by a steady-state vowel of variable duration, he found that as the noise duration
decreased, the percept changed from that of a voiceless fricative ([si]) to a voiceless stop ([ti]) to a
voiced stop ([di]). Of particular importance is the fact that he found that the fricative-stop and
voiced–voiceless boundaries were at shorter durations of burst when either the syllable was preceded
by a precursor sequence with short sounds (specifying a fast tempo) or when the steady-state vowel of
the test syllable was shorter. Thus, listeners seem to adjust for the duration of the following vowel
when interpreting either VOT or noise duration as a cue for voicing.

[9]Summerfield (1978) attempted to obtain evidence that the shift effect did reflect a normalization
for rate by altering the duration of the frication and whether it was perceived as [s] or [z]—

In summary, both the characteristics of the syllable itself and the characteristics of the speech context provide rate information that is used by the listener when processing VOT. It is reasonable to suppose that, because it is the context closest to the target syllable that is weighted more heavily, most importance would be given to the rate information conveyed by the target syllable itself. This, however, remains to be empirically determined.

Intervocalic Consonants.   In a set of production studies, Port (1976) examined the influence of changes in speech tempo on a number of cues for the voicing distinction in intervocalic stop consonants. In his first experiment, he studied the effects of speech rate on the production of six stops ([b], [p], [d], [t], [g], [k]) in medial position. To generate the speech, he asked speakers to produce each of the words "dipper," "dibber," "ditter," "didder," "dikker," and "digger," in the sentence frame "Pat tried to say———to his Pop" at three speech rates; neutral, the fastest possible, and the slowest possible. For all utterances, measurements were made of the duration of the sentence (to provide a measure of overall sentence rate), the closure duration for the medial stop, and the duration of the vowel [I] (defined as the segment beginning at the release burst of the [d] and ending at the onset of closure for the medial stop).

As expected, vowel duration was generally longer for the voiced than the voiceless stops (cf. House, 1961; Raphael, 1972) and closure duration was generally longer for the voiceless than the voiced stops (cf. Lisker, 1957).[10] One of the most interesting findings of the study is that although both slowing down speech and speeding it up had predictable effects on the durations of both voicing cues, the two rate manipulations did not lead to reciprocal consequences. When speech was slowed down, both closure duration and vowel duration increased for both the voiced and voiceless consonants, and by the same percentage as the total sentence duration. Thus, slowing speech seemed to simply stretch the individual segments, keeping constant their relative durations. Speeding up speech, however, had much more complicated effects on the speech signal. First, stop closure duration and vowel duration did decrease for both voiced and voiceless consonants, but the percentage of change was less than for the total sentence. Second, the contrast in both closure duration and in vowel duration between the two kinds of stops was weaker at the faster rate of speech. That is to say, there was a

---

manipulations that have predictable consequences if the shift is due to rate. However, none of these manipulations had any effect on the boundary location. Thus, although for simple CV syllables, syllable duration does seem to be the critical parameter influencing the voicing boundary, presumably by specifying rate, it is not clear just what information is the CVC syllable is responsible for the boundary shifts, and just how this information specifies rate.

[10]One exception is that there was no difference either in closure duration or preceding vowel duration between the phonological voiced ([d]) and voiceless ([t]) apical stops, suggesting that these were not phonetically distinct for the speakers in this study. For a detailed discussion of this finding, the reader is referred to Port (1976).

decrease in the extent to which the values associated with the voiced and voiceless stops differed. In fact, at the fast rate of speech, the difference in vowel duration for the two kinds of stops nearly disappeared.

In order to investigate more extensively this relative weakening of the cues for voicing, Port performed a second experiment, using only the medial contrast between [b] and [p]. In this study, speakers were asked to produce the words "deeber," "deeper," "dibber," and "dipper," in the frame used originally, at a fast and neutral speech tempo. The effect of increasing speech tempo on vowel duration is shown in Fig. 2.5 and the effect on closure duration is shown in Fig. 2.6. The figures reveal that, as in the previous study, with speeded speech there was a decrease in the absolute durations of both cues, with vowel duration showing a particularly large change in duration. In addition, there was again a reduction in the contrast for each cue between the voiced and voiceless stops at the fast rate of speech. However, there was one aspect of speech that actually increased in distinctiveness at the fast rate, namely, the presence or absence of glottal pulsing. Whereas in neutral speech 65% of the [b] segments and 1% of the [p] segments had no break in voicing, at the fast speech rate 89% of the [b] segments and 5% of the [p] segments had no break. Thus, this cue seems to

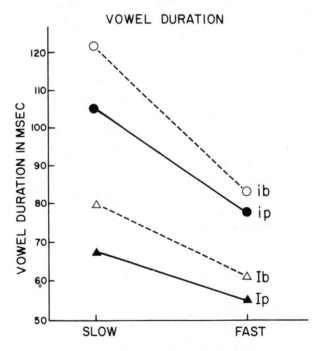

FIG. 2.5.   Mean vowel duration in msec for [i] and [I] before [b] and [p] at slow and fast tempos. (From Port, 1976. Reprinted by permission.)

STOP CLOSURE DURATION

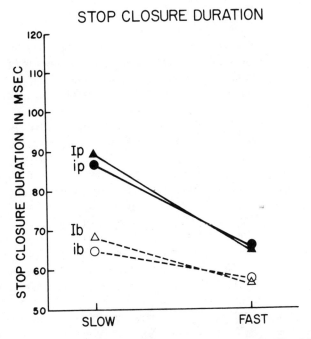

FIG. 2.6. Mean stop closure duration in msec for [b] and [p] after [i] and [I] at slow and fast tempos. (From Port, 1976. Reprinted by permission.)

differentiate the voiced and voiceless stops at both rates of speech, but perhaps even more so at the fast rate. This raises the very interesting possibility that listeners not only make the appropriate compensations for changes in the absolute value of a single cue at different rates of speech, but may also assign different relative weightings to cues at various rates. For example, whereas vowel duration and silence duration may be particularly important cues for neutral or slow speech, glottal pulsing may be the most salient cue at faster rates of speech.

Port (1976, 1978) has also performed a series of perceptual studies that examine the sensitivity of listeners to speech rate when processing cues for intervocalic voicing, in particular, the cue of closure duration. In one experiment, a speaker was asked to produce the sentence "I'm trying to say rabid" at a fast and slow rate of speech. The word "rabid" was then excised from both sentences and the slow "rabid" was manipulated in the following way. The word was electronically cut into two parts, one corresponding to "rab" and one to "bid" and a variable duration of silence (ranging from 10 to 120 msec) was inserted between the two segments. These tokens of the word were then spliced onto the slow and fast sentences and the newly created sentences were given to listeners to identify. As expected, closure duration was a sufficient cue for the voicing distinction, so that at relatively short durations "rabid" was heard and at relatively long durations "rapid" was heard.[11] Of primary interest is that the boundary between [b] and [p] changed as a function of sentence rate, and in the predicted direction. Whereas the [b]-[p] boundary for the slow carrier sentence was at about 75 msec closure duration, for the fast sentence it was at about 68 msec. Thus, when using closure duration as a cue for voicing, listeners do take into account the rate of the precursor string, just as they do when using VOT as a cue for voicing.[12]

In a following study, Port (1978) examined the relative contribution of the rate at which the carrier sentence is produced and the rate at which the target word itself is produced. He found that although both the tempo of the precursor string and the test word had some influence on the location of the phonetic boundary, the tempo of the test word itself was most important. Together with the Summerfield findings previously discussed, this implies that listeners take into account the rate information over a relatively long stretch of speech, but give increasingly more weight to segments more closely approximating the cue being processed.

Miller and Grosjean (in press) have recently extended Port's findings by investigating more directly the nature of the information in the precursor sentence that listeners using for specifying rate. The perceived rate of utterance depends not only on the articulation rate of the speech (i.e., the number of syllables per time spent articulating), but also on the pause time in the sentence. Furthermore, Grosjean and Lane (1976, and see Chapter 6, this volume) have shown that both variables contribute to a listener's estimation of the overall rate of a sentence, although articulation rate is a far more important variable than pause time. Miller and Grosjean attempted to determine whether this is also true when listeners are not judging speech rate, per se, but are adjusting for rate when interpreting a temporal cue, specifically, closure duration.

The stimuli for the experiment consisted of five versions of the naturally produced sentence "actually, the tiger that the man had to chase was rabid/rapid," in which both articulation rate and pause time were varied. Two sentences, one with no pauses and one with four pauses, had a relatively fast articulation rate; two sentences, one without pauses and one with four pauses, had a relatively slow articulation rate; and a fifth sentence had two pauses and a medium articulation rate. A "rabid-rapid" series was created by electronically editing the "rabid" from the medium-rate sentence so as to produce a series that varied in silence duration from 35 to 100 msec. Each of the resulting test words

---

[11]At the very shortest closure durations, subjects heard an apical flap instead of a voiced labial consonant. This suggests that closure duration may, under certain circumstances, be a cue for distinctions in place of articulation. For further details, see Port (1976).

[12]Souther and Diehl (1978) recently reported that for closure duration, as for VOT, the extent of the effect of precursor rate on the boundary depends on the match between the pitch of the precursor and target: As the pitch difference betwen the two is increased, the effect of the precursor tempo decreases.

was then electronically spliced onto each of the five test sentences, and subjects were asked to identify the target consonant as [b] or [p].

As in the studies of Port, the rate of the precursor sentence had an influence on the voicing judgments: As speech rate increased, listeners needed less silence to hear [p] instead of [b]. Interestingly, however, the global speech rate, that is, the rate determined by both articulation time and pause time, was not a very good predictor of voicing judgments. This was so because although both variables contributed to the effect, articulation rate was much more important than pause rate. In other words, when assigning a voicing value, listeners did not adjust for the global sentence rate (or total sentence duration, including pause time). Rather, they were particularly sensitive to the syllabic rate of the speech itself, and only secondarily affected by the amount of time spend pausing.

Together with the Grosjean and Lane (1976) data on the perception of rate, these data suggest that articulation rate and pause time interact in much the same way when influencing phonetic judgments and rate estimates. In both cases, it is the articulation time that is of prime importance. Even further support for this conclusion comes from an additional aspect of the Miller and Grosjean study, in which listeners were asked to estimate the tempo of the sentence, using a magnitude estimation procedure. As in the case of the [b]-[p] judgments, tempo estimates were affected primarily by the articulation rate of the sentence and less so by the pause time. Thus, at least to a first approximation, the information used to judge the tempo of a sentence is also used to adjust the way in which a phonetic value is assigned to a temporal cue.

Summary. We have seen that a number of temporal cues for the voiced-voiceless distinction, including VOT, closure duration, and preceding vowel duration, are systematically altered by changes in rate of speech and that, at least for some of these cues (VOT and closure duration), listeners make the appropriate compensation when listening to speech. Moreover, there is some indication that at different rates of speech different cues may be more or less distinctive, suggesting that listeners may alter the relative weighting they give to different cues in different contexts. Finally, there are data indicating that listeners use temporal variables specifying rate (e.g., articulation time, pause time) in much the same way when estimating speech tempo, per se, and when adjusting for speech rate while processing a temporal cue for a phonetic distinction.

Manner of Articulation

Although consonants (in English) can take on only one of two voicing values, they can take a number of manner values, including stop consonants (e.g., [b], [d], [g]), fricative (e.g., [ʃ], [ð], [θ], [v]), affricate ([tʃ], [dʒ]), nasal ([m], [n], [ŋ]), liquid ([r], [l]) and semivowel ([j], [w]). With respect to the issue of speech tempo, two manner contrasts have received most attention: the distinction between fricative and affricate ([ʃ] vs. [tʃ]) and the distinction between stop and semivowel ([b] vs. [w]).[13]

Fricative Versus Affricate.   There are a number of cues that signal the distinction between a fricative and an affricate consonant, including the duration of frication noise (Gerstman, 1957), the duration of the silence preceding the frication noise (Dorman, Raphael, & Liberman, 1976), and the onset characteristics of the noise (Cutting & Rosner, 1974; Gerstman, 1957). Two of these cues, frication duration and silence duration, have recently been studied with respect to articulation rate.

In a preliminary study on the [ʃ]–[tʃ] distinction, Dorman et al. (1976) found that the recorded utterance "please say shop" could be converted into "please say chop" by increasing the silence duration before the frication noise in "shop." That is to say, silence duration was an effective cue for the fricative-affricate distinction, with longer silence cueing the affricate. Of particular interest is that changing the tempo of the sentence changed the value of the silence duration at the [ʃ]–[tʃ] boundary. However, contrary to what might be expected, a longer, not a shorter, silence was required to cue the affricate at the faster rate of speech. As the reader will recall, exactly the opposite has been found for every other durational cue that has been studied, including silence duration as a cue for voicing. Both Port (1976, 1978) and Miller and Grosjean (in press) found that as speech rate was increased, less silence was required to hear a voiceless, as opposed to a voiced, stop.

To investigate further the seemingly paradoxical effect found by Dorman et al. (1976), Repp, Liberman, Eccardt, and Pesetsky (1978) conducted a more extensive study of the [ʃ]–[tʃ] contrast. Specifically, they examined the perception of this distinction in the sentence frame "why don't we say shop/chop again" by independently manipulating frication duration (60, 80, 100 msec), silence duration (0 to 100 msec in 10 msec steps), and speech rate (fast and slow). First, they found a trading relation between the two cues, such that as frication duration was increased (biasing the percept toward the fricative), silence duration needed to be increased (biasing the percept toward the affricate) to maintain a given percentage of affricate responses. Second, the paradoxical effect of Dorman et al. was replicated: At each frication duration, as speaking

---

[13]There are other manner contrasts that have been studied, although in less detail. First, as indicated in the foregoing, Ainsworth (1973) found that a contrast between a fricative ([si]) and a voiceless stop ([ti]), cued by burst duration, was sensitive to the duration of the following vowel. Second, Miller and Liberman (1978) found that a stop-nasal contrast between [b] and [m] cued primarily by the duration of nasal resonance, was also sensitive to syllable duration: As the duration of the syllable increased, presumably specifying a slower rate of articulation, a longer resonance was required to hear the nasal, as opposed to the stop, consonant.

rate increased, more silence was needed to maintain a given level of affricate indentification. Finally, at each of the two speech rates, the location of the [ʃ]-[tʃ] boundary was associated with a constant ratio of silence to noise duration. Thus, changing the rate of speech had the effect of changing the ratio of silence to noise necessary to perceive an affricate rather than a fricative.

Of course the critical issue raised by this study is why more, rather than less, silence is needed to hear the affricate at a faster rate of speech. The authors offer a tentative explanation based on the interaction of the two cues, silence duration and frication duration, in production. They suggest that when a speaker changes his or her rate of speech, he or she changes the duration of the frication relatively more than the duration of the silence.

A recent study by Isenberg (1978) provides support for this suggestion. He found that when the two words "dish" and "ditch" were produced in a sentence context at various rates of speech, increasing speech rate caused a decrease in the duration of the frication in both words and a decrease in the silence duration in "ditch" (there was no silence in "dish"). Furthermore, for "ditch," there was relatively more change in the frication noise than in the silence. Thus, as proposed by Repp et al., silence was relatively more stable with changes in speech rate than frication noise. To return now to the proposal of Repp et al., they hypothesized that when adjusting for speech tempo, the listener takes into account what should happen to the various cues as rate is changed. Specifically, the listener knows (tacitly) that if rate is increased, frication noise should decrease in duration more than silence. But in the perceptual experiment, as rate was increased, frication duration was held constant (at one of three levels). In effect, frication duration is very long compared to what is expected, and biases the percept toward the fricative. To compensate, the listener requires an increase in silence duration—just the result that was obtained.

Although the explanation proposed by Repp et al. provides a plausible account of their results, it does not reconcile their findings with those of Port (1976, 1978), and Miller and Grosjean (in press). It was found in these studies that when silence duration cues a voicing contrast, an increase in speaking rate leads to a decrease, not an increase, in the silence duration needed to convert a voiced to a voiceless stop. This occurs even though, in the case of voicing, variation in rate causes a larger change in vowel duration than in silence duration—analogous to the larger change in frication duration than in silence duration in the case of manner. Why silence duration is perceived in one way when it cues a manner distinction and in another way when it cues a voicing distinction remains as yet unresolved.

Regardless of the interpretation of the results, the findings of Repp et al. are of considerable importance. They reveal that compensations for rate of speech are not always straightforward, but involve complex adjustments by the listener for complex changes that occur in production. To ultimately sort out the various factors involved, it is necessary to consider the complete set of cues that signal a given distinction, rather than a single cue, and to directly compare the changes introduced as speech is produced at different rates of speech with the perceptual adjustments imposed by the listener.

Stop Versus Semivowel.   Another manner distinction that can be cued by a temporal variable is the distinction between a stop consonant (e.g., [b]) and a semivowel (e.g., [w]). In an early study on speech perception, Liberman, Delattre, Gerstman, and Cooper (1956) found that the duration of the initial formant transitions leading into the vowel is a critical manner cue: At shorter transition durations a stop consonant is heard, whereas at longer transition durations a semivowel is heard.

With the current interest in the effects of speech rate on segmental perception, investigators have begun to examine whether transition duration, as other temporal cues, is also perceived in a relative manner. The results of these studies suggest that it is. Ainsworth (1973), using synthetic speech, found that the duration of the sounds in a precursor sequence influenced the perception of a stop-semivowel distinction. Specifically, as the sounds in the precursor became longer (specifying a lower speech tempo), a longer initial transition was required to hear a semivowel instead of a stop consonant. And, using computer-edited natural speech, Minifie, Kuhl, and Stecher (1976) have recently obtained very similar results: Again, for faster speech, a relatively shorter transition was perceived as a semivowel rather than a stop.

In a recent series of studies, Miller and Liberman (1979) examined in more detail the effect of speech tempo on the perceived [b]-[w] distinction. For their first experiment they synthesized five series of sounds that ranged from [ba] to [wa]. The [b]-[w] distinction was cued by the duration of formant transition, ranging from 16 to 64 msec. The five series differed from each other only in total syllable duration, the shortest syllables having a duration of 80 msec and the longest syllables a duration of 296 msec. The variation in duration was accomplished by extending the steady-state portion of the syllable. Figure 2.7 shows that as syllable duration increased, the transition duration necessary to hear [w] also increased, resulting in a shift in the identification function toward a longer transition—a total shift of about 16 msec from the shortest to the longest syllable duration. Presumably, a longer syllable specified a slower rate of speech and, for a slower rate, [w] was specified by a relatively longer transition. Recall that an analogous interpretation was made by Summerfield for the effect of syllable duration on the location of the voiced–voiceless boundary.

In a second experiment, Miller and Liberman showed that the effect of subsequent information on the location of the [b]-[w] boundary is not confined to within a single syllable. When a [da] of variable duration was added to each member of a [ba–wa] series (so as to create [bada] or [wada]), the duration of the [da] was found to exert an influence on the phonetic boundary: Longer durations

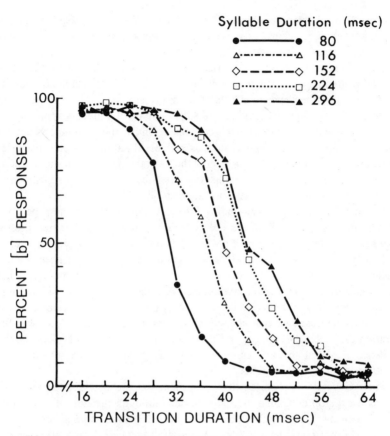

FIG. 2.7.   Mean percentage [b] responses as a function of syllable duration. (From Miller & Liberman, 1979. Copyright 1979 by The Psychonomic Society. Reprinted by permission.)

of [da] (presumably specifying a slower rate of speech) resulted in a longer transition at the boundary. Thus, rate of speech can be specified not only by the syllable containing the cue, but also by a following syllable. As might be expected, the effect due to variation in the [da] was considerably less than that due to variation in the target syllable itself.

Finally, in a third experiment, it was found that syllable duration, per se, is not the critical determinant of the perceived [b]-[w] contrast. Whereas adding steady-state information to each syllable (as in the first experiment) shifted the identification function toward a longer transition, adding final transitions (thus creating [bad] or [wad]) shifted the function in the opposite direction, toward a shorter transition. This effect was likewise interpreted in terms of adjustments for rate of speech. It was assumed that although the additional steady-state information specified a slower rate of speech, the added final transitions specified a faster rate of speech and, accordingly, relatively shorter transitions were perceived as [w]. Again, recall that Summerfield (1978) offered an analogous interpretation for the finding that adding a final fricative to a [bi–pi] series shifted the voiced–voiceless boundary toward a shorter, not a longer, VOT value. It should be emphasized that the opposite effects of adding steady-state information and final transition information on the perceived stop-semivowel boundary is an important finding. It reveals that the listener's compensation for speech tempo is not based solely on simple holistic factors such as syllable duration. Instead, the listener somehow takes into account not only the overall syllable duration, but also characteristics of the components that comprise the syllable—an adjustment that is certainly complex and, as yet, not understood.

Consider again the primary findings of the Miller and Liberman experiments; namely, that as the duration of a CV syllable increased, a longer transition was required to specify a semivowel ([w]) rather than a stop ([b]). It was proposed that this was because the longer syllable cued a slower rate of speech and the listener was making the appropriate compensation. This interpretation is based on the assumption that the slowing of speech leads to an increase in both overall syllable duration and transition duration. As we have mentioned earlier, numerous studies have shown that changes in rate result in modifications of syllable duration (e.g., Kozhevnikova & Chistovich, 1965). Moreover, there is recent evidence indicating that at least a portion of this change is due to alteration in the duration of formant transitions.

First, Gay (1978) reported that as speech was speeded up, the initial transitions for a stop consonant became shorter (although the rate of transition remained constant). Second, Miller and Baer (1980) found that as speech tempo decreased (and, consequently, syllable duration increased) there was some tendency for the F1 transition of [b] to lengthen and a pronounced increase in the F1 transition duration for [w]. Moreover, across a range of speech tempos, although most of the[b]'s had relatively short transitions and most of the[w]'s relatively long ones, transition duration alone did not completely distinguish the two consonants: There was a region of overlap, in which a given transition duration corresponded to some [b]'s and to some [w]'s. Of most interest is that within this region of ambiguity, the two consonants could be differentiated by considering overall syllable duration: If the syllable was short, the consonant was most likely [w], whereas if it was long, the consonant was most likely [b]. This pattern is in complete accord with the perceptual findings.

In the experiments reviewed so far on perceptual normalization for speech tempo, the listener has been under no pressure to respond quickly. This is quite unlike the natural listening situation, in which speech impinges on the listener at a rapid pace and places him under pressure to make a continuous string of phonetic decisions. The question arises, then, whether the listener would use rate information in making a phonetic judgment when under time constraints, especially if the rate information came *after* the cue being judged.

In an initial attempt to address this issue, Miller (in press) recently performed a speeded classification experiment in which she asked listeners to identify whether a syllable was [ba] or [wa] as quickly as possible. Her stimuli were three of the [ba–wa] series from the Miller and Liberman (1979) experiment which, as the reader will recall, differed from each other only in overall syllable duration. The results convincingly showed that, even under conditions of time pressure, listeners used information about syllable duration in making the phonetic decision. First, as in the original Miller and Liberman study, the boundary between [b] and [w] shifted toward a longer transition as syllable duration increased. Second, the overall response times to the syllables increased as syllable duration increased, indicating even more directly that listeners were not processing just the transition cue, but were waiting for information about the extent of the steady-state segment. Finally, response times not only increased with syllable duration at the intermediate transition durations near the boundary, but also for those longer transitions that were judged [w] almost 100% of the time, regardless of syllable duration. (There was no difference in response times for the three series within the [b] category). Thus, even when attempting to arrive at a phonetic decision quickly, the listener does not treat each acoustic segment as an independent event, but integrates information over a considerable stretch of speech.

One final point needs to be made. We have just seen that transition duration is a rate-dependent cue for a segmental distinction, namely, stop versus semivowel. As the reader will recall from the earlier discussion of vowels, transition duration can also specify rate of speech. Similarly, vowel duration, a rate-specific cue for vowel quality, also provides information about speaking tempo. Thus, a given acoustic property may serve two functions; first, specify a phonetic contrast and second, signal speaking rate. The problem for the listener is how to interpret a cue in relation to speech rate when rate is specified, at least in part, by the cue itself. However this is accomplished by the listener, it surely must be the case that judgments of phonetic structure and tempo are not independent, but are made simultaneously and interactively.

Summary

Although the temporal variation in the speech waveform that results from alterations in speech tempo primarily involves the vocalic segments of speech, those parameters corresponding to the consonants are affected as well. The variety of acoustic cues for consonantal distinctions that have been studied to date, including cues for manner of articulation, voicing, and the single-geminate distinction, all appear to be affected as the speaker changes tempo. Furthermore, the perceptual studies support the claim that the listener is sensitive to these changes, and properly compensates for them by processing the cues in relation to the rate of speech at which they were produced.

CONCLUDING REMARKS

Interest in the effects of speaking rate on the production and perception of segmental contrasts and, more generally, in the relation between prosodic and segmental aspects of speech, has grown considerably over the past few years. One reason is that it has become increasingly apparent that prosodic and segmental information is so intertwined in speech that only by studying both factors will it ultimately be possible to build a model of segmental perception.

This review has attempted to elucidate the nature of the interaction between segmental features and one prosodic parameter, speech tempo. We have seen that an alteration in speaking rate introduces complex modifications in a number of properties of speech that serve as cues for phonetic contrasts and that listeners adjust, at least within certain limits, to that variation when processing the phonetically relevant information. Moreover, it is apparent that rate does not affect the cues uniformly: The magnitude of effect varies across cues, as does the case of whether a cue becomes more or less distinctive with a change in speaking rate. Consequently, a thorough description of the set of cues that specifies any given segmental distinction, and the manner in which the listener processes these cues, cannot be rate-independent. Finally, we should note in closing that further study of speaking tempo, as well as other prosodic variables, will increase our understanding, not only of how these variables interact with segmental distinctions, but also of the nature of the acoustic cues themselves.

ACKNOWLEDGMENT

Preparation of this chapter and the author's research reported herein was supported by Grant NS 14394 from the National Institute of Neurological and Communicative Disorders and Stroke.

REFERENCES

Ainsworth, W. A. Duration as a cue in the recognition of synthetic vowels. *Journal of the Acoustical Society of America*, 1972, *51*, 648–651.

Ainsworth, W. A. Durational cues in the perception of certain consonants. *Proceedings of the British Acoustical Society*, 1973, *2*, 1–4.

Ainsworth, W. A. The influence of precursive sequences on the perception of synthesized vowels. *Language and Speech*, 1974, *17*, 103–109.

Bastian, J., Eimas, P. D., & Liberman, A. M. Identification and discrimination of a phonemic contrast induced by a silent interval. *Journal of the Acoustical Society of America*, 1961, *33*, 842. (Abstract)

Bennett, D. C. Spectral form and duration as cues in the recognition of English and German vowels. *Language and Speech*, 1968, *11*, 65–68.

Cohen, A., Slis, I. H., & 't Hart, J. Perceptual tolerance of isolated Dutch vowels. *Phonetica*, 1963, *9*, 65–78.

Cole, R. A., & Scott, B. Toward a theory of speech perception. *Psychological Review*, 1974, *81*, 348–375.

Cutting, J. E., & Rosner, B. S. Categories and boundaries in speech and music. *Perception and Psychophysics*, 1974, *16*, 564–570.

Delattre, P. C., Liberman, A. M., & Cooper, F. S. Acoustic loci and transitional cues for consonants. *Journal of the Acoustical Society of America*, 1955, *27*, 761–773.

Denes, P. Effect of duration on the perception of voicing. *Journal of the Acoustical Society of America*, 1955, *27*, 761–764.

Dorman, M. F., Raphael, L. J., & Liberman, A. M. Further observations on the role of silence in the perception of stop consonants. *Journal of the Acoustical Society of America*, 1976, *59*, S40. (Abstract)

Fowler, C. A. *Timing control in speech production*. Unpublished doctoral dissertation, University of Connecticut, 1977.

Fujisaki, H., Nakamura, K., & Imoto, T. Auditory perception of duration of speech and non-speech stimuli. In G. Fant & M. A. A. Tatham (Eds.), *Auditory analysis and perception of speech*. London: Academic Press, 1975.

Gaitenby, J. H. *The elastic word*. (SR-2, 3.1–3.12) Haskins Laboratories Status Report on Speech Research, 1965.

Gay, T. Effect of speaking rate on diphthong formant movements. *Journal of the Acoustical Society of America*, 1968, *44*, 1570–1573.

Gay, T. Effect of speaking rate on vowel formant movements. *Journal of the Acoustical Society of America*, 1978, *63*, 223–230.

Gay, T., & Hirose, H. Effect of speaking rate on labial consonant production. *Phonetica*, 1973, *27*, 44–56.

Gay, T., & Ushijima, T. Effect of speaking rate on stop consonant-vowel articulation. In G. Fant (Ed.), *Proceedings of the Speech Communication Seminar*. Stockholm: Almquist & Wiksell, 1974.

Gay, T., Ushijima, T., Hirose, H., & Cooper, F. S. Effect of speaking rate on labial consonant-vowel articulation. *Journal of Phonetics*, 1974, *2*, 47–63.

Gerstman, L. *Cues for distinguishing among fricatives, affricates, and stop consonants*. Unpublished doctoral dissertation, New York University, 1957.

Goldman-Eisler, F. *Psycholinguistics: Experiments in spontaneous speech*. New York: Academic Press, 1968.

Grosjean, F., & Lane, H. How the listener integrates the components of speaking rate. *Journal of Experimental Psychology: Human Perception and Performance*, 1976, *2*, 538–543.

Haggard, M. P., Ambler, S., & Callow, M. Pitch as a voicing cue. *Journal of the Acoustical Society of America*, 1970, *47*, 613–617.

Harris, K. S. Mechanisms of duration change. In G. Fant (Ed.), *Proceedings of the Speech Communication Seminar*. Stockholm: Almquist & Wiksell, 1974.

House, A. On vowel duration in English. *Journal of the Acoustical Society of America*, 1961, *33*, 1174–1178.

Huggins, A. W. F. Just noticeable differences for segment duration in natural speech. *Journal of the Acoustical Society of America*, 1972, *51*, 1270–1278. (a)

Huggins, A. W. F. On the perception of temporal phenomena in speech. *Journal of the Acoustical Society of America*, 1972, *51*, 1279-1290. (b)

Isenberg, D. Relative duration of stop closure and fricative noise across speaking rate. *Journal of the Acoustical Society of America*, 1978, *63*, S54. (Abstract)

Joos, M. *Acoustic Phonetics*. Linguistic Society of America Monograph, (Whole No. 23), Baltimore: Waverly Press, 1948.

Klatt, D. H. Interaction between two factors that influence vowel duration. *Journal of the Acoustical Society of America*, 1973, *54*, 1102-1104.

Klatt, D. H. Vowel lengthening is syntactially determined in a connected discourse. *Journal of Phonetics*, 1975, *3*, 129-140.

Klatt, D. H. Linguistic uses of segmental duration in English: Acoustic and perceptual evidence. *Journal of the Acoustical Society of America*, 1976, *59*, 1208-1221.

Kozhevnikova, V. A., & Chistovich, L. A. *Speech Articulation and Perception*. (Clearinghouse for Federal Technical and Scientific Information, trans.). Washington, D.C.: Joint Publications Research Service, 1965.

Kuehn, D. P., & Moll, K. L. A cineradiographic study of VC and CV articulatory velocities. *Journal of Phonetics*, 1976, *4*, 303-320.

Ladefoged, P., & Broadbent, D. E. Information conveyed by vowels. *Journal of the Acoustical Society of America*, 1957, *29*, 98-104.

Lehiste, I. *Suprasegmentals*. Cambridge, Mass.: MIT Press, 1970.

Liberman, A. M., Cooper, F. S., Shankweiler, D. P., & Studdert-Kennedy, M. Perception of the speech code. *Psychological Review*, 1967, *74*, 431-461.

Liberman, A. M., Delattre, P. C., Gerstman, L. J., & Cooper, F. S. Tempo of frequency change as a cue for distinguishing classes of speech sounds. *Journal of Experimental Psychology*, 1956, *52*, 127-137.

Lieberman, P. On the evolution of language: A unified view. *Cognition*, 1973, *2*, 59-94.

Lieberman, P., Crelin, E. S., & Klatt, D. H. Phonetic ability and related anatomy of the newborn, adult human, Neanderthal man, and the chimpanzee. *American Anthropologist*, 1972, *74*, 287-307.

Lindblom, B. Spectrographic study of vowel reduction. *Journal of the Acoustical Society of America*, 1963, *35*, 1773-1781.

Lindblom, B., & Rapp, K. *Some temporal regularities of spoken Swedish*. Papers from the Institute of Linguistics, University of Stockholm, 1973. (No. 21)

Lindblom, B. E. F., & Studdert-Kennedy, M. On the role of formant-transitions in vowel recognition. *Journal of the Acoustical Society of America*, 1967, *42*, 830-843.

Lisker, L. Closure duration and the intervocalic voiced-voiceless distinction in English. *Language*, 1957, *33*, 42-49.

Lisker, L. Is it VOT or first-formant transition detector? *Journal of the Acoustical Society of America*, 1975, *57*, 1547-1551.

Lisker, L. On buzzing the English [b]. *Journal of the Acoustical Society of America*, 1978, *63*, S20. (Abstract)

Lisker, L., & Abramson, A. S. A cross-language study of voicing in initial stops: Acoustical measurements. *Word*, 1964, *20*, 384-422.

Lisker, L., & Abramson, A. S. Some effects of context on voice onset time in English stops. *Language and Speech*, 1967, *10*, 1-28.

Lisker, L., & Abramson, A. S. The voicing dimension: Some experiments in comparative phonetics. *Proceedings of the 6th International Congress of Phonetic Sciences* (1967), Prague: Academia Publishing House of Czechoslavak Academy of Sciences, 1970.

Marcus, S. M. Distinguishing "slit" and "split"—an invariant timing cue in speech perception. *Perception and Psychophysics*, 1978, *23*, 58-60.

Mermelstein, P., Liberman, A. M., & Fowler, A. Perceptual assessment of vowel duration in consonantal context and its application to vowel identification. *Journal of the Acoustical Society of America*, 1977, *62*, S101. (Abstract)

Miller, J. L. Some effects of speaking rate on phonetic perception. *Phonetica,* in press.

Miller, J. L., & Baer, T. Unpublished study, 1980.

Miller, J. L., & Grosjean, F. How the components of speaking rate influence perception of the phonetic segments. *Journal of Experimental Psychology: Human Perception and Performance*, in press.

Miller, J. L. & Liberman, A. M. Unpublished study, 1978.

Miller, J. L., & Liberman, A. M. Some effects of later-occurring information on the perception of stop consonant and semivowel. *Perception and Psychophsics*, 1979, *25*, 457–465.

Minifie, F., Kuhl, P., & Stecher, B. Categorical perception of [b] and [w] during changes in rate of utterance. *Journal of the Acoustical Society of America*, 1976, *62*, S79. (Abstract)

Nooteboom, S. G. The perceptual reality of some prosodic durations. *Journal of Phonetics*, 1973, *1*, 25–45.

Oller, D. K. The effect of position in utterance on speech segment duration in English. *Journal of the Acoustical Society of America*, 1973, 54, 1235–1247.

Peterson, G. E., & Barney, H. L. Control methods used in a study of the vowels. *Journal of the Acoustical Society of America*, 1952, *24*, 175–184.

Peterson, G. E., & Lehiste, I. Duration of syllable nuclei in English. *Journal of the Acoustical Society of America*, 1960, *32*, 693–703.

Pickett, J. M., & Decker, L. R. Time factors in perception of a double consonant. *Language and Speech*, 1960, *3*, 11–17.

Port, R. F. *The influence of speaking tempo on the duration of stressed vowel and medial stop in English Trochee words*. Unpublished doctoral dissertation, University of Connecticut, 1976.

Port, R. F. Effects of word-internal versus word-external tempo on the voicing boundary for medial stop closure. *Journal of the Acoustical Society of America*, 1978, *63*, S20. (Abstract)

Raphael, L. J. Preceding vowel duration as a cue to the perception of the voicing characteristic of word-final consonants in American English. *Journal of the Acoustical Society of America*, 1972, *51*, 1296–1303.

Repp, B. H., Liberman, A. M., Eccardt, T., & Pesetsky, D. Perceptual integration of acoustic cues for stop, fricative, and affricate manner. *Journal of Experimental Psychology: Human Perception and Performance,* 1978, *4*, 621–636.

Shankweiler, D., Strange, W., & Verbrugge, R. Speech and the problem of perceptual constancy. In R. Shaw & J. Bransford (Eds.), *Perceiving, acting, and knowing*. Potomac, Md.: Lawrence Erlbaum Associates, 1977.

Souther, A., & Diehl, R. L. The effect of pitch change on rate normalization. *Journal of the Acoustical Society of America*, 1978, *64*, S20 (Abstract).

Stetson, R. H. *Motor phonetics*. Amsterdam: North-Holland, 1951.

Stevens, K. N., & House, A. S. Perturbation of vowel articulations by consonantal context: An acoustical study. *Journal of Speech and Hearing Research*, 1963, *6*, 111–128.

Stevens, K. N., & Klatt, D. H. Role of formant transitions in the voiced–voiceless distinction for stops. *Journal of the Acoustical Society of America*, 1974, *55*, 653–659.

Summerfield, A. Q. Towards a detailed model for the perception of voicing contrasts. In *Speech perception* (No. 3). Department of Psychology, Queen's University of Belfast, 1974.

Summerfield, A. Q. Aerodynamics versus mechanics in the control of voicing onset in consonant-vowel syllables. In *Speech perception* (No. 4). Department of Psychology, Queen's University of Belfast, 1975. (a)

Summerfield, A. Q. Cues, contexts, and complications in the perception of voicing contrasts. In *Speech perception* (No. 4). Department of Psychology, Queen's University of Belfast, 1975. (b)

Summerfield, A. Q. How a full account of segmental perception depends on prosody and vice versa. In A. Cohen & S. G. Nooteboom (Eds.), *Structure and process in speech perception*. New York: Springer-Verlag, 1975. (c)

Summerfield, A. Q. *Information processing analyses of perceptual adjustments to source and context variables in speech*. Unpublished doctoral dissertation, Queen's University of Belfast, 1975. (d)

Summerfield, A. Q. *On articulatory rate and perceptual constancy in phonetic perception*. Unpublished manuscript, 1978.

Summerfield, A. Q., & Haggard, M. P. Speech rate effects in the perception of voicing. In *Speech synthesis and perception* (No. 6). Psychology Laboratory, University of Cambridge, 1972.

Tiffany, W. R. Nonrandom sources of variation in vowel quality. *Journal of Speech and Hearing Research*, 1959, *2*, 305–317.

Umeda, N. Vowel duration in American English. *Journal of the Acoustical Society of America*, 1975, *58*, 434–445.

Verbrugge, R. R., & Isenberg, D. Syllable timing and vowel perception. *Journal of the Accoustical Society of America*, 1978, 63, S4. (Abstract)

Verbrugge, R. R., & Shankweiler, D. Prosodic information for vowel identity. *Journal of the Acoustical Society of America*, 1977, *61*, S39. (Abstract)

Verbrugge, R. R., Strange, W., Shankweiler, D. P., & Edman, T. R. What information enables a listener to map a talker's vowel space? *Journal of the Acoustical Society of America*, 1976, *60*, 198–212.

3

Birdsong and Speech: Evidence For Special Processing

Peter Marler
Susan Peters
Rockefeller University

Editors' Comments

A controversial idea in the field of speech is the hypothesis that the mechanisms of perception and production are species-specific adaptations, designed especially to serve the requirements of human communication. In actuality, the controversy is not so much whether there are any species-specific processes involved in human communication, but rather the level of processing at which they first become involved. Certainly, it is difficult to deny the existence of biologically determined constraints on the processes of production and the structure of the production system itself. In addition, most investigators ascribe to the belief that specializations of the human brain are responsible for our abilities to process and interpret the syntactic and semantic components of language. The question is still open, however, as to whether the perceptual processes that yield the initial phonetic representation involve species-specific mechanisms.

One approach to the issue of species-specificity in language processing has been to examine the acquisition of communication signals by nonhuman organisms. One of the best examples of this research is the study of song development in sparrows by Marler and his associates. In the present chapter by Marler and Peters, we find a discussion of their latest findings on song development in two species of sparrow: the swamp sparrow and the song sparrow. Although their data strongly implicate species-specific biological constraints, they (Marler & Peters, in this chapter) emphasize that these constraints, "should be viewed not so much as components for designing animals as efficient automata, but rather to provide developmental guidelines for learning [p. 78]." Marler and Peters also discuss how perception is elaborated by experience and the processes of production. In addition, they provide, as their title suggests, some forceful arguments for the idea that human speech, like the communication systems of other animals, is constrained by the biology of the human organism at all levels.

INTRODUCTION

An awesome task confronts the human infant as it embarks on the process of analyzing and understanding the complexities of adult speech. There is no simple isomorphism between sound structure and phonetic content. The infant has to come to grips with the problem of extracting phonetic information from exceedingly variable acoustic material, normalizing across speakers with vocal tracts of different sizes, and comprehending the structural variation of speaking at different rates (Fourcin, 1978). Moreover, as a prelude to participation in a system of social communication, the process of speech perception by infants is subject to some special constraints.

The infant must employ rules for the perceptual analysis and extraction of the linguistic content from speech more or less like those employed by speakers, if it is ever to extract the information intended for it. Moreover, the perceptual rules that the infant develops for speech analysis must surely have an impact upon its own subsequent speech production (Fry, 1966), raising the issue of sharing of common mechanisms for speech perception and production. The communicative potential of an infant's speech can only suffer if the rules employed reflect private or idiosyncratic habits adopted in processing the speech sounds of others. Seen in this light, it seems inevitable that the human organism will have evolved innate rules to guide the progression from stage to stage of the complicated unfoldings of the process of learning to perceive speech.

Although there has been progress in understanding perceptual development, especially in the visual domain, our understanding of many basic issues is still rudimentary. Processes of perceptual generalization, for example, as precursors to the formation of categories and the attachment of linguistic labels to them, still seem fraught with mystery (see Rosch & Lloyd, 1978). Crucial gaps in our knowledge are especially evident when we try to deal with the perceptual processing of the complex stimuli that animals use in the process of social communication. For example, we have little understanding of the development of the ability that birds display in perceptual processing of the complex sounds that they use in their vocal behavior. We refer here to the development of mechanisms specialized for particular subroutines within audition such as selective attentiveness to particular features of vocal stimuli. Our aim is to review some evidence for such special mechanisms, to indicate progress in analyzing contributions of innate processing to perceptual development, and to suggest that vocal perception in birds provides a useful ontogenetic model for furthering understanding of certain aspects of the development of speech perception in infants.

Innate Contributions to Perceptual Development

Given our ignorance as to which particular traits of structure or chemistry are responsible for the transmutations of mental imagery, and the innumerable developmental steps from the genes that make them possible, it is hardly surprising that we have so little grasp of genetic influences on the more subtle aspects of perceptual development. Yet the challenge must be faced if the mysteries of perception are ever to be fully understood. Perhaps the relative simplicity of perception in animals makes them a promising starting point.

It is a recurrent finding in studies of Lorenz, Tinbergen, and other ethologists that developing young animals manifest innate responsiveness to certain stimuli. Especial stimulus salience is typically associated with events that have particular biological significance for members of that species, such as predator detection or sexual communication. What kinds of mechanisms might mediate such preordained responsiveness? Perhaps specializations of the sensory surface might be involved as they are known to be in some invertebrate receptor systems (Marler & Hamilton, 1966). However, in vertebrates the dynamic selectivity of such innate responsiveness is sometimes such that it is hard to imagine peripheral sensory structures that could constrain responsiveness so narrowly. Thus, the concept of "innate release mechanisms" as developed by Lorenz and Tinbergen seeks to involve both peripheral and central influences in selective, innate perceptual discriminations (Baerends & Kruijt, 1973; Marler, 1961; Schleidt, 1962).

When an organism's life is dominated by a few special behavioral requirements, most environmental changes impinging on its receptors can be rejected or attenuated at an early stage of stimulus processing. The effect will be to focus immediate attention on the subset of stimuli that is biologically appropriate. In such cases innate release mechanisms can rely on peripheral specializations. However, with much sensory information rejected in the process of transduction, the focusing of responsiveness is obviously bought at considerable cost. The gain in selectivity is balanced by a loss of perceptual versatility. For organisms adapted to benefit from responsiveness to many kinds of environmental informa tion, such a price would be exhorbitant. Instead, more versatile receptor systems will be favored. The conditions for versatile sensory systems are met in many organisms. Cases in point are active, nonspecialized predators and species with elaborate social behavior. Above all, most higher vertebrates qualify, especially birds and mammals.

The essential feature of a "versatile" perceptual system is the dynamic quality of stimulus selectivity. The same receptor system can mediate selective responsiveness to many patterns of stimulation, the particular selection being adjusted according to changing needs of the organism. Sometimes these changes will reflect reversible, often cyclic changes in the hierarchically organized motivational states of an organism (Tinbergen, 1951). On other occasions there will be progressive noncyclical changes in the selectivity of responsiveness, such as accrue from the cumulative, learned experience of continuing interactions between organism and environment.

Although innate responsiveness plays a dominant role in the developing behavior of all organisms, enrichment through learning is often extensive. The challenge is to understand how genetic and environmental influences interact. The viewpoint has been expressed elsewhere that some "innate release mechanisms" as described by ethologists should be viewed not so much as components for designing animals as efficient automata, but rather to provide developmental guidelines for learning (Marler, Dooling, & Zoloth, 1980). If this is correct, there is promise in unifying concepts developed by ethologists for understanding innate behavior with those of psychologists arising from studies of animal learning.

According to our view, young birds and mammals have the potential to acquire responsiveness to virtually any perceptible feature of a stimulus object. In many circumstances they will nevertheless be prone to attend to certain features of natural situations in preference to others, namely those endowed with an innate salience. The effect will be to canalize perceptual development. Although idiosyncrasies of individual life histories within a species may result in many different types of perceptual organization, in species-typical environments adult perceptual organization is likely to be highly predictable in certain respects. Although the diversity may still be great, at certain levels of perceptual organization, most species members will share operational rules, the degree of sharing depending on the nature and timing of the innate constraints involved.

As guidelines for perceptual learning, rather than prescriptions for automata, the effects of "innate release mechanisms" of higher vertebrates will often be subtle. Such mechanisms are designed to operate in concert with stimulation from species-specific environments, physical and social. Out of this ecological interaction, the developing organization of perception of the external world of each species emerges in orderly and predictable procession, assured of the adaptiveness of its major lineaments, yet flexible enough to allow benefit from the vagaries of individual experience, experimentation and tutelage. We believe that the development of communicative behavior illustrates this process of ontogenetic interaction, and that it is well exemplified by avian vocal behavior and the development of vocal perception in birds.

AVIAN VOCAL BEHAVIOR

Within the basic vocal repertoires of birds, ranging in size from five to twenty or thirty functionally distinct acoustic signals, one finds alarm calls for various predators, food, aggression, locomotion and social signals, sounds given at different stages of courtship and calls peculiar to the relationships between parent and young (Nottebohm, 1975). In addition it is almost always possible to distinguish one complex set of vocal patterns, often consisting of long sequences of melodic sounds, characterized as the song. Usually, though not always, it is a male prerogative. Birdsong serves a variety of functions relating in one way or another to maintenance of the basic social organization of the reproductive phase of their life cycle. It is typically designed and delivered as a long-range signal, having to do with establishment and maintenance of territories, attraction and stimulation of mates, the structuring of populations, and training members of the next generation to sing.

Some bird songs are simple, with each individual male restricting its production to one single pattern. Even here, however, one finds variation at many levels, including local dialects, stable individual differences, and variations with the motivational state of the singer. Some features are always shared as species-specific universals. Songs of many sparrows fall into the category of relatively simple patterns, and just because of their relative simplicity they are favored research subjects.

At the other extreme of complexity are the almost unbelievably and unmanageably diverse song repertoires of such birds as thrushes and mockingbirds in some of which the song repertoire of an individual may be numbered in the hundreds and even thousands (Kroodsma, 1978). This extreme diversity is especially notable in songbirds that sing continuously for long periods of time without a break. The diversity seems to be designed primarily not for semantic enrichment but to reduce habituation. It thus serves to maintain the interest of the audience, whether it be a rival male or a female in the course of seduction (e.g. Kroodsma, 1976). There are various rules for the organized delivery of these large song repertoires, apparently also designed to maintain a continuing level of acoustic novelty in the stimuli presented to others (e.g. Nelson, 1973). Analogies to phonological rules abound (Beer, 1976), but it is doubtful if there are parallels with grammar or lexical syntax (Marler, 1977).

The songbird syrinx is a remarkable instrument, in many ways more versatile than the mammalian larynx. Although there is still much to learn about how it functions, syringeal function is much better understood since the work of Greenewalt (1968). He showed that it operates, at least part of the time, not by modulation of resonant properties of post syringeal air cavities, but rather as a consequence of active driving by the syringeal membranes. This was confirmed by Hersh (1966), who demonstrated that several songbirds vocalizing in helium air showed no change of pitch. With songbird syringes placed at the convergence of the two bronchi, and vibrating membranes on each limb, it is possible for them to produce harmonically unrelated sounds simultaneously, which helps in understanding the acoustic complexity of bird songs. The complicated sounds that birds make are produced for others to perceive them, thus raising some of the same issues that arise in the development of speech perception.

The Perception of Birdsong

How much of the acoustic detail of song is in fact sensed by birds? One kind of answer stems from studies of their ability to imitate. Secondly, there have been extensive playback studies with wild and captive birds, presenting them with recordings of songs that are either unmodified, or transformed and degraded in various ways, in some cases electronically synthesized, again telling us something about which details of song are perceived, and in which situations they have communicative significance. Finally, a picture is emerging of the basic psychophysics of bird hearing, as revealed by physiological techniques, and by conditioning procedures analogous to those used in behavioral studies of mammalian or human audition (Dooling, 1980; Konishi, 1978; Saunders, Else, & Bock, 1978).

The burden of much of this research is that a great deal of the acoustic detail of bird vocalizations is in fact perceived and responded to by the birds (Emlen, 1972; Falls, 1969; Kroodsma, 1977a). This is clearly the case with species differences in bird song. In some songbirds, there are local dialects, and playback studies reveal responsiveness to them. We know that certain features of songs are learned and reproduced with great accuracy. Alongside the acoustic features that characterize species and dialect, others are unique to each individual. These arise as a consequence of the intrusion of vocal invention or improvization into the developmental process, relegated to certain parts of the signal. Experienced subjects are responsive to these, personally identifying companions in the society in which they live. Birds are responsive to variations in song complexity or repertoire size. In some cases this is known to correlate with a male's age, and may be important for females in the selection of the best available mate (e.g. Nottebohm & Nottebohm, 1978; Yasukawa, in press).

There is a hierarchy of meaningful features at different levels of organization of singing behavior. They are present as a kind of overlay of acoustic properties, embedded in a single string of sounds, much as a spoken sentence of speech carries in parallel information about the linguistic message, the affective state of the speaker, gender and personal identity, membership in a cultural community, and personality. In both speech and song, it is a challenge for the organism to process this information without confusion between levels. The bird case is simpler, and may thus be more manageable in some respects, while still complicated enough to give a window on the principles involved.

We want to focus here on what seems at first sight a relatively simple problem, namely the ability to discriminate conspecific sounds from others, a significant issue for many birds, and perhaps more important for infants of our own species than is often thought. Vocal learning has proved to play a significant role in song development in every species of songbird tested so far. That is to say, song is abnormal when birds are reared without access to models of their own species song (Konishi & Nottebohm, 1969; Marler & Mundinger, 1971;

Nottebohm, 1972; Thorpe, 1961). In some, vocal plasticity is persistent (e.g. Marler, Mundinger, Waser, & Lutjen, 1972; Nottebohm & Nottebohm, 1978). In other species, vocal learning is constrained to well-defined sensitive periods during youth or infancy, often for about a month or so (e.g. Immelmann, 1969; Kroodsma, 1978; Marler, 1970). Song productions are atypical if normal models are withheld during this period, and may remain so, irrespective of whether there is further access to normal models later in life or not.

Avian Vocal Learning

Among the many variations of the vocal learning process in songbirds certain basic features recur. Firstly, there is often a strongly emphasized infantile phase of song learning (Kroodsma, 1978). Secondly, there is a widespread tendency for the learning to proceed in two phases, one sensory, the other sensorimotor. Although these two phases may interdigitate in time, they are often clearly separated. In the white-crowned sparrow for example, the first sensory phase falls between 10 and 50 days of age. However, the bird does not sing at this time. Instead, singing begins some weeks or even months later, so that the sensorimotor phase is guided from memory (Marler, 1970).

A white-crowned sparrow that has been exposed to a normal model during the sensitive period will begin subsong some 50 or 100 days later. This is a soft, rambling, exceedingly variable pattern of vocal production that gradually crystallizes over a period of weeks. At first it bears no relationship to the model. Then it begins to include renditions of syllables from the model along with many others, in a variable order. These finally assume a specific and detailed correspondence with certain features of the normal song, which is typically a series of introductory whistles followed by a terminal, syllabic trill.

In the white-crowned sparrow, features of the learned dialect are especially embodied in the latter part of the song. The song introduction exhibits more signs of improvised individuality than the concluding trill. Precise imitation tends to be limited to this second, trill portion of the white-crowned sparrow song (Marler, 1970). Reproduction of features of learned models is thus selective. It is rare to find slavish imitation of models in their entirety in learned bird songs. Even such famous mimics as the mockingbird recast their imitations into their own version of the overall temporal organization.

The third notable characteristic of birdsong learning is that of selectivity. It is well known that mockingbirds and starlings mimic other species. However, these are exceptions, and in nature the vast majority of songbirds refrain from mimicry of other species, even though rare interspecific mimicry may indicate a physical ability to produce sounds of other birds (e.g., Eberhardt & Baptista, 1977). If song learning is indeed universal among songbirds, how do they minimize cross-species imitation?

At least two kinds of mechanisms are involved. In one case exogenous constraints of a social nature are employed, as in species such as the bullfinch and the zebra finch (Immelmann, 1969; Nicolai, 1959). A young bullfinch can be persuaded in the laboratory to learn an enormous variety of natural and artificial sounds (Thorpe, 1955). In nature, it will learn only from the vocal productions of the father. Illustrating a second type of mechanism, some species possess endogenous, physiological mechanisms for constraining the choice of models for vocal imitation. The white-crowned sparrow is a typical example (Konishi, 1978; Marler, 1970). If during the sensitive period, a young male white-crown is given a choice of two recorded songs, one of his own species, the other of a different species present and singing in his natural habitat, such as the song sparrow, he will accept the conspecific model and reject the alien one. Interestingly, song development proceeds significantly faster if a conspecific model has been presented at the appropriate time than when acceptable models have been withheld. If alien song alone is presented, he will again reject it, and develop the innate song of an untrained social isolate.

At this point, one begins to wonder what a bird's first perception of the song of its species is like. Is there equal attentiveness to all audible sounds, or is there some innate perceptual selectivity? What of the possibility that motor constraints are involved in the selectivity of song learning, so that many different sounds are learned during the sensitive period, only to be subject to severe filtering when they are transformed into motor activity? Could the syrinx of each species be differently designed so that each can only produce its own song? The extraordinary versatility of the songbird syrinx argues against this position, but it must be taken seriously (Lemon, 1975). If, on the other hand, there is innate perceptual selectivity manifest at first encounters with song, are birds responsive to the entire spectrum of species-specific traits or to some subset?

In early investigations of selective birdsong learning (Marler, 1970; Thorpe, 1958) there was no separation of sensory and motor constraints and no specification of the effective stimulus features. Furthermore, there was no final resolution of the question of innateness, because the experiments were all conducted with birds taken after hatching, leaving open the possibility that responsiveness might have been shaped by very early prior experience.

Innate Mechanisms for Selective Vocal Learning

In setting out to design a new study that would clarify some of these unresolved issues, we chose a pair of sparrow species that seemed ideal for the purpose (Marler & Peters, 1977). Within the extensive, continent-wide range of the abundant song sparrow, the less common swamp sparrow lives in pockets, surrounded by and mingled with members of the other species. Both species learn their songs early in life while still on the natal territory or close to it (Mulligan, 1966; Kroodsma, 1977b). Thus both species, and particularly the less ubiquitous swamp sparrow, face the problem of discriminating their own song from the other's during the song learning process.

The song of the swamp sparrow, simpler than that of the song sparrow, consists of a trill of identical multinote syllables delivered at a steady rate. Song sparrow song is composed of alternating phrases of two types, trills of repeated syllables, and unrepeated note complexes. The terminology we use in song description is illustrated in Fig. 3.1. As a further difference, swamp sparrow trills are highly regular, whereas those within song sparrow songs, although sometimes given at a steady rate, are often either accelerating or decelerating. Despite the differences, songs of the two species are similar in note duration and song length. They overlap considerably in frequency range, although there are slight differences (see Fig. 3.1).

In both species, the notes and syllables from which a song is constructed are endowed with a high degree of individuality. Swamp sparrow syllables are composed of tonal up-slurred and down-slurred whistles combined with short notes of steady pitch. Some components of song sparrow syllables share these characteristics, but others are consistently different in the presence of rapid frequency modulations, which are lacking from notes of the swamp sparrow.

Techniques for computer speech editing (Zoloth, Miller, Peters & Dooling, in press) were used to generate series of synthetic songs by reshuffling components from normal songs of the two species. The artificial patterns were designed to represent the basic temporal and organizational features of songs of the two species, with intermediates between them.

Strong emphasis was placed in this design on the temporal organization of components, an avian equivalent of phonological syntax. Swamp sparrow-like patterns consisted of single phrases composed of identical syllables repeated at a constant tempo, either slow or fast. For another category of patterns, we retained the one-phrase swamp sparrow structure but arranged the syllables in either an accelerated or decelerated manner. A variable tempo, and the presence of more than one phrase, were taken to be the main distinguishing features of the song sparrow song. Thus the most song sparrow-like synthetic song was composed of two trills, each with a different syllable type and a different tempo, the first accelerating and the second constant. Other variants of this two-parted pattern included first trills with a decelerating tempo coupled with second trills of constant tempo, and some in which both parts were given at steady but different rates. All together, 10 such patterns were devised, each assembled from different natural syllables (see Fig. 3.1).

To explore the possibility of species-specific properties in the constituent syllables, two different sets of these ten patterns were created. One set was synthesized from swamp sparrow syllables, the other from song sparrow syllables. These training songs were then presented in bouts as they are normally delivered. In a first experiment our subjects were eight young swamp sparrow males and five young song sparrow males. They had been taken from nests in the wild when they were between 3 and 10 days old and subsequently hand reared to independence. They were given each of the 20 song types, 52 times per day (a

NORMAL SONGS

SWAMP SPARROW

SONG SPARROW

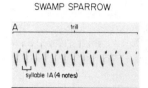

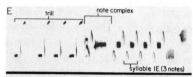

1975 TRAINING SONGS

SWAMP SPARROW SYLLABLES

SONG SPARROW SYLLABLES

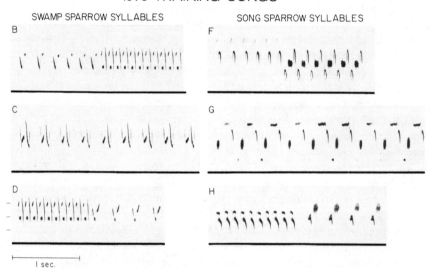

I sec.

FIG. 3.1. *1975 Training Songs.* A and E are examples of normal songs. Syllable 1A, composed of four notes, is the unit of repetition in the steady-rate swamp sparrow trill. An accelerated trill is shown in song E, along with a note complex and syllable 1E, composed of three notes. Songs B, C, and D are training songs constructed with swamp sparrow syllables; F, G, and H are training songs constructed with song sparrow syllables. Songs B and F contain syllables arranged in a two-parted, accelerated-fast pattern (song sparrow-like). Syllable 1A from the normal swamp sparrow song has been used in the first part of Song B. Syllable 1E from the normal song sparrow song has been used in the second part of song F. Songs C and G are one-parted, slow patterns (swamp sparrow-like). Songs D and H are composed of syllables arranged in a two-parted, steady-fast, steady-slow pattern, which thus contains both song sparrow and swamp sparrow temporal features. Frequency is indicated at 2 kHz intervals, and the time marker indicates one second.

total of about 1000 songs per day) during what we already know to be the sensitive period for song learning in these birds, between 20 and 50 days of age. After training was completed they were then separated in acoustical chambers on normal photoperiods through fall and winter. They came into full song the following spring, 100–200 days after termination of training. In addition, three males of each species were collected and raised as described for the trained birds, but without tutoring of any kind. For the sake of clarity, we present results for the two species separately.

Selective Learning in the Swamp Sparrow

As in nature, each male swamp sparrow sang several different song types. Tutored birds learned a great deal from the models presented during the sensitive period. One group of eight males sang a total of 18 songs representing 19 syllable types. We compared these syllables with the models that the birds had heard during the training period and judged that 12 out of 19 were close copies. In every case, copies matched swamp sparrow syllables that had been presented as models. Song sparrow syllable models were all rejected by swamp sparrows. The choice was made with little regard for temporal patterning: Swamp sparrows learned syllables from two-parted songs, from accelerated or decelerated patterns (song sparrow-like features) as well as from swamp sparrow-like patterns (see Table 3.1). Although this species selected conspecific syllables for learning without reference to temporal pattern, phrase structure of the models did have a subtle influence on the selection of particular syllables. The swamp sparrows copied from both one-and two-part songs, but only one of the 12 learned syllables was from the second part of a two-parted song. Thus the swamp sparrows showed some tendency to focus on syllables in the first part of any song learned, whether swamp sparrow-like or not.

Otherwise, the swamp sparrows were largely unresponsive to temporal organization of the models we presented to them during infancy. When they began to sing, however, some 100 to 200 days later it became clear that they possessed more information about song structure than was evident earlier.

In 14 of the 18 crystallized songs, the swamp sparrows gave simple, one-parted steady-rate trills, composed either of improvised or learned syllables. Even a syllable copied by a swamp sparrow from the accelerated phrase of a two-parted tutor model was rendered into a one-parted constant-rate trill. In those few instances when copied swamp sparrow syllables were rendered with an accelerated tempo (10%) or incorporated into a two-part song (10%), the production did not necessarily correspond exactly to the temporal or organizational features of the model song (Table 3.2). An innate basis for the temporal organization of swamp sparrow song is further indicated by the performance of the three untrained birds whose improvised syllables were all delivered in a one-parted, steady-rate trill.

TABLE 3.1

Imitations by Swamp and Song Sparrows of Tutor Songs Comprising
Song Syllables of the Two Species Assembled in Different Patterns

| | | *One Part Song* | | | | *Two-Part Songs* | | | | | | *Total Number of Copied Syllables* |
| | | | | | | *First Part* | | | | *Second Part* | | |
		A^a	*D*	*F*	*S*	*A*	*D*	*F*	*S*	*F*	*S*	*Syllables*
Swamp Sparrow Learning	Number of swamp sparrow syllables copied by swamp sparrows	2	1	—	1	3	1	1	2	1	—	12
	Number of song sparrow syllables copied by swamp sparrows	—	—	—	—	—	—	—	—	—	—	0
Song Sparrow Learning	Number of swamp sparrow syllables copied by song sparrows	1	—	—	2	1	4	—	1	2	—	11
	Number of song sparrow syllables copied by song sparrows	1	1	1	2	2	—	—	1	3	—	11

[a] A, D, F, and S represent accelerating, decelerating, fast and slow, respectively.

We conclude that swamp sparrows are virtually unresponsive in infancy to the organizational features of the species-specific song manipulated in this experiment. When production begins, however, it becomes clear that they possess more innate information about species-specific song structure than is apparent from the selectivity of their early learning. This additional organizational information only becomes manifest at the time that they begin to sing. At this stage, swamp sparrows proceed to incorporate the syllabic structures acquired earlier into the overall syntactical pattern. They behave as though there is an advantage in dividing the process into stages, with the acquisition of the smaller acoustic units accomplished before a complete commitment is made to higher levels of temporal organization. As we have noted, untrained birds also generate elements of the species-specific song organization, in their case constructed from syllables that are developed without reference to auditory information other than from their own production. A repeat experiment used as subjects swamp sparrows that were taken, not as nestlings, but as eggs from wild nests and foster-reared by canaries. These were trained with the same tapes at the same age, with the same result. The swamp sparrows learned only swamp sparrow syllables with no obvious attention paid to the syntactical organization. Evidently the selective learning of the swamp sparrow is truly innate.

Vocal Learning in the Song Sparrow

A sample of five song sparrow males sang a total of 32 songs, which represented 89 syllable types. Twenty-two proved to match tutor models. However, they were indiscriminate in which syllable types they accepted. Half were copies of song sparrow syllables and the other half copies of swamp sparrow syllables. This surprised us insofar as there is no evidence that song sparrows copy swamp sparrow songs in nature. Like the swamp sparrows, the song sparrows learned to sing tutor syllables largely without reference to the temporal pattern in which they were arranged although, as indicated in the following section, the inclusion of more complex patterns leads to a somewhat different result. The song sparrows selected their 11 conspecific syllables equally often from one-parted (5 learned syllables) or two-parted models (6 learned syllables). On the other hand, they tended to choose swamp sparrow syllables from two-parted songs (8 out of 11 swamp sparrow syllable copies), though with no preference for the first or second part. It is as though the infant song sparrows ignored organizational features when learning conspecific syllables, but found swamp sparrow syllables

TABLE 3.2.
Swamp Sparrow Renditions of Crystallized Syllables
in Relation to Tutor Song Patterning

	SYLLABLE COPY SOURCE										
	One-Part Song				Two-Part Song				Second Part		Noncopy
							First Part				
SYLLABLE RENDITION:	A	D	F	S	A	D	F	S	F	S	
One-Part Song Constant Tempo	1	1		1	2[a]		1	2			6[a]
One-Part Song Accelerated Tempo	1				1						
First of Two-Part Song Constant Tempo											2[b]
Second of Two-Part Song Constant Tempo						1			1		

[a] Includes one simple, constant tempo song with the first intersyllable interval being slightly longer than the following intersyllable interval.
[b] Includes second rendition of noncopy syllable also sung in one-part constant tempo song. Thus there was a total 7 non-copied syllables.

more attractive when presented in a song sparrow-like phrase structure. This hints at a moderate responsiveness to temporal organization in infancy that is lacking in the swamp sparrow, and we have further evidence that this does indeed exist. In a later experiment, male song sparrows were trained in infancy with field-recorded songs of both their own species and swamp sparrows, unmodified in any way. Although they still learned a few swamp sparrow syllables, they overwhelmingly favored those of their own species. Evidently the simplified "synthetic" song sparrow songs used in the previous experiment were deficient in some aspects of temporal organization. With the added complexities of more typical song sparrow song, more selectivity became evident.

With one exception, the trained song sparrows sang complex multipartite songs. In the first experiment learned song and swamp sparrow syllables were typically sung as trills and incorporated into songs along with improvised syllables. A readiness to reassemble syllables learned from different models is again evident. Of the songs that contained renditions of learned syllables, a quarter of them included both song and swamp sparrow syllables in the same song, something the subjects had never heard (See Fig. 3.2, Song L).

As indicated, temporal and organizational features of the model song were responded to by this species in infancy, and features of tutor songs did affect the patterns in which the learned syllables were reproduced. In the song sparrows, about half of the renditions of learned syllables matched the timing and tempo of the model. Also, those syllables learned from the first part of two-parted models were sung significantly more often as the first trill in the crystallized song, even if the other syllables in the song were improvised; similarly all those syllables learned from the second part of the model song appeared as second trills in the produced song. However, as with the swamp sparrows, song sparrows rarely produced a completely faithful copy of an entire tutor song. As evidence of a relative lack of dependence on the structural organization of a model when it departed too much from the species-specific pattern, song sparrows produced only one example of a one-parted song ($1/32 = 3\%$), although two thirds ($8/12 = 66\%$) of the synthetic song patterns heard by each subject in the training regimen had a one-parted structure (Table 3.3).

The features of the songs of five local wild song sparrows were examined and compared to the songs of the trained and untrained male song sparrows (Table 3.4). The results of our analysis of the wild song agree with Kroodsma (1977b). Ninety percent of the normal song sparrow songs started with a trill. The second phrase was most often an unrepeated note complex and the subsequent phrases alternated between trill and note complex. Alternation of phrase type occurred at 122 out of 130 phrase changes or 94% of the time. Likewise, two trills in succession were found in only 7 of 49 songs. The phrase types were present in equal proportions within a song.

The three untrained song sparrows all sang multipartite songs (Table 3.4) and sang equal proportions of trill and note complex. Thus they were able to generate

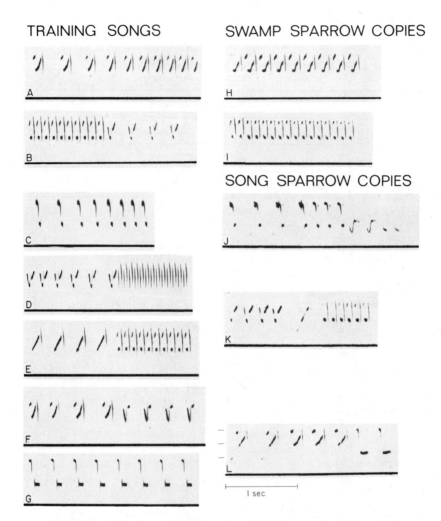

FIG. 3.2. *Illustrations of Some Imitations of 1975 Training Songs.* Songs A–G are training songs. A, B, D, E, and F are composed of swamp sparrow syllables; C and G are composed of song sparrow syllables. Songs H and I are swamp sparrow copies of the adjacent training songs A and B. Note that the swamp sparrows learned the syllable unit from an accelerated temporal pattern (A) and a two-parted song (B), but in both cases recast it into a steady-rate, one-parted trill. Songs J, K, and L are copies of the adjacent training songs C–G and are sung by song sparrows. In song J the song sparrow has copied both the syllable unit and temporal pattern of the training song, with an improvised ending added. Song K includes copies from two training songs D and E. Note that the first part of K was learned from a decelerated pattern but is sung in an accelerated temporal pattern. Song L also contains syllables learned from two different training songs. Note that this song incorporates copies of both song sparrow and swamp sparrow syllables drawn from different models. Frequency is indicated at 2 kHz intervals; the time marker equals one second.

TABLE 3.3
Song Sparrow Rendition of Crystallized Syllables
in Relation to Tutor Song Patterning

		SYLLABLE COPY SOURCE										
Phrase Structure:		*One-Part Song*				*Two-Part Songs*						
						First Part				*Second Part*		*Noncopy*
Temporal Pattern:		*A*	*D*	*F*	*S*	*A*	*D*	*F*	*S*	*F*	*S*	
Syllable Rendition												
One-Part Song	A					X						
	D											
	F											
	S											
First Trill in	A	(+)				+ +	X	X				7
Multipartite Song	D						X					1
	F						X					
	S		(+)		XX		(X)					12
Second Trill in	A	(+)										1
Multipartite Song	D											
	F							+X(XX)				5
	S				+		(X)				+ + +	7
Third Trill in	A											
Multipartite Song	D											
	F			+								2
	S				+							2
Fourth Trill in	A											
Multipartite Song	D											
	F											
	S											1
Note Complexes Within Song		X	(+)							(X)		37

X Indicates copy of swamp sparrow syllable
+ Indicates copy of song sparrow syllable
( ) Indicates copied syllables with 2 or 3 renditions (4 syllables in 9 renditions)
Eight noncopy syllable types had two different renditions.
A total of 89 syllable types occurred in 102 renditions.

some of the species-specific organizational features of their normal song innately. Nevertheless, they deviated from the normal in that they were just as likely to start a song with either phrase type. However, they did alternate phrase types 86% of the time and only 5 of 22 songs combined 2 trills in succession.

The birds trained with the synthetic songs did start songs with a trill 81% of the time, and the second phrase of 77% of these songs was a trill. However, 19 of the 32 songs contained two trills in succession. In addition, the trained birds sang twice as many trills per song as note complexes, and alternated phrase types only 57% of the time. Thus another sign of an influence of training on song structure is the following: Although in the songs of normal song sparrows and untrained birds, trills and note complexes are present in equal proportion and are delivered in an alternating fashion, our trained birds tended to sing two trills in succession and sang fewer note complexes than normal. This parallels the two-parted phrase structure of the model songs, in which note complexes were essentially absent.

Infant song sparrows are clearly more responsive than swamp sparrows to the gross syntactical features of their species song. In contrast with the swamp sparrow, they rely on information at this level of structure rather than at the syllabic level as a basis for selective learning. Although we have yet to define the organizational features to which they respond innately, it appears from the results we already have, and from the singing of untrained birds (cf. Kroodsma, 1977b) that the instructions are inadequate to sustain fully normal singing. At least some aspects of normal song structure must be learned.

Song sparrow vocal learning again appears to proceed in stages. Syntactical information is used to select models. These are then reduced to syllabic units and committed to memory in such a way that, although some syllables may be produced in their original arrangements, others are recombined from a variety of

TABLE 3.4
Song Characteristics of Wild, Untrained, and Trained Song Sparrows

	Wild	Untrained	Trained
	N = 5	N = 3	N = 5
Number of songs analyzed	49	22	32
Average song duration	2.45 SD = .262	2.19 SD = .405	2.13 SD = .419
Songs with trill as first phrase	44 (90%)	10 (45%)	26 (81%)
Songs with note complex as second phrase	34 (80%)	7 (32%)	7 (23%)
Average number of phrases/song	4	3.5	3
Number phrase type alternation/possible alternation	122/130 (94%)	49/57 (86%)	33/58 (57%)
Number songs with two trills in succession	7 (14%)	5 (23%)	19 (59%)
Ratio number trills: number note complexes	1.2	1.0	2.2

sources. The learned syllables, mingled with others that are invented de novo, are then used as the elements from which larger scale patterns are created. The information on which this patterning is based comes partly from the models, as we have shown, and is partly innately generated. Innate information may be brought to bear by way of motor programs, manifest only as the bird begins to sing, relatively late in the developmental process. However, there may also be an early perceptual component that awaits further elucidation.

Selective Vocal Learning:
A Perceptual or a Motor Phenomenon?

As already indicated, the selectivity of swamp sparrow song learning could be a perceptual or a motor phenomenon. One way of separating these possibilities is to look for physiological measures of auditory responsiveness applicable at a young age. Any sign of selective responsiveness in songbirds at an age prior to the development of singing, would point to a perceptual component. Working with heart-rate changes, Dooling (1980) has found that, as in mammals, presentation of a salient stimulus results in an acceleration of heart rate followed by a deceleration phase. The latter, in particular, seems to be a correlate of the attention-catching quality of the stimulus. The more salient the stimulus is, the longer the deceleration phase before the heart rate returns to baseline.

Dooling and Searcy (1980) presented complete natural songs to song sparrows and swamp sparrows, while using songs of canaries as a control sound. They were able to show that at 20 days swamp sparrows discriminate clearly between the different stimuli, responding more strongly to conspecific song than to alien song. By contrast, song sparrows discriminate more weakly, which is consonant with their readiness to learn syllables of both species in our experiment. Although the discrimination is weak and not statistically significant, like the swamp sparrows, song sparrows also tend to favor their conspecific song (Fig. 3.3).

There have been some preliminary tests on the acoustic basis for the swamp sparrow discrimination, which leads to rejection of song sparrow syllables. Swamp sparrow songs tend to be pitched somewhat higher than those of song sparrows, with the average minimum frequency transposed about 13%. In 1976 we imposed such a transposition on song sparrow syllables by rerecording 1975 training songs at a slightly faster tape speed. This raised the syllable pitch as well as decreasing the note and song duration. When these were presented to young swamp sparrows in a choice situation, they still preferred swamp sparrow syllables, and rejected the transposed song sparrow syllables.

Attention is currently focused on the frequency modulations present in many song sparrow syllables, but lacking from those of swamp sparrows. In order to explore the significance of this species song difference, we created a new set of synthetic songs in 1977.

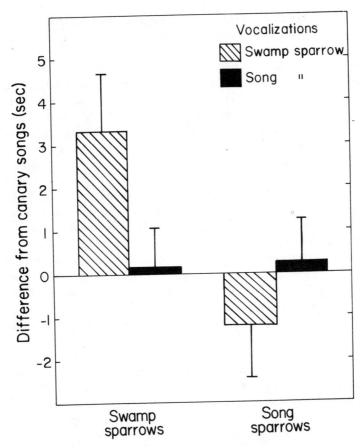

FIG. 3.3.   Cardiac responses of song and swamp sparrows to conspecific songs and to the songs of the other sparrow are shown relative to each species' response to neutral canary song. Vertical bars represent ± 1 standard error. From Dooling and Searcy, 1980.

One group of swamp sparrows was trained with the following four-syllable designs: (1) "hybrid" syllables were created by picking out song sparrow notes in which the frequency modulations were prominent, and inserting them into the middle of swamp sparrow syllables, replacing an original swamp sparrow note by a song sparrow note; (2) syllables to serve as controls for the previous set were formed by selecting components from different swamp sparrow syllables, and recombining these fragments into new arrangements; (3) a version of [1] in which only the individual song sparrow syllable components were transposed upward in frequency by 13% and then combined with normal swamp sparrow notes to create another set of "hybrid" syllables; (4) normal swamp sparrow syllables. These syllables were then arranged in a normal swamp sparrow trill pattern. The trained swamp sparrows learned to sing syllables from all four design sets, including those that contained frequency modulated elements, as shown in Fig. 3.4.

Another group of swamp sparrows was trained with three sets of song types: (1) sequences of song sparrow imitations of swamp sparrow syllables derived from a previous experiment; (2) a re-edited version of a field recording of a rare, two-parted swamp sparrow song that incorporates frequency-modulated features into its syllables; (3) two-parted songs composed of one trill of song sparrow syllables that had been transposed upward in frequency by 13% and another of normal swamp sparrow syllables. This was the first time during the course of our experiments that swamp sparrows were exposed to a "hybrid" song containing syllables of both species. Again, the swamp sparrows learned to sing syllables from all three sets. That they learned the song sparrow-sung swamp sparrow syllables indicated that their previous avoidance of song sparrow syllables was not due to some acoustic voicing feature imposed automatically on all vocalizations of the song sparrow. Another point of information gained from this experiment was that swamp sparrows would learn the transposed song syllables, that they had previously avoided, when these syllables were played in close conjunction with swamp sparrow syllables.

Thus swamp sparrows will learn to sing song sparrow syllable components when they are embedded in "hybrid" syllables and entire song sparrow syllables when closely associated in time with swamp sparrow syllables as in "hybrid" songs. In current experiments, seven swamp sparrow males were trained during their sensitive period with the following: (1) two natural song sparrow songs; (2) two natural song sparrow songs in which a trill phrase was replaced by a trill composed of swamp sparrow syllables; (3) two natural song sparrow songs in which a note complex was replaced by a combination of either one or three unrepeated swamp sparrow syllables; (4) two natural song sparrow songs in which the introductory syllables were replaced by swamp sparrow syllables; (5) two songs each composed of 11 different swamp sparrow syllables delivered at a steady tempo without repetition. By varying the position, temporal form and number of swamp sparrow syllables embedded in natural song sparrow songs, we hope to discover the temporal constraints on the ability of swamp sparrow syllables to render associated song sparrow syllables acceptable to the swamp sparrow. In addition, the two songs composed of unrepeated swamp sparrow syllables will test whether the swamp sparrow required a succession of identical multinote clusters in order to define one syllable as an acceptable, coherent unit for imitation.

Meanwhile, the results already obtained tend to reinforce the conclusion that the selectivity of swamp sparrow learning of song syllables is primarily perceptual rather than a reflection of motor constraints. Evidently swamp sparrows are quite capable of reproducing song sparrow syllables, when they are presented in the right acoustic context. Thus the current evidence points towards perceptual

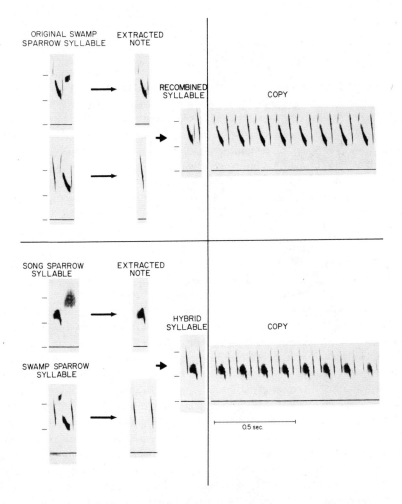

FIG. 3.4. *Illustration of an Imitation by a Swamp Sparrow of a "Hybridized" Syllable.* The top section of this figure illustrates training syllables created from notes extracted from two normal swamp sparrow syllables. The bottom section illustrates a hybrid training syllable created from the notes of a swamp sparrow syllable and a song sparrow syllable. As shown, these recombined syllables, arranged into one-parted steady-rate trills for training, were imitated by swamp sparrows. The copies shown are sections of one-parted, steady-rate trills sung by swamp sparrows.

constraints as the primary determinants of the selectivity of the swamp sparrow song learning process.

Enrichment of Avian Vocal Perception from Infancy to Adulthood

To explore adult responsiveness to the syntactical features of song, some of the same computer-edited sounds were presented to experienced wild birds in the field (Peters, Searcy, & Marler, 1980). We found adult swamp sparrows still primarily responsive to information at the level of the syllable. The only hint of responsiveness to temporal patterning was the somewhat greater effectiveness of a simple trill as compared with an accelerating series. This is perhaps not too surprising in view of the simplicity of the temporal patterning of their song, and the fact that rather similar, simple trills are used by other sympatric bird species as well, providing a less-than-ideal vehicle for species-specificity.

The usual method of testing was to map a male's territory and then place two loudspeakers well within the boundaries, through which two song types would be played in alternation. Males approached when a conspecific song was played and showed every sign of attacking the speaker. Samplings of distance from the speakers proved to be the most sensitive measures.

First, we were able to show that each species responds most strongly to natural conspecific songs. Furthermore, our normal synthetic songs were just as effective as field recordings, demonstrating that the computer manipulations were not introducing unacceptable distortions. In particular, our most normal synthetic song sparrow song composed of song sparrow syllables in an accelerating series followed by a rapid trill, was not distinguished from a normal song by wild song sparrows under these experimental conditions.

Adult song sparrows tested with a variety of synthetic songs proved to be highly responsive to features of temporal pattern. They reacted much more strongly to conspecific syllables organized in a song sparrow-like pattern, as compared with a simple, swamp sparrow-like trill. This is a striking contrast with the infantile condition. Adult song sparrows were also highly discriminating with regard to syllable type, responding more strongly to a song formed from conspecific syllables than to one made of swamp sparrow syllables, irrespective of overall temporal patterning.

Multiple Developmental Stages of Song Perception

It is clear that the vocal perception of song sparrows is considerably more elaborate in adulthood than in infancy. In addition to the features already tested they are likely to prove responsive to other aspects of song such as the individual features of familiar neighbors. What intervenes between infancy and adulthood to result in this enrichment? One contribution undoubtedly derives from interaction with adults of their own species and experience of their song. Another possible source for some of this syntactical information is feedback from the bird's own vocal production.

The birds behave as though it is advantageous to withhold innate information about the temporal organization of song until a still more basic issue has been dealt with, namely the acquisition of a repertoire of basic units at the level of the syllable. Our experiments suggest that the process of syllable learning is largely completed before the birds proceed to the next stage, by which time they are provided with the raw material with which to construct larger scale patterns.

As already noted, species differences in song organization then become evident as the birds actually start to sing. What is the physiological origin of this syntactical information? Does it originate as a central, endogenous "motor tape" in the brain, or is it a manifestation of another kind of auditory predisposition that guides motor development by sensory feedback? Information is needed on the behavior of swamp and song sparrows deafened prior to the development of singing. Konishi has demonstrated a general tendency for some sparrows treated in this way to revert to a very basic, elementary pattern of singing in which most species-specific features are erased, thus implicating auditory mechanisms in the genesis of species-specific temporal organization (e.g. Konishi, 1965a, 1965b; Mulligan, 1966).

To explore the significance of auditory feedback in song production for both song and swamp sparrows, we deafened two male song sparrows and seven male swamp sparrows around 2 days of age. All stages of song development, from subsong through crystallized song, are being recorded and compared to the corresponding stages of normal birds. We shall be especially interested to see if any species-specific song features arise when the birds cannot hear their own voices. If not, this will implicate auditory mechanisms in the generation of species-specific song organization, either directly, or indirectly, by their influence on conditions for manifestation of a motor program.

Sensory mechanisms delineating temporal organization of song, if there are such, might be latent even in infancy, but only activated during actions of singing. In this case, we could entertain notions of a motor-contingent feedback mechanism, such that special auditory predispositions are only activated as some immediate, time-locked correlate of singing behavior. The work of Held (1965) has introduced us to a similar concept in other domains of sensorimotor development. Visual stimulation that a moving kitten experiences from the environment has very different consequences for sensorimotor development if the kitten is passively transported rather than moving of its own accord.

The development of vocal perception in these sparrows appears to proceed in steps, with different innate mechanisms becoming engaged in the learning process at different stages. Perhaps we should entertain more generally the idea of innate hierarchical programs for the development of the perception of complex stimuli? One can conceive of advantages to such a strategy in speech development. On the one hand, such programs should enable the infant to proceed quickly and surely through the stages of a very complex process. Most important, such rules will increase the likelihood that all human infants tackle the problem in the same general way, thus reducing the likelihood of private, nonuniversal solutions to perceptual problems that could only be a hindrance to the free and efficient use of speaking and of speech perception for purposes of social communication.

GENES AND COMMUNICATION

The effectiveness of a communication system will obviously be enhanced if signal senders and receivers use closely matched procedures. The complexities of social organization in most higher animals are such that the requirement for uniform rules will extend far beyond a sexually bonded pair, or mother and young, to include families, larger social groupings, and in some degree all species members. To the extent that the apparatus, rules and procedures are heritable, it follows inevitably that individual variations of lesser or greater effectiveness will be subject to natural selection.

There is an extensive literature on the phylogeny of signaling actions in animals, a major theme in ethological research since Lorenz's (1941) classical analysis of display behaviors in ducks. Ethologists have properly emphasized the dominant role of genetic mechanisms. Some feel, however, that the importance of learning has been underplayed. According to this view the focus in past research on the morphology of signaling behaviors, rather than on what they mean to others, has led to overemphasis on the inherited component of communicative interchange in animals. Whereas many signal actions develop innately, it seems probable that, at least in higher animals, learning plays an important role in the acquisition and development of abilities to derive functionally appropriate "assessments" of situations or signals (Green & Marler, 1979).

If we compare the current state of understanding of the development of human communication, an opposite bias emerges. Few hesitate to acknowledge the dominant or even exclusive role of individual experience in the ontogeny of language. This may stem in part from our introspective access to processes both of encoding information into speech, and of decoding speech signals, as well as our awareness of the diversity of human languages and dialects and the problems of crosscultural communication. In the minds of many, this environmentalist viewpoint extends to the development of all human signaling behavior. This extension is less appropriate than many suppose. Innate, universal, species-specific components in human signaling behavior are widespread. They are present in human facial expressions (e.g. Eibl-Eibesfeldt, 1972; Ekman, 1973).

They intrude extensively even into human speech behavior (e.g. Aslin & Pisoni, in press; Eimas, 1975; Eimas & Tartter, 1979), although as users we are rarely conscious of them.

If our understanding of the development of speech behavior is to progress, we need to acknowledge the indispensable role of hereditary influences in human communication. We also need more emphasis on the importance in animals of cultural and other environmental influences. In recent years the burgeoning of interest in nativistic interpretations of human communicative behavior, together with reappraisals of the possibility of scientific study of cognition in animals (Griffin, 1976; Premack, 1976) gives promise of a more sensible balance.

Development of Perception

There are many examples of close evolutionary interactions between the structure of signals and sensory receptors. Such interactions are most evident in species with highly specialized receptor systems. Harmony between lepidopteran pheromones and their olfactory systems, and the matched frequency tuning of frog songs and their auditory systems are good illustrations (Capranica, 1976; Schneider, 1977). When service of receptors is required not only for communication but also for other functions, mechanisms of signal perception become embedded in more basic perceptual operations. Studies of perceptual development in general thus come to bear directly on the ontogeny of communication. This is a theme with an extensive literature in both philosophy and psychology (e.g. Boring, 1942; Gibson, 1966, 1969; Sutherland, 1973; Uhr, 1966; Warnock, 1967).

We are here viewing perception as involving not just the ability to sense changes in the environment, but also to organize and interpret that which is sensed and to act on the basis of those interpretations. The transformations from sensation to percept are many and profound. Carl Popper (Popper & Eccles, 1977) goes so far as to suggest that "our sense organs should be regarded as auxiliaries to our brain. The brain in turn is programmed to select a fitting and relevant model of our environment as we move along, to be interpreted by the mind [p. 91]." If perception is viewed as incorporating the formation, storage, and retrieval of structural descriptions of the external world, with many different potential descriptive domains (Sutherland, 1973), "there must exist a set of rules that makes it possible to map from one domain onto another [p. 159]." Students of perception hypothesize that something equivalent to the building up of structural representations or "schemata" of the external world must be involved (Craik, 1943; Gregory, 1974). In the construction of such schemata, redundancies are reduced or eliminated, a necessary step if the organism is to cope quickly and efficiently with changes in complex environments. The perceptual system seems typically to discard information that is not to some degree *coherent*

(Attneave, 1954). In ways that are still mysterious, objects and events become classified into categories, with boundaries separating them (Rosch & Lloyd, 1978).

Aside from the purely sensory aspects of interaction with the external world, there is a growing appreciation of the importance, in the ontogeny of perceptual schemata, of motor involvement (Turvey, 1977; Weimer, 1977). There is an obvious contribution from actions that directly aid the gathering of sensations, such as searching movements with the eyes or the hands (e.g. Hebb, 1949; Yarbus, 1967). There is also evidence that more intimate functional involvement with the environment participates in the emergence of perceptual categories, as when successfully negotiating obstacles or manipulating and retrieving objects (Nelson, 1974; Rosch, 1973, 1975). Indeed, the original conceptualization of environmental reconstructions or "schemata" in the brain was inspired by Henry Head's studies of the abnormal perceptions that brain-damaged patients have of the spatial-temporal position of their limbs in space (Oldfield & Zangwill, 1942–43). The concept was extended to include perception of the external world, a process viewed as intimately associated with awareness of posture and the location of the body in space. According to this view, experiences are registered as a cumulative and continuously updated record. This record may either be referred to the body or, in the case of external stimuli, projected into space.

Bartlett (1932) developed the concept further. Again, he viewed schemata as operating outside the subject's awareness and he expressly distinguished them from conscious images. Bartlett's (1932) definition of the "schema" is as: "an active organization of past reactions, or of past experiences, which must always be supposed to be operating in any well-adapted organic response [p. 201]." The active response to a situation is judged to be as important as the passive sensations associated with it. Given the intimate involvement of schemata with both perception and action, it is but a small step to the invocation of similar concepts in the analysis of communication.

Common Mechanisms for Perception and Production

There would be economy in designing communicative physiology around brain mechanisms that serve both the perception of signals and also their production. One line of argument in favor derives from studies of effects of temperature on the behavior of cold-blooded animals. In a pioneering study, Walker (1957) demonstrated that a critical species-specific difference between the calling songs of male tree crickets lies in the rate of pulsation of their stridulatory sounds. Within groups of sympatric cricket species, he found that females respond selectively to conspecific male songs by approaching the loudspeaker. It is well known that song pulse rates are temperature dependent in a regular fashion, and Walker was able to show that the responsiveness of females to pulse rate changes in parallel fashion, so maintaining specific discrimination over a range of temperatures that would otherwise cause confusion between species. The shared temperature dependence of both male song production and female song responsiveness would be intelligible if it were mediated by a common mechanism such as a sensorimotor template.

There are similar parallels in frogs. Several properties of frog calls are temperature-dependent (e.g. Schneider, 1967, 1974, 1977). Gerhardt (1978), working with tree frogs, has shown that species-specific pulse-repetition rates and pulse durations in male calling are highly dependent on temperature, and that female responsiveness for each species studied marches in parallel.

Study of the behavior of hybrid crickets leads to a similar interpretation. Having demonstrated that the calling songs of hybrids are uniquely different from songs of both parental species, Bentley and Hoy went on to show that hybrid females prefer hybrid male songs to either of the two parental male songs (Bentley & Hoy, 1972; Hoy, 1974; Hoy, Hahn, & Paul, 1977; Hoy & Paul, 1973). Common genetic control of signal production and reception is indicated (Hoy et al., 1977).

Studies of vocal communication and development in birds have provided another type of evidence in favor of sensorimotor neural templates as shared mechanisms for producing and perceiving learned bird songs.

Learning plays a role in the development of avian vocal perceptions even in species whose patterns of production are not only innate but develop in the absence of auditory feedback, such as the domestic chicken (Konishi, 1963). In spite of this apparent lack of plasticity in the motor coordination of sound production, there are strong hints that chickens learn much of their mature perception of conspecific sounds (Evans, 1972; Evans & Mattson, 1972; Guyomarc'h, 1972, 1974a, 1974b).

In birds with more plastic vocal behavior than chickens, a variety of lines of evidence indicate that they engage in extensive perceptual learning. As we have indicated, some young birds demonstrate an innate ability for song recognition. But songbirds also develop responsiveness to many details of the male territorial song such as local dialects, individual differences, and variations associated with changing motivation (e.g. Brooks & Falls, 1975a, 1975b; Falls, 1969; Falls & Brooks, 1975; Kroodsma, 1977a; Milligan & Verner, 1971).

This vocal perceptual learning interacts in turn with vocal production: It plays some role in motor aspects of vocal development in all songbirds, such that their vocal behavior is abnormal if reared in social isolation (Konishi & Nottebohm, 1969; Marler & Mundinger, 1971; Thorpe, 1961). The extreme abnormality of the singing behavior of males of some songbirds deafened in youth, before singing, is further evidence of a crucial role for audition in vocal development (Konishi, 1965a, 1965b; 1966; Marler, Konishi, Lutjen, & Waser, 1973; Marler & Waser, 1977). In one closely related group of sparrows, deafening has been found to eliminate many species song differences. Such data implicate audition in guiding species-specific signal production by way of auditory "schemata" or "templates" to which feedback from singing is matched.

Sensorimotor interplay is also indicated by the tendency for the initiation of the sensory phase of song learning to precede production in many birds. When singing begins, some time after the initiation of perceptual vocal learning, there is a gradual transition from subsong to full song. This proceeds without the necessity of further access to models. Thus many birds learn to sing from memory. A series of developmental vocal transformations occurs such as might be expected if the bird were improving skill at controlling the operation of the complex syringeal apparatus, thereby achieving a better and better match with the memory of sounds heard earlier in life. We can conceive of the auditory information used in this matching process as embodied in sensory templates that are modifiable through auditory experience (Marler, 1970, 1976).

A further role for perceptual mechanisms in avian vocal development is implied by the selectivity of initial stages of the learning process. As we have seen in the swamp sparrow, some birds have an innate auditory predisposition to learn certain classes of sounds more readily than others. If recent studies are any guide, the initial perceptual specifications are simple and incomplete. These specifications, although lacking in many details, are sufficient to endow the singing of a naive young male with more normal traits than is the case if he is deafened. Given auditory experience with normal species-specific songs, additional features are memorized, and also manifested in learned song patterns when the male begins singing later. The learned song is a closer match to the wild type than that of a bird without this experience, so that we may confidently postulate an engram or schema of the learned song, then used template fashion during the process of learning to sing. In the brain of an adult bird equivalent processes will presumably be used in song recognition as well as in song production (Marler 1976).

That mechanisms exist in the brains of nonsinging females with some similar properties is indicated by the elicitation of female song after treatment with male sex hormones. In the white-crowned sparrow, a species with well-marked song dialects, the normal male song is learned (Marler, 1970; Marler & Tamura, 1964). A female who hears a local dialect in her youth will not only sing under the influence of testosterone, but will render that particular dialect (Kern & King, 1972; Konishi, 1965b). This acquired information is presumably normally used in the process of mate selection by female sparrows which prefer to settle within the natal dialect area (Baker & Mewaldt, 1978; Milligan & Verner, 1971). Thus, a sensorimotor template is indicated that guides both perceptual and motor development, shared by males and females, though normally put to different uses by the two sexes.

Learning plays a major role in development of this mechanism. Its neuroanatomical nature is unexplored. It may comprise few or many physiological components, with separate elements selecting different acoustic features from external sounds and from the animal's own vocal performance. Components exhibiting developmental plasticity might be distinct from or identical with those that underlie the innate selective perception of an untrained bird. Mechanisms might operate in series or in parallel, with control shifting from one to another as learning takes place. Whatever its particular physiological nature, there must be a unity of operation to the sensory template mechanism as a whole, subserving both vocal perception and production. It seems conceivable that they operate in analogous fashion to the developing "schemata" for control of perception and movement that physiologists are beginning to infer, however dimly, from interactions between operations in different parts of the mammalian brain (Evarts, Bizzi, Burke, DeLong, & Thach, 1971; Mountcastle, 1976).

There is a remarkable parallel here with aspects of the "motor theory" of speech perception as developed by Liberman, Cooper, Shankweiler, & Studdert-Kennedy (1967). In Fant's seminal taxonomy of "distinctive features" of speech patterns, acoustic criteria were mingled with production operations (Jakobson, Fant, & Halle, 1952). Noting that some anomalies of speech sound recognition disappear if one thinks of them in terms not of acoustic features but of central commands for the vocal gestures producing them, Liberman and his colleagues proposed that common mechanisms underlie both perception and production. They suggested (Liberman et al., 1967) that we "think in terms of overlapping activity of several neural networks—those that supply control signals to the articulators and those that process incoming neural patterns from the ear—and suppose that information can be correlated by these networks and passed through them in either directions [p. 454]."

In the original form of the "motor theory" there was no commitment to any particular kind of ontogenetic history. There has been a tendency to adduce developmental primacy for mechanisms of sound production in view of our tendency to make use of gestures of tongue and palate that exhibit a degree of acoustic stability. In the modal tongue positions for producing labial, dental, and velar consonants, for example, there is very little variation in the sounds produced with errors of tongue placement (Lieberman, 1977; Stevens, 1977). In some accounts of the motor theory the metaphor is used of an internalized dynamic representation of the vocal tract and its operation, terms immediately reminiscent of perceptual "schemata."

With the discovery that prespeech infants are responsive to some of the same distinctions between phonemes that adults respect (Eimas, Siqueland, Jusczyk, & Vigorito, 1971; Juscyzk, Chapter 4, this volume), it now seems reasonable to think of auditory rather than motor predispositions as taking the initiative in development of the very complex task of analyzing speech sounds. According to this interpretation, speech perceptions would first be elaborated in infancy. Then speaking would begin, guided by memories of what has been learned, much as has been postulated in the learning of birdsong. There will follow a period of overlap between the ability to learn new speech perceptions and new productions, as mature speech behavior emerges.

Common mechanisms are postulated, developing during the early conjoint operations of speaking and listening to speech, which then take part in the control of both kinds of operation in the mature organism. Processes of encoding and decoding would thus employ some of the same brain mechanisms, an illustration of the kind of economy we may expect to be widespread.

Using examples from auditory communication, we can make a case for overlap or even correspondence between the biologist's *sensory template* and the psychologist's *schema*. At least partly because we are conscious of the operation of our own external auditory feedback channel, the argument seems intuitively plausible in this case. Even with audition, however, it is likely that the bulk of sensorimotor matching occurs unconsciously. It is worth remembering that Head emphasized the unconscious nature of brain "schemata" for bodily movements and their proprioceptive feedback patterns in his orginal conception.

Something similar may operate unconsciously with visual communication. Adult humans and chimpanzees, for example, are remarkably clever at imitating what they see others doing (e.g. Hayes & Hayes, 1952). This imitation extends to facial expressions. Recent studies have shown that a 2-week old human infant can imitate both facial and manual gestures, a result which implies a remarkable ability on the baby's part. It must first perceive the configuration of the stimulus face and then generate a matching motor output. This could only be achieved by reference to patterns of previous proprioceptive experience from the infant's own unseen facial movements, or by direct mapping onto an appropriate motor output (Meltzoff & Moore, 1977). At least as adults we are not conscious of either kind of operation. The sensorimotor brain mechanisms implied by this behavior of the infant must surely become elaborated and enriched by developing visual experience during ontogeny in concordance with growing skill in operation of the visual signaling apparatus. It is economical to postulate that shared mechanisms are involved in both perception and production of such visual signals.

Development of Human Vocal Perception

Although the communicative behavior of higher organisms is heavily influenced by learning, there is nevertheless recurring evidence of perceptual constraints emerging early in life. In some cases these are known to be innate. We view these indications as crucial to understanding how perceptual abilities develop (Marler et al., 1980). The importance of shared rules for encoding and decoding of signals is obvious if communication is to operate efficiently. To the extent that signaling behaviors are modified and elaborated through learning, it becomes more difficult to ensure that an adequate degree of rule sharing for production and perception will persist among all communicants, especially with signals as complex as speech and human facial expressions. However, with both processes performed by common mechanisms, which develop with some close degree of genetic control, we can begin to conceptualize how this might be accomplished.

Innate instructions to the young organism as to how to embark on the process of perceptual analysis are valuable both in ensuring a choice of efficient procedures, and in encouraging all species members to tackle the problem in the same basic fashion. It is our view that classical ethological illustrations of innate responsiveness in animals are often better interpreted as innate instructions for embarking on a certain trajectory of perceptual learning, rather than for designing animals as behavioral automata (Marler, 1979; Marler et al., 1980). To the extent that this strategy of innately guided perceptual development is successful, it will ensure a degree of rule sharing, while still allowing freedom for learned variability in both signal and production.

Whether or not there is something special about the neural processing of speech as compared with other sounds will continue to be a much debated topic. Fragmentary though they are, the data on animal perception of conspecific vocal sounds suggest an affirmative answer to this question. It is tempting to view the perceptual biases that monkeys show in responding to vocal stimuli of their own species as animal analogies of phonetic perception in man. As applied to monkeys, the comparative method illustrates nicely how the same vocal stimulus may be processed in the equivalent of a phonetic mode by one species—that of the vocalizer—and in an auditory mode by another (Peterson, Beecher, Zoloth, Moody, & Stebbins, 1978; Zoloth, Petersen, Beecher, Green, Marler, Moody, & Stebbins, 1979). We are assuming that perception based on a generally salient cue, such as fundamental frequency, is analogous to auditory processing. Involvement of more specialized acoustic features, also known to encode communicative information such as the position of a frequency inflection in a call, would be the monkey's equivalent of phonetic processing.

In the case of song perception in birds, innate, species-specific predispositions come into play in development, serving to guide and constrain the processes of song learning. The ontogeny of vocal perception in monkeys has yet to be studied. Juscyzk (Chapter 4, this volume) reviews the literature implicating innate predispositions in the development of speech perception in human infants. In both cases, we know the perceptual predispositions involved to be malleable. Discriminations that are difficult for the human infant at a younger age, such as those involving the fricatives [sa] and [za] are made with ease at 6 months (Eilers & Minifie, 1975; Eilers, Wilson, & Moore, 1977).

The properties of speech sounds on which adult responsiveness is based are obviously more complex and abstract than those that infants repond to, sometimes so changed that the original predispositions of infancy are no longer evident. The [ra]-[la] distinction that Japanese adults find so difficult, unemployed in Japanese, is easier for infants, though only American infants have been tested so far as we know (Eimas, 1975). Special predispositions that infants employ in speech processing must surely play a significant ontogenetic role in setting the trajectory of the perceptual learning process (cf. Aslin & Pisoni, in press).

One way in which such trajectories may be achieved is indicated in a study by Kuhl and Miller (1975). The formant patterns that distinguish different vowel sounds are complicated by variations in the fundamental frequency of the voice within and between speakers. These must be a serious distraction for an infant embarking on the linguistic analysis of speech. Given the importance of vowel coding in speech, we might perhaps expect a predisposition at some phase of development to focus more strongly on formant patterns than on pitch (Kuhl & Miller, 1975).

By independently varying the two features in sounds presented to infants, while monitoring high-amplitude sucking, Kuhl and Miller obtained indications that variations in formant pattern are indeed more salient or arresting for human infants than variations in pitch. When formant patterns were varying randomly, the infants habituated rather slowly and were more distracted from attending to a pitch change than in the opposite condition, when they were required to attend to a vowel change in the face of random pitch variations. This is not to say that they are unresponsive to pitch variations—far from it. Variation in fundamental frequency is a striking feature of "baby talk"—the particular speech mode mothers often adopt when speaking to infants (Sachs, Brown, & Salerno, 1976). However, the salience of pitch changes to infants of this age seems to be lower than that of variations in vowel patterns under these test conditions, although it would be desirable to ascertain that pitch and vowel are in fact being scaled in ways that are more or less equivalent for the infant's auditory capabilities. Such hierarchies of salience would impose some order on the process of learning to extract different features from the complex stimuli that speech sounds present, insofar as success using certain dimensions in sorting speech sounds probably leads an infant to persevere with them, at least for a time, in further speech sound discriminations (cf. Mackintosh, 1974, p. 615). Experiments using a conditioned head-turning response suggest that by 6 months of age, infants can perceive similarity between vowels produced by different size vocal tracts and between a fricative consonant when it occurs in different vowel environments and spoken by different talkers. One may assume that innate responsiveness to simple properties of vowel formants becomes modified and enriched as, with further experience of speech behavior, the infant acquires the ability to normalize across speakers.

Human infants thus bring well-defined perceptual predispositions to the task of developing responsiveness to the immensely complex pattern of sound stimuli that speech represents. Some predispositions are innately manifest in initial encounters, developing without prior experience of the stimuli involved. Although these innate contributions are clear, we are hardly tempted to view them as developmental instructions for designing infants as automata. It seems natural to think of them as helping the infant to learn, by providing initial instructions that set a trajectory for the development of adult perceptual abilities. On the one hand, such predispositions must help the infant to proceed quickly and surely through the stages of a very complex process. Perhaps most important of all, such rules will increase the likelihood that all human infants tackle the problem in roughly the same way. The result will be a reduced likelihood of private, nonuniversal solutions to perceptual problems that could only be a hindrance to the free and efficient use of speaking and of speech perception in the service of social communication.

ACKNOWLEDGMENTS

Research reported in this paper was supported by grants PHS M14651 and NSF BNS 77 16894, and PHS S07 RR-0765-12 to Rockefeller University.

REFERENCES

Aslin, R. N., & Pisoni, D. B. Some Developmental processes in speech perception. In G. H. Yeni-Komschian, J. F. Kavanagh, & C. A. Ferguson (Eds.), *Child Phonology. (Vol. 2). Perception.* New York, Academic Press, 1980.

Attneave, F. Some informational aspects of visual perception. *Psychological Review,* 1954, *61,* 183–193.

Baerends, G. P., & Kruijt, J. P. Stimulus selection. In R. A. Hinde & J. Stevenson-Hinde (Eds.), *Constraints on learning.* Cambridge: Cambridge University Press, 1973.

Baker, M. C., & Mewaldt, L. R. Song dialects as a barrier to dispersal in white-crowned sparrows, *Zonotrichia leucophrys nuttalli. Evolution,* 1978, *32,* 712–722.

Bartlett, F. C. *Remembering: A Study in experimental and social psychology.* London & New York: Cambridge University Press, 1932.

Beer, C. Some complexities in the communication behavior of gulls. In S. R. Harnad, H. D. Steklis, & J. Lancaster (Eds.). *Origins and evolution of language and speech,* New York: New York Academy of Sciences, 1976.

Bentley, D. R., & Hoy, R. R. Genetic control of cricket song patterns. *Animal Behaviour,* 1972, *20,* 478–492.

Boring, E. G. *Sensation and perception in the history of experimental psychology.* New York: Appleton-Century-Crofts, 1942.

Brooks, R. J., & Falls, J. B. Individual recognition by song in white-throated sparrows: I. Discrimination of songs of neighbors and strangers. *Canadian Journal of Zoology,* 1975, *53,* 879–888. (a)

Brooks, R. J., & Falls, J. B. Individual recognition by song in white-throated sparrows: III. Song features used in individual recognition. *Canadian Journal of Zoology,* 1975, *53,* 1749–1761. (b)

Capranica, R. R. Morphology and physiology of the auditory system. In R. Llinas & W. Precht (Eds.), *Frog neurobiology.* Berlin: Springer-Verlag, 1976.

Craik, K. J. W. *The nature of explanation.* Cambridge: Cambridge University Press, 1943.

Dooling, R. J. Behavior and psychophysics of hearing in birds. In A. N. Popper & R. R. Fay (Eds.), *Comparative studies of hearing in vertebrates.* New York: Springer-Verlag, 1980.

Dooling, R. J., & Searcy, M. A. Early perceptual selectivity in the swamp sparrow. *Developmental Psychobiology*, 1980, *13*, 499–506.

Eberhardt, C., & Baptista, L. F. Intraspecific and interspecific song mimesis in California song sparrows. *Bird-Banding*, 1977, *48*, 193–205.

Eibl-Eibesfeldt, I. Similarities and differences between cultures in expressive movements. In R. A. Hinde (Ed.), *Non-verbal communication*. Cambridge: Cambridge University Press, 1972.

Eilers, R. E., & Minifie, F. D. Fricative discrimination in early infancy. *Journal of Speech and Hearing Research*, 1975, *18*, 158–167.

Eilers, R. E., Wilson, W. R., & Moore, J. M. Developmental changes in speech discrimination in infants. *Journal of Speech and Hearing Research*, 1977, *20*, 766–780.

Eimas, P. D. Speech perception in early infancy. In L. B. Cohen & P. Salapatek (Eds.), *Infant perception: From sensation to cognition*. New York: Academic Press, 1975.

Eimas, P. D., Siqueland, E. R., Jusczyk, P., & Vigorito, J. Speech perception in infants. *Science*, 1971, *171*, 303–306.

Eimas, P., & Tartter, V. C. On the development of speech perception: Mechanisms and analogies. In H. W. Reese & L. P. Lipsett (Eds.), *Advances in child development and behavior* (Vol. 13). New York: Academic Press, 1979.

Ekman, P. Cross-cultural studies of facial expression. In P. Ekman (Ed.), *Darwin and facial expression*. New York: Academic Press, 1973.

Emlen, S. T. An experimental analysis of the parameters of bird song eliciting species recognition. *Behaviour*, 1972, *41*, 130–171.

Evans, R. M. Development of an auditory discrimination in domestic chicks (*Gallus gallus*). *Animal Behaviour*, 1972, *20*, 77–87.

Evans, R. M., & Mattson, M. E. Development of selective responses to individual maternal vocalizations in young *Gallus gallus*. *Canadian Journal of Zoology*, 1972, *50*, 777–780.

Evarts, V., Bizzi, E., Burke, R. E., DeLong, M., & Thach, W. T. Jr. Central control of movement. *Neuroscience Research Program Bulletin* (No. 1), *9*, 1971.

Falls, J. B. Function of territoral song in the white-throated sparrow. In R. A. Hinde (Ed.), *Bird vocalizations*. Cambridge: Cambridge University Press, 1969.

Falls, J. B., & Brooks, R. J. Individual recognition by song in white-throated sparrows. II. Effects of location. *Canadian Journal of Zoology*, 1975, *53*, 1412–1420.

Fourcin, A. J. Acoustic patterns and speech acquisition. In N. Waterson & C. Snow (Eds.), *The development of communication*. New York: John Wiley & Sons, 1978.

Fry, D. B. The development of the phonological system in the normal and deaf child. In F. Smith & G. A. Miller (Eds.), *The genesis of language: A psycholinguistic approach*. Cambridge, Mass.: MIT Press, 1966.

Gerhardt, H. C. Temperature coupling in the vocal communication system of the gray tree frog, *Hyla versicolor*. *Science*, 1978, *199*, 992–994.

Gibson, E. J. *Principles of perception learning and development*. Englewood Cliffs, N.J.: Prentice-Hall, Inc., 1969.

Gibson, J. J. *The senses considered as perceptual systems*. Boston: Houghton Mifflin, 1966.

Green, S., & Marler, P. The analysis of animal communication. In P. Marler & J. Vandenbergh (Eds.), *Social behavior and communication*. New York: Plenum Press, 1979.

Greenewalt, C. H. *Bird song: Acoustics and physiology*. Washington, D.C.: Smithsonian Institution Press, 1968.

Gregory, R. L. *Concepts and mechanisms of perception*. New York: Charles Scribner & Sons, 1974.

Griffin, D. R. *The question of animal awareness*. New York: Rockefeller University Press, 1976.

Guyomarc'h, J.-C. Les bases ontogenétiques de l'attractivité du gloussement maternel chez la poule domestique. *Revue du Comportement Animal*, 1972, *6*, 79–94.

Guyomarc'h, J.-C. L'empreinte auditive prénatale chez le poussin domestique. *Revue du Comportement Animal*, 1974, *8*, 3-6. (a)

Guyomarc'h, J.-C. Le rôle de l'expérience sur la sémantique du cri d'offrance alimentaire chez le poussin. *Revue du Comportement Animal*, 1974, *9*, 219-236. (b)

Hayes, K. J., & Hayes, C. Imitation in a home raised chimpanzee. *Journal of Comparative and Physiological Psychology*, 1952, *45*, 450-459.

Hebb, D. O. *The organization of behavior*. New York: Wiley & Sons, 1949.

Held, R. Plasticity in sensory-motor systems. *Scientific American*, 1965, *213*, 84-94.

Hersh, G. L. *Bird voices and resonant tuning in air/helium mixtures*. Unpublished doctoral dissertation, University of California, Berkeley, 1966.

Hoy, R. R. Genetic control of acoustic behavior in crickets. *American Zoologist*, 1974, *14*, 1067-1080.

Hoy, R. R., Hahn, J., & Paul, R. C. Hybrid cricket auditory behavior: Evidence for genetic coupling in animal communication. *Science*, 1977, *195*, 82-84.

Hoy, R. R., & Paul, R. C. Genetic control of song specificity in crickets. *Science*, 1973, *180*, 82-83.

Immelmann, K. Song development in the zebra finch and other Estrildid finches. In R. A. Hinde (Ed.), *Bird vocalizations*. London & New York: Cambridge University Press, 1969.

Jakobson, R., Fant, C. G. M., & Halle, M. *Preliminaries to speech analysis*. Cambridge, Mass.: MIT Press, 1952.

Kern, M. C., & King, J. R. Testosterone-induced singing in female white-crowned sparrows. *Condor*, 1972, *74*, 206-209.

Konishi, M. The role of auditory feedback in the vocal behavior of the domestic fowl. *Zeitschrift für Tierpsychologie*, 1963, *20*, 349-367.

Konishi, M. Effects of deafening on song development in American robins and black-headed grosbeaks. *Zeitschrift für Tierpsychologie*, 1965, *22*, 584-599. (a)

Konishi, M. The role of auditory feedback in the control of vocalization in the white-crowned sparrow. *Zeitschrift für Tierpsychologie*, 1965, *22*, 770-783. (b)

Konishi, M. Effects of deafening on song development in two species of juncos. *Condor*, 1966, *66*, 85-102.

Konishi, M. Ethological aspects of auditory pattern recognition. In R. Held, H. W. Leibowitz, & H.-L. Teuber (Eds.), *Handbook of sensory physiology, Vol. VIII: Perception*. Berlin: Springer-Verlag, 1978.

Konishi, M., & Nottebohm, F. Experimental studies in the ontogeny of avian vocalization. In R. A. Hinde (Ed.), *Bird vocalizations*. London & New York: Cambridge University Press, 1969.

Kroodsma, D. E. Reproductive development in a female songbird: Differential stimulation by quality of male song. *Science*, 1976, *192*, 575.

Kroodsma, D. E. The effect of large song repertoires on neighbor "recognition" in male song sparrows. *Condor*, 1977, *78*, 97-99. (a)

Kroodsma, D. E. A re-evaluation of song development in the song sparrow. *Animal Behaviour*, 1977, *25*, 390-399. (b)

Kroodsma, D. E. Aspects of learning in the ontogeny of bird song: Where, from whom, when, how many, which and how accurately? In G. Burghardt & M. Bekoff (Eds.), *Ontogeny of behavior*. New York: Garland Publishing Co., 1978.

Kuhl, P. K., & Miller, J. D. Speech perception by the chinchilla: Voiced-voiceless distinction in alveolar plosive consonants. *Science*, 1975, *190*, 69-72.

Lemon, R. E. How birds develop dialects. *Condor*, 1975, *77*, 385-406.

Liberman, A. M., Cooper, F. S., Shankweiler, D., & Studdert-Kennedy, M. Perception of the speech code. *Psychological Review*, 1967, *74*, 431-461.

Lieberman, P. *Speech physiology and acoustic phonetics: An introduction*. New York: MacMillan, 1977.

Lorenz, K. Vergleichende Bewegungstudien bei Anatiden. *Journal für Ornithologie*, 1941, *89*, 194–294.

Mackintosh, N. J. *The psychology of animal learning*. New York: Academic Press, 1974.

Marler, P. The filtering of external stimuli during instinctive behavior. In W. H. Thorpe & O. L. Zangwill (Eds.), *Current problems in animal behavior*. Cambridge: Cambridge University Press, 1961.

Marler, P. A comparative approach to vocal learning: Song development in white-crowned sparrows. *Journal of Comparative and Physiological Psychology*, 1970, *71*, 1–25.

Marler, P. Sensory templates in species-specific behavior. In J. Fentress (Ed.), *Simpler networks: An approach to patterned behavior and its foundations*. New York: Sinauer Associates, 1976.

Marler, P. The structure of animal communication sounds. In T. H. Bullock (Ed.), *Recognition of complex acoustic signals*. Berlin: Dahlem Konferenzen, 1977.

Marler, P. Development of auditory perception in relation to vocal behavior. In M. von Cranach, K. Poppa, W. Lepenies, & D. Ploog (Eds.), *Human ethology: Claims and limits of a new discipline*. Cambridge: Cambridge University Press, 1979.

Marler, P., Dooling, R., & Zoloth, S. Comparative perspectives on ethology and behavioral development. In M. Bornstein (Ed.), *Comparative methods in psychology*. New York: Sinauer Associates, 1980.

Marler, P., & Hamilton, W. J. III. *Mechanisms of animal behavior*. New York: John Wiley & Sons, 1966.

Marler, P., Konishi, M., Lutjen, A., & Waser, M. S. Effects of continuous noise on avian hearing and vocal development. *Proceedings of the National Academy of Science*, 1973, *70*, 1393–1396.

Marler, P., & Mundinger, P. Vocal learning in birds. In H. Moltz (Ed.), *Ontogeny of vertebrate behavior*. New York: Academic Press, 1971.

Marler, P., Mundinger, P., Waser, M. S., & Lutjen, A. Effects of acoustical stimulation and deprivation on song development in the red-winged blackbird (*Agelaius phoeniceus*). *Animal Behaviour*, 1972, *20*, 586–606.

Marler, P., & Peters, S. Selective vocal learning in a sparrow. *Science*, 1977, *198*, 519–521.

Marler, P., & Tamura, M. Culturally transmitted patterns of vocal behavior in sparrows. *Science*, 1964, *146*, 1483–1486.

Marler, P., & Waser, M. S. The role of auditory feedback in canary song development. *Journal of Comparative and Physiological Psychology*, 1977, *91*, 8–16.

Meltzoff, A., & Moore, M. K. Imitation of facial and manual gestures by human neonates. *Science*, 1977, *198*, 75–78.

Milligan, M., & Verner, J. Interpopulation song dialect discrimination in the white-crowned sparrow. *Condor*, 1971, *73*, 208–213.

Mountcastle, V. The world around us: Neural command functions for selective attention. *N.R.P. Bulletin 14*, April, 1976. (Supplement)

Mulligan, J. A. Singing behavior and its development in the song sparrow, *Melospiza melodia*. Berkeley: University of California, Publications in Zoology, 1966, *81*, 1–76.

Nelson, K. Does the holistic study of behavior have a future? In P. P. G. Bateson & P. H. Klopfer (Eds.), *Perspectives in ethology*. New York: Plenum Press, 1973.

Nelson, K. Concept word and sentence: Interrelations in acquisition and development. *Psychological Review*, 1974, *81*, 267–285.

Nicolai, J. Familientradition in der Gesangsentwicklung des Gimpels (*Pyrrhula pyrrhula* L.). *Journal für Ornithologie*, 1959, *100*, 39–46.

Nottebohm, F. The origins of vocal learning. *American Naturalist*, 1972, *106*, 116–140.

Nottebohm, F. Vocal behavior in birds. In D. Farner (Ed.), *Avian Biology*, (Vol. V). New York: Academic Press, 1975.

Nottebohm, F., & Nottebohm, M. E. Relationship between song repertoire and age in the canary, *Serinus canarius*. *Zeitschrift für Tierpsychologie*, 1978, *46*, 298–305.

Oldfield, R. C., & Zangwill, O. L. Head's concept of the schema and its application in contemporary British psychology. I-IV. *British Journal of Psychology*, 1942-43, *32*, 267-286; *33*, pp. 58-64, 113-129, 143-147.

Peters, S., Searcy, W., & Marler, P. Species song discrimination in choice experiments with territorial male swamp and song sparrows. *Animal Behaviour*, 1980, *28*, 393-404.

Petersen, M. R., Beecher, M. D., Zoloth, S. R., Moody, D. B., & Stebbins, W. C. Neural lateralization of species-specific vocalizations by Japanese macaques (*Macaca fuscata*). *Science*, 1978, *202*, 324-327.

Popper, K., & Eccles, J. C. *The self and its brain.* New York: Springer International, 1977.

Premack, D. *Intelligence in ape and man.* New York: John Wiley & Sons, 1976.

Rosch, E. On the internal structure of perceptual and semantic categories. In T. E. Moore (Ed.), *Cognitive development and the acquisition of language.* New York: Academic Press, 1973.

Rosch, E. Universals and cultural specifics in human categorization. In R. Breslin, S. Bochner, & W. Lonner (Eds.), *Cultural perspectives on learning.* New York: Sage/Halsted, 1975.

Rosch, E., & Lloyd, B. B., (Eds.). *Cognition and categorization.* Hillsdale, N.J.: Lawrence Erlbaum Associates, 1978.

Sachs, J., Brown, R. T., & Salerno, R. A. Adults' speech to children. In W. von Raffler-Engel & T. Lebrum (Eds.), *Baby talk and infant speech.* Lisse, Netherlands: Swetz & Zeitlinger, 1976.

Saunders, J. C., Else, D. V., & Bock, G. R. Frequency selectivity in the parakeet (*Melopsittacus undulatus*) studied with psychophysical tuning curve. *Journal of Comparative and Physiological Psychology*, 1978, 92, 406-415.

Schleidt, W. Die historische Entwicklung der Begriffe "Angeborenes auslosendes Schema" und "Angeborener Auslosmechanismus" in der Ethologie. *Zeitschrift für Tierpsychologie*, 1962, *19*, 697-722.

Schneider, H. Rufe and Rufverhalten des Laubfrosches, *Hyla arborea arborea* (L.). *Zeitschrift für vergleichende Physiologie,* 1967, *57,* 174-189.

Schneider, H. Structure of the mating calls and relationships of the European tree frogs (Hylidae, Anura). *Oekologia*, 1974, *14*, 99-110.

Schneider, H. The acoustic behavior and physiology of vocalization in the European tree frog, *Hyla arborea* (L.). In D. H. Taylor & S. I. Guttman (Eds.)., *The reproductive biology of amphibians.* New York: Plenum Publishing Company, 1977.

Stevens, K. N. Quantal nature of speech. In E. E. David, Jr. & P. B. Denes (Eds.), *Human communication: A unified view.* New York: McGraw-Hill, 1972.

Sutherland, N. S. Object recognition. In E. C. Carterette & M. P. Friedman (Eds.), *Handbook of perception* (Vol. III). New York: Academic Press, 1973.

Thorpe, W. H. Comments on "The Bird Fancyer's Delight": Together with notes on imitation in the sub-song of the chaffinch. *Ibis*, 1955, *97*, 247-251.

Thorpe, W. H. The learning of song patterns by birds, with especial reference to the song of the chaffinch, *Fringilla coelebs. Ibis*, 1958, *100*, 535-570.

Thorpe, W. H. *Bird Song.* Cambridge: Cambridge University Press, 1961.

Tinbergen, N. *The study of instinct.* Oxford: Oxford University Press, 1951.

Turvey, M. T. Preliminaries to a theory of action with reference to vision. In R. Shaw & J. Bransford (Eds.), *Perceiving, acting, and knowing.* New York: John Wiley & Sons, 1977.

Uhr, L. *Pattern recognition.* New York: Wiley & Sons, 1966.

Walker, T. J. Specificity in the response of female tree crickets (Orthoptera, Gryllidae, Oecanthinae) to calling songs of the males. *Annals of the Entomological Society of America*, 1957, *50*, 626-633.

Warnock, G. J. *The philosophy of perception.* Oxford: Oxford University Press, 1967.

Weimer, W. B. A conceptual framework for cognitive psychology: Motor theories of the mind. In R. Shaw & J. Bransford (Eds.), *Perceiving, acting, and knowing.* Hillsdale, N.J.: Lawrence Erlbaum Associates, 1977.

Yarbus, A. L. *Eye movements and vision*. New York: Plenum Press, 1967.

Yasukawa, K. Song repertoires and sexual selection in the red-winged blackbird. *Nature*, in press.

Zoloth, S. R., Miller, R., Dooling, R. J., & Peters, S. A mini-computer system for the synthesis of animal vocalizations. *Zeitschrift für Tierpsychologie*, in press.

Zoloth, S. R., Petersen, M. R., Beecher, M. D., Green, S., Marler, P., Moody, D., & Stebbins, W. Species-specific perceptual processing of vocal sounds by monkeys. *Science*, 1979, *204*, 870–873.

4

Infant Speech Perception:
A Critical Appraisal

Peter W. Jusczyk
Dalhousie University

Editors' Comments

One of the research developments of the 1970s that has strongly influenced our ideas about speech and its processing is the study of infant speech perception. From the time of the original work by Moffitt (1971) a number of investigators have tried to explicate the basic perceptual abilities that the infant brings to the language acquisition situation, and the extent to which these abilities are both biologically determined and capable of modification by experiential factors.

Jusczyk, one of the earliest investigators in the field, has provided a comprehensive review and critique of the infant speech literature, along with his own more recent findings. Moreover, he has discussed a number of the critical issues, including the implications of infant data for theories of adult perception, the nature and limitations of the current methodologies available for the study of infant speech perception, and the extent to which the remarkable perceptual abilities of the young infant reflect the operation of species-specific mechanisms that have evolved especially for the development and processing of language. This chapter, together with Chapter 3 by Marler and Peters, provides a wide range of data and discussion on issues that have been and continue to be central to our understanding of the development of communication systems in general, and speech in particular.

INTRODUCTION

Human infants are not the most cooperative of experimental subjects. The investigator who works with them must learn to accept the fact that experimental sessions will be frequently terminated because his or her subjects are crying, sleeping, or just generally disinterested. Further problems are posed by the infants' lack of an adequate language for communication; thus the experimenter is forced to devise alternative ways of conveying instructions and obtaining responses from subjects. Given the array of potential frustrations that an investigator could encounter, why would anyone ever be tempted to study the speech perception capacities of human infants?

There would appear to be two obvious answers to such a question. First, knowledge of the infant's speech perception capacities is necessary for understanding how the infant acquires language. Second, knowledge of what the infant's capacities are may provide insights as to the mechanisms underlying speech perception by adults as well as by infants. Both of these concerns have guided investigators in the field, and over the past 10 years some gains have been made with respect to each one. However, as with any new field of research, there has been some tendency for investigators to draw conclusions from experimental results that, in retrospect, appear to be stronger than the data warrant. In this chapter, I undertake a critical examination of many of the findings from infant speech perception studies and evaluate the implications that such findings have both for language acquisition and the nature of the mechanisms underlying speech perception. In what follows, I consider several aspects of the infant's speech perception capacities including: (1) the variety of contrasts that the infant can discriminate; (2) the range of situations to which the infant is able to apply his or her capacities for analyzing speech; and (3) the possible bases for the infant's speech processing abilities. In my conclusions, I try to summarize the gains that have been made in understanding the infant's speech perception capacities, and to relate the implications that research in this area has for theories of language acquisition as well as for theories of speech perception.

THE VARIETY OF CONTRASTS
THAT INFANTS DISCRIMINATE

By a wide margin, most studies of infant speech perception have focused upon the variety of speech contrasts that infants are capable of discriminating. Although much attention has been given to the infant's perception of cues for voicing and place-of-articulation (place) for stop consonants, some consideration has also been given to cues relevant to distinguishing among vowels, liquids, glides, fricatives, and nasals. Moreover, some researchers have even stepped beyond the bounds of contrasts normally found in the infant's native language, to examine the discriminability of foreign language contrasts. In this section, I review much of the work relating to the variety of contrasts that infants have been shown to discriminate. For ease of discussion, I survey the studies bearing on the perception of each phonetic contrast separately, beginning with voicing.

Consonants

Voicing.   The speech cues that have received the most attention from investigators of infant speech perception are those relating to the discrimination of voicing distinctions, and in particular, to one of the major cues for voicing, namely voice-onset-time (VOT). A number of factors have contributed to the interest in VOT including: (1) studies with adults (e.g., Liberman, Harris, Kinney, & Lane, 1961) demonstrating that the perception of speech sounds differing in VOT is categorical (i.e., subjects are only slightly better at discriminating sounds differing in VOT than they are at differentially labeling them); (2) observations of 11 diverse languages that indicated that, with only slight variations, speakers' productions clustered around the same three values of VOT (Lisker & Abramson, 1964). More specifically, the demonstrations of categorical perception and strong cross-language similarities in production suggested the existence of underlying constraints on the perception and production of VOT. Questions about the nature and origins of such constraints were difficult to assess with adult subjects given their long history of contact with language. Thus, when new advances were made in the methods of assessing the perceptual capacities of young infants (e.g., Graham & Clifton, 1966; Siqueland & DeLucia, 1969), it was quite natural that investigators turned to this linguistically naive population for information about the nature of constraints on the perception of VOT.

It is worth considering that when Eimas, Siqueland, Jusczyk, and Vigorito (1971) began their study of the perception of VOT by young infants, very little, if anything, was known about how categorical perception developed in the child. Thus, when their study was first undertaken there were at least two interesting possibilities. On the one hand, categorical perception of a speech dimension like VOT might be the result of innate constraints on the perceptual system. On the other hand, categorical perception might develop gradually as a result of the child's experience in hearing and producing speech sounds differing in VOT. By this latter notion, one might suppose that although, initially, young infants are capable of making many distinctions along the VOT continuum, they gradually learn to ignore subtle differences between tokens, and focus only on major differences relevant to distinguishing between words in their native language.

Because the issue of the origins of categorical perception was of some interest to them, Eimas et al. (1971) examined the discrimination of VOT differences by two age groups, 1-month-olds and 4-month-olds. The procedure that they used was a modified version of the high-amplitude sucking (HAS) technique developed previously by Siqueland and DeLucia (1969). Briefly, the experimenter makes the presentation of one of a pair of auditory stimuli contingent upon the infant's rate of sucking, such that a suck that exceeds a predetermined criterion level results in the presentation of one speech sound. Typically, the infant's sucking pattern will show a slow but steady increase in rate of responding, followed by a leveling off of the rate for several minutes, and then a decline in sucking. When the infant's rate declines by some prearranged measure, the auditory stimulus is changed to the second member of the pair. The infant's discrimination of the two stimuli is inferred from an increase in sucking rate (relative to that of control subjects) upon presentation of the second stimulus. (For further details about the procedure and its rationale, the reader should consult Williams & Golenski, 1978.)

In order to address the question of whether or not infants' discrimination of VOT is categorical, Eimas et al. (1971) examined performance with several different VOT pairs. For each pair, the two stimuli differed from each other by a constant amount: 20 msec of VOT. The pairs themselves were chosen so that one pair opposed stimuli chosen from different VOT categories (i.e., +20 msec [ba] vs. +40 msec [pa]) and the other pairs consisted of stimuli chosen from within the same VOT category (i.e., -20 msec [ba] vs. 0 msec [ba] or +60 msec [pa] vs. +80 msec [pa]). Eimas et al.'s results showed that both 1-month- and 4-month-olds discriminated the "Between-categories" pair (+20/+40), but that neither age group discriminated the "Within-categories" pairs (-20/0 or +60/ +80).

On the basis of their results, Eimas et al. drew the following conclusions: (1) that the mechanisms underlying the infant's discrimination of VOT differences may well be part of the biological makeup of the organism (i.e., they are presumably innate); (2) that the infants were perceiving the sounds in a manner approximating categorical perception; and (3) that the findings suggested perception in a linguistic mode. Looking back on these claims, it would appear that the first of them is quite secure. It is difficult to envision any sort of a learning account for these results given the limited exposure that these infants had to language. On the other hand, both the second and third claims bear closer examination.

The second claim—that infants were perceiving the sounds in a manner approximating categorical perception—is one that is open to misinterpretation. Traditionally, categorical perception has been defined in terms of a match between labeling and discrimination data such that the region of highest discriminability coincides with the category boundary as determined from the labeling data (e.g., see Studdert-Kennedy, Liberman, Harris, & Cooper, 1970). Judging by these criteria, the Eimas et al. (1971) study provides only half of the information (viz., information about infants' discriminative capacities) necessary for establishing whether infants have categorical perception of VOT. Because they did not collect the relevant data about the way in which infants "label" stimuli selected from various points along the VOT continuum, Eimas et al. could not justifiably claim to have found categorical perception of these sounds. However, the fact that infants, like adults, did discriminate pairs from different adult VOT categories but not ones from within the same category, suggested that the same kinds of processes might be operating in both age groups. For this reason, Eimas et al. claimed that infants perceived the sounds in a manner *approximating* categorical perception. Nevertheless, it might be more appropriate to say that what Eimas et al. found was evidence for *categorical discrimination* of VOT differences by infants.

The third claim made by Eimas et al.—that their findings suggested perception in a linguistic mode—is the most questionable of the three. This claim was based both upon the finding that infants' discrimination of VOT differences corresponded to that for adults and the assumption that categorical perception was unique to speech sounds. However, recent studies with nonspeech stimuli (e.g., Cutting & Rosner, 1974; Miller, Wier, Pastore, Kelley, & Dooling, 1976; Pisoni, 1977) demonstrate that categorical perception is not limited to speech. Consequently, it need not be the case that infants' discrimination of VOT differences is accomplished by means of mechanisms specialized for the perception of speech. In fact, the findings showing that chinchillas, too, respond to VOT differences in a manner similar to humans (Kuhl & Miller, 1975a, 1978) suggest that any underlying mechanisms likely reflect general constraints imposed upon the mammalian auditory system. Thus, the Eimas et al. results do not provide much support for the contention that infants are exhibiting perception in a linguistic mode.[1]

The Eimas et al. study showed that infants had the capacity to distinguish between two modes of voicing along the VOT continuum, i.e., between voiced ([pa] or the English /ba/) and voiceless ([pʰa]) segments. However, as noted earlier, Lisker and Abramson (1964) found evidence for at least three modes of voicing. The third category, prevoiced, is not one employed in English, but is used in a number of other languages, including Thai. Given the initial results, which strongly implied an innate basis for the voiced–voiceless distinction, it was only natural to expect that infants would also discriminate contrasts between prevoiced and voiced tokens. Eimas (1975b) reported on two attempts to determine whether infants were sensitive to prevoiced/voiced contrasts. His results were equivocal for several reasons. First of all, the VOT differences (80 msec) that he employed were much larger than those used for the comparable voiced–voiceless distinction (20 msec). Second, although he did find evidence that one group of infants could distinguish a prevoiced–voiced contrast (−70 msec/+10 msec), the performance of this group was not reliably different from one that received a contrast from within the prevoiced category (−150 msec/−70 msec). Thus, the results suggested that infants were sensitive to contrasts between prevoiced and voiced syllables, but there was no evidence that infants' discrimination of these contrasts was categorical.

One possible explanation for the discrepancy that Eimas observed between the prevoiced–voiced and voiced–voiceless distinctions was that even the limited exposure that 2-month-olds have to language might be sufficient to exert a

---

[1]It should be noted that later claims that infants perceive speech in a linguistic mode (e.g., Eimas, 1975a) were not based solely on these grounds, but on additional evidence as well (e.g., Eimas, 1974; 1975b). The extent to which this additional evidence provides support for the linguistic mode claim is discussed in subsequent sections.

change in sensitivity for certain speech contrasts. Thus, because infants in English-speaking environments would only rarely be exposed to information in prevoiced–voiced region of the VOT continuum, their sensitivity to such information might become attenuated (see Aslin & Pisoni, 1978, for similar suggestions about the possible effects of linguistic experience on speech perception). It is clear that linguistic experience does affect adults' sensitivity to information along speech continua like VOT, as demonstrated by the studies of Lisker and Abramson (1970) and Williams (1977b, 1977c). However, it is more probable that the discrepancies observed by Eimas are due to some other factor, perhaps the size of the VOT differences that he used, because several recent studies (e.g., Aslin, Hennessy, Pisoni, & Perey, 1979; Lasky, Syrdal-Lasky, & Klein, 1975; Streeter, 1976) suggest that a 2-month exposure to language is unlikely to result in a pronounced change in sensitivity along the VOT continuum (although, for an opposing view see Eilers, Gavin, & Wilson, 1979).

Though his own results were equivocal, several other studies have borne out Eimas' (1975b) contention that infants are sensitive to VOT differences in the prevoiced–voiced boundary region. Lasky et al. (1975) investigated the discrimination of VOT contrasts by Guatemalan infants. In contrast to the earlier study by Eimas et al., they employed a heart-rate dishabituation procedure. This paradigm is based upon the assumption that cardiac deceleration serves as an index of the infant's orienting response to a novel stimulus (Sokolov, 1963). Although a marked deceleration in heart rate may be observed during the first few presentations of the stimulus, the amount of decrement declines with repeated exposure to the stimulus (i.e., the heart-rate response habituates). Following heart-rate habituation to a particular stimulus, if a second stimulus is introduced and is recognized as novel in some way, then a marked deceleration in heart rate might again occur (i.e., heart-rate dishabituation). It is this deceleration to the second stimulus, following habituation to the first stimulus, which serves as an index of the infant's ability to discriminate the two stimuli. Using this measure, Lasky et al. reported that Guatemalan infants 4 to 6½ months old of Spanish-speaking parents exhibit two regions of high sensitivity to VOT differences. One region, between +20 and +60 msec, was coincident with the voiced–voiceless distinction; the other, between −20 and −60 msec, was coincident with the prevoiced–voiced distinction. These results are interesting not only because they imply that infants discriminate three modes of voicing along the VOT continuum, but also because of a discrepancy observed between the discrimination of VOT differences by the infants and Spanish-speaking adults. The adults gave evidence of only one VOT boundary in the region of 0 msec, in contrast to the two boundaries that Lasky et al. inferred from the infant discrimination data. Moreover, despite 4 to 6½ months of experience in a Spanish-speaking environment, the infants did not display discrimination of a contrast (−20/+20 msec) selected from the region of highest sensitivity for Spanish-speaking adults.

On the basis of Lasky et al.'s (1975) results, it would appear that the linguistic environment has little effect on the infant's sensitivity to VOT differences during the first few months of life. This conclusion is bolstered by findings from another study with infants from a non-English-speaking environment. Streeter (1976) found that Kikuyu infants also discriminated both prevoiced-voiced and voiced-voiceless contrasts. Again, what is interesting about these results is that one of these contrasts, the voiced-voiceless one, is not one that occurs in the linguistic environment to which these infants are exposed.

Despite the fact that studies with infants from three diverse language environments (English, Spanish, and Kikuyu) display a remarkable agreement with respect to the regions of highest sensitivity to VOT differences, the suggestion that there is an innate basis for the detection of VOT has not gone unchallenged. Eilers and her associates (Eilers, Gavin, & Wilson, 1979; Eilers, Wilson, & Moore, 1979) have argued that extensive experience with language may be a prerequisite for the discrimination of some VOT contrasts. Eilers bases her argument largely on results, which she obtained in her own studies of VOT discrimination by 6-month-olds. She has employed a visually reinforced head-turning measure to assess infant's discriminative capacities. With this procedure, infants are reinforced for turning their heads when they detect a change in auditory stimulation. When Eilers employed this paradigm with 6-month-olds from an English-speaking environment, she found no evidence for the discrimination of the prevoiced-voiced contrast. On the other hand, she did find evidence that infants from a Spanish-speaking environment discriminated both the prevoiced-voiced and the voiced-voiceless contrast. On the basis of these findings, Eilers et al. (1979) concluded that the voiced-voiceless distinction might have special acoustic properties that make it readily discriminable for infants regardless of their linguistic background, but that the prevoiced-voiced contrast develops only if infants experience it in their linguistic environment.

Eilers' findings would appear to present a problem for the view that some innate mechanism underlies the discrimination of VOT differences by infants. However, Aslin and Pisoni (1980) have suggested that some methodological problems, such as too small a number of test trials, may have led Eilers to underestimate the ability of infants from English-speaking backgrounds to discriminate the prevoiced-voiced contrast. In support of their position, they cite evidence from their own laboratory (Aslin et al., 1979) that 6-month-olds from English-speaking environments are sensitive to both prevoiced-voiced and voiced-voiceless distinctions. Aslin et al. employed a variant of the head-turning paradigm in conjunction with an adaptive staircase procedure for assessing absolute thresholds. To implement this procedure, they first trained infants to respond to a contrast between two endpoints of a continuum; one endpoint sound served as the background stimulus and the other as the change stimulus. Each time the infant correctly detected a change stimulus on two successive trials, the VOT difference between it and the background stimulus was diminished by 20 msec.

On the other hand, whenever the infant failed to discriminate the difference between the background and change stimuli, the VOT difference was increased by 20 msec. By proceeding in this fashion, Aslin et al. were able to obtain an estimate of the point along the continuum at which infants failed to distinguish the change stimulus from the background. Their results suggest the existence of two boundaries along the VOT continuum. Figure 4.1 provides an indication of the estimated boundaries for a number of individual subjects in their study. Though there are some individual differences, one boundary occurs in the neighborhood of -25 msec (which fits well with the estimates of the prevoiced-voiced boundary) and the other is located around $+25$ msec (which approximates the voiced–voiceless boundary). Thus, these results suggest that 6-month-old infants from English-speaking families are sensitive to three modes of voicing. Moreover, Aslin et al.'s data collected from observations of individual subjects concurs with findings obtained using group measures in previous studies (i.e., Eimas, 1975a; Eimas et al., 1971; Lasky et al., 1975; Streeter, 1976).

At first glance, it might appear that Aslin et al. (1979) have actually provided data concerning the way in which infants label the VOT stimuli. Thus, one is tempted to conclude that when an infant does not detect a change stimulus from the background stimulus, it is because both stimuli have the same label. By similar reasoning, one might expect that when the infant does detect a change stimulus it is given the same label as the original change endpoint stimulus, and thus the infant makes a head-turn. However, whereas the first portion of the argument appears to be sound, the second portion is not. As Aslin (personal communication) has noted, an infant who learns to make a head-turn to a change stimulus may be learning to respond to any change against the background. There is no a priori reason to expect that the infant "labels" all such changes as the same. For instance, the infant might distinguish between the various change stimuli. Presumably, one could attempt to settle the issue by testing whether infants really do distinguish between the different change stimuli. However, not only would such extensive testing be impractical with 6-month-olds, but it is not clear that such testing would provide an unambiguous answer as to how the stimuli are "labeled" by the infant.[2] Consequently, the labeling data necessary to establish the claims of categorical perception of VOT information by infants are still not available.[3]

---

[2]For instance, suppose one were to find that infants did distinguish some of the change stimuli from each other. We know that adults, under some circumstances, can make within-category discriminations (Carney, Widin, & Viemeister, 1977; Pisoni & Lazarus, 1974; Pisoni & Tash, 1974; Samuel, 1977). Thus, a finding that infants could distinguish between some of the change stimuli would not guarantee that they would not assign the same label to the stimuli.

[3]What is really required here is a conditioned discrimination procedure in which infants are trained to make two distinct responses to the endpoints of a continuum such as the two-alternative forced-choice method suggested by Aslin, Perey, Hennessy, and Pisoni, 1977. This would allow infants the option of performing no response for a stimulus they deem to be unlike either of the two endpoints.

To summarize to this point, research on the perception of VOT differences between stop consonants indicates the following: (1) infants are sensitive to three modes of voicing differences along the VOT continuum; (2) the discrimination of VOT differences by infants is categorical; (3) the perception of VOT information during early infancy is relatively unaffected by the specific language environment of the infant; (4) the mechanisms responsible for infants' discrimination of VOT are apparently innately determined.

Thus far I have only reviewed studies relating to the perception of voicing differences between stop consonant contrasts. Some limited data also exist concerning the perception of voicing differences between fricatives. Eilers (1977; Eilers, Wilson, & Moore, 1977) has examined the perception of [sa]/[za] contrasts by infants of different ages. In a study with 3-month-old infants employing the high amplitude sucking paradigm, Eilers (1977) found no evidence for the discrimination of a [sa]/[za] contrast, although infants did discriminate an [as]/[az] contrast. In a subsequent study with 6-month-olds employing the headturning paradigm, Eilers et al. (1977) reported that infants in this age group did distinguish [sa] from [za]. On the basis of these two studies, it would appear that the discrimination of voicing differences in fricatives develops with increasing experience with language. However, such a conclusion would be premature because a number of questions have been raised regarding the procedure and method of analysis employed in the study with 3-month-olds. For example, Eimas and Tartter (1979) have suggested that the high amplitude sucking criterion employed by Eilers may have led to response suppression in some subjects, thus effectively lowering the probability of finding significant effects. Moreover, Eilers' method of testing for significant recovery after shift to the second stimulus involves a comparison of infants' sucking rates for the 4 minutes preceding shift and the 4 minutes succeeding shift. Because marked changes in sucking occur, by definition, between the third and second minutes before shift, the measure she uses is much more variable. Therefore, Eilers' measure is less sensitive than measures employed by other investigators using this paradigm (e.g., Eimas, 1974; Jusczyk, 1977). The use of a less sensitive measure reduces the probability of finding evidence that infants can distinguish a particular contrast. Thus, some caution must be exercised in interpreting these results, and any firm conclusions regarding infants' sensitivity to voicing differences in fricatives must await further testing.

Place. Information regarding the perception of place-of-articulation contrasts has played a prominent role in the formulation of theories of speech perception. It has long been held that invariant acoustic cues do not exist for the perception of place-of-articulation in stop consonants (Liberman, Cooper, Shankweiler, & Studdert-Kennedy, 1967). In support of their position, Liberman et al. cite several sources of evidence, two of the most prominent being: (1) instances in which different acoustic cues give rise to the perception of the same phonetic segment; and (2) cases in which the same acoustic segment, depending

GROUP I

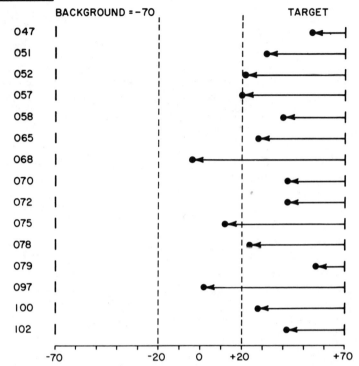

GROUP II

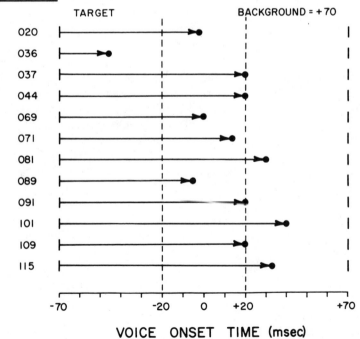

VOICE ONSET TIME (msec)

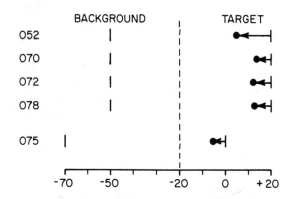

GROUP I

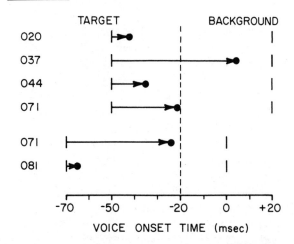

GROUP II

VOICE ONSET TIME (msec)

FIG. 4.1. Shows the staircase data obtained from infants in the study by Aslin, Hennessy, Pisoni, and Perey (1979). The data from 27 infants who completed the full range VOT series (−70 msec to +70 msec) is shown on the left. Note that the predominant boundary location (as indicated by the dots) coincides with the voiced–voiceless boundary in English. On the right-hand side, the data are shown for infants tested on several VOT series whose range (as indicated by the vertical bars) spanned only a portion of the −70 msec to +70 msec continuum. About half of the infants tested provide evidence of a boundary in the prevoiced–voiced region. (Used with permission of the authors.)

on the context in which it occurs, leads to the perception of different phonetic segments. Thus, with respect to the first issue, they note that the second format transitions, which cue the perception of [d] differ considerably for the syllables [di] and [du], yet the [d] heard in both syllables is the same perceptually. With respect to the second issue, they point to the fact that the same burst of noise that cues a perception of [p] before [i] will be heard as [k] if it occurs before [a] (Liberman, DeLattre, & Cooper, 1952; Schatz, 1954).

The finding that potential acoustic cues for place-of-articulation vary dramatically in different vowel contexts has been an important justification for the claim that specialized processing mechanisms for the perception of speech exist. However, recently there have been several investigations, using new methods of analyzing speech information, which purport to show the existence of invariant acoustic cues for the perception of place (Searle, Jacobson, & Rayment, 1979; Stevens & Blumstein, 1978). If these findings are supported by further research, then they would serve to undermine one of the important bases for claiming that specialized mechanisms for processing speech do exist.

Given the pivotal role that information about the perception of place-of-articulation has for theories of speech perception, it is not surprising that place contrasts have been extensively studied by investigators of infant speech perception. Moffit (1971) conducted the first investigation in this area. Using the heart-rate dishabituation measure, he showed that 5-month-old infants were capable of discriminating synthetic tokens of [ba] and [ga].

Moffit's findings were replicated by Morse (1972), who employed the HAS measure in testing 2-month-old infants. In addition to examining the discriminability of the [ba]/[ga] contrast, Morse also attempted to provide evidence about the mechanisms underlying the infant's perception of this contrast. Thus, Morse tested infants for their ability to discriminate the same acoustic information (formant transition differences) in both speech and nonspeech contexts. For infants in the speech conditions, the formant transition information was presented in the context of syllables [ba] and [ga]. For infants in the nonspeech conditions, the same second- and third-formant transition information was presented by using stimuli from which information regarding the first formant or the vocalic portions of the second and third formants had been removed. These latter sounds are not perceived as speech by adults (Mattingly, Liberman, Syrdal, & Halwes, 1971); rather they have a bird-like quality and are usually referred to as "chirps." Morse believed that finding a difference in the way in which infants responded to speech and nonspeech contexts (as Mattingly et al. had demonstrated for adults) would provide evidence that infants perceive place cues in a linguistically relevant manner. Unfortunately, his results were somewhat equivocal. The overall analysis of his data suggested no differences in responsiveness to the speech and nonspeech contexts. A subsequent analysis indicated that for infants who received the nonspeech sounds, performance was bimodally distributed with about half of the infants showing evidence of discrimination, and half not. The bimodal performance of the nonspeech group contrasted with that of the speech group, which displayed small but consistent increases in sucking during the postshift period. Morse took this as evidence that infants respond differently to speech and nonspeech stimuli. However, there are real problems associated with trying to interpret the postshift performance of individual subjects in the high-amplitude sucking procedure. Spurious increases and decreases in sucking might occur for any number of reasons (e.g., lapses of attention, discomfort, fatigue, etc.). It is not unusual to find marked differences in postshift performance for subjects in a given experimental group. Consequently, it is not clear how the bimodal performance of subjects in the nonspeech condition should be interpreted. Were the nonspeech sounds less discriminable for the infants or less interesting? And if the latter, were they less interesting because they were not speech, or for some other reason such as their shorter duration? In view of these concerns, caution must be exercised in interpreting Morse's data as support for the claim that infants process speech in a linguistically relevant manner.

A more convincing demonstration that infants may process the same acoustic information differently in speech and nonspeech contexts was provided by Eimas (1974). He, too, examined the infant's capacity for discriminating formant transition differences in both speech and nonspeech contexts. However, unlike Morse's study, his investigation was designed to test whether infants might display categorical discrimination for formant transition cues. Eimas selected his synthetic stimuli in such a way that he could present either "between-category" ([bae] vs. [dae]) or "within-category" ([bae$_1$] vs. [bae$_2$]) pairs. Because he employed syllables composed of only two formants, the only difference between members of any stimulus pair lay in the frequency values for the second formant transitions. The physical difference in Hz for the pair members of the between-category and within-category contrasts was approximately the same. In order to provide comparable nonspeech pairs, whose members differed physically in the same way as the speech pairs, Eimas utilized chirps generated from the speech stimuli by presenting only the second-formant transition information. This allowed him to test whether infants might exhibit categorical discrimination for the same physical contrast in both a speech and nonspeech context.[4] His results indicated a difference in the way in which infants reacted to the speech and

---

[4]The underlying assumption behind using only second-formant transition information for chirp controls is that the only physical differences between the stimuli relevant for auditory processing are contained in this portion of the signal. The first-formant transition information does not differ for the stimuli and is omitted because it is considered to be redundant. However, it is possible that the information of most relevance to the auditory processing system is not the absolute frequency of the second-formant transition but rather the relation of the second-formant transition to that of the first formant. Research in our laboratory (Jusczyk, Smith, & Murphy, 1980) suggests that there may be marked differences in adults' perception of chirps with and without first-formant transitions. These results may force us to re-examine the assumption that acoustic differences between speech stimuli can be adequately modeled by nonspeech chirps without first formant transitions.

nonspeech contrasts. For the speech contrasts, infants discriminated the between-category contrasts but not the within-category contrasts. Thus, for the speech contrasts discrimination performance was categorical. By comparison, there was no evidence that discrimination of the nonspeech stimuli was categorical.[5]

With his study, Eimas (1974) was able to extend what was previously known about the infant's perception of place-of-articulation in several directions. First, he provided evidence about the infant's ability to discriminate two different place contrasts—both the [bae]/[dae] contrast mentioned earlier and, in an earlier experiment, the [dae]/[gae] contrast. Second, he demonstrated that, as is the case for VOT, the infant's discrimination of these contrasts is categorical. Third, he found that infants, like adults (see Mattingly et al., 1971), respond differently to the same acoustic changes when they occur in speech versus nonspeech contexts. This latter finding was perhaps the most important for it was, and still remains, the strongest evidence in favor of the claim that infants may utilize specialized mechanisms for processing speech sounds.

Eimas' finding that differences exist in infants' responsiveness to similar changes in speech and nonspeech sounds, received additional support from a study conducted by Till (1976). He used a heart-rate dishabituation measure to explore the infant's sensitivity to changes in formant structure for speech and nonspeech contrasts. The speech contrasts consisted of synthetic tokens of [ba] and [da], whereas the nonspeech sounds were identical except that the first-formant pattern was inverted. Till found that infants displayed categorical discrimination for the speech contrasts, but not for the nonspeech ones. Hence, Till, like Eimas, claimed that infants respond differently to the same acoustic changes depending on whether their context is speech or nonspeech.[6]

To this point, we have limited our discussion of the perception of place contrasts by infants to studies in which place information was signaled by formant transition differences. However, we know that there are a number of other cues that are linked to the perception of place information (see, for example, the excellent discussion of this point by Dorman, Studdert-Kennedy, & Raphael, 1977). Miller, Morse, and Dorman (1977) examined the infant's sensitivity to one of these cues, viz. burst information. Using the heart-rate paradigm, they presented infants with a contrast between the syllables [bu] and [gu]. The stimuli

---

[5]There were no reliable differences between the groups receiving the various nonspeech contrasts, though only one of the two groups performed significantly better than controls. The other group, although in the right direction, did not differ from the controls. However, Eimas reported testing an additional group of infants on this contrast with the result that it was reliably discriminated.

[6]Because he did employ stimuli that included first formant information, Till's nonspeech stimuli might appear to escape the criticisms we made in footnote 4. However, his stimulus manipulation did disturb the relationship between the first formant and the other formants for the nonspeech contrasts. Thus, any mechanism that responded to information about the relationship between formants would be disturbed, or perhaps inactivated by Till's manipulation.

differed only in the nature of the initial burst cue. Both stimuli were derived from the same natural speech token of [bu]; however, for the [gu] stimulus the initial b-burst was removed and replaced by a g-burst. Miller et al.'s results indicated that this initial burst difference was a sufficient basis for the infant's discrimination of the two syllables. Thus, it would appear that infants can utilize information from either bursts or formant transitions in order to discriminate changes in place-of-articulation.

In the natural environment, bursts and formant transitions covary, and so a listener might use either cue or some integral combination of the two. Stevens and Blumstein (1978) have argued in favor of the latter possibility, suggesting that invariant spectral properties characteristic of a given stop consonant might be found in the combination of bursts and the onsets of formant transitions. If Stevens and Blumstein are correct, then one might expect to find that under some circumstances, syllables containing both burst and formant transitions are more discriminable than syllables possessing only one of these cues. Williams and Bush (1978) sought to test this hypothesis. Therefore, they examined the discrimination performance of a group of infants presented with a [da]/[ga] contrast cued by both bursts and formant transitions in comparison to a second group for whom the contrast was cued by formant transitions alone. Their results provided weak support for the hypothesis, because the performance of the group presented with both cues was marginally (p = .063) better than that of the group presented with the single cue. Regrettably, Williams and Bush did not collect data on the discrimination of a burst-cued pair, nor did they explore the consequences of pitting the burst cues against the formant transition cues (i.e., by interchanging the bursts). Hence, it is impossible to draw any firm conclusions regarding the importance that the infant attaches to burst and formant transition cues singly, or in combination.

Before concluding our discussion of the infant's capacity for distinguishing stop consonant contrasts differing in place-of-articulation, we note that other studies have demonstrated that infants are also sensitive to such contrasts occurring in either medial or final positions of utterances (Jusczyk, 1977; Jusczyk & Thompson, 1978; Williams, 1977a). We defer consideration of these studies because they are examined at length in a later section.

In summary, then, research on the infant's perception of place differences for stop consonants indicates: (1) that infants are sensitive to place differences; (2) that they are capable of discriminating place differences on the basis of burst cues, formant transition cues, or some combination of the two; (3) that the discrimination of at least one of these cues, formant transitions, is categorical; and (4) that differences exist in infants' responsiveness to what appears to be the same acoustic information in speech and nonspeech contexts.

Additional evidence exists regarding the infant's perception of place contrasts for other manners of articulation such as nasals, glides, and fricatives. Specifically, Eimas and Miller (1977) have reported that infants distinguish a [ma]/[na]

contrast when it is cued by formant transition differences. Similarly, Jusczyk, Copan, and Thompson (1978) have shown that infants discriminate the glides [w] and [y] on the basis of formant transition differences. Thus, findings from these two studies are consistent with previous ones for the discrimination of stop consonant differences.

The situation with respect to fricatives is a little more complicated. Using the head-turning paradigm with 6- and 12-month-old infants, Eilers et al. (1977) studied the perception of a variety of fricative contrasts, some of which involved place-of-articulation differences. Of most relevance to us here was the performance of subjects for the contrasts [sa]/[ʃa], [fa]/[θa], and [fi]/[θi].[7] In line with previous findings for 2- to 4-month-olds (Eilers & Minifie, 1975), Eilers et al. (1977) found that both the 6-month-olds and the 12-month-olds discriminated the [sa]/[ʃa] pair. By contrast, neither age group showed evidence of discriminating the [fa]/[θa] and only the 12-month-olds discriminated the [fi]/[θi] pair.[8] Eilers et al. (1977) took these results to be an indication that developmental changes occur in the infant's ability to detect some fricative contrasts during the first year. However, another interpretation is possible. Eilers et al. reported that the [θi] and [θa] tokens were only correctly identified by a group of adult listeners 70% and 60% of the time, respectively. Although such poor labeling performance may be characteristic for such tokens (e.g., Carden, Levitt, & Jusczyk, 1979; Miller & Nicely, 1955), it may be especially important in the context of the infant experiments given the small number of test trials (three change trials and three control trials), which were employed by Eilers et al. (1977). Hence, these contrasts may have been difficult ones for the infants and a greater number of observations may have been necessary to obtain reliable evidence for discrimination. This suggestion has received empirical support from two recent studies. Holmberg, Morgan, and Kuhl (1977) tested 6-month-olds using the head-turning paradigm. They reported evidence that infants could detect a [f]/[θ] contrast in both the initial ([fa] vs. [θa]) and final ([af] vs. [aθ]) positions of syllables. Significantly, Holmberg et al. (1977) employed a different criterion for successful discrimination performance than that used by Eilers et al. Holmberg et al.'s measure was more akin to a training paradigm in that infants were tested repeatedly until they attained a performance level of 8 correct responses out of 10 trials (5 change and 5 control trials). On average, it took Holmberg et al.'s subjects 68 trials to achieve this criterion (this was about twice as long as it took for them to master a

---

[7]One other contrast that involved a place-of-articulation contrast [sa]/[va] also differed on other dimensions such as voicing. For the record, it is noted that infants of both age groups in this study, as well as a group of 2- to 4-month-olds tested using the HAS paradigm in a previous study, (Eilers & Minifie, 1975) did discriminate the [sa]/[va] contrast.

[8]Again these same contrasts were not discriminated by a group of 2- to 4-month-olds tested with the HAS procedure (Eilers, 1977).

[sa]/[ʃa] contrast). Thus, whereas the [fa]/[θa] contrast is undoubtedly a difficult one, Holmberg et al. have provided an indication that 6-month-olds will discriminate it if the appropriate test conditions hold.

Further support for the claim that infants can discriminate a [fa]/[θa] contrast comes from a series of experiments reported by Jusczyk, Murray, and Bayly (1979). The first of these experiments employed synthetic speech tokens and was designed to compare the perception of place-of-articulation in stops and fricatives. The stimulus tokens for this study were selected from two synthetic speech continua (one from [da] to [ba], the other from [θa] to [fa]). Both continua were constructed by varying the onset frequencies of the second- and third-formant-transitions. In fact, the only difference between the two continua was that 130 msec of ambiguous neutral frication (i.e., noise with a center frequency midway between [fa] and [θa] frication) was added to the beginning of each of the stimuli from one of the continua to produce the [θa]/[fa] continuum. In all other respects, the stimulus parameters of the stop continuum matched those of the fricative continuum. Prior research with adult subjects (Carden, Levitt, & Jusczyk, 1979) had established that the place boundaries for the two continua differed (i.e., the place boundary for the nine point stop continuum was about 4.5, whereas for fricatives, it was approximately 5.6). Thus the same formant transition values (i.e., those of stimulus #5 on both continua) that signaled a *dental* place response for fricatives (i.e., [θa]), actually cued a *labial* place for stops (i.e., [ba]). This finding suggested that, for adults, decisions about place-of-articulation are dependent on judgments about manner-of-articulation (i.e., whether the sound that one just heard was a stop or a fricative). Hence, Jusczyk et al. (1979) designed their first experiment not only to test whether 2-month olds discriminate [fa] from [θa], but also to explore the possibility that place information is dependent on manner for infants, too. They chose their stimulus pairs in such a way that the formant transition differences between stimulus pair members might signal a "between-category" contrast for one manner of articulation, but a "within-category" contrast for the other manner. For example, because the place boundary for stops is approximately 4.5, then a contrast between stimulus #2 ([da]) and stimulus #5 ([ba]) would be a between-category contrast, but with respect to the place boundary for fricatives (approximately 5.6), both of these stimulus values would be chosen from within the same category (i.e., both would be labeled by adults as [θa]). Similarly, a pairing between stimulus #5 and stimulus #8 would constitute a "between-category" contrast for fricatives, but a "within-category" contrast for stops (i.e., both were labeled by adults as [ba]).

The results, which Jusczyk et al. (1979) obtained are shown in Fig. 4.2. A reliable increase in sucking, relative to the control groups, occurred for the stimulus pairing "2 versus 5" for both the stops and the fricatives. There was no evidence that infants could discriminate the "5 versus 8" contrast for either fricatives or stops. Thus, in contrast to adults, the infants did not give evidence

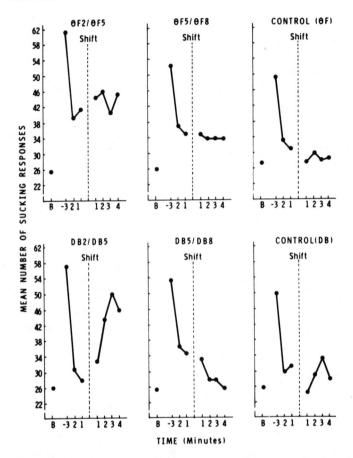

FIG. 4.2.   Mean number of high-amplitude sucking responses as a function of time and experimental group. Time is measured with reference to the moment of the stimulus shift, marked by the vertical dashed line. The baseline rate of sucking is indicated by the letter "B."

that their perception of place information is dependent upon manner. Instead, infants appear to have only a single boundary location for discriminating changes in place, and that location is in the region previously observed for stops.

One possible explanation of Jusczyk et al.'s results is that the place boundaries for stops and fricatives might be initially coincident, but that linguistic experience results in a slight shifting of the boundary location for fricatives. If this were the case, then many of the natural tokens of [θa] and [fa] would fall on the same side of the infant's boundary, and would therefore be difficult for the infant to discriminate until linguistic experience caused the boundary to shift. This would account for the difficulties that Eilers et al. and Holmberg et al. had in demonstrating the discrimination of [θa]/[fa] contrasts by infants. However, an alternative explanation is also possible. In preparing their stimuli, Jusczyk et al. varied only the formant transition cues; the frication noise cue was held constant. Whereas, for adults, place information for fricatives is carried primarily by formant transition cues, frication information is not without its effect (Harris, 1958). Both kinds of information may be required for infants to distinguish [θa] from [fa]. Finally, it is also possible that because Jusczyk et al. used a computer-generated frication noise, the infants did not integrate the noise cue with the rest of the syllables (even though the adults that Carden et al. [1979] tested did integrate the noise with the syllables). If this were the case, then one would expect the infants to discriminate only the pairing that crossed the stop boundary, as they did.

In order to assess more carefully the possible contribution of frication information to the infant's perception of fricative contrasts, Jusczyk et al. (1979) ran an experiment with natural speech tokens. They presented one group of infants with a contrast between [θa] and [fa], and a second group with the same tokens but modified so that the frication was removed from both tokens. The stimuli for this latter group were both perceived by adults as sounding like [ba]. Thus, the expectation for these two groups was that if frication differences were important to the infant's perception of [θa]/[fa] contrasts, then the first group, but not the second group, would show evidence of discrimination. In addition to these first two groups of subjects, Jusczyk et al. tested two other groups on the analogous *voiced* fricative contrasts. Accordingly, one group received a contrast between tokens of [ða] and [va], and a second group received the same contrast only without the accompanying frication cues. This latter contrast was of some interest because, unlike the case with voiced fricatives, removing the frication from the voiced fricative pair does not cause each to be perceived by adults as the same syllable [ba], but rather as the distinct syllables [da] and [ba].[9] Hence, the expectation for the groups receiving the voiced or modified voiced fricative pairs was that both groups would show evidence of discrimination. The results confirmed the expectations for both the voiced and voiceless fricative groups, i.e., both groups receiving the voiced fricative contrasts and the group receiving the voiceless fricative contrast that included frication information showed evidence of discrimination. Only the group receiving the modified voiceless fricative contrast did not display evidence of discrimination.

This second experiment suggests that infants can distinguish [θa] from [fa] when the appropriate frication information is present, but it leaves unspecified the precise role that frication information plays in the infant's perception of place differences. For instance, do frication differences provide a sufficient basis for the discrimination of place contrasts, or do they constitute necessary information

---

[9]Research with adult subjects by Carden, Levitt, & Jusczyk (1979) indicates that the place boundary for the voiced fricative pair [ða] and [va] is more nearly coincident with the boundary for stops than is the boundary for the voiceless fricatives [θa] and [fa].

that must be integrated with other kinds of information such as formant transitions? In order to resolve this issue, Jusczyk et al. conducted a third experiment. One group of infants received stimuli composed only of the frication noises of [fa] and [θa] prefixed to the vowel [a] (in other words, the formant transitions were removed from both syllables). This test comparison enabled Jusczyk et al. to determine whether infants are capable of discriminating [fa] from [θa] solely on the basis of frication differences. In fact, infants did discriminate this contrast, suggesting that frication differences may be a sufficient cue for infants to discriminate [fa] from [θa]. However, in order to better understand the relationship that exists between frication and formant transition information in the perception of fricative contrasts by infants, Jusczyk et al. tested an additional group. For this group, they employed a stimulus pairing between a [fa] stimulus and a special hybrid stimulus produced by taking a [θa] stimulus and substituting the frication portion of a [fa] for the frication portion of the [θa]. These stimulus pair members, then, differed only in terms of whether the formant transitions were appropriate to [fa] or [θa]. (Recall that in their second experiment, Jusczyk et al. had shown that when the frication information was removed, infants did not discriminate the [f] formant transitions plus [a] from those of [θ] plus [a].) By examining this last test pair, Jusczyk and his colleagues sought to determine whether the presence of frication could serve as a suitable context for distinguishing the [fa] transitions from those of [θa]. In other words, does the discrimination of [fa] transitions from [θa] transitions in some way depend on their occurrence in a fricative context? The results indicated that infants did discriminate this last test pair. It would appear, then, that the mechanism underlying the infant's discrimination of the place-of-articulation difference between [fa] and [θa] is one which is sensitive to information about manner of articulation (i.e., whether frication is present or not). Thus, although frication differences between [fa] and [θa] are a sufficient basis for distinguishing between these syllables, such differences are apparently not a necessary basis. Rather, the mechanism that underlies the discrimination of place differences in fricatives is obviously a complicated one that utilizes information about several factors, including frication and formant transitions. Future research in this area may help to specify more precisely the way in which these factors interact in perception.

To summarize the situation with respect to fricatives, there is evidence to suggest that infants, as young as two months of age, do detect place contrasts for both voiced (i.e., [ða]/[va]) and voiceless (i.e., [sa]/[ʃa] and [θa]/[fa]) pairs. Moreover, it appears that frication information on plays an important role in infants' discrimination of place contrasts between fricatives.

Other Consonantal Contrasts.   Information also exists regarding the infant's ability to discriminate a variety of other speech contrasts. For the most part, these studies have focused on the infant's ability to make distinctions based upon some aspect of the manner of articulation. For example, Eimas and Miller (1980) have explored the 2- to 4-month old's capacity for detecting an oral/nasal distinction. By manipulating the amount of nasal resonance present and the starting frequency of the first formant, Eimas and Miller were able to construct a synthetic speech continuum ranging from [ma] to [ba]. They chose their stimulus pairs such that two of the pairs were within-category pairs (either $[ma_1]/[ma_2]$ or $[ba_1]/[ba_2]$) and the other two were between-category pairs (i.e., [ba]/[ma]). The overall pattern of their results indicated that the only reliable difference occurred between subjects in the "between-category" group and those in the control group. The discrimination performance of subjects in the "within-category" group did not differ reliably from that of either the control or "between-category" groups. A closer inspection of the data revealed that only one of the two between-category groups actually differed significantly from the control group. Eimas and Miller attributed the lower performance of the other between-category group to sampling error.[10] Some support for this assertion was provided when an additional group of infants, tested on the same stimulus pair, did show reliable evidence of discrimination.

The fact that performance on the "within-category" pairs did not differ reliably from that on the "between-category" pairs implies that the infant's discrimination of the oral/nasal distinction is not categorical. In this respect, the infants differ from adults who do show categorical perception for the same stimuli (Miller & Eimas, 1977). One interpretation of this discrepancy between infants and adults is that infants are better able to make "within-category" discriminations along the oral/nasal continuum. This interpretation is the one favored by Eimas and Miller, who further suggest that linguistic experience may function to reduce the capacity to make "within-category" discriminations along this continuum. However, some caution is necessary in making this sort of interpretation because, although in the right direction, the difference between the control and the "within-category" groups was not significant. Pending further experimentation, the best that one can say is that infants make discriminations between oral and nasal stops and that these discriminations do not appear to be categorical. Therefore, in contrast to the situation for voicing and place-of-articulation, there is at present no evidence that infants discriminate manner-of-articulation in a categorical fashion.

Hillenbrand, Minifie, and Edwards (1979) also investigated the infant's ability to make distinctions on the basis of changes in manner-of-articulation.

---

[10]More specifically, they argued that the oral/nasal boundary location for some of the subjects in this group may have fallen outside of the range of values for the stimulus pair tested. The fact that marked fluctuations might occur in the location of the oral/nasal boundary for infants appears to contrast to findings with other speech continua. In previous studies, whatever individual differences might have occurred in boundary location were not large enough to affect discrimination performance (e.g., Eimas, 1974). One possible interpretation of this difference between the oral/nasal continuum and other speech continua is that the oral/nasal boundary may be less clearly marked in the acoustic signal than are boundaries on other continua.

Their investigation focused upon whether infants are sensitive to cues for a distinction among stops, glides, and dipthongs. The parameter, which they varied, was that of tempo of spectral change. This is a complex cue consisting of both formant transition duration and rate of frequency change. For stops such as [bɛ], formant transition durations are very short (~35 msec) and therefore the rate of frequency change is quite high; for glides such as [wɛ], formant transition durations are longer (~120 msec) and the rate of frequency change more gradual; for dipthongs the formant transitions are still longer (~250 msec) and the corresponding rate of frequency change even more gradual. Hillenbrand et al. used the head-turning paradigm to test a group of 6- to 8-month-olds. Their results indicated that infants did discriminate contrasts among [bɛ], [wɛ], and [uɛ] when the stimuli were computer-modified natural tokens. Results for synthetic speech tokens were similar with the exception that most infants failed to discriminate the [wɛ]/[uɛ] pair. However, because Hillenbrand et al. employed only a 6 trial (3 change and 3 control) measure of discrimination performance, it is likely that with a more sensitive measure infants would have discriminated the synthetic [wɛ]/[uɛ] pair. Regardless, Hillenbrand et al.'s study demonstrates that infants are able to make manner distinctions based upon tempo of spectral change.

Several other phonetic contrasts have been studied that have some interesting ramifications for understanding the ways in which speech perception develops. For example, Eimas (1975a) has investigated the infant's capacity to distinguish [ra] and [la]. This contrast is of some interest because cross-language research with adults had suggested marked differences in the way in which it is perceived by Japanese and American speakers (Miyawaki, Strange, Verbrugge, Liberman, Jenkins, & Fujimura, 1975). The distinction between [ra] and [la] is signaled by changes in the initial steady-state frequency of the third formant. Hence, one can construct a continuum from [ra] to [la] by varying the starting frequency of the third-formant. Miyawaki et al. found that, for native American speakers, changes in third formant starting frequency are perceived in a categorical manner when such changes occur in the context of speech sounds. If, on the other hand, a nonspeech context is provided (i.e., only isolated third formants occurred), then such changes are perceived in a continuous manner (i.e., within-category discrimination of the stimuli is quite good). For native Japanese speakers the results were somewhat different. Although these speakers behaved similarly to the Americans when the third-formant changes occurred in a nonspeech context, their discrimination performance for the same changes in a speech context diverged markedly from that of the Americans. Native Japanese speakers exhibited poor discrimination performance for the speech contrasts and gave no indication that some stimulus pairs were more discriminable than others.

The difference between Japanese and American speakers for the speech contrasts was apparently the result of linguistic experience: The [ra]/[la] distinction occurs in English but not in Japanese. Yet, it is not clear which direction that linguistic experience operates in. Is the [ra]/[la] distinction acquired by American speakers as a result of their experience with the language, or does the absence of relevant linguistic experience cause Japanese speakers to lose an ability they once had as some, such as Strange and Jenkins, (1978) have suggested? Eimas (1975a) endeavored to address this issue by testing a group of 2- to 3-month-old infants for the ability to discriminate changes in third-formant starting frequencies for both speech and nonspeech stimuli. As in his previous investigation of place-of-articulation (Eimas, 1974), he chose his stimulus pairs for the speech condition so that some pairings were between members of the same phonetic category (e.g., $[ra_1]$ vs. $[ra_2]$), whereas others involved members of different phonetic categories (e.g., [ra] vs. [la]). The nonspeech pairs were identical to the speech pairs except that all first- and second-formant information had been deleted.

Eimas found evidence for categorical discrimination of third formant starting frequencies for speech sounds, but not for nonspeech sounds. For the latter sounds, discrimination appeared to be continuous because performance was about equal on all the stimulus pairs.[11] These findings fit well with those from Eimas' previous work on the perception of place cues in both speech and nonspeech contexts. In both studies, clear-cut differences emerged in the way in which infants responded to the same acoustic changes in speech and nonspeech contexts.[12] It is the existence of these differences that has led Eimas to argue that infants may be endowed with mechanisms specialized for speech processing.

Eimas' data also bear on the question as to how linguistic experience affects the discrimination of [ra] and [la]. The finding that infants, like American adults, display categorical discrimination for the [ra]/[la] distinction, suggests that the ability to perceive this contrast is probably innate. Thus, one might hypothesize (as Eimas does) that the absence of specific experience with the [ra]/[la] contrast in the Japanese environment results in a loss of sensitivity to this contrast. One possible objection to this line of argument is that data regarding the Japanese infant's discrimination of [ra]/[la] do not exist at present. Thus, one must assume, perhaps not unreasonably, that Japanese infants will behave like their American counterparts. Although this assumption gains some support from pre-

---

[11]One slight discrepancy was observed between discrimination performance for the nonspeech sounds in this study and that of the earlier study with place (Eimas, 1974). Although each of the nonspeech groups in the place study performed reliably better than the control group, such was not the case for the present study. In fact, only when the data for all three nonspeech groups were pooled was the difference between them and the control group significant. One possible explanation for this difference, which Eimas mentions, is that the [r-1] nonspeech stimuli were less discriminable than the [b-d] nonspeech stimuli.

[12]Again, for reasons stated earlier (cf. footnote 4), it is possible that the relevant acoustic information may have been omitted from the nonspeech pairs. If so, then claims that the same acoustic information is discriminated in a different manner for speech and nonspeech contexts would not hold.

vious cross-cultural investigations that tend to show strong similarities in the discrimination performance of infants from different linguistic environments (e.g., Eilers & Oller, 1978; Lasky et al., 1975; Streeter, 1976), it remains an assumption in the absence of data for Japanese infants. Hence, it is only safe to say that Eimas' data suggest that linguistic experience can, in some instances, lead to a loss of discriminative capacity.[13]

The notion that infants may actually lose discriminative capacities with increasing linguistic experience would also seem to be supported by Trehub's (1976a) research on the perception of [řa] and [za]. This fricative contrast is one that occurs in Czech but not English. Using natural speech tokens obtained from Czech speakers, Trehub employed the HAS procedure to test 1- to 4-month-old infants from English-speaking environments. She found evidence that the contrast was discriminable for the infants. Subsequently, she tested a group of English-speaking adults with no knowledge of Czech on the same contrast. Her results indicated that the adults had considerable difficulty with this contrast (i.e., there were many more confusions than for a comparable English contrast), although discrimination performance was reliably above chance. Because the procedure that she used with adults was an analogue to that of the infants, Trehub took these findings to be an indication of a loss of discriminative capacity on the part of the adults. However, there are some difficulties with this interpretation. First of all, we have no way of establishing a priori whether or not the task is the same for infants and adults. Although ostensibly the tasks may appear similar, adults' greater experience makes it likely that they approach the task with different expectations than the infants. This raises doubts about whether the tasks are truly the same, and, as Flavell and Wohlwill (1969) have warned, there are real difficulties in drawing conclusions about the development of specific abilities when different tasks are used. A second difficulty with Trehub's interpretation is that although English speakers did not perform as well on the [řa]/[za] pairs as on a comparable English pair, they *did* discriminate the Czech pair. Thus, it is clear that the adults did not completely lose their capacity to discriminate this contrast; rather they are merely less sensitive to it than to a

---

[13]The degree of permanence and the extent of the loss of discriminative capacity as a result of linguistic experience is a matter of some debate (see, for example, Pisoni, Aslin, Perey, & Hennessy, 1979; Strange & Jenkins, 1978). Strange and Jenkins reported little success in modifying phonetic perception of foreign language contrasts by the use of laboratory training techniques. However, in a more recent series of studies, Pisoni et al. present convincing evidence that English-speaking subjects can, with little or no training, utilize information about a third voicing category, prevoicing, despite the fact that it does not occur in their native language. Whether Pisoni et al.'s procedures yield similar results for other phonetic categories remains to be seen. Still, their results to date suggest caution in attributing any loss of discriminative capacity to the atrophy of some physiological mechanism. Rather, it seems likely that such losses might best be ascribed to attentional factors whereby with increasing linguistic experience one tends to focus only on those acoustic attributes that are relevant to making distinctions in one's own native language.

particular English contrast—[ri]/[li].[14] (Again this is in line with Pisoni et al.'s (1979) findings; see footnote 13.) In conclusion, then, we are again forced to say that these data only suggest a loss of some discriminative abilities with increasing linguistic experience.

Vowels

In the study of speech perception, vowels have always provided an interesting counterpoint to stop consonants. In contrast to stop consonant sounds, vowels appear to be perceived in a manner much more analogous to that of many nonspeech sounds. This is perhaps best evidenced by repeated findings that vowels tend to be perceived continuously (i.e., within-category discrimination tends to be considerably better than chance) rather than categorically (e.g., Fry, Abramson, Eimas, & Liberman, 1962; Pisoni, 1973, 1975; Stevens, Liberman, Studdert-Kennedy, & Öhman, 1969). Although it has been demonstrated that the degree to which both consonants and vowels are perceived in a continuous manner is subject to experimental manipulation (see for example, Carney, Widin, & Viemeister, 1977; Pisoni, 1973, 1975; Pisoni & Lazarus, 1974; Repp, Healy, & Crowder, 1978; Samuel, 1977), claims about differences between the perception of vowels and consonants appear to be well founded (Perey & Pisoni, 1977). For this reason, it is of interest to know whether any interesting differences occur in the infant's perception of vowels and consonants.

The earliest study in this area was one conducted with 1- to 4-month-olds by Trehub (1973b), using the HAS paradigm. She investigated the perception of two vowel contrasts ([a]/[i] and [i]/[u]) involving natural speech tokens. For one of these, [a]/[i], she also examined the consequences of presenting the contrast in the context of an accompanying stop consonant ([pa]/[pi] or [ta]/[ti]). Her results indicated that infants were able to distinguish all of the contrasts. Moreover, there was no evidence of differences between subjects who received the [a]/[i] contrast in isolation and those who received it with an accompanying stop consonant.

Trehub's findings with respect to the [a]/[i] distinction were replicated by Kuhl and Miller (1975b), who showed that infants could discriminate this contrast even in the face of irrelevant pitch changes.[15] Subsequent work by Kuhl (1976) using the head-turning paradigm, indicates that 6-month-olds are able to perceive the [a]/[i] contrast despite continuous changes in intonation and speakers. Kuhl (1977) also reported similar findings for 6-month-olds presented in an [a]/[ɔ] contrast.

---

[14]In this regard, one wonders about how great the difference between the English and Czech contrasts would have been if a more difficult English contrast (e.g., [θa]/[fa]) had been chosen.

[15]This result is discussed more fully in a subsequent section of this chapter.

The infant's capacity for discriminating vowel contrasts is apparently not limited to those occurring in his linguistic environment. Trehub (1976a) presented 1- to 4-month-old infants from English-speaking backgrounds with a [pa]/[pã] contrast. This contrast, which involves a distinction between non-nasalized and nasalized vowels, occurs in both Polish and French but not in English. This particular contrast was of some interest because according to Jakobson (1968) it is one of the last distinctions that speakers learn to accurately produce. Despite the fact that her subjects had little or no pre-exposure to this distinction, Trehub found evidence that they could discriminate it.

Further support for the notion that infants can distinguish vowel contrasts not native to their linguistic background, comes from a recent study by Eilers and Oller (1978). They used the headturning procedure with 6- to 8-month-old infants from English-speaking and Spanish speaking backgrounds. Both groups of infants were presented with two different vowel contrasts; one ([bIt]/[bit]) of which is native to English, and the other ([bej]/[be]) native to Spanish. Eilers and Oller's results suggest that both contrasts were discriminable for infants from both the English-speaking and the Spanish-speaking environments. Moreover, there was evidently no indication that linguistic experience had any effect on discrimination performance (i.e., infants from Spanish-speaking environments were no more likely to discriminate the Spanish contrast than were infants from English-speaking environments).

Thus, the evidence reviewed to this point demonstrates that infants are capable of discriminating a variety of different vowel contrasts from a very early age. However, none of the studies discussed has specifically addressed the issue as to whether the infant's discrimination of any of these vowel contrasts was of a continuous or a categorical nature. Information on this point is available in the form of two studies by Swoboda and his colleagues. In the first of these studies (Swoboda, Morse, & Leavitt, 1976), 2-month-olds were tested with the HAS procedure on their ability to discriminate various contrasts along a vowel continuum running from [i] to [I]. Two of the contrasts were selected to be "within-category" distinctions (either $[I_1]/[I_3]$ or $[i_5]/[i_7]$ and the third contrast involved a "between-category" distinction ($[I_3]/[i_5]$). Swoboda et al. found that infants discriminated not only the "between-category" items but the "within-category" items as well. Moreover, there was no evidence that performance of subjects receiving the "between-category" items was any better than that for subjects with the "within-category" items. Therefore, these results strongly implied that infants' discrimination of contrasts on the [I]/[i] continuum is continuous rather than categorical.

One factor that may have influenced Swoboda et al.'s results was the fact that they employed vowels with rather long durations (240 msec). Studies with adults suggest that the use of long vowel durations increases the likelihood of finding continuous (i.e., good within-category) discrimination (Pisoni, 1973, 1975; Repp et al., 1978). By contrast, when vowel durations are short, the discrimination data appear to be more categorical in nature. The most widely accepted account (Fujisaki & Kawashima, 1970; Pisoni, 1973, 1975) for these results is one that posits both acoustic and phonetic memory codes for speech information. Information in the acoustic code is deemed to decay more rapidly than that in the phonetic code. Consequently, procedures that reduce the availability of acoustic information are more likely to lead to categorical-like discrimination. In order to determine whether infants might be similarly affected by such procedures, Swoboda, Kass, Morse, and Leavitt (1978) employed vowels with very short durations (60 msec). Essentially, the stimulus pairs they used were identical to the ones in the Swoboda et al. (1976) study, the only difference being the stimulus durations. The results obtained with the new shortened stimuli were somewhat equivocal. An examination of the postshift performance indicated that subjects in the "between-category" condition, but not those in the "within-category" condition, displayed a reliable increase in sucking. However, a comparison of the postshift performance of the two groups revealed no reliable differences between them. Swoboda et al. were able to find some weak evidence for a difference between the groups when the postshift performance of each was compared to that of the control group in the Swoboda et al. (1976) study.[16] Specifically, the between-category group differed reliably from the control, whereas the within-category group did not (although again the between- and within-category groups did not differ reliably from each other). Swoboda et al. took these results to imply that short duration vowels are discriminated by infants in a more categorical-like fashion than are long duration vowels. But the data are not terribly convincing, they are at best suggestive. Any conclusive statements as to whether infants perceive short duration vowels more categorically require further experimentation with additional controls included.[17]

---

[16]Swoboda, Kass, Morse, and Leavitt (1978) were forced to adopt this rather unorthodox procedure because they had not included a no-shift control group in their study.

[17]Swoboda et al. (1978) also tried to use another method of assessing whether availability of acoustic information might affect the categoricalness of vowel discriminations. They reasoned that the duration of the delay interval between the last preshift stimulus and the first postshift stimulus might have similar consequences to the delay intervals that Pisoni (1973) used in his tasks with adults. Pisoni found that as delay interval increased, discrimination performance decreased for both "between-" and "within-category" pairs. Swoboda et al. found some evidence that discrimination performance decreased as the interval between the last preshift and the first preshift stimulus increased, but only for subjects in the "between-category" group. These results are difficult to interpret for a number of reasons. First, one might have expected to find greater evidence of a correlation in the "within-category" group because acoustic information is presumed to decay faster and this group presumably does not have access to differential phonetic information. Second, the duration of the delay intervals (5 to 10 seconds and beyond) that Swoboda et al. were able to report on were much longer than those employed by Pisoni (.25 to 2.0 seconds). Third, there is a possible confound in the data because the longer the child delays in making the first suck after shift, the less time the child has left in the first postshift minute to display an increase in sucking rate.

In conclusion, the studies of vowel discrimination reveal that infants are capable of distinguishing a variety of vowel contrasts, both native and nonnative to their linguistic environment. Moreover, there is evidence to suggest that for infants, like adults, vowels are discriminated in a continuous manner.

CONTEXTS TO WHICH THE INFANT'S SPEECH PERCEPTION CAPACITIES CAN BE APPLIED

Thus far the data we have examined pertain, for the most part, only to a limited aspect of speech perception, viz. the capacity for distinguishing items on the basis of initial segment differences. But the speech perception capacities of the mature language user are far more extensive than merely detecting initial segment differences. For example, distinctions are also made on the basis of information contained in medial and final segments, and in some cases, information that spans a number of segments (e.g., the distinction between récord and record). In addition, despite large individual differences in the way in which speech sounds are articulated, the mature listener is able to recognize the same phonetic segment across a number of different speakers. Moreover, the mature listener also displays an ability to segment the nearly continuous acoustic stream that he or she hears into discrete segments corresponding to words. To what extent might the infant exhibit similar abilities? The answer is not immediately obvious because a number of factors, especially attentional ones, could combine to limit the infant in the first few months of life to processing information about only the initial segments of utterances. In this section, we review the evidence regarding the range of situations for which infants are able to display some speech processing capability.

Perception of Suprasegmental Information

One problem that has received considerable attention concerns the infant's responsiveness to suprasegmental information such as stress and intonation. In the past, a number of investigators had hypothesized that infants might actually respond to differences in suprasegmental information before they respond to phonetic distinctions (Crystal, 1970; Kaplan & Kaplan, 1971; Lewis, 1951). This seems unlikely given that it appears that infants respond to phonetic contrasts right from birth. Nevertheless, interest in the infant's sensitivity to suprasegmental information has remained high, due to a growing appreciation of the important functions served by such information in speech. For example, changes in intonation contour have been shown to differentiate interrogative and declarative sentences (Lieberman, 1967). Similarly, variations in amplitude, pitch contours, and duration affect not only the assignment of lexical stress in multisyllabic utterances (e.g., Fry, 1958; Morton & Jassem, 1965), but also influence the perception of phrase boundaries (Streeter, 1978).

The simplest situation in which the infant's perception of suprasegmental cues has been studied is one which involves the discrimination of two syllables on the basis of pitch (fundamental frequency) contour. Morse (1972) tested 2-month-olds on their ability to discriminate a syllable with a falling pitch contour [ba−] from one with a rising contour [ba+]. He found that infants could discriminate this contrast as evidenced by their postshift performance for the high amplitude sucking procedure.

An interesting extension of Morse's study was conducted by Kuhl and Miller (1975b). As in the earlier Morse study, these investigators examined one group of infants for their ability to discriminate two vowel segments on the basis of pitch contours.[18] In addition, they tested a second group of infants for whom the relevant contrast was again pitch contour, but this time the contrast was accompanied by an irrelevant variation in vowels (i.e., for these subjects the vowels varied between [a] and [i]). In agreement with Morse's results, Kuhl and Miller found that when the vowels did not vary irrelevantly, the infants detected change in pitch contour. However, when irrelevant vowel changes did occur, there was no evidence for discrimination. Moreover, infants *did* respond to a vowel contrast in the midst of irrelevant pitch changes, Notice that this pattern of results is precisely the opposite of what might have been anticipated if it were true that infants respond to suprasegmental information prior to phonetic distinctions. That is, if infants really were more attuned to suprasegmental information, then one might have expected it to be easier for them to ignore the irrelevant vowel changes. Kuhl and Miller took their results to be an indication that vowel changes are actually more salient for infants than pitch changes. However, this conclusion may be a bit premature because it is not clear that the two kinds of changes (pitch and vowel) were equally discriminable. Specifically, it would appear that the pitch changes may have been less discriminable. Recent evidence by Carrell and Smith (1979) suggests that when discriminability for the two types of changes is equated, irrelevant vowel changes are no more likely to interfere with pitch discrimination than irrelevant pitch changes are to interfere with vowel discrimination.

The two studies reviewed thus far demonstrate that, in at least some circumstances, infants are sensitive to one aspect of suprasegmental information, viz. pitch contour. However, both studies have focused upon the infant's capacity to detect pitch contour differences between single syllables. More typically, though, suprasegmental information is conveyed across a number of syllables or words in natural speech settings. Several investigators have explored the infant's responsiveness to suprasegmental information in these types of contexts. Juscyzk

---

[18]In contrast to Morse (1972), their pitch contour difference involved a contrast between a monotone and a rise-fall contour.

and Thompson (1978) employed the HAS procedures to test 2-month-olds' ability to detect a change in the syllable-stress pattern of bisyllabic utterances (e.g., [dába] vs. [dabá]). Syllable stress can be produced by increasing either singly or in combination, the pitch, amplitude, or duration of a syllable (Fry, 1958; McClean & Tiffany, 1973; Morton & Jassem, 1965). To ensure that their subjects would have the maximum opportunity to detect the syllable-stress change, Jusczyk and Thompson varied all three parameters in combination. Their results were quite clear; every infant exhibited a greater increase in sucking during the postshift period for the stress change condition than for the control condition. Thus, when syllable-stress changes are cued by concurrent increases in the parameters of pitch, amplitude, and duration, infants will respond to such changes. Moreover, there is also evidence that infants can detect syllable-stress differences cued by only one of these parameters. Spring and Dale (1977) also tested infants on their ability to discriminate two bisyllabic utterances from one another solely on the basis of syllable-stress cues. In accord with Jusczyk and Thompson's results, Spring and Dale found that when all three parameters of syllable stress varied naturally, infants detected the syllable-stress change. More importantly, Spring and Dale found in a second experiment, that the duration parameter alone was sufficient to cue the infant's detection of the stress difference. This latter finding, along with the earlier ones that show that infants are sensitive to pitch contour differences (Kuhl & Miller, 1975b; Morse, 1972), suggest a potentially fruitful direction for further research in this area; namely, an investigation of whether the infants might treat the various ways of signaling a stress change as being equivalent in some respect. For example, could an infant who has learned to respond to a stress difference cued by syllable duration generalize to a situation in which the difference is cued by a pitch change? Adults are apparently able to employ such trading relations between stress cues (Morton & Jassem, 1965), and so it would be of some interest to know when and if infants might exhibit this ability.

Finally, there has been an attempt to examine the infant's perception of suprasegmental information carried over a string of words. Kaplan (1969) used a heart rate variability measure to investigate 4- to 8-month-olds' discrimination of falling versus rising intonation contours for the utterances, "See the cat." She found that both age groups showed reliable changes in heart rate variability when shifts in intonation patterns occurred. However, the 4-month-olds displayed a decrease in heart rate variability, whereas the 8-month olds gave evidence of increased variability. Because Kaplan's index of discriminability was increased heart rate variability, she concluded that only the 8-month-olds discriminated the contrast. But, Morse (1978) has questioned Kaplan's interpretation of the 4-month-olds' data in light of the findings reviewed previously. Hence, it would appear that further testing is necessary to establish conclusively when infants can respond to intonation contour differences for sentences.

In conclusion, research on the infant's sensitivity to suprasegmental information has only just begun. Although it is clear that infants are responsive to dimensions such as pitch contour, amplitude changes, and durational differences, much remains to be discovered about the ways in which such information can be employed by infants in segmenting the stream of speech.

Discrimination beyond Initial Segments

In a very methodical manner, the Russian investigator, Shvachkin (1973) examined the ability of 1-year-old infants to make various types of phonemic distinctions. As a result of his inquiry, he outlined a timetable of the order in which various phonemic contrasts might be acquired. One of the observations he made was that contrasts that were discriminable for 1-year-olds in the syllable-initial positions of utterances were often not discriminable in syllable-final positions of utterances. Shvachkin claimed that the reason for this discrepancy was that children learning language initially focus on information at the beginning of utterances. Although the task that Shvachkin used to infer discriminability was considerably more complex than present-day measures, his belief that contrasts in initial positions might be easier than those in final positions does have some empirical support.[19] Malecot (1958) has shown that under some circumstances (viz. when the contrasts occur between *unreleased* stop consonants) discriminability of stop consonant contrasts is less for syllable-final pairs than for syllable-initial pairs.

Knowledge of the infant's capacity to discriminate phonetic contrasts in other than syllable-initial positions is important not only for what it can reveal about the infant's information-processing capacities, but also because this knowledge can affect our understanding of the course of language acquisition. Over the last few years, a number of investigators have begun to study how the infant copes with speech information that occurs in noninitial positions of utterances.

Jusczyk and his colleagues have investigated the infant's sensitivity to place-of-articulation contrasts occurring in various positions in utterances. In one study, Jusczyk (1977) examined the 2-month old's ability to detect a [d]/[g] contrast occurring in the final segments of pairs of synthetic speech syllables (e.g., [bag] vs. [bad]). To gain some appreciation of factors that might affect the infant's ability to detect such differences, Jusczyk actually employed several different contrasts in his study and tested each group of infants on two different stimulus pairs. All groups of infants were presented with a [bag]/[bad] contrast during one test session and with one of the following stimulus pairings during another test session: (1) [bag]/[bam]; (2) [ag]/[ad]; (3) [dab]/[gab]; (4) control

---

[19]In Shvachkin's task, children had to learn to associate a nonsense word to a particular item and then be able to correctly pick out the item from a group of objects when asked for it by name. In other words, as Garnica (1973) has observed, the child must categorize each phoneme in such a way as to allow him or her to distinguish it from all other phonemes and thereby recognize it when it occurs. Thus, there are considerable memory demands imposed upon Shvachkin's subjects in addition to the requirement that they be able to make the phonemic distinction. For this reason, his measure is likely to be less sensitive than present-day ones.

(e.g., [bag]/[bag]). The [bag]/[bam] contrast was included in order to see whether a contrast between items differing on two dimensions (in this case place and nasality) might be more discriminable than a pair differing only on place. The [ad]/[ag] pairing was chosen to evaluate whether the inclusion of a common consonantal segment, [b], would render the [d]/[g] contrast less discriminable in the [bad]/[bag] pair. The [dab]/[gab] pair was selected to examine whether infants found the [d]/[g] contrast more discriminable in the syllable-initial or syllable-final position. Jusczyk's results showed that the infants discriminated all of the contrasts. Moreover, there was no evidence that any of the stimulus pairs was more discriminable than any of the others. Thus, there was no indication that contrasts involving more than one dimension are more discriminable, or that the inclusion of an additional common phonetic segment impairs discriminability, or that syllable-initial contrasts are easier than syllable-final ones for infants. Of course, the possibility exists that the insensitivity of the HAS procedure may have obscured some real differences between the stimulus pairs. Nevertheless, the fact remains that infants can discriminate final-segment contrasts differing only on a single dimension, i.e., place-of-articulation.

Jusczyk's (1977) finding that syllable-initial contrasts are no more discriminable than syllable-final contrasts stands in apparent contradiction to Shvachkin's report. Thus, it seems as though discriminability per se was not the reason for Shvachkin's subjects' difficulty with pairs differing in final segments. However, one qualification is necessary here. Jusczyk employed stimuli in which the final stops were accompanied by release bursts. Yet, oftentimes in natural speech settings, and perhaps in Shvachkin's, release bursts are omitted from final segments. As Malecot's (1958) data show, segments without bursts tend to be less discriminable than those with bursts. Consequently, it is possible that had he employed syllable-final contrasts *without release bursts,* Jusczyk would have found that such contrasts were less discriminable for infants than syllable-initial contrasts. Some empirical support for this notion comes from an investigation by Williams (1977a). She also used the HAS procedure to test the 2-month-old's discrimination of syllable-initial ([da]/[ga]) and syllable-final ([ad]/[ag]) contrasts. Contrary to Jusczyk, she employed consonants *without* release bursts for her syllable-final pair. Her results indicated that although the syllable-initial contrast was discriminated, the syllable-final contrast was not. Clearly, a true understanding of the importance of release-burst cues for the infant's discrimination of syllable-final contrasts can only be established by a direct comparison of the discriminability of the same contrast both with and without release bursts. Nevertheless, the results of the Jusczyk and Williams studies suggest that release burst information may be critical for the detection of place-of-articulation differences between final segments of syllables.

In another investigation, Jusczyk and Thompson (1978) assessed the consequences of positioning a place-of-articulation contrast (i.e., [b]/[g]) in multisyllabic items. By utilizing multisyllabic stimuli, Jusczyk and Thompson were able to examine several factors simultaneously. First of all, they could determine the effects of locating a phonetic contrast in either the initial (e.g., [bada] vs. [gada]) or medial ([daba] vs. [daga]) position of a bisyllabic utterance. Second, they could observe whether suprasegmental information interacts in any interesting way with phonetic information to affect the discriminability of the contrasts. For instance, does syllable stress serve to call attention to a phonetic contrast that might otherwise be unnoticed (e.g., is a [dabá]/[dagá] contrast more discriminable than a [dába]/[dága] contrast)?

Jusczyk and Thompson found that 2-month-olds were able to detect the [b]/[g] in either the initial or medial portion of the bisyllabic utterances, regardless of whether or not the contrast occurred in a stressed or unstressed syllable. Furthermore, there was no indication that contrasts that appeared in stressed syllables were any more discriminable than those in unstressed syllables.[20]

Williams has reported similar findings, but for a different place-of-articulation contrast. She examined the discrimination of a [d]/[g] contrast in the medial position of bisyllabic utterances both when the contrast occurred between stressed (e.g., [agá]/[adá]) and unstressed (e.g., [ága]/[áda]) syllables. In accordance with Jusczyk and Thompson's results, she found that infants were able to discriminate the contrast in both stressed and unstressed syllables.[21] Moreover, there was no evidence that syllable stress had any effect on discriminability.

Although it might appear that syllable stress is of no consequence for detecting phonetic distinctions, both studies discussed thus far employed contrasts between stop consonants. There are several characteristics of stops that prominently mark their appearance in an utterance, chief among them being a silent interval (for vocal tract closure) followed by an abrupt onset of spectral energy. It is possible that these characteristics are sufficient to call attention to stop segments so that syllable stress would produce no appreciable gain in discriminability. Thus, one might look to contrasts between phonetic segments that lack silent closures and abrupt onsets for evidence of an effect of syllable stress. Jusczyk, Copan, and Thompson (1978) have examined one such contrast involving the glide pair [w]/[y]. Their experimental design was basically the same as Jusczyk and Thompson's, viz. discriminability of the contrast was tested for initial and

---

[20]Again it is possible that the HAS procedure is just too insensitive to pick up subtle differences in discriminability, or it may be the case that differences in discriminability would have emerged for stressed versus unstressed syllables if more complicated stimuli (e.g., four-syllable utterances) had been employed.

[21]The results described here pertain to stimuli generated in the same manner as Jusczyk and Thompson's with a period of silent closure preceding the stop consonants as is typically the case for natural speech. However, Williams also tested infants on a stimulus pair in which she substituted a period of glottal pulsing for the silent closure interval. Under these circumstances, she found that infants did not discriminate the [d]/[g]. The reason for this failure to discriminate is not clear. Williams' own hypothesis that a silent closure period is necessary for infants to discriminate medial contrasts is inadequate in light of Jusczyk, Copan, and Thompson's (1978) findings for glide contrasts in medial positions.

medial locations in bisyllabic utterances and in both stressed and unstressed syllables. Their results were in agreement with the earlier ones for stop consonant contrasts. Infants showed reliable evidence of discriminating the [w]/[y] contrast in all situations, and there was no indication that syllable stress improved discrimination performance. On the basis of these results, Jusczyk et al. (1978) argued that syllable stress may have little or no effect on the infant's ability to perceive phonetic contrasts in these situations in which one meaningless utterance is pitted against another.[22]

To summarize to this point, the infant is able to discriminate place-of-articulation contrasts in a variety of different locations in an utterance, in both stressed and unstressed segments. It is clear from the studies previously reviewed that the infant's speech processing capacities extend beyond the perception of initial segment differences. Still, it would be useful to know whether the ability that the infant displays for processing place-of-articulation distinctions extends to other kinds of phonetic contrasts. In fact, some consideration has been given to the infant's ability to perceive voicing contrasts in medial and final positions of utterances.

Eilers and her colleagues have investigated the infant's perception of the voiced–voiceless distinction for both stops and fricatives in the syllable-final position. In one study (Eilers, 1977), she used the HAS paradigm to explore the 2-month-old's sensitivity to information considered to be important in cueing the [at]/[ad] and [as]/[az] distinctions. Her results basically showed that both contrasts were discriminable for the infants. However, because the voiced-voiceless distinction in a syllable final position is cued by vowel duration differences as well as VOT differences, Eilers also tried to assess the infant's sensitivity to each component. An analysis of this sort could certainly yield critical information about the infant's ability to utilize two different sources of information about the same phonetic contrast, particularly because vowel duration cues might possibly be learned as a property of local dialect. Unfortunately, for reasons discussed earlier, Eiler's use of the HAS procedure makes her results difficult to interpret because it is biased against finding reliable evidence for discrimination. Moreover, her use of natural, as opposed to synthetic speech tokens, creates an additional problem because, as she herself admits, it was not possible to gain full control over all the important stimulus parameters. For these reasons, it is difficult to evaluate her claims that voicing-during-closure is not sufficient for distinguishing [s]/[z] in final position, but is sufficient for distinguishing [t]/[d]. Similar sorts of criticisms can be made of the work of Eilers, Wilson, and Moore (1977) because they employed the same stimuli and used a six-trial head-turning measure to infer discriminability. Thus, although Eilers and her colleagues have addressed some important issues, the only conclusion that we can safely draw

---

[22]However, they did leave open the possibility that syllable stress may play a role in language-learning situations in which attention is also taxed by semantic and syntactic considerations.

from their work is that infants do discriminate voicing contrasts for stops and fricatives in syllable-final positions.

Trehub (1973a; 1976b) has studied the discrimination of voicing contrasts in multisyllabic utterances. She used the HAS procedure to test 1- to 4-month-olds for their ability to discriminate a [b]/[p] contrast embedded in bisyllabic and trisyllabic utterances. She found that infants were able to discriminate voicing contrasts in bisyllables (e.g., [aba]/[apa] and [kaba]/[kapa]) provided that the individual syllable durations were 500 msec long. For contrasts presented in bisyllabic and trisyllabic utterances with syllable durations of 300 msec, there was no evidence for discrimination, even when the contrast occurred in a stressed syllable. Just why it is that infants could discriminate the voicing contrasts in the 500 msec syllables but not the 300 msec ones is unclear. Trehub's explanation is that temporal constraints are imposed upon speech-processing capacities that limit the infant's ability to process speech at rapid rates. But this seems unlikely considering that the infants in Jusczyk and Thompson's (1978) study discriminated contrasts in syllables with duration of only 208 msec. Another possibility is that the 500 msec and 300 msec syllables differed as to the presence of some critical feature. However, this cannot be determined without further information about the exact nature of the natural speech tokens that were used. Therefore, we can say nothing further than that, under some circumstances, infants display the capacity to detect voicing differences in bisyllabic utterances.

In conclusion, the studies reviewed in this subsection indicates that infants do process speech information beyond the initial segments of utterances, and that their ability to do so is apparently not related in any direct way to the occurrence of syllable stress.

Recognition of Constancy

Certainly one of the most important issues in speech perception is that of perceptual constancy. How is it that one is able to recognize the same phonetic segment when its acoustic characteristics change depending on what other phonetic segments occur with it or which vocal tract produced it? There are at least three possible solutions to this problem. One is to find evidence of some invariant acoustic properties, which appear in all the variations of a particular phonetic segment regardless of what the surrounding segments are or which vocal tract uttered them. As we noted earlier, there are real difficulties with this approach because the search for acoustic invariants has been generally fruitless (Liberman et al., 1967; but see Searle et al., 1979; Stevens & Blumstein, 1978, Chapter 1, this volume). A second possible solution is to demonstrate that the invariance occurs as a result of the way in which the brain is structured, i.e., there are specialized mechanisms for detecting phonetic segments. Although the first results from studies of selective adaptation suggest the existence of such mechanisms (e.g., Cooper, 1974a; Eimas, Cooper, & Corbit, 1973), more recent results present problems for this view (e.g., Ades, 1974; Cooper, 1974b; Remez, 1979; Simon & Studdert-Kennedy, 1978). The third solution to the constancy problem differs from the first two views because it postulates no invariants—either in the signal or in the head. Instead, it assumes that constancy is the result of learning the appropriate equivalence classes. By this latter view then, one might expect to find that infants are initially without perceptual constancy for phonetic segments and thus must acquire it in learning language. Although it is difficult to see how developmental data could help to decide between the first two solutions to the constancy problem, such data could help to separate the first two solutions from the third.

There have been several attempts to study the perceptual constancy problem with infants. The first of these was an ambitious investigation conducted by Fodor, Garrett, and Brill (1975) with 4-month-olds. They trained the infants to make head-turning responses to speech sounds under two conditions. In one condition, head turns were reinforced if they occurred in response to either of two items chosen from the same phonetic category (e.g., /pi/ and /pu/), but no reinforcement was given for responses to an item from another phonetic category (e.g., /ka/). In the second condition, the reinforced items came from different phonetic categories (e.g., /pi/ and /ka/) and the nonreinforced item was a member of the same phonetic category as one of the reinforced items (e.g., /pu/). Fodor et al. hypothesized that if the infants had perceptual constancy for phonetic segments, then the first condition should be easier to learn than the second one.

One interesting facet of their study was the fact that they selected their stimulus syllables so that the items from the different phonetic categories actually shared an important acoustic feature, viz. burst-cue frequency. Previous work by Liberman, DeLattre, Cooper, and Gerstman (1954) and by Schatz (1954) had shown that if the burst cue from /pi/ is removed and placed before the vowel /a/, the resulting percept is actually /ka/. Hence, by choosing stimuli of this type, Fodor et al. hoped to undercut the hypothesis that infants might show better performance for same phonetic category pairs because they were responding to an invariant acoustic property like burst-frequency-cue. Such a hypothesis would necessarily predict that in some instances performance on the different category pairs would actually be better because some of these pairs more closely shared the burst-frequency-cue.[23]

Fodor et al.'s results provided some support for the position that infants have perceptual constancy for phonetic segments. Infants showed reliably better performance on the headturning measure when the reinforced sounds came from the same phonetic category (e.g., /pi/ and /pu/) than when the items were from different phonetic categories (e.g., /pi/ and/ka/). However, the infants never did

---

[23]Although Fodor et al.'s (1975) argument on this point is basically sound, they did not provide any detailed information about the natural speech tokens that they used. Thus, it is possible that there may have been other invariant acoustic cues shared only by the same phonetic category members.

achieve a very high level of accuracy even with the same phonetic category items. Several factors may be responsible for this low level of performance, including the fact that the head-turning procedure is difficult to implement effectively in infants under 5½ months of age (Kuhl, 1978). Nevertheless, considering the low performance levels obtained in this study, it is perhaps best to interpret the results as providing weak support for the view that infants have perceptual constancy for phonetic segments.

A more convincing demonstration that infants possess at least some measure of perceptual constancy for phonetic segments comes from a series of studies by Kuhl and her colleagues (Kuhl, 1976; 1977; Holmberg, Morgan, & Kuhl, 1977). Kuhl has explored the constancy problem with 6-month-olds using the head-turning paradigm. In one study (Kuhl, 1976), she examined the degree to which infants would display perceptual constancy for the vowels /a/ and /i/. Kuhl's method was to use a single token from each category to train the head-turning response (i.e., infants had to make a head turn when the background vowel stimulus changed to the other vowel). When the infants had acquired this response, Kuhl gradually introduced variations in the tokens for each category. She began by introducing changes in pitch contour, and then by incorporating tokens from different speakers. Eventually, both pitch contour changes and speaker variations were included in the same test series. At this stage, infants were required to respond to the vowel contrast despite the fact that random changes occurred in the pitch contours and speakers of the tokens. Kuhl found that her subjects continued to respond to the [a]/[i] contrast even when such changes took place. In a second investigation, she reported very similar results when an [a]/[ɔ] contrast was tested (Kuhl, 1977). The only difference between the two studies was that more trials were necessary for infants to master the [a]/[ɔ] contrast when changes of pitch contour and speaker's voices occurred. Kuhl attributed this difference to the fact that estimates of vowel space (e.g., Peterson & Barney, 1952) show some overlap for [a] and [ɔ] tokens, but none for [a] and [i]. The difference in difficulty for pairs aside, Kuhl has demonstrated that 6-month-olds do possess some measure of perceptual constancy for vowels in that they can learn to ignore irrelevant variations in pitch contours or speaker's voices.

More recently, Kuhl and her coworkers (Holmberg et al., 1977) have extended the bounds of their investigation to include the fricative contrasts [s]/[ʃ] and [f]/[θ]. Fricatives were chosen because their acoustic cues vary to some extent depending on their vowel context, although they are much less susceptible to such influences than stop consonants. Thus, Holmberg et al. examined the 6-month-old's capacity to cope with the variance that arises from pairing fricatives with different vowels. In addition, they once again presented another source of variation by introducing tokens collected from different speakers. Their results indicated that infants were able to contend with both sources of variation; i.e., they were able to discriminate both the [s]/[ʃ] and [f]/[θ] even when the vowel context and speaker's voice changed constantly.

It should be pointed out that the procedure that Kuhl and her colleagues have employed is not really a generalization procedure demonstrating that infants have innate categories for phonetic segments. Rather, it is a transfer of training or learning paradigm, because she reinforced all responses. What Kuhl and her associates have demonstrated in these experiments is that it is possible to train infants to ignore changes in speaking voices, pitch contours, and vowel contexts in order to respond to phonetic contrasts. Although it is extremely unlikely that infants would have been able to master such a task without recognizing commonality between the different tokens of the same phonetic segment, it is important to test for such a possibility. One way to do this would be to employ the same set of tokens used in any of the experiments but to require infants to learn an arbitrary grouping of these tokens (i.e., one in which tokens from the two phonetic categories are mixed and assigned to two new categories not based on phonetic properties).[24] If infants failed to learn the arbitrary groupings, or learned them only with considerably more difficulty than they did the phonetic groupings, one could be fairly safe in claiming that they recognize a similarity among tokens from the same phonetic category. Even in the absence of such comparisons, though, Kuhl's data strongly suggest that infants do possess a degree of perceptual constancy for some phonetic segments. Should similar findings occur for other kinds of phonetic segments, such as stop consonants, then there would be some reason to favor a solution to the perceptual constancy problem based on innate factors over one that relies on learning equivalence classes.

POSSIBLE BASES FOR THE INFANT'S SPEECH-PROCESSING ABILITIES

What kinds of mechanisms underlie the infant's speech-processing abilities? Are there mechanisms devoted exclusively to processing speech, or are all mechanisms used in speech perception also employed in processing other kinds of acoustic signals? In this section, we review the evidence both for and against the claim that infants possess specialized mechanisms for processing speech.

The initial basis for the claim that infants might possess specialized speech-processing mechanisms was Eimas et al.'s (1971) finding that infants discriminate VOT information in a categorical manner. The argument in this instance was that categorical perception occurs only for speech sounds. Therefore, the demonstration that infants as young as 1 month old had this presumed language-specific capacity implied the existence of some underlying mechanism specialized for dealing with the perception of speech sounds. However, this argument has been undercut not only by studies with adults demonstrating categorical perception for some nonspeech sounds (Cutting & Rosner, 1974; Miller et al., 1976; Pisoni,

---

[24]Kuhl (1978) has apparently adopted this procedure in an experiment in progress.

1977), but also by several studies in which infants' discrimination of nonspeech sounds was investigated. In the first of these, Jusczyk, Rosner, Cutting, Foard, and Smith (1977) examined the 2-month-old's discrimination of sinewave stimuli differing in rise times. Previous work by Cutting and Rosner (1974) and Cutting, Rosner, and Foard (1976) had shown that adults typically hear these sounds as being produced by a musical stringed instrument. Moreover, their perception of these sounds is categorical such that sinewave tones with rise times of less than 35 msec are labeled as being produced by a plucked stringed instrument, and those with longer rise times by a bowed stringed instrument. Using the HAS procedure, Jusczyk et al. (1977) demonstrated that the 2-month-old's discrimination of these sounds was also categorical. That is, the infants discriminated a 30-msec rise time contrast only when the stimulus pair members were chosen from the opposite sides of the adult category boundary (e.g., 30 msec vs. 60 msec of rise time). Stimulus pairs chosen from within either the pluck (0 msec vs. 30 msec) or bow (60 msec vs. 90 msec) categories were not discriminated. Thus, by demonstrating that infants display categorical discrimination for certain nonspeech contrasts, Jusczyk et al. helped to undermine the claim that categorical discrimination occurs only for speech sounds.

More recently, there have been several attempts to demonstrate specifically that the underlying basis for the infant's categorical discrimination of VOT information is psychoacoustic. Pisoni (1977) has advanced the argument that the perception of VOT information may have its origin in a basic property of the auditory system to respond to differences in the temporal order of events. His own research (Pisoni, 1977) and that of Hirsch (1959; Hirsch & Sherrick, 1961) has shown that adults cannot identify the temporal order of two distinct acoustic events when their onsets are separated by less than about 25 msec. In effect, the two onsets are perceived as occurring simultaneously. By contrast, when the onsets of two events differ by more than 25 msec, then they are perceived as occurring successively and ordered in time. Pisoni demonstrated this in his own research using a set of nonspeech stimuli differing in the relative onsets of two-component tones.[25] He found evidence for three perceptual categories corresponding to whether the onset of one of the tones was perceived as leading, occurring simultaneously with, or lagging behind the onset of the other tone. Not only was the perception of these stimuli categorical but the locations of the boundaries for the lead, simultaneous, and lag categories fit well with those observed along the VOT continuum. On the basis of this correspondence between the adult's perception of the speech and nonspeech stimuli, Pisoni argued that categorical perception for VOT information may be a consequence of the

---

[25]Each stimulus consisted of a 500 Hz tone paired with a 1500 Hz tone. The onset of the 500 Hz tone with respect to the 1500 Hz tone was varied systemically in 10 msec steps to produce the tone-onset-time continuum employed by Pisoni (1977) and Jusczyk, Pisoni, Walley, and Murray (1980) in their experiments.

way the auditory system responds to differences in the temporal order of acoustic events.

Jusczyk, Pisoni, Walley, and Murray (1980) sought to determine whether a similar explanation could account for the infant's categorical discrimination of VOT information. Accordingly, they presented 2-month-old infants with contrasts between stimuli selected from various locations along the tone-onset-time (TOT) continuum employed by Pisoni. The stimulus pairs were chosen so that three of the pairings consisted of stimuli chosen from within the same adult category (i.e. $lead_1/lead_2$, $simultaneous_1/simultaneous_2$, lag_1/lag_2) whereas the other two pairings were composed of stimuli chosen from different categories (i.e., lead/simultaneous and simultaneous/lag). Their results indicated that infants, like adults, discriminate differences in the relative onsets of two-component tones and that they, too, appear to have three perceptual categories along the tone-onset-time continuum. However, one difference between infants and adults is the fact that, for the infants, the regions of highest discriminability along this continuum appear to be shifted toward slightly larger stimulus values. Specifically, Jusczyk et al. (1980) had predicted that infants would discriminate pairs of items chosen from the opposite sides of the adult category boundaries, which are located at about -20 and $+20$ msec on the continuum. In fact, infants discriminated only the $-70/-40$ msec and $+40/+70$ msec contrasts; pairings that were, for adults, "within-category" contrasts (lead and lag respectively). Thus, in contrast to the findings for adult subjects (where both boundaries occur in the neighborhood of $+25$ msec), there appears to be a slight discrepancy in the location of the infant's category boundaries (inferred from the discrimination data) for the speech (between 20 and 40 msec VOT) and nonspeech (between 40 and 70 msec TOT) stimuli. Some caution is necessary in interpreting this discrepancy, because the HAS measure does not permit an exact specification of the infant's sensitivity to stimulus differences. Nevertheless, Jusczyk et al. (1980) recognized that temporal order information might not be the only property that young infants respond to in discriminating VOT. Rather, they argued that temporal order information might be combined with other psychoacoustic cues, such as the presence or absence of an Fl transition (Stevens & Klatt, 1974), to yield the perception of VOT differences.[26]

---

[26]Mehler and Bertoncini (1978) also claim to have found evidence to suggest that infants have a threshold somewhere in the neighborhood of ± 30 msec for perceiving simultaneity. Their stimuli consisted of three identical beats such that the interval between the first and last beat was held constant at 600 msec. Mehler and his colleagues systematically varied the temporal location of the middle beat. For adult subjects, displacements of less than 30 msec from the point midway between the first and last beats resulted in the perception of three equally spaced beats. Larger displacements, however, had the effect of changing the percept to one of a couple of beats followed by a single one or vice versa depending on the direction of the displacement. Mehler tested infants on these same stimuli using an HAS measure. He found that infants discriminated pairs of three-beat stimuli when the members were chosed from opposite sides of the ± 30 msec range, but not when both members were

An explanation of the perception of VOT information in terms of psychoacoustic properties has a certain appeal because it can account for a number of diverse findings, such as why chinchillas should display categorical perception for VOT (Kuhl & Miller, 1978). In fact, Jusczyk et al. (1980) suggest that a psychophysical explanation for VOT perception could account for why cross-language similarities are observed for infants but not for adults. According to their hypothesis, infants might respond to speech signals initially purely on the psychoacoustic properties of the stimuli. Thus, at this point one would expect to observe marked similarities in the way that infants from diverse linguistic backgrounds respond to speech contrasts. Later, experience in the language-learning environment might direct infants to take advantage of other kinds of prominent acoustic attributes that appear regularly in certain phonetic environments as a consequence of constraints imposed by the phonological features of the language. Different weighting could be assigned to these acoustic cues according to their usefulness in marking a salient contrast in the language. A change in the relative weightings of the cues for a particular phonetic contrast could result in a shift in the region of highest sensitivity along a given stimulus continuum. Hence, differences in the relative weights assigned to the various acoustic cues for some phonetic distinction such as voicing, could account for the cross-language differences present in adult speakers.[27]

The studies of nonspeech contrasts lend some evidence to the view that infants may be responding to speech on the basis of some well-defined psychoacoustic properties. Categorical discrimination is present for certain classes of nonspeech sounds as well as for speech. Moreover, in addition to the similarities that Jusczyk et al. (1980) noted for the infant's sensitivity to VOT and to temporal cues, parallels can be drawn between the results of Jusczyk et al. (1977) and those of Hillenbrand, Minifie, and Edwards (1979). Specifically, the rise-time dimension investigated by Jusczyk et al. (1979) with sinewave stimuli involves the detection of the rate of frequency change; a factor which Hillenbrand et al. showed to be important in making the stop–glide distinction. At present, then, nonspeech analogues have been found for two types of phonetic dimensions. It remains to be seen if similar evidence can be adduced for other phonetic dimensions. As we remarked earlier, some dimensions such as place-of-articulation, may not be amenable to an analysis into well-defined acoustic properties (but see

---

selected from within the ±30 msec range. Mehler took this to be evidence that infants have thresholds for simultaneity at about −30 and +30 msec. However, other interpretations of his results are also possible. For example, one might argue that what Mehler has demonstrated is related not to the infant's perception of simultaneity, but rather to the perception of regular intervals. If this were the case, then one might expect to find changes in the infant's threshold as the interval between the first and last beats increases or decreases.

[27]A detailed discussion of the possible effects of environmental input on perceptual mechanisms and the attendant consequences for developmental changes in speech perception is available in a recent chapter by Aslin and Pisoni (1978).

Searle et al., 1979; Stevens & Blumstein, 1978). Yet, even with dimensions as difficult to specify acoustically as place, there has been some progress made in devising nonspeech stimuli that may parallel this dimension. Bailey, Summerfield, and Dorman (1977) were able to use sinewave analogues to formant patterns in order to construct a set of nonspeech stimuli with many of the spectrotemporal properties thought to be relevant to distinguishing [b] from [d]. Bailey et al. had hoped to ascertain whether the spectro-temporal characteristics of their stimuli were sufficient to account for categorization along the place continuum or whether an appeal to a specialized level of phonetic processing was necessary. More specifically, would the category boundary for nonspeech stimuli coincide with that for speech stimuli with similar spectro-temporal properties? If not, then one might conclude that different processes are involved in the perception of similar spectro-temporal properties in speech and nonspeech contexts. Unfortunately, Bailey et al.'s results were equivocal, so further testing will be required to resolve this matter.

The attack on the notion that infants possess mechanisms specialized for speech processing has taken the form of demonstrating that results thought to be explicable only by recourse to phonetic mechanisms have a psychophysical explanation. Although measurable gains have been made along these lines over the last few years, there are still differences observed in infants' responsiveness to speech and nonspeech sounds that need to be explained. For example, Eimas (1974; 1975a, 1975b) and Till (1976) have reported that infants respond differently to the same acoustic distinctions depending on the context, i.e., speech or nonspeech. However, as we noted earlier (cf., footnote 4), some questions can be raised as to whether or not the same information is actually present in the speech and nonspeech stimuli. Hence, it may be the case that had three formant chirps been used in the Eimas studies, no differences would have emerged between the speech and nonspeech stimuli. Therefore, the issue of whether infants do respond to the same acoustic contrasts differently for speech and nonspeech contexts remains in doubt.

Similar comments apply to another difference that is said to occur in the way in which infants deal with speech and nonspeech sounds, viz., hemispheric asymmetries in processing. Both electrophysiological (Molfese, 1972; Molfese, Freeman, & Palermo, 1975; Molfese, Nunez, Seibert, & Ramanaiah, 1976) and behavioral (Entus, 1977; Glanville, Best, & Levenson, 1977) indices have been employed in measuring hemispheric asymmetries during infancy. The evidence to date suggests a *left* hemisphere advantage for speech contrasts and a *right* hemisphere advantage for nonspeech contrasts. However, these studies have, for the most part, employed nonspeech stimuli of little complexity—usually musical tones. In the one study in which complex nonspeech stimuli were used (Molfese et al., 1976), there were overall amplitude differences in the auditory evoked potentials of the two hemispheres but neither hemisphere responded differentially to the speech and nonspeech stimuli. Thus, until further investigations are undertaken using complex nonspeech stimuli (such as those employed by Jusczyk et al., 1980), the import of findings showing that infants have a left hemisphere advantage for speech is difficult to assess.[28]

One additional set of research findings that would seem to demand an explanation based upon specialized phonetic processing mechanisms is that which deals with perceptual constancy (e.g., Fodor et al., 1975; Holmberg et al., 1977; Kuhl, 1976, 1977). In particular, Fodor et al. tried to demonstrate that infants were responding to stimulus items on the basis of phonetic rather than acoustic similarities. The only way to provide a psychoacoustic explanation for the infants' behavior in that situation is to show that acoustic invariants really are present in the kinds of items that Fodor et al. chose. Thus, this whole issue hinges upon how successful Searle et al. (1979), Stevens and Blumstein (1978), and others are in isolating invariant acoustic cues for place-of-articulation.

Finally, Bertoncini and Mehler (reported in Mehler & Bertoncini, 1978) have tried to determine the extent to which the syllable has special status as a perceptual unit for the infant. They note that syllables typically exhibit a structure of alternating consonants and vowels and suggest that virtually no natural languages contain instances of three consecutive consonants in a single word. Details of their study are sketchy, but Bertoncini and Mehler claim that infants respond differentially to changes between CVC stimuli than they do for equivalent changes between CCC stimuli. Specifically, infants showed larger increases in sucking rates for the first postshift minutes following a change from one CVC item to another than they did for comparable CCC changes. Bertoncini and Mehler take this to be an indication that the syllable has a special status in perception for the infant: an interpretation that favors the claim for a special mode of processing for speech. However, it is not clear that their interpretation is correct, because it appears that both types of contrasts were discriminated by the infants. Moreover, the postshift levels of sucking were identical, thus raising the possibility of a ceiling effect in the case of CCC contrast, especially because the preshift levels of sucking were considerably higher for this group. A more detailed description of this study is necessary before its implications can be adequately assessed.

In conclusion, although the early studies of infant speech perception seemed to point to the existence of specialized phonetic processing mechanisms, some of the more recent investigations suggest that an account based upon general psychoacoustic mechanisms is preferable. While not all findings cited in support of specialized phonetic mechanisms have been given a psychophysical account, considerable progress has been made in this direction.

---

[28]It is worth noting that adults do display a left-hemisphere advantage for some sets of complex nonspeech sounds (e.g., Bever & Chiarello, 1974; Blechner, 1976).

CONCLUSIONS

Implications for Language Acquisition

Curiously, speech perception has often been ignored by most researchers in the field of language acquisition, yet its importance to the language learning process is undeniable. For a child to learn a word and its meaning, he or she must first be made able to recognize the word. Ten years ago, there was little comprehension of how the child came to distinguish between different utterances. In the interim, much has been learned about the perceptual capacities that the infant possesses for processing speech. Our knowledge of these capacities has given us a foothold toward understanding one critical aspect of language acquisition—how the child is able to decode the stream of speech into usable segments.

We now know that infants are able to perceive a wide variety of phonetic contrasts long before they actually produce these contrasts in their own babbling. Thus, we can say with certainty that the view that infants learn to perceive differences in speech sounds by first discriminating among the sounds in their own productions is wrong. Nor, is a long period of exposure to speech sounds of a particular language necessary for infants to discriminate a particular set of phonetic contrasts. Rather, the cross-language investigations demonstrate that infants are capable of distinguishing between phonetic segments that do not appear in their native linguistic environment (e.g., Aslin et al., 1979; Eilers & Oller, 1978; Lasky et al., 1975; Streeter, 1976; Trehub, 1976a). Judging from the existing data, it appears that infants are innately endowed with mechanisms necessary for making phonetic distinctions in any natural language, at least to a first approximation. To be sure, experience plays a role in tuning those mechanisms to respond to particular values along a given psychoacoustic dimension. The values chosen for any particular language must be a consequence of its phonological structure and would be those optimal for distinguishing between phonetic segments in that language. At the present time, we know little about this process. There are no developmental data to indicate when a shift in sensitivity occurs from a set of initial values along some psychoacoustic continuum to those values used by speakers of a particular language.

Our understanding of how the infant begins to decode speech has also advanced on several other fronts. For instance, there is ample evidence that infants have the capacity to process information beyond the initial segments of utterances (e.g., Eilers, 1977; Jusczyk, 1977; Jusczyk & Thompson, 1978; Williams, 1977a). Moreover, they respond not only to phonetic distinctions but to suprasegmental contrasts as well (d.g., Morse, 1972); Spring & Dale, 1977). Thus, the infant's discriminative capacities for speech are very well developed by the time language learning is thought to begin. These capacities would allow the infants to recognize differences between utterances that he or she is likely to hear.

Yet the speech decoding process obviously involves more than just making distinctions between utterances. One must also be able to recognize similarities between utterances as well. Although research on this problem has scarcely begun, it appears that the infant may also possess a remarkable capacity to recognize similarities between utterances spoken by different speakers and with different inflections (e.g., Holmberg et al., 1977; Kuhl, 1976; 1977). If so, then it would not be necessary to provide an account of how the infant *learns* to recognize the same word spoken by different speakers (though we would still work to discover the nature of the mechanism that allows the infant to perceive the invariance).

One major problem in speech decoding that has yet to be dealt with is how the infant is able to segment the stream of speech into word-sized units. Perhaps this is not surprising in view of the fact that we do not fully understand how adults go about segmenting speech either. Suprasegmental information may play a key role in this process, and the infant research to date has been limited largely to examining the discrimination of suprasegmental contrasts. What is required is a better understanding of the degree to which infants can recognize equivalences between different ways of conveying suprasegmental information. We also need to know more about factors that might lead the infant to treat a particular piece of information as a unit rather than several units. Of course, it may turn out in the end that suprasegmental cues are not the chief means by which the infant locates word boundaries in utterances. Instead, it is possible that the infant begins by recognizing words in isolation and only when he or she gains mastery over them in that context, can the word be recognized in running speech. Unfortunately, we are as yet unable to provide an answer to this problem.

Implications for Theories of Speech Perception

Data gathered from studies with infants serve to constrain theories of speech perception. For, any explanation of why adults behave the way they do when presented with certain speech information should also be able to account for any similarities or differences that occur in the infant's behavior, given the same information. Whenever correspondences are observed between the behaviors of infants and adults, investigators are prompted to seek out a common mechanism to explain their behaviors. Thus, when infants were found to have categorical discrimination for sounds differing in VOT, a new constraint was imposed upon any model for categorical perception, viz. the range of abilities that such a model could draw upon were restricted to those within the capability of the infant. This constraint necessitates an account based upon sensory and perceptual mechanisms rather than higher order cognitive ones. For this reason, it was quite important to test whether infants would also show evidence for categorical discrimination of nonspeech contrasts. Without such data from infants, it would be possible to fashion an alternative explanation for why adults display categorical perception for nonspeech sounds. Specifically, one could claim that adults' long experience with speech allows them to interpret the nonspeech sounds by analogy to certain speech contrasts. However, this kind of explanation is almost certainly excluded by the demonstration that 2-month-olds with their limited exposure to speech also display categorical discrimination for the same nonspeech sounds.

In a similar vein, if future research efforts continue to show that infants display the capacity for perceptual constancy for speech sounds, this will surely constrain any accounts of how adults achieve constancy. Again the clear suggestion would be that constancy must be the result of innate sensory and perceptual mechanisms.

But if correspondences between infants and adults serve to constrain theories of speech perception, then so also do discrepancies that arise between these age groups. For example, consider the situation with respect to whether the perception of VOT differences can be explained simply by reference to the way in which temporal order information is processed. Looking only at adults, the fit between the data for speech and nonspeech contrasts is remarkably close. However, the infant data show a slight divergence between responses to temporal information in speech and nonspeech contrasts. This raises the possibility that temporal order information is not the only cue used in discriminating VOT (a possibility that might have been overlooked if only the adult data had been collected).

Other kinds of discrepancies between infants and adults have an important bearing on theories of speech perception. Knowledge of just when shifts in the location of phonetic boundaries occur may help to illuminate the degree to which higher order information, such as the knowledge of particular phonological constraints, may affect speech perception. Thus, by observing what kinds of cognitive changes are happening in parallel with changes in speech perception, we might gain some insight as to the role that certain cognitive factors might assume in the adult's processing of speech.

ACKNOWLEDGMENT

I would like to thank David Pisoni and Linda Smith for their comments on an earlier version of this manuscript. In addition, I would also like to acknowledge my debt to Nancy Beattie for the care and effort that she extended in typing all drafts of the manuscript. This paper was written while the author was receiving support from N.S.E.R.C. grant A-0282.

REFERENCES

Ades, A. E. How phonetic is selective adaptation? Experiments on syllable position and vowel environment. *Perception & Psychophysics*, 1974, *16*, 61–66.
Aslin, R. N. Personal communication. April 1979.

Aslin, R. N., Hennessy, B., Pisoni, D. B., & Perey, A. J. *Individual infants' discrimination of voice onset time: Evidence for three modes of voicing.* Paper presented at the biennial meeting of the Society for Research in Child Development, San Francisco, 1979.

Aslin, R. N., Perey, A. J., Hennessey, B., & Pisoni, D. B. *Perceptual analysis of speech sounds by prelinguistic infants: A first report.* Paper presented at the 94th Meeting of the Acoustical Society of America, Miami Beach, December 1977.

Aslin, R. N., & Pisoni, D. B. *Some developmental processes in speech perception.* Paper presented at N.I.C.H.D. conference in Child Phonology: Perception, Production and Deviation, Bethesda, 1978.

Aslin, R. N., & Pisoni, D. B. Effects of early linguistic experience on speech discrimination by infants: A critique of Eilers, Gavin and Wilson, 1979. *Child Development,* 1980, *51,* 107–112.

Bailey, P. J., Summerfield, Q., & Dorman, M. On the identification of sine-wave analogues of certain speech sounds (SR-51/52). *Haskins Laboratories: Status Report on Speech Research,* New Haven: Conn., 1977.

Bever, T. G., & Chiarello, R. J. Cerebral dominance in musicians and nonmusicians. *Science,* 1974, *185,* 537–539.

Blechner, M. J. Right-ear advantage for musical stimuli differing in rise-time (SR–47). *Haskins Laboratories: Status Report on Speech Research,* New Haven: Conn., 1976.

Carden, G., Levitt, A., & Jusczyk, P. W. *Manner judgments affect the locus of the labial/dental boundary for stops and fricatives.* Paper presented at the 97th Meeting of the Acoustical Society of America, Cambridge, Mass., June 1979.

Carney, A. E., Widin, G. P., & Viemeister, N. F. Noncategorical perception of stop consonants differing in VOT. *Journal of the Acoustical Society of America,* 1977, *62,* 961–970.

Carrell, T. D., & Smith, L. B. *Some perceptual dependencies between vowel color and pitch.* Paper presented at the 97th Meeting of the Acoustical Society of America, Cambridge, Mass., June 1979.

Cooper, W. E. Adaptation of phonetic feature analyzers for place of articulation. *Journal of the Acoustical Society for America,* 1974, *56,* 617–627. (a)

Cooper, W. E. Contingent feature analysis in speech perception. *Perception & Psychophysics,* 1974, *16,* 201–204. (b)

Crystal, D. Prosodic system and language acquisition. In M. Didier (Ed.), *Prosodic Feature Analysis.* Montreal: Didier, 1970.

Cutting, J. E., & Rosner, B. S. Categories and boundaries in speech and music. *Perception & Psychophysics,* 1974, *16,* 564–571.

Cutting, J. E., Rosner, B. S., & Foard, C. F. Perceptual categories for musiclike sounds: Implications for theories of speech perception. *Quarterly Journal of Experimental Psychology,* 1976, *28,* 361–378.

Dorman, M., Studdert-Kennedy, M., & Raphael, L. J. Stop consonant recognition: Release bursts and formant transitions as functionally equivalent context-dependent cues. *Perception & Psychophysics,* 1977, *22,* 109–122.

Eilers, R. E. Context-sensitive perception of naturally produced stop and fricative consonants by infants. *Journal of the Acoustical Society of America,* 1977, *61,* 1321–1336.

Eilers, R. E., Gavin, W., & Wilson, W. R. Linguistic experience and phonemic perception in infancy: A cross-linguistic study. *Child Development,* 1979, *50,* 14–18.

Eilers, R. E., & Minifie, F. D. Fricative discrimination in early infancy. *Journal of Speech and Hearing Research,* 1975, *18,* 158–167.

Eilers, R. E., & Oller, D. K. *A cross-linguistic study of infant speech perception.* Paper presented at the Southeastern Conference on Human Development, Atlanta, Ga., 1978.

Eilers, R. E., Wilson, W. R., & Moore, J. M. Developmental changes in speech discrimination in infants. *Journal of Speech and Hearing Research,* 1977 *20,* 766–780.

Eilers, R. E., Wilson, W. R., & Moore, J. M. Speech discrimination in the language-innocent and the language-wise: A study in the perception of voice-onset time. *Journal of Child Language*, 1979, *6*, 1-18.

Eimas, P. D. Auditory and linguistic processing of cues for place of articulation by infants. *Perception & Psychophysics*, 1974, *16*, 513-521.

Eimas, P. D. Auditory and phonetic coding of the cues for speech: Discrimination of the [r−1] distinction of young infants. *Perception & Psychophysics*, 1975, *18*, 341-347. (a)

Eimas, P. D. Speech perception in early infancy. In L. B. Cohen & P. Salapatek (Eds.), *Infant Perception*. New York: Academic Press, 1975. (b)

Eimas, P. D., Cooper, W. E., & Corbit, J. D. Some properties of linguistic feature detectors. *Perception & Psychophysics*, 1973, *13*, 247-252.

Eimas, P. D., & Miller, J. L. *Perception of initial nasal and stop consonants by young infants.* Unpublished manuscript, 1977.

Eimas, P. D., & Miller, J. L. Discrimination of the information for manner of articulation by young infants. *Infant Behavior & Development*, 1980, *3*, 367-375.

Eimas, P. D., Siqueland, E. R., Jusczyk, P., & Vigorito, J. Speech perception in infants. *Science*, 1971, *171*, 303-306.

Eimas, P. D., & Tartter, V. C. On the development of speech perception: Mechanisms and analogies. In H. W. Reese & L. P. Lipsitt (Eds.), *Advances in child development and behavior* (Vol. 13). New York: Academic Press, 1979.

Entus, A. K. Hemispheric asymmetry in processing of dichotically presented speech and nonspeech stimuli by infants. In S. Segalowitz & F. Gruber (Eds.), *Language development and neurological theory*. New York: Academic Press, 1977.

Flavell, J. H., & Wohlwill, J. F. Formal and functional aspects of cognitive development. In D. Elkind & J. H. Flavell (Eds.), *Studies in cognitive development*. New York: Oxford University Press, 1969.

Fodor, J. A., Garrett, M. F., & Brill, S. L. Pi ka pu: The perception of speech sounds by prelinguistic infants. *Perception & Psychophysics*, 1975, *18*, 74-78.

Fry, D. B. Experiments in the perception of stress. *Language & Speech*, 1958. *1*, 126-152.

Fry, D. B., Abramson, A. S., Eimas, P. D., & Liberman, A. M. The identification and discrimination of synthetic vowels. *Language & Speech*, 1962, *5*, 171-189.

Fujisaki, H., & Kawashima, T. Some experiments on speech perception and a model for the perceptual mechanism. *Annual Report of the Engineering Research Institute*. Tokyo: University of Tokyo, 1970, *29*, 207-214.

Garnica, O. K. The development of phonemic speech perception. In T. E. Moore (Ed.), *Cognitive development and the acquisition of language*. New York: Academic Press, 1973.

Glanville, B., Best, C., & Levenson, R. A cardiac measure of cerebral asymmetries in infant auditory perception. *Developmental Psychology*, 1977, *13*, 54-59.

Graham, F. K., & Clifton, R. K. Heart rate change as a component of the orienting response. *Psychological Bulletin*, 1966, *65*, 305-320.

Harris, K. S. Cues for the discrimination of American English fricatives in spoken syllables. *Language & Speech*, 1958, *1*, 1-7.

Hillenbrand, J., Minifie, F. D., & Edwards, T. J. *Tempo of frequency change as a cue in speech sound discrimination by infants. Journal of Speech & Hearing Research*, 1979, 22, 147-165.

Hirsch, I. J. Auditory perception of temporal order. *Journal of the Acoustical Society of America*, 1959, *31*, 759-767.

Hirsch, I. J., & Sherrick, C. E. Perceived order in different sense modalities. *Journal of Experimental Psychology*, 1961, *62*, 423-432.

Holmberg, T. L., Morgan, K. A., & Kuhl, P. K. *Speech perception in early infancy: Discrimination of fricative consonants.* Paper presented at the 94th Meeting of the Acoustical Society of America, Miami Beach, December 1977.

Jakobson, R. *Child language, aphasia and phonological universals*. The Hague: Mouton, 1968.

Jusczyk, P. W. Perception of syllable-final stop consonants by two-month-old infants. *Perception & Psychophysics*, 1977, *21*, 450–454.

Jusczyk, P. W., Copan, H. C., & Thompson, E. J. Perception by two-month olds of glide contrasts in multisyllabic utterances. *Perception & Psychophysics*, 1978, *24*, 515–520.

Jusczyk, P. W., Murray, J., & Bayly, J. *Perception of place-of articulation in fricatives and stops by infants.* Paper presented at the biennial meeting of the Society for Research in Child Development, San Francisco, March 1979.

Jusczyk, P. W., Pisoni, D. B., Walley, A., & Murray, J. Discrimination of relative onset-time of two-component tones by infants. *Journal of the Acoustical Society of America*, 1980, *67*, 262–270.

Jusczyk, P. W., Rosner, B. S., Cutting, J. E., Foard, C. F., & Smith, L. B. Categorical perception of nonspeech sounds by two-month old infants. *Perception & Psychophysics*, 1977, *21*, 50–54.

Jusczyk, P. W., Smith, L. B., & Murphy, C. *Perceived similarities of speech and nonspeech sounds.* Paper presented at the 99th Meeting of the Acoustical Society of America, Atlanta, April 1980.

Jusczyk, P. W., & Thompson, E. Perception of a phonetic contrast of multisyllabic utterances by two-month old infants. *Perception & Psychophysics*, 1978, *23*, 105–109.

Kaplan, E. L., *The role of intonation in the acquisition of language.* Unpublished doctoral dissertation, Cornell University, 1969.

Kaplan, E. L., & Kaplan, G. The prelinguistic child. In J. Eliot (Ed.), *Human development and cognitive processes.* New York: Holt, Rinehart & Winston, 1971.

Kuhl, P. K. *Speech perception in early infancy: Perceptual constancy for vowel categories.* Paper presented at the 92nd Meeting of the Acoustical Society of America, San Diego, November 1976.

Kuhl, P. K. *Speech perception of early infancy: Perceptual constancy for the vowel categories /a/ and /ɔ/.* Paper presented at the 93rd meeting of the Acoustical Society of America, State College, Pa., June 1977.

Kuhl, P. K. *Perceptual constancy for speech-sound categories.* Paper presented at the N.I.C.H.D. conference on Child Phonology: Perception, Production, and Deviation, Bethesda, Md., May 1978.

Kuhl, P. K., & Miller, J. D. Speech perception by the chinchilla: Voiced–voiceless distinction in alveolar-plosive consonants. *Science*, 1975, *190*, 69–72. (a)

Kuhl, P. K., & Miller, J. D. Speech perception in early infancy: Discrimination of speech-sound categories. *Journal of the Acoustical Society of America*, 1975, *58*, S56(Abstract). (b)

Kuhl, P. K., & Miller, J. D. Speech perception by the chinchilla: Identification functions for synthetic VOT stimuli. *Journal of the Acoustical Society of America*, 1978, *63*, 905–917.

Lasky, R. E., Syrdal-Lasky, A., & Klein, R. E. VOT discrimination by four and six and a half month old infants from Spanish environments. *Journal of Experimental Child Psychology*, 1975, *20*, 215–225.

Lewis, M. M. *Infant speech: A study of the beginnings of language* (2nd ed.). New York: Harcourt, Brace & World, 1951.

Liberman, A. M., Cooper, F. S., Shankweiler, D. P., & Studdert-Kennedy, M. Perception of the speech code. *Psychological Review*, 1967, *74*, 431–461.

Liberman, A. M., DeLattre, P. C., & Cooper, F. S. The role of selected stimulus variables in the perception of unvoiced stop consonants. *American Journal of Psychology*, 1952, *65*, 497–516.

Liberman, A. M., DeLattre, P. C., Cooper, F. S., & Gerstman, L. J. The role of consonant–vowel transitions in the perception of stop and nasal consonants. *Psychological Monographs*, 1954, *68*, 1–13.

Liberman, A. M., Harris, K. S., Kinney, J. A., & Lane, H. The discrimination of relative-onset time of the components of certain speech and nonspeech patterns. *Journal of Experimental Psychology*, 1961, *61*, 379–388.

Lieberman, P. *Intonation, perception and language.* Cambridge: MIT Press, 1967.

Lisker, L., & Abramson, A. A cross-language study of voicing in initial stops: Acoustical measurements. *Word*, 1964, *20*, 384–422.

Lisker, L., & Abramson, A. S. The voicing dimension: Some experiments in comparative phonetics. In *Proceedings of the Sixth International Congress of Phonetic Sciences*, Prague, 1967. Prague: Academia, 1970.

Malecot, A. The role of releases in the identification of released final stops. *Language*, 1958, *34*, 370–380.

Mattingly, I. G., Liberman, A. M., Syrdal, A. K., & Halwes, T. Discrimination in speech and nonspeech modes. *Cognitive Psychology*, 1971, *2*, 131–157.

McClean, M. D., & Tiffany, W. R. The acoustic parameters of stress in relation to syllable position, speech loudness and rate. *Language & Speech*, 1973, *16*, 283–290.

Mehler, J., & Bertoncini, J. Infants' perception of speech and other acoustic stimuli. In J. Morton & J. Marshall (Eds.), *Psycholinguistic Series II*. London: Elek Science Books, 1978.

Miller, C., Morse, P., & Dorman, M. Cardiac indices of infant speech perception: Orienting and burst discrimination. *Quarterly Journal of Experimental Psychology*, 1977, *29*, 533–545.

Miller, G. A., & Nicely, P. E. An analysis of perceptual confusions among some English consonants. *Journal of the Acoustical Society of America*, 1955, *27*, 338–352.

Miller, J. D., Wier, L., Pastore, R., Kelly, W., & Dooling, R. Discrimination and labeling of noise-buzz sequences with varying noise-lead times. *Journal of the Acoustical Society of America*, 1976, *60*, 410–417.

Miller, J. L., & Eimas, P. D. Studies on the perception of place and manner of articulation: A comparison of the labial-alveolar and nasal-stop distinctions. *Journal of the Acoustical Society of America*, 1977, *61*, 835–845.

Miyawaki, K., Strange, W., Verbrugge, R., Liberman, A. M., Jenkins, J. J., & Fujimura, O. An effect of linguistic experience: The discrimination of [r] and [l] by native speakers of Japanese and English. *Perception & Psychophysics*, 1975, *18*, 331–340.

Moffit, A. R. Consonant cue perception by twenty-two twenty-four-week-old infants. *Child Development*, 1971, *42*, 717–732.

Molfese, D. *Cerebral asymmetry in infants, children, and adults: Auditory evoked responses to speech and music stimuli*. Unpublished doctoral dissertation, Pennsylvania State University, 1972.

Molfese, D., Freeman, R., & Palermo, D. The ontogeny of brain lateralization for speech and nonspeech stimuli. *Brain and Language*, 1975, *2*, 356–368.

Molfese, D. L., Nunez, V., Seibert, S. M., & Ramanaiah, N. V. Cerebral asymmetry: Changes in factors affecting its development. *Annals of the New York Academy of Sciences*, 1976, *280*, 821–833.

Morse, P. A. The discrimination of speech and nonspeech stimuli in early infancy. *Journal of Experimental Child Psychology*, 1972, *14*, 477–492.

Morse, P. A. *The infancy of infant speech perception: The first decade of research*. Unpublished manuscript, 1978.

Morton, J., & Jassem, W. Acoustic correlates of stress. *Language & Speech*, 1965, *8*, 159–181.

Perey, A. J., & Pisoni, D. B. *Dual processing vs. response limitation accounts of categorical perception: A reply to McMillan, Kaplan & Creelman*. Paper presented at 94th Meeting of the Acousical Society of America, Miami Beach, December 1977.

Peterson, G. E., & Barney, H. L. Control methods used in a study of the vowels. *Journal of the Acoustical Society of America*, 1952, *24*, 175–184.

Pisoni, D. B. Auditory and phonetic memory codes in the discrimination of consonants and vowels. *Perception and Psychophysics*, 1973, *13*, 253–260.

Pisoni, D. B. Auditory short-term memory and vowel perception. *Memory and Cognition*, 1975, *3*, 7–18.

Pisoni, D. B. Identification and discrimination of the relative onset-time of two-component tones:

Implications for voicing perception in stops. *Journal of the Acoustical Society of America,* 1977, *61,* 1352–1361.

Pisoni, D. B., Aslin, R. N., Perey, A. J., & Hennessy, B. L. *Identification and discrimination of a new linguistic contrast: Some effects of laboratory training on speech perception.* Manuscript submitted for publication, 1979.

Pisoni, D. B., & Lazarus, J. H. Categorical and noncategorical modes of speech perception along the voicing continuum. *Journal of the Acoustical Society of America,* 1974, *55,* 328–333.

Pisoni, D. B., & Tash, J. Reaction times to comparisons within and across phonetic categories. *Perception & Psychophysics,* 1974, *15,* 285–290.

Remez, R. E. Adaptation of the category boundary between speech and nonspeech: A case against feature detectors. *Cognitive Psychology,* 1979, *11,* 38–57.

Repp, B. H., Healy, A. F., & Crowder, R. G. Categories and context in the perception of isolated steady-state vowels (SR–54). *Haskins Laboratories: Status Report on Speech Research,* New Haven: Conn., 1978.

Samuel, A. The effect of discrimination training on speech perception: Noncategorical perception. *Perception & Psychophysics,* 1977, *21,* 321–330.

Schatz, C. D. The role of context in the perception of stops. *Language,* 1954, *30,* 47–56.

Searle, C. L., Jacobson, J. Z., & Rayment, S. G. Phoneme recognition based on human audition. *Journal of the Acoustical Society of America,* 1979, *65,* 799–809.

Shvachkin, N. K. The development of phonemic speech perception in early childhood. Reprinted in C. A. Ferguson & D. I. Slobin (Eds.), *Studies of Child Language Development.* New York: Holt, Rinehart & Winston, 1973.

Simon, H. J., & Studdert-Kennedy, M. Selective anchoring and adaptation of phonetic and non-phonetic continua. *Journal of the Acoustical Society of America,* 1978, *64,* 1338–1357.

Siqueland, E. R., & DeLucia, C. A. Visual reinforcement of non-nutritive sucking in human infants. *Science,* 1969, *165,* 1144–1146.

Sokolov, E. N. *Perception and the conditioned reflex.* New York: MacMillan, 1963.

Spring, D., & Dale, P. The discrimination of linguistic stress in early infancy. *Journal of Speech and Hearing Research,* 1977, *20,* 224–231.

Stevens, K. N., & Blumstein, S. E. Invariant cues for place-of-articulation in stop consonants. *Journal of the Acoustical Society of America,* 1978, *64,* 1358–1368.

Stevens, K. N., & Klatt, D. H. Role of formant transitions in the voiced-voiceless distinction for stops. *Journal of the Acoustical Society of America,* 1974, *55,* 653–659.

Stevens, K. N., Liberman, A. M., Studdert-Kennedy, M., & Öhman, S. Cross-language study of vowel perception. *Language & Speech,* 1969, *12,* 1–23.

Strange, W., & Jenkins, J. J. The role of linguistic experience in the perception of speech. In R. D. Walk & H. L. Pick (Eds.), *Perception and experience.* New York: Plenum Press, 1978.

Streeter, L. A. Language perception of two-month old infants shows effects of both innate mechanisms and experience. *Nature,* 1976, *259,* 39–41.

Streeter, L. A. Acoustic determinants of phrase boundary perception. *Journal of the Acoustical Society of America,* 1978, *64,* 1582–1592.

Studdert-Kennedy, M., Liberman, A. M., Harris, K. S., & Cooper, F. S. Motor theory of speech perception: A reply to Lane's critical review. *Psychological Review,* 1970, *77,* 234–249.

Swoboda, P., Kass, J., Morse, P., & Leavitt, L. Memory factors in infant vowel discrimination of normal and at risk infants. *Child Development,* 1978, *49,* 332–339.

Swoboda, P. J., Morse, P. A., & Leavitt, L. A. Continuous vowel discrimination in normal and at risk infants. *Child Development,* 1976, *47,* 459–465.

Till, J. A. *Infants' discrimination of speech and nonspeech stimuli.* Paper presented at the annual meeting of the American Speech and Hearing Association, Houston, November 1976.

Trehub, S. E. *Auditory-linguistic sensitivity in infants.* Unpublished doctoral dissertation, McGill University, 1973. (a)

Trehub, S. E. Infant's sensitivity to vowel and tonal contrasts. *Developmental Psychology,* 1973, *9,* 91–96. (b)

Trehub, S. E. The discrimination of foreign speech contrasts by infants and adults. *Child Development,* 1976, *47,* 466–472. (a)

Trehub, S. E. *Infants' discrimination of multisyllabic stimuli: The role of temporal factors.* Paper presented at the annual convention of the American Speech and Hearing Association, Houston, November 1976. (b)

Williams, L. *The effects of phonetic environment and stress placement on infant discrimination of place of stop consonant articulation.* Paper presented at the Second Annual Boston University Conference on Language Development, Boston, October 1977. (a)

Williams, L. The perception of stop consonant by Spanish-English bilinguals. *Perception & Psychophysics,* 1977, *21,* 289–297. (b)

Williams, L. The voicing contrast in Spanish. *Journal of Phonetics,* 1977, *5,* 169–184. (c)

Williams, L., & Bush, M. The discrimination by young infants of voiced stop consonants with and without release bursts. *Journal of the Acoustical Society of America,* 1978, *63,* 1223–1225.

Williams, L., & Golenski, J. Infant speech sound discrimination: The effects of contingent versus non-contingent stimulus presentation. *Child Development,* 1978, *49,* 213–217.

5 Possible Psychoacoustic Factors in Speech Perception

Richard E. Pastore
SUNY-Binghamton

Editors' Comments

A common approach in the past among researchers directly concerned with perception of speech was to invoke a number of phenomena of speech perception, such as categorical perception or the more general issue of perceptual discontinuities, which could not readily be explained in terms of general auditory principles, as evidence for the existence of specialized processors. An alternative approach, as exemplified by Pastore's discussion, is to attempt to apply the principles of psychoacoustics in a systematic manner to the "facts" of speech, and to invoke specialized speech processors only in those instances when the laws of psychoacoustics proved wholly inadequate as explanatory principles. A major difference between the two positions is the degree to which one will hold to the possibility that more general auditory laws apply before yielding to the assumption of specialized mechanisms.

Despite the psychoacoustician's faith that the phenomena of speech can and will eventually be explicable in terms of the basic laws of psychoacoustics, Pastore has made it abundantly clear that there is, at present, insufficient knowledge to accommodate the fine grain of many of the findings in speech perception. His discussion is important in that it not only demonstrates the present shortcomings of the psychoacoustic approach to speech, but also describes future research that will be necessary if we are to determine whether and to what extent the perceptual events of speech can be described within the domain of psychoacoustics.

INTRODUCTION

The major premise of this chapter is that the perception of speech stimuli involves both a psychoacoustic analysis common to the processing of many nonspeech acoustic stimuli, and subsequent higher stages, or levels of organization, which probably are unique to the human perception of its species-specific speech stimuli. This premise is consistent with the majority of current research on phonetic perception. The major difference in this basic supposition between most research on phonetic perception and the present approach is the assumed degree of involvement and importance of the initial psychoacoustic analysis. It is our belief that, with a sufficient understanding of the perception of nonphonetic stimuli, many (but not all) aspects of the perception of phonetic segments currently attributed to unique speech analyzers will be found to be the result of a psychoacoustic analysis. The goals of this chapter are first to summarize those aspects of psychoacoustic knowledge and theory that probably are relevant to the study of speech perception, and then, with the context provided by this summary, to examine some aspects of speech perception that, with further investigation, might prove to have a psychoacoustic basis.

Before we can begin discussing the perception of speech and nonspeech (or phonetic and nonphonetic) stimuli, it is necessary to address questions concerning the meaning of these, and related, terms. At present, it is not possible to provide more than a brief general discussion of the manner in which these terms usually are employed. We can characterize some terms by their exclusion from the classes of stimuli that define other terms. The terms *nonphonetic* and *nonspeech* define those classes of auditory stimuli that are excluded from the classes of stimuli categorized respectively as *phonetic* and *speech*. The term *phonetic* is used to characterize the basic perceived units of speech, that is, the individual phones. The term *speech* is used to characterize stimuli that are produced by the human vocal apparatus (or by various synthetic means) and that abstractly convey meaning. From this class of stimuli, we must exclude all nonlinguistic stimuli (cough, laugh, cry, musical stimuli, etc.), yet must include a large class of synthetically produced speech stimuli perceived as conveying linguistic meaning, but that cannot be produced by the normal human vocal apparatus. A *phonetic mode* or *speech mode* describes a type of processing or a perceptual organization that is uniquely involved in the human perception of speech stimuli. Such modes typically are assumed to exist as an analysis stage beyond a preliminary psychoacoustic processing of the speech stimuli. A linguistic feature detector is a subset of such a unique mode of stimulus processing that is automatically activated by a specific (but usually undefined) set of characteristics of a speech waveform.

At this point we have a series of constructs, some of which we have at least loosely characterized. These constructs are in general use, and the current literature cannot be addressed adequately without reference to them. Thus, in our discussion we use these terms in the manner that they have been employed in the current literature (summarized in the foregoing), with the expectation that this and future discussions will lead to a more precise characterization of their meaning.

PSYCHOACOUSTICS

Temporal Attributes

Audition is very much a temporally defined sensory modality, in terms of both the nature of the physical stimuli and the processing of those stimuli by the human auditory system. All major parameters of acoustic stimuli are defined as a function of time. Intensity is measured in terms of total energy (or power) per unit time. Frequency is the rate of vibration (the number of vibrations per unit time) of molecules in the transmitting medium. Phase is the temporal delay in one waveform relative to another waveform of the same frequency (or, for certain phase relationships, relative to a harmonically related frequency) scaled in proportion to the temporal period of the waveform. Spectral complexity is the number of sinusoidal components in the waveform, and thus also is defined as a function of time. Finally, for any given sinusoidal waveform (or even the mixture of n sinusoidal waveforms [$n = 1,2,\ldots$]), the spectral purity of the waveform (and thus the mixture) is proportional to the duration of the waveform. For instance, a 1000 Hz tone will have half-power (-3 dB) bandwidths of 1, 10, 100, and 1000 Hz for durations of 1000, 100, 10, and 1 msec, respectively—i.e., the spectrum is described by a Sinc or (Sine x)/x function. For relatively brief waveforms, this inverse relationship between effective bandwidth and duration may become an important parameter for the auditory system (and is discussed later).

Temporal Resolution

Time is also an important parameter in the processing of acoustic stimuli. For instance, Hirsh (1959) has shown that the onsets of two waveforms must differ by at least approximately 2 msec for the observer to report a nonsimultaneous onset, and others have reported that two clicks delivered to the same ear will be perceived as a single click unless the two clicks are separated by at least approximately 2 msec (e.g., Wallach, Newman, & Rosenzweig, 1949). Although these results might lead one to conclude that the auditory system has a resolving power of only a few milliseconds, this conclusion probably is too simplistic. Rather, the temporal resolving power of the auditory system seems to depend on the nature of the specific task. For instance, when time differences are coded in terms of interaural phase differences for sinusoids, trained observers can detect differences of as little as 10 to 20 μsec (e.g., Julesz & Hirsh, 1972). When one component in a complex waveform is delayed relative to other components in an otherwise constant or "frozen" (e.g., computer-generated) waveform, the component need be delayed by only 1–2 msec in order for subjects to detect the differences between the waveforms (Green, 1971). When the task is changed from the detection of the presence or absence of temporal differences between waveforms to the identification of the nature of the temporal difference, the "temporal resolving power" of the auditory system is found to be much poorer. Hirsh (1959) has found that a difference in onset of at least approximately 17 msec is required for observers to identify the order of onset of two stimuli. (This applies whether the stimuli are equal in loudness or differ in loudness by 20 phons). This temporal order threshold is equivalent in magnitude to the category boundaries for labeling noise-buzz sequences (Miller, Wier, Pastore, Kelly, & Dooling, 1976) and for voiced and voiceless stops in CV syllables (e.g., Liberman, Harris, Kinney, & Lane, 1961). When temporal order identification involves repeated sequences of four discrete components, untrained subjects require minimal component durations of approximately 125 msec when the components are common vowels (e.g., Thomas, Hill, Carroll, & Garcia, 1970; Warren & Acroff, 1976) and approximately 200 msec when the components are either nonrelated, nonphonetic sounds (e.g., tones, buzzes [Warren, 1968]) or specific bursts of computer-generated noise (Warren & Acroff, 1976). However, one would expect that observers with considerable experience with the bursts of "frozen" computer-generated noise might yield lower temporal limits or thresholds, probably more in line with the thresholds for vowel stimuli. This type of threshold might be characterized as the minimal duration for the perception of physically discrete sounds as being discrete (Warren & Acroff, 1976). Thus, although the auditory system does appear to be characterized by the concept of a temporal threshold that is measurable and relatively stable, it is clear that there are a number of different temporal thresholds, each determined by a different type (and, probably, level) of task requirement.

Temporal Integration

Time is also an important parameter for the auditory system in terms of the integration of energy. For measurements of absolute threshold for intensity, one finds that $I \times T$ is a constant for a specific range of T (where I is intensity per unit time and T is the duration of the stimulus). In general, this auditory analogue to Block's Law in vision holds for a range of stimulus durations between approximately 10 and 200 msec (e.g., Blodgett, Jeffress, & Taylor, 1958), although some researchers have claimed that the upper limit is not a constant 200 msec, but that the value depends on the frequency of the signal (e.g., Campbell & Counter, 1968). Others have found support for a constant upper limit independent of frequency (e.g., Zwicker & Wright, 1963; Zwislocki, 1960), although that limit may be somewhat longer than previously assumed (e.g., 250 msec [Sheeley & Bilger, 1964; Stiegel & Bilger, 1975]). The lower limit on temporal integration may reflect simply a spread in energy (see foregoing) to frequencies beyond the limits of the peripheral auditory filter (i.e., the critical band). The upper limit may reflect some unit of sensory processing time for which an important parameter is the total energy (I × T) at the given frequency. In simultaneous masking, a similar relationship has been found for constant detection performance, where the required total stimulus energy is constant for stimulus durations between 10 and 150 msec (Green, Birdsall, & Tanner, 1957). This type of finding has led some investigators to model the auditory system in terms of a leaky (e.g., imperfect) integration of energy (e.g., Jeffress, 1964, 1967).

We return to this notion of constant energy as an important parameter for the auditory system when we discuss the concept of signal-to-noise ratio. At this point, it is important to note that the findings just discussed must be considered when one performs an experiment manipulating the duration of components of a complex waveform, whether or not that waveform is phonetic in nature. Duration and frequency are considered "primary auditory parameters" of phonetic stimuli. Changes in the duration of a component will alter both the total energy in that component (thus possibly its detectability or discriminability) and the relative spectral concentration (or spread) in energy of that component. This may alter the perceptual properties of that stimulus component, but in a manner that is in addition to the obvious manipulation of duration.

Interstimulus Interactions

Investigations of the perception of phonetic stimuli often propose alternative, nonphonetic psychoacoustic hypotheses involving seemingly simple models of masking, which actually involve some very specific implicit assumptions about the nature of masking (e.g., see next section). However, masking involves a complex set of stimulus interactions, which are still somewhat poorly understood. Thus, it is not surprising that these simple "psychoacoustic explanations" of phonetic phenomena seldom are found to be adequate in predicting phonetic interactions. Enough currently is known about the nature of masking to allow some realistic preliminary evaluations of its possible role in the perception of phonetic distinctions.

Masking may be defined as the interference with the perception of one signal (or aspect of a stimulus) caused by the presence of a second stimulus, called the masker. This seemingly simple definition of masking encompasses a multitude of different types of interactions, many of which probably involve very different sets of factors. One can better understand the complexity of masking by separately examining subsets of this class of interaction phenomena, and by consistently using different terms for these various subsets. The term *masking* is used for interactions involving the detection of the presence or absence of a signal, whereas the term *recognition masking* is used when the task involves the identification of specific aspects of a signal whose presence is not in question. (Although the distinction between masking and recognition masking is very important, these two types of stimulus interaction may represent a subdivision on a continuum rather than the existence of two discrete classes of task-related interactions, because the differences between detection, discrimination, and recognition are not always discrete—something we discuss later.) Both masking and recognition masking can be subdivided into simultaneous and nonsimultaneous masking—a distinction that is based on the temporal relation between the signal and the masker. These may be subdivided, respectively, into continuous and gated simultaneous masking, and backward and forward nonsimultaneous masking. Although further distinctions can be made, their apparent importance to the perception of phonetic segments is, most likely, marginal.

Masking

Masking is the interference with the detection of a signal due to the presence of a second stimulus. Detection refers to the ability to accurately report the presence or absence of a signal. Discrimination refers to the ability to accurately report the presence or absence of differences in the parameters of a signal that always is present. Recognition refers to the ability to identify the manner in which two stimuli differ. One could argue that the detection of a masked stimulus involves the discrimination of the effects of the masker plus the signal from the masker alone—this notion is the basis for models of signal detection theory. We use the term *masking* to refer to cross-stimulus interference effects associated with detection tasks and those discrimination tasks that may be interpreted as detection-type tasks.

In general, there are two basic types of models for masking. One type of model, cited earlier, was developed as an auditory application of statistical decision theory. It assumes that the effects of a signal are superimposed upon (and mixed with) the effects of "noise" in the environment and in the processing system. The task of the subject is to determine the likelihood that a given observation is a result of "signal-plus-noise" relative to the likelihood that it is the result of "noise-alone" (e.g., Green & Swets, 1966; Pastore & Scheirer, 1974). In a masking situation, the masker is simply another source of "noise." The second type of model has its origins in the vision and in the memory literature. It assumes that the masker disrupts either the memorial image of the stimulus or the processing of that memorial image. Many papers on phonetic perception that posit a "psychoacoustic" hypothesis involving masking (e.g., Repp, 1978) assume the validity of this latter type of model (although that assumption may not be explicit). Finally, Durlach and Braida (1969) have incorporated these two types of approaches as different stages in their model of observer behavior. Where appropriate, we compare the two types of models of masking in our discussion of the various types of masking.

Simultaneous Masking.   Simultaneous masking refers to the condition in which the masker is physically present throughout all time intervals that might contain the signal. When the masker and the signal are both sinusoids, one generally finds that, other things being equal, low-frequency maskers are more effective than high-frequency maskers, and the closer the signal and masker are in frequency, the greater the amount of masking (Wegel & Lane, 1924). However, when the signal and masker interact to produce beats, combination tones, or difference tones (i.e., making other things unequal), the amount of masking is reduced relative to maskers of similar frequency and intensity.

When the masker is a complex waveform or noise, it is primarily the masker energy within a band of frequencies surrounding the signal that masks the signal (Fletcher, 1940). This band of frequencies is called the critical band, and represents a kind of peripheral filter for the auditory system. As a rough approximation, the amount of masking (dB elevation in threshold due to the masker) is equal to the total amount of suprathreshold energy in the critical band of the signal (e.g., Hawkins & Stevens, 1950). Expressed mathematically,

$$M = E - T = (No - T)f', \tag{1}$$

where M is the amount of masking in dB, or the difference between the masked (E) and absolute (T) thresholds of the signal, *No* is the average power of the noise per unit bandwidth (i.e., power per one Hz bandwidth), and f' is the width of the critical band in Hz. In general, the width of the critical band is approximately constant for frequencies below 500 Hz, and is approximately proportional to the center frequency for higher frequencies. The critical band either can be measured indirectly using Eq. 1 and solving for f', or can be measured directly in terms of the predictable presence/absence of interstimulus interactions across frequencies. The critical band, when measured directly, is approximately 2.5 times larger than when measured indirectly and is approximately 25 times larger than the frequency difference limen for the given frequency (Zwicker, Flottorp, & Stevens, 1957).

If we assume that T is negligibly small relative to E and to *No* (and thus T may be dropped from Eq. 1), and that f' is a constant that is difficult to measure but that is dependent only on the frequency of the signal [thus f' = c(f)], we obtain the relationship

$$c(f) = E/No, \tag{2a}$$

which, expressed in dB, becomes:

$$10 \log c(f) = (10 \log E) - (10 \log No). \tag{2b}$$

c(f) is known as the signal-to-noise ratio and, at a given frequency, should be constant for constant performance. For a theoretical model of a perfectly efficient human observer (i.e., an ideal observer) in a Yes-No task,

$$10 \log d' = 10 \log (E/No) + C, \qquad\qquad (3)$$

where d' is the measure of observer sensitivity from the Gaussian Equal Variance Model of Signal Detection Theory (e.g., Green & Swets, 1966). This relationship is based upon the assumption that the effects of the signal and the masker are summated at a peripheral level, thus requiring that the observer discriminate between events that reflect only the effects of the masker and events that reflect the combined effects of the signal and the masker. As noted previously, the auditory system integrates energy in time, and thus E and No must be expressed as an average per unit time (arbitrarily set at one second). For example, assume that we have a gated 20 msec segment of a 3150 Hz sinusoid, which is masked by a continuous Gaussian noise. Using a sound level meter with a third octave filter set at 3.15 kHz (730 Hz bandwidth), we measure the continuous signal and noise to be 70 and 71 dB SPL, respectively. 10(log E) is 53 dB: 10(log It) = 70 + (10 log 0.02) = 70 − 17 = 53. 10 log No is 42.4 dB: 10(log I/f) = 71 − (10 log 730) = 71 − 28.6 = 42.4. Thus, 10 log E/No value of 10.6. Typically, a d' of approximately 1.0 is found for 10 log E/No values between approximately 9 and 12 (Green & Swets, 1966). Thus, with relatively continuous maskers, one can expect to find a relatively constant relationship between masker intensity and its effects on the signal.

This simple relationship is complicated when the masker is gated on or off in temporal proximity to the signal. Elliott (1965) found that the amount of masking associated with a 500 msec noise masker was greatest when the 10 msec tonal signal was presented near the onset or offset of the masker, and was minimal (but still significant) when presented during the temporally central portion of the masker. Others (e.g., Green, 1969; Green & Sewall, 1962) have found that simultaneous maskers gated on and off with the potential signal cause greater masking than the same broad-band maskers whose onsets and offsets are not in temporal proximity to the signal (and thus are essentially continuous). However, this superiority of gated over continuous masking has not always been found (e.g., Tucker, Williams, & Jeffress, 1968). Masking between the acoustic components of individual phonetic segments often may be considered to involve a gated, rather than continuous, type of masking.

Nonsimultaneous Masking.   Nonsimultaneous masking refers to those conditions in which the physical presentation of the signal and masker do not overlap in time. Forward masking is the condition in which the masker is presented before the signal, with the masking effect extending forward in time. Backward masking is the opposite temporal condition, where the effects of the later occurring masker extend backward in time (at least in terms of the physical stimuli). Both backward and forward masking are dependent on the time interval between the two stimuli (e.g., in forward masking, the time interval between masker offset and signal onset). For any given signal and masker, the amount of masking decreases with increased interstimulus interval, ISI, although for very brief signal and masker there may be less masking at an ISI of 1 msec than at an ISI of 5 msec (Penner, 1974). In general, large nonsimultaneous masking effects are found only for ISIs of up to approximately 20 to 40 msec, although masking can be measured to ISIs of 200 to 400 msec (Elliott, 1971) and even 1000 msec for backward masking (Samoilova, 1959). The forward masking paradigm typically yields far less masking than a simultaneous masking paradigm, with the amount of forward masking growing as a slower function of masker intensity (e.g., a 20 dB increase in masker intensity may yield only an 8 dB increase in forward masking but will yield a 20 dB increase in simultaneous masking). To be effective, the masker must be presented in the same earphone as the signal (Elliott, 1971), and must be within a frequency range somewhat greater than the critical bandwidth for the signal (Weber, 1978a). These and other findings have led to the conjecture that forward masking is related primarily to the peripheral processing of the stimuli (e.g., Weber, 1978b), and probably is related to a temporal integration of energy (Zwislocki, 1969).

Backward masking usually is found to be a more effective interference paradigm than forward masking (e.g., Elliott, 1971), and is believed to involve a more central processing of the stimuli (e.g., Weber, 1978b). Thus, although the intensity of the masker is still an important parameter, its frequency only need be within several critical bands of the signal (Weber, 1978a), and the masker can be presented to the other earphone (although the amount of masking from contralateral presentation will be reduced relative to the ipsilateral presentation [Elliott, 1971]). Furthermore, unlike simultaneous masking, where all contralateral cues appear to be lacking in effect (Pastore, Freda, & Barnett, 1977), the amount of backward masking can be reduced significantly by presenting, in the nonsignal earphone, any cue that provides temporal information about the potential signal (Puleo & Pastore, 1977). Thus, backward masking probably involves a high degree of temporal uncertainty. Other recent research from our laboratory indicates that stimulus change is an important factor in backward masking, with masker onsets and masker offsets being two types of stimulus change that can interfere with signal detection and discrimination (e.g., Pastore & MacLatchy, 1974; 1975). It is quite probable that backward masking is one factor influencing the perception of inital position consonants, and thus may be a major psychoacoustic factor in the categorical perception of some initial position consonants, as well as the perception of other phonetic segments (e.g., Pisoni, 1975). In our later discussion of categorical perception, we return to this conjecture, and use the foregoing discussion to propose a test of this hypothesis. Finally, if forward masking equally is a factor in the perception of final position consonants, one would expect to find that the perception of initial and final position consonants would exhibit similar temporal patterns of interactions, with the interactions occurring under more restricted conditions for final position consonants.

Recognition Masking.   Recognition masking is the interference with the differential identification of the properties of signals due to the presence of another stimulus. Because stimuli can differ in myriad ways, it is difficult to make the relatively simple types of summary generalizations about recognition masking that we have made about masking. Also, recognition masking has been subject to systematic investigation less often than simple masking. However, some generalizations are possible, especially in comparing masking and recognition masking. Hawkins and Stevens (1950) investigated both the masking and recognition masking effects of white noise on speech. In general, beyond levels near absolute threshold, a 10 dB change in the intensity of the masking noise caused a 10 dB change in threshold. Also, masking for speech waveforms closely corresponded to the masking of pure tones at 500, 1000, and 2000 Hz., whereas typically, the threshold for detecting the presence or absence of a speech signal is approximately 10 to 12 dB below the intelligibility or recognition threshold for the same speech waveforms. This classic discrepancy between masked detection threshold and masked recognition threshold is not unique to the perception of speech. Pastore (1973) investigated the detectability and discriminability of periodically and aperiodically interrupted noise waveforms masked by a continuous Gaussian noise. Again, the threshold for discriminating the periodic versus the aperiodic waveforms (with equal average periods) was approximately 10 to 12 dB higher than the threshold for detecting the presence of the interrupted waveform. In general, it would appear that the identification of the nature of differences between stimuli is a far more complex and demanding task than detecting a difference between two waveforms. Thus, as previously described, although the threshold for detecting the nonsimultaneous onset of two stimuli is only 1 to 2 msec, the threshold for temporal order identification is on the order of 15 to 20 msec (i.e., approximately 10 dB different [Hirsh, 1959]). However, there may be instances where one does not find this classic difference between detection and recognition performance.

Nonsimultaneous recognition masking is the interference with the identification, recognition, or discrimination of aspects of a signal when that signal is presented in nonsimultaneous temporal proximity to a second stimulus (or masker). This definition differs somewhat from some current definitions of nonsimultaneous recognition masking in that it does not specify the assumed nature of the mechanism. For instance, basing their notions on models of interference for visual stimuli, Kallman and Massaro (1978) define auditory backward recognition masking as "the ability of a masking sound to terminate further resolution of a test sound presented slightly earlier in time." This definition is far more restrictive (in a nonmeasurable manner) than our definition in that it requires the cessation of processing of the test signal due to the presentation of the masker.

Our definition allows for the existence of such discrete types of interaction, as well as other types of interaction more typical of the psychoacoustic literature. For instance, effects of the masker may summate with the effects of the signal (as was described for masking). Alternatively, the masker may serve to increase the uncertainty of the observer as to the parameters of the signal to be extracted (the concept of uncertainty is discussed in the following section). Note that both process-termination models and summation of effects models predict that the amount of backward recognition masking should decrease as the signal-to-masker interval increases, and both assume that the processing of a signal need not be completed at the offset of the physical signal. Furthermore, as is typical of most controversies, the question of the appropriate characterization of nonsimultaneous recognition masking is not easily resolved. For instance, the processing-termination notion should be effective for backward, but not forward, recognition masking, and thus predicts that, "other things being equal," backward recognition masking will be more effective than forward recognition masking—a finding reported by Massaro (1973). A model based upon the summation of stimulus information in time would not predict any major differences between backward and forward recognition masking, and such results have been reported by Cudahy and Leshowitz (1974). These discrepant findings might be attributable to procedural differences. However, they clearly do not justify the acceptance or rejection of either of the two types of models.

Massaro (1975, 1976) has argued that backward recognition masking occurs because the masker overrides all information held in a Preperceptual Auditory Storage (PAS), thus terminating access to that information for further analysis. However, Sparks (1976) recently found that backward recognition masking increases as one increases the similarity between the masker and the target stimulus. These results are consistent with models based on summation of information and the discrimination of a signal-plus-noise from noise alone. Kallman and Massaro (1978) have now replicated the Sparks results, and explain these similarity effects in terms of a second stage of memory (the Synthesized Auditory Memory or SAM) to which information is transferred from PAS at a constant rate. In backward recognition masking, the masking stimulus both interferes with the contents of SAM to an extent depending upon its similarity to the stimulus, and overrides all of PAS.

It should be obvious to the reader that there are several schools of thought concerning the nature of nonsimultaneous recognition masking, and that the phenomenon is far from simple. Thus, one may be only setting up an untenable hypothesis when one states that if backward masking were involved in the perception of sequentially presented phonetic components, then the onset of the second should simply wipe out the PAS representation of the first and thus cease its processing. Rather, one should attempt to make specific predictions concerning the nature of interactions based upon our knowledge of the many factors underlying nonsimultaneous masking.

Methodology

One major type of problem in trying to examine both psychoacoustics and phonetic perception arises from differences in the use of terms and methods. We already have dealt with one such difference in the models that are assumed to be implied by the term *masking*. In this section, we deal with differences in methodologies, some of which also cause differences in the meaning of terms.

Subject Uncertainty

Let's take a simple discrimination task—for the moment we will not be concerned whether it involves AX, ABX, AXB, or some other procedure. There are a number of different ways in which we can employ these tasks. In a "High Uncertainty Situation," one might: (1) employ a group of subjects who have had little or no experience with the stimuli and/or the procedure; (2) employ 10 to 20 different stimulus comparisons within a block of trials; and (3) collect a limited amount of data from each subject (usually no more than several hundred trials). Here, statistical power is achieved through the use of a reasonably large pool of subjects. Also, the use of more than approximately seven stimulus comparisons represents a load on the use of short-term memory for naive subjects, thus increasing uncertainty. This procedure is typical of speech research. In a "Low Uncertainty Situation," one: (1) gives the subjects considerable practice with the stimuli and task; (2) uses a limited number of stimulus comparisons within a block of trials; and (3) does not collect any data until performance has reached a stable level (e.g., an assumed asymptotic level). The use of such trained subjects for a sufficient period of time imposes a practical limitation on the number of subjects that can be run, and statistical power is obtained by collecting a large number of trials per subject. This procedure is typical of psychoacoustics research. In a "Very Low Uncertainty Situation," one practices subjects for months, or even years, until one is quite sure that performance has reached an asymptote. This procedure is very costly, and thus seldom employed (see Watson [1976] for an example of the use of this procedure). Although all three approaches yield measures of discrimination, one should not expect that these measures will necessarily be equivalent, in that each is used to answer a different question. The High Uncertainty Situation provides information about the stimulus information subjects most readily use when faced with the task. Here, one can expect the results to be weighted toward the use of cues with which the subjects are most familiar. Those cues will tend to be the ones that are most important in defining and differentiating the aspects of the acoustic stimuli important for linguistic communication. The Low and Very Low Uncertainty Situations, on the other hand, yield assessments of the stimulus information subjects can use to optimize performance. Here, one can expect a heavier weighting for cues which better differentiate between the stimuli being compared, with the cues approaching (for Low Uncertainty), or probably achieving (for Very Low Uncertainty), an optimal weighting. An excellent example of the differences between the High and Low Uncertainty situation may be found in the study of within-category discrimination of unvoiced stop consonants (in CV syllables) varying in voice onset time (VOT). In High Uncertainty situations, stimuli differing by a small, constant time (e.g., 2 msec) are generally found to be discriminated uniformly at chance, whereas in a Low Uncertainty situation, these same stimuli generally are discriminated at above chance levels, and appear to approximately follow the predictions of Weber's Law (Carney, Widin, & Viemeister, 1977; Pisoni & Lazarus, 1974; Samuel, 1977). Obviously, in high and low uncertainty situations, there is an elevation (or discontinuity) in the discrimination function at the category boundary. One cannot claim that discrimination measured in a low uncertainty situation is more or less valid than discrimination measured in a high uncertainty situation. Each is measuring a different level of human discrimination capability, and each measure provides estimates that should be valid indicators of discrimination for that level of processing—but not necessarily for the other level (although 100% discriminability in a high uncertainty condition should yield 100% discriminability in a low uncertainty condition). Each procedure limits the conclusions we may reach based upon our obtained results. In a high uncertainty situation, one cannot conclude that chance performance is an indication that the given stimuli are perceptually equivalent and indistinguishable. On the other hand, low uncertainty situations usually exist only in a laboratory, and the results may not be easily generalized to typical functioning in more realistic situations. Thus, measurements of frequency and/or intensity difference limen, when made under low uncertainty situations, may have only limited predictive value for examining the processing of speech stimuli, or other complex stimuli, in high uncertainty situations—even if that processing is based upon the discrimination of differences in frequency, or intensity, or both.

Detection and Discrimination Procedures

Most of the procedures employed in psychoacoustic research are based upon detailed models of stimulus processing under each procedure, with those models typically having been subjected to empirical tests. Two of the more common psychoacoustic procedures are the single interval Yes–No (Y–N) and the Two-Interval Temporal Forced-Choice (2IFC) procedures. In the Yes–No procedure, the subject must report whether or not a target stimulus was present during the single observation interval, whereas in the 2IFC procedure the subject must indicate which of the two observation intervals contained the signal. One can expect, on both theoretical and empirical grounds, that d' performance measures from a Yes–No and a 2IFC task will differ by a factor of $\sqrt{2}$ (e.g., d' for 2IFC $= \sqrt{2}\, d'$ for Y–N; (see Egan & Clarke, 1966, for explanation and discussion), and that the logarithm of d' from a Yes–No detection task will be a linear function of

10 log E/No (see Green & Swets, 1966). The advantages to the 2IFC procedure are its inherently bias-free nature and the existence of a strong theoretical basis for its use (e.g., Green & Swets, 1966).

Many of the procedures employed to study phonetic perception were developed (or adopted) because of the belief that one cannot easily describe phonetic stimuli as differing along a continuum in the simple manner that is characteristic of frequency or intensity of tonal stimuli. Thus, whereas an AX (or Same–Different) procedure can be employed to study categorical perception, a 2IFC task would seem to be inappropriate. Instead, matching procedures such as ABX, AXB, and Oddity tasks have been employed, thus avoiding the problem of having to specify a continuum. Only recently have these procedures been subjected to theoretical modeling (e.g., Macmillan, Kaplan, & Creelman, 1977). This analysis has shown that, relative to a Yes–No procedure, ABX tends to underestimate performance when discriminations are difficult (e.g., within-category discriminations in categorical perception studies) and overestimate performance when the discriminations are relatively easy (e.g., cross-category discriminations). In no way does this analysis claim that the matching procedures (e.g., ABX) are invalid. Rather, this theoretical (Kaplan, Macmillan, & Creelman, 1978) and empirical (Creelman & Macmillan, 1978; Pastore, Friedman, & Baffuto, 1976) work provides a basis for cross-procedure comparisons, such that the results obtained with these procedures can be better evaluated relative to the results obtained with more conventional procedures.

We should note that it is possible, and in fact easy, to employ a 2IFC procedure in a categorical perception task with phonetic stimuli varying in VOT. We have employed this procedure in a study involving a natural speech example of [pa], which was edited on the Haskins PCM2 system (Pastore, 1978a). We first presented extreme stimuli, describing each as having either a long aspirated noise (20 msec) or a short aspirated noise (1 msec). We then presented pairs of the stimuli from along the continuum in a random order, asking our subjects to indicate which of the two stimuli had the longer (or shorter) aspirated noise. Without either practice or feedback, the subjects (all experienced in psychoacoustic tasks) were able to perform the task in a stable and consistent manner, yielding data consistent with that expected on the basis of previously published research on categorical perception of voicing in initial stops employing ABX procedures. Thus, by appropriately posing the question to the subjects, one can, under some circumstances, employ a 2IFC procedure with phonetic stimuli, and thereby take advantage of the strong theoretical base inherent to this psychophysical procedure.

Labeling and Scaling Procedures

One seemingly simple way to study the perception of stimuli varying along a given physical continuum is to ask subjects to assign labels that describe their perception of stimuli drawn from along the continuum. However, any conclusions based upon the results of such a procedure must depend upon the assumptions being made about the nature of the underlying continuum and the behavior of the subjects in performing such tasks—whether or not those assumptions are stated explicitly. Fortunately, the nature of identification task behavior, and, thus, the relationships between detection, discrimination, identification, and scaling task results, have been both modeled and studied extensively for the intensity continuum by Durlach and Braida (e.g., Braida & Durlach, 1972; Durlach & Braida, 1969; Pynn, Braida, & Durlach, 1972). This model and associated research provides a strong theoretical framework for interpreting much recent research on identification and discrimination of phonetic segments.

The Durlach–Braida model is based upon both Thurstone's "Law of Categorical Judgment" (applied in a manner similar to Signal Detection Theory), and the notion of internal noise as developed in the applications of Signal Detection Theory. According to the model, the input waveforms are transformed by the auditory system into sensations that are subjected to noise (i.e., sensation noise). The sensations (or sensory traces) are stored while they are transformed into a decision variable, which then is compared to the response criteria to determine the appropriate response. The response criteria are based upon the context established by the range of the total set of stimuli employed in the study, as well as by the frequency and recency of presentation of the various stimuli within that set. The encoding and storage of this context information involves a context-coding mode of processing. The processes in the model are assumed to be subjected to memory noise (e.g., memory variability and failure), both at the stage where the sensory trace is maintained (e.g., through a rehearsal process in the sensory-trace stage), and in the specifications and storage of the general context of sounds in the experiment (context-coding mode) that establishes the response criteria. The sensory-trace noise involves such factors as a drift in the trace along the continuum, and interference from other stimuli. The context-coding noise involves such factors as an inability to accurately determine the stimulus context, and a limited ability to precisely determine the relationship between the sensory trace and the context.

The model, described in detail by Durlach and Braida (1969), has a number of implications that are important to the issues discussed in this chapter. First, in single interval tasks (e.g., magnitude estimation, category scaling, absolute identification) the sensitivity to any set of stimuli should be independent of the experimental task. Braida and Durlach (1972) have confirmed that total sensitivity under Absolute Identification and Category Scaling tasks are equivalent, but total sensitivity in both is appreciably greater than total sensitivity exhibited in Magnitude Estimation tasks—the latter deviating from the predictions of the model. Second, in single interval tasks, a large total range of stimuli should cause the classic discrepancy between discrimination and identification sensitivity. However, when the stimuli are closely spaced, one should not find differences between discrimination and identification performance sensitivity. Testing this implication of the theory, Pynn, Braida, and Durlach (1972) obtained results that were in general agreement with this prediction. Third, in multiple interval roving-standard tasks (e.g., 2IFC, AX, where A = S1, S2, . . . , Sn), the imperfections of memory become an important limitation to sensitivity only when both the total range of stimuli and the time interval between stimuli are large. This prediction was generally confirmed by Berliner and Durlach (1973). However, this third implication is not consistent with the models that claim memory is a major factor in the categorical perception of stimuli varying in VOT (e.g., Fujisaki & Kawashima, 1969; Pisoni, 1975). In studies of VOT, the range of VOT usually is relatively small (e.g., 30 msec or less; see next section for discussion of Categorical Perception). Finally, in comparing the results of single interval identification tasks, the model predicts equivalent results (subject to appropriate scale factors (e.g., $\sqrt{2}$ for 2IFC)) if the range of stimuli is identical across the two tasks, and the interstimulus interval in the two interval task is large. However, if the interstimulus interval is short, total observer sensitivity for the two types of tasks should not be equivalent. This prediction also was generally confirmed by Berliner and Durlach (1973).

In subjecting this theory to empirical verification, it was noted that discrimination performance at the edges or ends of the continuum defined by the stimulus set is better than predicted (e.g., Braida & Durlach, 1972). The magnitude of this "edge effect" was found to decrease as the range of the stimulus set was decreased (Berliner & Durlach, 1973). The "edge effect" was believed to involve the context-coding stage, with the continuum edges acting as references or anchors that improve the context coding, thus reducing that form of memory noise and improving discriminability in the region of the anchors. Subsequent research supported the notion that edges and other standards or reference stimuli tend to improve performance in various tasks (i.e., identification and discrimination) in the vicinity of the standard, except when the standard is in close proximity to other standards (Berliner, Durlach, & Braida, 1977). This notion serves as the basis of the Common Factor Model for Categorical Perception, which we have proposed (see following section).

Theoretical Constructs

Researchers studying psychoacoustics, auditory perception, and speech perception tend to differ in terms of the nature of the constructs employed in theorizing. In psychoacoustics, most constructs are assumed to be relatively peripheral in nature, and are used to provide theoretical organization for relatively small bodies of knowledge. Examples of psychoacoustic constructs include absolute thresholds, masked thresholds, and the critical band. In general, the philosophy seems to require that the constructs be well defined by the data, and that new constructs, or higher order constructs, are hypothesized only when other explanations of results are not possible. For many psychologists, this philosophy is too conservative. In auditory perception some theoretical constructs have been borrowed from models of memory. Consequently, theories of auditory perception have tended to emphasize multistage models, with each stage possessing certain assumed properties. Often, when data are not consistent with the assumed properties of a given construct, new constructs are conjectured. An example of this approach is the description of recognition masking in terms of PAS and SAM (Kallman & Massaro, 1978). For most researchers in psychoacoustics, these constructs are too far removed from the data to be very useful. In speech perception, theoretical constructs are assumed to be of a higher order in nature, and usually are intended to provide an organization for relatively large subsections of the processing of speech stimuli. Linguistic and auditory feature detectors represent one such type of construct. Usually, such constructs are based upon some relative broad conceptions of speech processing, with subsequent research directed toward mapping the specific characteristics of the construct. From the perspective of the more conservative psychoacousticians, such constructs often seem ill-defined. Each of these approaches to theory construction often serves as a source for criticism from researchers in the other areas, yet each approach has merits, and each has problems.

PERCEPTION OF SPEECH AND OTHER COMPLEX STIMULI

Categorical Perception

The phenomenon known as categorical perception once was touted as a clear example of a phenomenon that was both a critical component in and unique to the perception of speech (e.g., Mattingly, 1972; Studdert-Kennedy, Liberman, Harris, & Cooper, 1970). Recent research has tended to contradict the claims about the uniqueness of this phenomenon, thus modifying our conception of the phenomenon, but not changing its role as underlying the perception of many phonetic distinctions.

Categorical perception was conjectured to occur (Studdert-Kennedy, Liberman, Harris, & Cooper, 1970) when stimuli along a continuum "are responded to, *and can only be responded to, in absolute terms* [p. 234; italics theirs]." Thus, the ability to discriminate between two stimuli should be based solely on the ability of the subject to differentially label the stimuli. According to Studdert-Kennedy et al. (1970), the operational criteria for the existence of categorical perception are: (1) distinct labeling categories separated by a sharp boundary; (2) chance performance for discriminating stimuli drawn from within the same category; (3) a peak in discrimination performance at the category boundary; and (4) close correspondence between discrimination performance and the predicted discriminability based upon the labeling performance. This phenomenon is characteristic of the perception of a number of speech continua, including the continua for voiced and voiceless initial position stop consonants (Liberman, Harris, Kinney, & Lane, 1961) and the continua for initial position consonants differing in place of articulation (Liberman, Harris, Hoffman, & Griffith, 1957). Our discussion focuses primarily on these two contrasts inasmuch as they have been the most extensively studied and the findings are representative of other phonetic contrasts.

According to one purely phonetic interpretation of this phenomenon, the stimuli, once recognized as speech, are recoded and processed in a phonetically discrete categorical nature with the loss of the more primitive auditory properties (the phonetic recoding process may be assumed to involve either higher level abstract categorization processes [e.g., Studdert-Kennedy et al., 1970] or phonetic feature detection [e.g., Eimas, 1975]). With the loss of the auditory properties, the only source of information available for discriminating the stimuli would be their differential categorization by the phonetic processor. Based upon subsequent research (see following) demonstrating categorical perception for nonphonetic stimuli, we recently proposed an alternative model for categorical perception. We proposed that one will tend to find categorical perception whenever there is a relatively precise, stable reference along a continuum (Pastore, Ahroon, Baffuto, Friedman, Puleo, & Fink, 1977). Such a reference would provide greater information to the system for discriminating between stimuli than would be available elsewhere on the continuum—thus creating a discrimination peak at the location of the reference. The reference also may be used as a criterion or anchor point for labeling or scaling stimuli along the continuum. The reference may be in the form of a threshold (e.g., fusion threshold for visual stimuli varying in interruption rate [Pastore, 1976]), or in the form of a stable, continuous stimulus (e.g., a tone of fixed intensity for an intensity continuum [Pastore et al., 1977] or the grave line, $\diagdown$ in the letters v or y for the relative length of the acute line, $\diagup$ [Pastore, 1978a]). The Braida–Durlach "edge effect" is another example of the effects of a reference. Our model is discussed further in terms of its specific predictions for phonetic stimuli that have exhibited categorical characteristics.

Before discussing the nature of phonetic stimuli that exhibit categorical perception, it is of value to re-examine the criteria for categorical perception in the context of the Durlach–Braida model discussed earlier. According to that model, total measured sensitivity should be equivalent for identification and discrimination tasks, and thus one should be able to predict discrimination performance from identification performance along the continuum—subject to appropriate scale factors associated with the discrimination procedures. The model predicts that one should find a close correspondence between the actual discrimination performance and discrimination performance predicted from the identification task (criterion d in Studdert-Kennedy et al.'s [1970] definition). Also, a distinct labeling boundary (criterion a) should be associated with a discrimination peak (criterion c), thus these criteria of Studdert-Kennedy can be combined to form a single criterion (*a-c-d*). This reduces the four Studdert-Kennedy criteria (see foregoing) to two, (*a-c-d*) and (*b*).

Macmillan (Macmillan et al., 1977) has shown that the discrimination procedures often employed in categorical perception studies relative to more common procedures tend to overestimate discriminability when discriminability is relatively good, and tend to underestimate discriminability when the discrimination task is difficult. This would tend to enhance the probability of finding chance performance within categories and would tend to cause discrimination performance to be greater than predicted near the category boundary (an often-reported finding). Finally, when uncertainty in the situation is reduced by employing well-practiced subjects, chance performance has not been found within categories, even for the phonetic stimuli claimed to exhibit categorical perception (e.g., Carney et al., 1977; Pisoni & Lazarus, 1974; Samuel, 1977). Thus, known acoustic and phonetic continua meet only the first (*a-c-d*) criterion for categorical perception, and may better be described as exhibiting a "category boundary effect" (Wood, 1976). This still leaves us with an important characteristic of the given continua, and with the difficult task of trying to identify the acoustic basis for the reference that is responsible for the category boundary effect. (For historical accuracy, we use the term *categorical perception* when all four of Studdert-Kennedy et al.'s [1970] criteria were met, and the term *category boundary effect* when the reduced criteria were met. Based upon the logic summarized previously, the two terms should be viewed as being synonymous.)

Perception of Phonetic Contrasts

Voicing

The role of F1-transitions in the definition of initial position CV syllables contrasting in voicing was studied by Liberman, Delattre, and Cooper (1958). Shortening the F1-transition of voiced consonants by approximately 20 msec (i.e., eliminating the first 10 to 30 msec of the transition) while maintaining the temporal position of the release burst had the effect of changing the perception of voiced initial consonants to their unvoiced counterparts. We should note that the procedure of cutting back the F1-transition not only shortens the duration of the transition, but also raises its starting frequency. When the F1-transition was cut back, the substitution of noise for the harmonics in the F2- and F3-transitions improved the voiceless perception of the stimuli. However, in the absence of the F1-transition cutback, this substitution of noise for the F2- and F3-transitions (or even for all three formant transitions) was ineffective in changing the perception of the stimuli from voiced to voiceless. Thus, the presence of a F1-transition is important in determining the voicing value of phonetic stimuli. (The F1-transition also influences the degree to which stimuli are perceived as consonantal in nature [Delattre, Liberman, & Cooper, 1955]). In a similar vein, Lisker, Liberman,

Erickson, Dechovitz, and Mandler (1978) have shown that manipulations of the duration and extent of the first formant transition leads to significant changes in the VOT boundary (i.e., interval between release burst and voicing onset) for the voiced–voiceless distinction (e.g., between /da/ and /ta/). Furthermore, only at longer F1-transition durations do the higher formant transitions have any effect on this VOT boundary (and even then, that effect is small). (For discussion of alternative cues for the voiced–voiceless, see Stevens & Klatt, 1974.)

Stop consonants, contrasting in voicing in the initial position of CV syllables, have been reported to be perceived categorically when the stimuli are varied in terms of VOT, which is defined as the time between the release of stop closure and the onset of voicing (e.g., Liberman, Harris, Eimas, Lisker, & Bastian, 1961). Miller, Wier, Pastore, Kelly, and Dooling (1976) have found categorical perception for analogous nonphonetic stimuli, specifically, Gaussian noise and filtered pulse-trains (buzz) in place of the aspirated noise and the vowel formants (although noise and buzz had simultaneous offsets). Miller et al.'s stimuli were not perceived as being speech, but exhibited labeling and discrimination functions that matched those found with analogous voiced and voiceless stop consonants in CV syllables. However, neither the noise stimuli in isolation, nor stimuli with the noise substituted for the buzz, exhibited categorical perception. So, it is the perception of the noise in relationship to the buzz that is important for categorical perception. Miller et al. conjectured that categorical perception for this, and related, continua involves a masked threshold. Subthreshold stimuli do not have detectable noise stimuli, and are discriminated at chance; suprathreshold stimuli have a detectable noise and the discrimination functions follow Weber's Law. Discriminability between a subthreshold and a suprathreshold stimulus should be relatively good, because the discrimination is across the perceptual discontinuity of the masked threshold—a discontinuity upon which labels may easily be anchored. Note that this analysis could be valid for thresholds of either masking or recognition masking. For instance, one possibility is that both onsets were always clearly detectable, but that the subjects simply could not identify which stimulus had the earlier onset (i.e., recognition masking).

Recently, Pisoni (1977) demonstrated categorical perception for tonal stimuli differing in relative time of onset. This would appear to be a clear demonstration of categorical perception involving the temporal order threshold described by Hirsh (1959). However, because the low-frequency tone (500 Hz) always was 12 dB more intense than the high-frequency tone (1500 Hz), one cannot completely rule out the possibility that the perception of the onset of the high-frequency tone was masked by the more intense low-frequency tone for relatively brief stimulus onset asynchronies. That possibility would be eliminated only if the identical results were obtained either with both stimuli equal in intensity, or with the high-frequency tone more intense. This experimental manipulation would significantly alter the expected masking pattern but, based upon Hirsh's finding of intensity independence, should not alter temporal order identification.

Although these studies of categorical perception for the initial components of time-varying nonphonetic stimuli clearly demonstrate that such categorical perception is not unique to phonetic stimuli, they do not provide a complete explanation of the phenomenon for phonetic stimuli varying in VOT. The most likely psychoacoustic explanations are: (1) a limitation on temporal order identification; (2) a backward masking of the aspirated noise; and (3) a backward recognition masking of the aspirated noise. These alternatives should be subjected to experimental test based upon the psychoacoustic relationships summarized earlier. In studies involving VOT, one is varying the total duration of the aspirated noise, with the maximum duration typically being less than 100 msec. The shortening of this component of CV syllables increases the spread in energy across frequency. However, because the aspirated noise is spectrally broad, encompassing several critical bands, it is doubtful that those changes in effective bandwidth would be perceptually significant. Because the durations of the aspirated noise are within the limits for temporal integration, reductions in duration lead to proportional reductions in the effective intensity of the noise. Although this change in intensity should not affect the threshold for temporal order identification (see foregoing, and Hirsh, 1959), it should be important if categorical perception is based upon a threshold for detecting the presence of the noise, or identifying the nature of the noise. If that threshold is based upon some type of simultaneous masking, we should find a relatively perfect trading (+3 dB per halving of duration) between duration and instantaneous intensity. However, it is more likely that backward masking defines the threshold (e.g., masking from the vowel formants), and so there should be a far less than perfect trading relationship. This is because the effectiveness of backward masking is an inverse function of the temporal distance from the onset of the masker. Therefore, shortening the duration of the aspirated noise by eliminating its first n-msec serves to remove that portion of the stimulus least subjected to backward masking, leaving the noise cue concentrated in the more effective temporal region for backward masking. With backward masking, the effects of shortening the duration of the noise cue can be overcome only by increasing the intensity of the noise by an amount predicted by temporal summation plus the increase in backward masking effectiveness.

To summarize, if alternative (1) is valid, manipulating the intensity of the aspirated noise should have no effect on the location of the category boundary. However, if alternatives (2) or (3) are valid, raising the intensity of the aspirated noise (with vowel constant) should move the category boundary toward shorter VOTs. Repp (1979) has reported finding just such an intensity-dependent relationship. Also, because contralateral timing cues are effective in reducing backward masking (but not simultaneous or forward masking), we would expect that a contralateral timing cue should lead to significantly improved discrimination along the VOT continuum. We have found such a relationship using a sinusoidal cue (3 KHz) and natural speech edited with the Haskins PCM2 system (Pastore, 1978b). We also would expect such a cue, which partially counteracts backward masking, to shift the category boundary toward shorter VOT—a hypothesis we currently are testing. However, because we do not know what effects such a cue would have in either a backward recognition masking situation or a temporal order identification situation, we cannot interpret these findings as favoring the backward masking hypothesis, although these findings certainly are consistent with such an hypothesis. Probably the most direct tests of these hypotheses would be a measurement of the detection and recognition thresholds for several durations of aspirated noise in CV context. If either the detection or the recognition results predict the category boundaries for the continuum (VOT and intensity) involving the stimuli, then those results would be strong support for the given hypothesis. To the best of our knowledge, this experiment has not yet been conducted. Such experiments could provide strong support for a psychoacoustic explanation for the VOT category boundary effect for initial stops. However, if such experiments fail to exhibit the types of phonetic results predicted from the perception of nonphonetic stimuli, we will have strong support for positing a uniquely phonetic explanation, with a much better understanding of the specific characteristics that must be unique.

Place of Articulation

The first demonstration of categorical perception was with two formant CV syllables that varied in the extent and direction of the F2-transition (Liberman, Harris, Hoffman, & Griffith, 1957), signaling differences in place of articulation. The consonant of the CV syllables was perceived as [d], [g], or [b], with discrimination performance being considerably better for stimuli separated by a phonetic boundary than for stimuli drawn from within a single phonetic category. In this experiment the consonant [b] was characterized by a sharply rising second formant transition (e.g., more rapid change in frequency than found in the F1-transition), whereas [d] was characterized by more gradually rising, steady-state, or gradually falling F2-transitions, and [g] by falling F2-transitions. A superficial examination of the physical stimulus patterns might lead one to conjecture that the [d]−[g] boundary corresponds to the detection of falling versus rising F2-transitions, whereas the [d]−[b] boundary corresponds to detection of less rapid versus more rapid F2-transitions. However, other research on the physical characteristics of auditory cues associated with the place of articulation would seem to indicate that the phonetic boundaries are not so simply defined. For instance, Mattingly, Liberman, Syrdal, and Halwes (1971) studied two-formant synthetic CV syllables with a varying F2-transition. They found that [d] was characterized by a slightly rising, or a steady–state, or a slightly falling F2-transition. As the rate of frequency change in the F2-transition became more rapid, the perception of [b] or [g] became stronger, yet the stimuli became less feasible for the human articulatory system to produce (Mattingly, 1972). Single formant versions of these stimuli consisting of F2 alone, which were perceived as nonspeech "bleats," did not exhibit categorical perception (Mattingly et al., 1971).

Delattre, Liberman, and Cooper (1955) studied the perceptual consequences of manipulating the F2-transitions in two formant synthesized stimuli. Keeping F1 (and the 50 msec F1-transition) constant and the beginning of the F2-transition fixed at 1800 Hz (the theoretical "starting locus" for [d]), they varied the frequency of the steady-state portion of F2 (and thus the direction and extent of the F2-transition). The initial consonant was perceived as [d], [g], [d], and [b], respectively, as the F2 was increased from 720 Hz to 2520 Hz. With the elimination of the first 50 msec of these F2-transitions by substituting silence (together with a 50 msec delay in the onset of the F1-transition), all stimuli were perceived as [d]. However, if the F2-transitions were shorter than 50 msec, not all stimuli were perceived as [d]. The critical parameter for perceiving all stimuli as [d] appears to be that the F2-transition be 50% of the original F2-transition, measured from the original common starting locus (frequency) to the steady-state frequency of the second formant—so long as the original F2-transition was at least 80 msec in duration. Similar findings were reported for series of stimuli based upon a [b] and a [g] locus, although there was not any silent interval (or second formant cutback) for which only [g] was heard with the [g] locus series.

The foregoing summarized conclusions must be limited by the nature of the manipulations performed on the physical stimuli, namely: (1) the fixed starting locus of the F2-transition (which corresponds to the position of the articulating system set to begin the production of the consonant); and (2) the substitution of silence for voicing during the initial portion of the stimuli. For these factors to be important for perception, the auditory system must be able to compute a more appropriate duration (in the absence of stimulation, how can the listener know when the appropriate "silent interval" begins?) and, from this, compute the appropriate starting locus of the articulatory system (because one must know the theoretical duration of an FM glide to compute the hypothesized starting locus). That is, the notion of a system based upon a common starting locus, or an initial starting frequency, may make sense in the context of both the initial position of the articulatory system in producing such stimuli, and the synthesis of an artificially produced set of stimuli, but not in terms of a perceptual system that must deal with individual stimuli differing in terms of the duration, rate, and extent of the second formant transition. (Although the initial release burst might be a cue for the duration of the transition, it does not appear that a release burst was employed in this study. Also, any perceptual algorithm based upon the interval between the release burst and voicing onset [i.e., VOT] would have to be fairly complex [e.g., Lisker et al., 1978].) With the information available in the Delattre study, a 40 msec transition falling from 1000 to 720 Hz might actually have originated 50 msec earlier (before a 50 msec silent interval) at 1800 Hz, or 60 to 80 msec earlier (before a 60 to 80 msec silent interval) at 3000 Hz. It would make more sense to examine the perceptual representation of FM glides varying in direction, duration, ending frequency, and extent. Research into such perception only recently has begun and, in the future, may provide an alternative, possibly more perceptually realistic, hypothesis concerning the nature of the transitional cue for consonants. In the next section we examine the psychoacoustics of stimuli whose spectral envelope is systematically altered as a function of time. We should note, however, that the Delattre study does provide a very important mapping of the range of physical stimuli varying in the duration and extent of F2-transitions (with delayed F1) in the perceptual phonetic space.

FM Glides in Isolation.   Psychoacoustic examinations of the perception of FM glides has been quite limited, although interest in possible psychoacoustic bases of phonetic perception has motivated a number of recent investigations. These investigations have employed FM glides presented in isolation, and FM glides in the context of both leading and trailing tones (corresponding to the initial and final frequencies of the glide), but only a very limited number have studied glides in the restricted context of leading or trailing tones. Within the context of both leading and trailing tones, Nàbělek and Hirsh (1969) have found that brief silent intervals between tones are perceived as being approximately equivalent to the interval being filled with a transitional FM glide. Also, thresholds (f') for detecting the presence of a brief glide tend to be considerably larger when the glide occurs near the beginning, rather than near the center or end of the complex stimulus (Tsumura, Sone, & Nimura, 1973). Although these and similar studies (e.g., Nàbělek, 1976) are important in their own right, and may be important for understanding connected speech, the use of leading tones makes the results difficult to generalize to the study of initial position consonants.

Pollack (1968) studied the ability of subjects to identify the direction of isolated FM glides as a function of the stimulus duration (t) and the rate of change in frequency (f'/t, where f' is the total change in frequency). Pollack measured the 75% recognition thresholds for correct identifications. Over an initial range of stimulus duration from 500 msec to 4.0 sec, rate of frequency (f'/t) and duration (t) exhibited a nearly perfect trading relationship. That is, total frequency change [$f' = (f'/t) \times (t)$] was approximately constant at threshold. (Over a range of durations from 75 msec to 10 sec, Sergeant & Harris [1962] found a similar, although somewhat less perfect, trading relationship). The magnitude of the change in frequency at recognition threshold was approximately a constant proportion of the starting frequency, and was nearly equivalent to the frequency recognition threshold for tonal stimuli with identical starting frequencies. When starting frequency was varied randomly across trials, Pollack found that the total frequency change at threshold for the glides increased by 40 to 80%, and thus was somewhat poorer than the thresholds for tonal stimuli. Finally, Pollack found some evidence that brief glides (e.g., less than 30 msec) may be processed differently than longer glides. With the longer glides, subjects appear to exhibit some ability to track, and respond more to the changing frequency. With brief glides, the subjects may respond more to the total spectral pattern of the stimuli. Whereas such discrimination studies tell us a great deal about psychophysical differences between glides and tones, they tell us very little about the perceptual consequences of a monotonic change in frequency across time.

Brady, House, and Stevens (1961) studied the perception of isolated, single moving resonances stimulated by a short train of pulses with a repetition rate of 100 cps. The resonances were varied in a linear fashion between terminal frequencies of 1500 and 1000 Hz over a duration of from 10 to 80 msec. Subjects adjusted the frequency of an equivalently stationary resonance until the two stimuli were judged to be most alike. This study demonstrated that the perception of a changing resonance corresponds neither to a following of the changing frequency, nor to the subjective impression of a simple frequency average, but rather to some form of weighted average. Subjects tended to adjust the stationary resonance to roughly match the terminal frequency of the time varying resonance stimulus, whether the stimuli were rising or falling across the fixed frequency range. However, brief stimuli involving only one or two pulses tended to be matched to frequencies 50 to 100 Hz short of the terminal frequency (i.e., frequencies closer to the mean frequency of the glide). For brief resonance glides, the addition of a stationary leading resonance shifted the matched frequency to the mean frequency of the changing resonance (when a 20 msec change was stimulated by two pulses) or even to the initial frequency of the resonance (when a 10 msec change was stimulated by a single pulse).

In an analogous study, Whittaker (1978) attempted to investigate the perceptual consequences of linear changes in frequency by having subjects match tonal stimuli to the perceived pitch of glides. Although also finding the absence of a simple relationship between physical spectrum and perceived pitch, Whittaker's results differed from the Brady results in several respects. Glides rising in frequency (upglides) that cover a range of greater than 20 Hz tend to be perceived as having a pitch quality corresponding to frequencies higher than the highest frequency in the glide. The magnitude of this perceptual overestimate of pitch is positively correlated with both the duration of the glide and the total range of frequencies covered by the glide. Glides falling in frequency (downglides), on the other hand, have a pitch corresponding to frequencies slightly below the mean frequency in the glide. Furthermore, as either the duration or the frequency extent of the downglide is increased, the pitch-matched frequency tends to better match the mean frequency in the glide. Finally, when the frequency range or extent of the glides are narrow (e.g., 10 Hz or less), both upglides and downglides were perceived as having a pitch quality equivalent to a somewhat lower frequency than any frequency in the glide. The stimuli employed in the Brady and the Whittaker studies differ significantly along many physical dimensions. It is impossible to explain the difference in the results without further investigation. If these or similar types of perceptual relationships are applicable to glides in the presence of relatively stable following components (e.g., vowel formants), one would have to expect that any category boundary based upon the perception of the pitch quality of the transition in relation to the following stimulus would not directly correspond to the simple physical characteristics of the stimulus spectrum as determined by visual inspection of the spectogram—yet this is one common source of acoustical hypotheses to explain the perception of these phonetic stimuli.

Finally, how susceptible are isolated glides to the effects of masking? To date, this question has been addressed only for simultaneous masking. Ronken (1973) studied the masking effect of tone glides on brief tonal signals. Nàbĕlek (1976) measured the masked thresholds for downglides with initial frequencies of 1.0kHz in a broad band white noise masker. In general, glides have higher masked thresholds than tones. Furthermore, the masked threshold appears to be correlated with the rate of frequency change in the glide. Nàbĕlek (1978) extended the foregoing investigation to employ both upglides and downglides over a broader range of frequencies. For glide durations of greater than 10 msec, both types of glides have higher thresholds (by 5 to 10 dB) than tones with equivalent duration and a frequency equal to the terminal frequency in the glides. Furthermore, as the frequency range covered by the glide increases, the masked threshold increases. These general findings also have been reported by Collins and Cullen (1978). Nàbĕlek (1978) further found that for durations between approximately 10 and 200 msec, downglides have higher masked thresholds than upglides. At durations greater than approximately 200 msec, the masked thresholds for the two types of glides are equal and, at durations greater than one second, masked thresholds for glides are lower than masked thresholds for tones. At very short durations (less than 10 msec), the masked thresholds for tones and glides are equivalent. These differences between masked thresholds for tones and glides are consistent with the notion that the width of the glide (and the tone) spectrum is correlated with the spectral density (I/Hz) of the stimulus, and thus with the signal-to-noise ratio. That is, for any given duration and total intensity, the spectrum of the glides is broader than the spectrum of the tones and accordingly has less power per unit bandwidth. This broader spread in energy over frequency means that, at any given duration, a glide is more likely (than a tone) to exceed the width of a single critical band. Because stimulus energy is integrated in time (for t less than approximately 250 msec) primarily within a critical band of frequencies, the energy in the glide outside the critical band is effectively lost. Thus, the effective total intensity of the glide will be reduced by this spread in power beyond the critical band. Following the same logic, spectrally broad glides will have a lower effective intensity than spectrally narrow glides. Finally, at very brief durations (e.g., t < 10 msec), the spectrum of the tones and glides may be sufficiently broad to make other differences between tones and glides negligible.

Cullen and Collins (1978) investigated the masked thresholds for pairs of isolated glides roughly corresponding in frequency to a pair of "average" F1- and F2-formant transitions, as well as pairs of tones equivalent in frequency to the average frequency of the glides. The masked thresholds for brief stimuli (5 and 10 msec) were approximately equivalent, and therefore were independent of the nature of the stimulus. At durations of 35 msec or longer (35, 50, 90, 120 msec, no other durations being employed), the masked thresholds for pairs of either parallel glides (both upglides or downglides), or nonparallel glides (up-glides with downglides), were equal to the masked thresholds for single glides and were considerably poorer than the masked thresholds for tones.

FM Glides as Transitions to Stimuli.   The studies discussed in the immediate foregoing section primarily concern isolated glides—tonal analogues to isolated formant transitions or "chirps." It has been shown that chirps are not perceived in the same manner as the identical waveform in phonetic context (i.e., when followed by vowel formants, i.e., Dorman, 1974). For a number of reasons, ranging from nonsimultaneous masking effects (see the section on nonsimultane-ous masking) to implications of the Durlach-Braida model (see the section on labeling and scaling procedures, especially the "edge effect"), we would expect the perception of a glide to be altered by the context provided by a trailing tone that is equal in frequency to the termination of the glide. For instance, trailing stimuli can, under certain circumstances, provide a reference against which one may judge the relative characteristics of the glides. Then, rather than having to judge the absolute frequency (or intensity) of the glide (or the frequency [or intensity] relative to some memorial representation), one may make a direct comparison.

Trailing stimuli also may serve to mask the initial transition, especially if the initial transition and trailing stimuli are spectrally different. In the presence of such differences, the subject must be able to identify and extract the appropriate characteristics of the transition in the context of a large set of different and changing stimulus parameters. An example of these types of effects may be found in an interpretation of a set of studies examining intensity discrimination for initial stimuli. If the initial stimulus involves a change in frequency leading to the trailing stimulus, the subject must extract information concerning changes in intensity from the context provided by simultaneous uncorrelated changes in frequency (a task involving a high degree of stimulus parameter uncertainty). The discrimination would be easier if the trailing stimulus were a spectral con-tinuation of the initial stimulus. Furthermore, if the trailing stimulus also is identical in intensity to the unincremented or undecremented intensity of the initial stimulus (thus minimizing stimulus parameter uncertainty), discriminabil-ity should be optimal. These are precisely the findings reported by Dorman (1974) and Cutting (Cutting & Dorman, 1976) for synthetic CV syllables, and by Pastore (Pastore, Ahroon, Wolz, Puleo, & Berger, 1975) for both tonal and glide analogues to the Dorman stimuli. Under conditions similar to the Dorman and the Pastore intensity discrimination studies, we have found a similar pattern of results in a frequency discrimination study (Pastore, Friedman, & Barnett, 1978). The task of the subjects was to identify which of two tones (60 msec initial stimuli) was higher in frequency. The stimuli were presented either in isolation or in the presence of identical 240 msec trailing tones. When the trailing tone was identical in frequency to one of the two initial tones, the task was much easier than when the initial tones were presented in isolation. Here, the trailing tone acted as a useful reference for the subjects, allowing the subjects to respond on the basis of which of the initial tones differed from the trailing tone. On the other hand, when there was a highly detectable change in frequency between each of the two initial tones and the trailing tone, large differences in frequency were required before subjects could identify which of two initial tones was higher in frequency. This interference was found for a broad range of frequency differences (e.g., up to 1000 Hz) between the initial and trailing frequencies. We suspect that performance would be much poorer with spectrally changing stimuli (e.g., glides), but have not yet run those conditions.

Bailey, Summerfield, and Dorman (1977) investigated the identification of sinusoidal analogues to three formant CV syllables, approximately a [bo-do] and a [bε-dε] place continuum. The stimuli were presented in an *AXB* format, where *A* and *B* were the terminal stimuli from the continuum under investigation and *X* was selected from the set of intermediate stimuli. The task of the subjects was to identify *X* as being more like *A* or more like *B*. The subjects were all given three blocks of identification and six blocks of discrimination trials with feedback, then nine blocks of each type of trial without feedback. Only the last six blocks of each type of trial were included in the results. Each block of trials involved two presentations of each stimulus comparison, once for each possible ordering of *A* and *B*. It was found that some subjects perceived the stimuli as being speech-like, whereas others did not. These two groups of subjects systematically yielded differences in the patterns of results, both from the identification tasks and from the discrimination tasks (differences in both the sharpness and the location of the category boundary). These results were interpreted as demonstrating differences between an acoustic and a higher level phonetic mode of processing the stimuli. Whereas this may in fact be the case, there are several alternative interpretations. First, although the subjects were given practice with the stimuli, this practice was minimal by psychoacoustic standards (there were a total of 24 and 34 presentations of each stimulus/subject for identification and discrimination respectively, including both practice and nonpractice trials), and so may be considered to be examples of high uncertainty situations (see the section on subject uncertainty). The feedback, being based upon the spectral similarity of the physical stimuli, rather than being based upon any subjective psychoacoustic distances between stimuli, may have served to confuse the subjects. It may be that some subjects were able to successfully ignore the effects of feedback by viewing the stimuli as being speech-like. Alternatively, it is possible that the major difference between the two groups of subjects was solely a difference in the types of stimulus information the subjects tended to weigh more heavily in performing the task. Although these latter two hypotheses involve differences in the ''modes of processing'' between the two groups, these differences are not interesting either in an acoustic or in a phonetic sense. These hypotheses are quite consistent with our knowledge of the behavior of subjects in such measurement tasks, so are as likely as the hypothesis that the data are indicative of higher order differences in processing acoustic and phonetic stimuli.

FM glides do not allow for the same simplicity of specification as allowed by sinusoidal stimuli, and consequently do not allow for the same precision in theoretical interpretation. There is far less empirically derived knowledge concerning the perception of isolated glides than isolated tones, and even less knowledge concerning the perceptual interaction between glides and either leading or trailing stimuli. In the absence of such knowledge, it is difficult to generate reasonable hypotheses concerning possible psychoacoustic bases for the perception of initial place distinctions. Obviously, far more research is required before we will be able to generate such reasonable hypotheses, yet such knowledge and hypotheses are critical for understanding precisely how the perception of such phonetic stimuli differs from the perception of analogous nonphonetic stimuli (and thus what constitutes the characteristics of the appropriate feature detector).

In our discussions, we have dealt only with initial position consonants. Mattingly (Mattingly et al., 1971) studied the perception of nonphonetic bleats in initial and final position, and found the perception of the two classes of stimuli to differ. Given the psychoacoustic differences between forward and backward interference effects, the Mattingly results are not entirely surprising. However, our knowledge of the psychoacoustics of trailing glides is even more inadequate than our limited knowledge of initial position glides. Thus, we certainly are not in a position to propose a specific model for a psychoacoustic basis for the perception of such nonphonetic stimuli. Rather, we can only suggest the types of questions whose answers might be important for developing a reasonable and testable model for initial and final position place cues for consonants. For selected samples of F1 and F2, what are the minimal changes in starting (or, for final position, ending) frequency necessary for the detection of the presence of a transition or glide as a function of the duration of that transition or glide? Also, for each F1 and F2, what are the minimal starting (or ending) frequencies necessary for the accurate identification of the transition as rising or falling relative to the steady-state F1 or F2? Finally, are these results correlated with the phonetic boundaries found for analogous speech stimuli, and, if not, might there be a reasonable psychoacoustic explanation for the differences? In the context of this type of detailed analysis, significant unexplained aspects of phoneme perception may be attributed to specialized feature detectors, with that hypothetical construct then being reasonably well characterized.

Alternative Spectral Cues.   Stevens and Blumstein (e.g., 1978, Chapter 1, this volume) have investigated an alternative hypothesis concerning the nature of auditory cues that characterize initial position stops differing in terms of place of articulation. This hypothesis is based upon the supposition that the auditory system is responding to integral patterns or configurations of acoustic events that occur at the release of a stop (i.e., the first 5 to 25 msec), rather than analyzing, tracking, and responding to each of the separate formant transitions. The stop onset spectra are believed to be invariant for each consonant, and thus are independent of the following vowel formants. In this framework, formant transitions are not primary cues for signaling place of articulation, but rather serve to smoothly join the onset spectra with the vowel formants (Cole & Scott, 1974; Stevens & Blumstein, 1978). Stevens and Blumstein (1978; Blumstein & Stevens, 1977, 1978) have shown that the addition of appropriate burst cues to four formant stimuli sharpens the category boundaries of stops relative to the same stimuli without the burst cues (i.e., cued only by the formant transitions).

It is reasonably clear that abrupt changes in energy or in the spectral distribution of energy are salient stimulus characteristics for the auditory system. However, the auditory system appears to respond to abrupt changes in a manner that is far less precise, in terms of spectral composition, than it does for more continuous stimuli—even when compensating for the differences in bandwidth between brief and longer stimuli. Thus, one would expect that onset bursts would provide less precise spectral information than formant transitions. It is possible that the bursts in the Stevens–Blumstein labeling study acted as cues that informed the subjects when the transitional cues were to begin, and might even have provided some crude information about the potential starting locus of the formant transitions (the role of cues is briefly discussed in the context of backward masking). That is, the burst cues may have acted to make transitional information more salient for the subjects without providing direct information about the phonetic category of the stimuli. Alternatively, the spectral information in the burst cues may have been sufficiently precise to allow for an appropriate response from the subjects in terms of an overall, integral acoustic pattern characterizing the consonants—as claimed by Stevens and Blumstein (1978). If the latter is the case, then this research may have some potentially interesting implications for the psychoacoustic investigation of nonsimultaneous masking and recognition masking. We agree with Stevens and Blumstein (1978) that their hypothesis warrants further investigation.

Manner of Articulation.

Categorical perception also has been reported for sawtooth waveforms differing in rise time (Cutting & Rosner, 1974). Stimuli with rapid rise-time stimuli were perceived as "plucked," whereas the longer rise-time stimuli were perceived as "bowed." These stimuli were intended to be analagous to differences in the onsets of phonetic stimuli contrasting in manner of articulation; specifically, a *shop–chop* continuum that is perceived categorically. It is not obvious what the critical acoustic properties might be. It is possible that the steady-state sawtooth waveform masked its own onset when the onset was rapid, creating a situation somewhat analogous to that hypothesized by

Miller for the voiced–voiceless distinction. However, it is more likely that the spectral characteristics of rapid versus slow onsets were the important parameters. The most rapid onsets would be characterized by a brief, broad band spread in energy (thus the "plucked" label), followed by a narrowing in bandwidth to the steady-state spectrum. The slow onsets would not cause a broad spread in intensity with time. Given differences in the intensity of the various components of a sawtooth waveform (and differences in human threshold across frequency), some components in the slowly rising stimuli probably were audible before others, leading to the impression of a smooth transition from a narrow band signal to the broader band steady-state waveform (and thus the "bowed" label). The transition from "plucked" to "bowed" perception would probably be related to perceived spectral bandwidth of the final, steady-state waveform, which may serve as a standard or reference against which one might judge the transition. If this post hoc analysis is correct, then one should be able to substitute other complex waveforms such as a square-wave, or a pulse train, or possibly even a band-limited noise for the sawtooth waveform, and obtain similar results. Also, one should shift the category boundary to longer rise times by decreasing the bandwidth of the sawtooth (i.e., by filtering the sawtooth). One also might hypothesize that the sawtooth stimuli "activated" specialized feature detectors sensitive to certain onset characteristics. However, this last statement is a relatively meaningless relabeling of a finding, unless one can begin to understand exactly what characteristics of a stimulus are necessary for activating such detectors.

Other Topics

Many aspects of both speech and nonspeech perception have been ignored in this chapter. Space does not permit a detailed discussion of these topics. However, a few brief comments on some of these topics seems in order before we finish our discussion.

Silence

Silence has been conjectured to be an important parameter in the perception of phonetic stimuli (e.g., Dorman, Raphael, Liberman, & Repp, 1975; Liberman, Harris, Eimas, Lisker, & Bastian, 1961; Lisker, 1957). For instance, increasing the duration of the silent interval between /s/ and /lit/ changes the perception of the stimulus from SLIT to SPLIT (Marcus, 1978). Similarly, sufficient silence before /sh/ in SAY SHOP changes the perception to SAY CHOP (Dorman, Raphael, & Liberman, 1979). Recently, Repp, Liberman, Eccardt, & Pesetsky (1978) reported finding a "trading relationship" (more appropriately described as a proportional dependency) between the duration of the initial stimulus and the silent duration between the stimuli, with the dependent measure being the location of the perceptual boundary between the two phonetic categories. Erickson,

Fitch, Halwes, and Liberman (1977) found a similar "trading relationship" between spectral cues and silence duration in defining the identification boundary between /s/-/lIt/ and /s/-/plIt/. Obviously, these all are acoustically complex situations, and any attempt at an adequate, plausible psychoacoustic explanation would be extremely difficult at this time—even with space permitting. However, a few comments might help to place this research in a slightly different perspective. In the stimuli, silence is a temporal interval that is devoid of energy (actually, that has "minimal" energy) at all auditory frequencies. Thus, a temporal interval does not contain any physical stimulus to serve as a source of interference for preceding and trailing stimulus components. This allows for a maximum persistence of the sensory/perceptual effects of the preceding stimulus and serves to segregate the preceding and trailing stimulus components. In natural settings, silent intervals are temporal periods when environmental sounds typically dominate over, and mask, any weak phonetic sounds that might be present. It is only in a laboratory that silences always are truly devoid of nonphonetic acoustic sounds. Silent intervals are defined by an offset of the initial stimulus and the onset of the trailing stimulus, both of which may be spectrally complex, yet perceptually subtle events, and require a relatively interference-free period of time for adequate processing.

Obviously, these conjectures are based upon general knowledge of how the auditory system functions, and are not based upon specific knowledge about functioning in these types of stimulus situations. If the persistence of the sensory trace across the silent interval is important, then filling the silent interval with a phonetically irrelevant, moderately low-level masking stimulus (e.g., white noise) should eliminate effective persistence. If the important factor is a stimulus-specific, persistence-related interaction between leading and trailing stimuli, with the critical silence duration being determined by the threshold for the interaction, such a masker should reduce the persistence of the sensory trace, shortening the duration of the necessary interval. If subtle offset (onset) characteristics of leading (trailing) stimuli are important, a moderate-level masker should make those characteristics more difficult to extract (i.e., should decrease the signal-to-noise ratio), and should require a longer interval (with sufficient masker, possibly even an infinite time interval). If the silent interval simply serves as a perceptual marker, then filling it with a low-level masker should either have no effect, or it should decrease the saliency of the interval and lead to a longer required interval. (We should note that if we are dealing with a unique phonetic feature system, then the phonetically irrelevant noise should have no effect.) A second manipulation might be to change the intensity of the acoustic segment preceding the phonetic component temporally defining the beginning of silence (e.g., V1 in a V1C1–C2V2 pair of syllables separated by silence, [−]). This could be accomplished by amplifying the vowel with a speech editing program, or by increasing the duration of the vowel (at least for vowel duration within the normal limits for temporal integration). This should increase the amount of masking from V1, making any subtle characteristics of C1 even more difficult to extract, yet should not diminish the persistence of the effects of C1 in time. Finally, one could use other means to designate, or cue, the separation of the presilence and postsilence stimuli. One could use a different type of cue (e.g., high-frequency, low-intensity tone [e.g., 12 kHz]), which should not mask any stimuli in the phonetically important frequency range. Alternatively, one could use interaural phase relationships (0 and 180 degrees) to differentially lateralize (and thus cue) the presilence and postsilence stimulus components (e.g., Jeffress, 1972). Such investigation should lead to an identification of the nature of the role played by silence in the perception of phonetic, and complex nonphonetic, stimuli.

Selective Adaptation

Eimas and Corbit (1973) conjectured that the uniformity across languages in the perception and production of voicing distinctions in initial stops (i.e., categorical perception) may be indicative of processing by a specialized perceptual structure that may be differentially tuned to detect and respond to the acoustic consequences of modes of speech production. They further conjectured that the repeated presentation of a stimulus with a given feature value should fatigue the detector tuned to that feature value, and thereby reduce its sensitivity. The consequences of this fatigue-induced decrease in sensitivity should be a temporary shift in the behaviorally measured category boundary. The assumption is that stimuli near a category boundary have the potential to activate either of the feature detectors separated by that boundary. If one of the feature detectors is adapted or fatigued, it will have a lower probability of activation, resulting in a category boundary shift toward the adapting stimulus. Eimas and Corbit found that the repeated presentation of a stimulus from a VOT continuum resulted in a shift in the category boundary, measured in terms of both identification and discrimination performance. The shift in category boundary was toward the adapting stimulus. These results were interpreted as supporting the hypothesized existence of linguistic feature detectors.

Eimas, Cooper, and Corbit (1973) subsequently demonstrated an analogous selective adaptation when the adapting stimulus and the test stimuli were presented to separate ears. These results were interpreted as indicating that selective adaptation involves central, rather than peripheral, stimulus processing. (We should note that the major efferent fibers to the cochlea originate in the relatively peripheral superior olivary complex, with the majority of neurons having a contralateral origin. Thus, the finding of selective adaptation with contralateral presentation of the adapting stimulus need not necessarily imply the involvement of central processes—although in this case, the more central interpretation probably is correct.) Eimas, Cooper, and Corbit also found that the initial 50 msec of a voiced stop consonant, when presented in isolation, was not effective in significantly shifting the category boundary for the linguistic continuum. These results lend support to the notion that selective adaptation involves the fatigue of a linguistic feature detector, rather than a detector sensitive to specific acoustic components of the stimuli.

Subsequent work by Tartter and Eimas (1975) investigated selective adaptation for stop consonants differing in place of articulation. They found that isolated initial F2- and F3-transitions, or such transitions with inappropriate F1-transitions, could be used as effective adapting stimuli. Adaptation occurred when the adapting stimuli were not heard as speech, as long as the adapting transitions were appropriate for the continuum of the test stimuli. Pisoni and Tash (1975) found that final position stop consonants could be employed as adapting stimuli for a continuum of initial position consonants, so long as the nature of the transitions were acoustically identical.

What seemed to be relatively simple, straightforward evidence for the existence of linguistic feature detectors has turned out to be complex. Recent research on this problem has tended to revolve around two major issues. One is whether selective adaptation primarily involves a shift in response criterion, or an actual change in sensory/perceptual processing. The second major issue tacitly assumes that the adaptation involves a temporary alteration (e.g., fatiguing) of the sensory or perceptual processes, which are the basis of the perception of speech stimuli, and attempts to identify the locus of adaptation. The latter issue is, in reality, quite complex. It is clear from the work summarized earlier, and from other research (e.g., Ades, 1974; Cooper, 1975; Cooper & Blumstein, 1974; Ganong, 1977; Sawusch & Pisoni, 1974) that the acoustic characteristics of the stimuli are important for obtaining selective adaptation. With this information, a number of different conjectures have been developed about the locus of the fatiguing effect. One view is that the fatigue alters only limited aspects of the feature detectors; one possibility is a shift in the thresholds (or perceptual criteria) imposed upon the incoming acoustic information for activation of the given feature detectors. Some researchers have hypothesized that there may be some additional alteration involving the higher order linguistic feature-detection unit (e.g., Tartter & Eimas, 1975). Others have argued that the results indicate an alteration of the sensory processes that provide stimulus information to higher order linguistic units. Obviously, this aspect of the selective adaptation phenomenon is quite complex, and is far from resolved. For this paper, we focus, albeit briefly, on the other major issue.

Cole and Cooper (1976) attempted to determine whether the selective adaptation effects involve actual changes in sensory/perceptual processes, or simply changes in response criteria. They computed d', the measure of sensitivity from the Gaussian, Equal Variance Model of Signal Detection (Green & Swets, 1966). However, this study failed to generate a ROC curved to evaluate the assumptions of the model, and did not evaluate the criteria—which would have indicated whether the assumptions of the model should have been a major concern (Pastore & Scheirer, 1974). If the assumptions of the model are not valid, then criterion placement would be correlated with d'. Wood (1976) later used Luce's Choice

Model (Luce, 1963) to address this same question, and found support for the hypothesis that selective adaptation involves changes in processing capability. However, Diehl, Lang, and Parker (1978) have found selective adaptation effects that are more consistent with the notion of criterion changes than with the notion of fatigue-induced changes in sensory/perceptual capabilities.

These selective adaptation results would seem to be consistent with an alternative sensory/processing hypothesis, which we feel merits consideration. Based upon the Durlach–Braida model and the research investigating that model, it has been established that the repeated presentation of a stimulus can establish that stimulus as a temporary reference. Reference can create categorical perception along a continuum (Pastore et al., 1977), improving stimulus discriminability and serving as a basis for differential labeling behavior. This hypothesis should be considered as an alternative to the fatigue hypothesis, which has dominated the theorizing concerning the basis of the effects known as selective adaptation.

CONCLUDING REMARKS

The study of auditory perception and the study of speech perception too often have been treated as largely nonoverlapping fields. Auditory perception (or psychoacoustics) research has developed some excellent methodology and stimulus control to permit the study of relatively simple stimulus situations. Most models for psychoacoustic perception are based upon processes that are assumed to be primarily peripheral in nature. Speech perception research has tended to focus on the physical analysis of speech signals, with the perceptual consequences of variability along dimensions of the physical stimuli (or on the production mechanism and its relationship to the physical nature of the speech signal, which have been ignored in this chapter). Most of the models for speech perception are based upon processes that are higher order theoretical constructs. In the opinion of many speech researchers, results from individual psychoacoustic studies tend to involve such limited stimulus conditions that it is difficult to generalize to the study of speech perception. As a result, auditory perception often is assumed to involve a relatively direct transformation of the physical characteristic of the waveform, with these characteristics often being identified by visual inspection of spectograms. At the same time, many psychoacoustic researchers tend to view speech stimuli as being far too complex to allow for the controlled analysis typical of their work with simple stimuli. The results of speech perception research thus often is ignored, and the hypotheses of higher order constructs, such as feature detectors, concomitantly are viewed as little more than an explanation by renaming. However, the lack of concerted efforts to integrate the two fields probably has hurt them both.

Examining the two fields, we have come to believe that the preliminary acoustic analysis of speech stimuli probably can account for much more of speech perception than typically assumed by speech researchers, and much less than typically assumed by psychoacoustic researchers. It is generally accepted that speech waveforms are subject to the same general principles of analysis as any other acoustic waveforms, and any higher order organization of speech perception must be imposed upon the information transformed by that analysis. From the perspective of a psychoacoustician, this means that speech perception studies have identified perceptually important characteristics of stimuli, which should be studied under rigorously controlled conditions. These characteristics are at least as relevant as many of the somewhat esoteric factors now studied by psychoacousticians (including the author). For speech perception research, the general principles derived from psychoacoustic research need more careful examination to determine their relevance to the processing of phonetic stimuli. Efforts should be made to find more realistic explanations for speech perception based upon psychoacoustic principles before falling back upon higher order constructs. When this is done, the remaining constructs will be better delineated, and therefore have increased predictive value. This chapter is simply a preliminary, limited attempt by the author to integrate some aspects of the two fields, and to bring into focus a few relevant considerations. Inevitably, it leaves a great many questions unanswered, but does address how one might begin to search out the answers.

ACKNOWLEDGMENTS

The author thanks Edward Cudahy, David Pisoni, and Neil Macmillan for detailed critiques of earlier drafts of this manuscript. Comments by Robert Sorkin, Bruno Repp, Laura Harris, Janet Cohen, and Charlotte MacLatchy also were quite helpful in preparing this manuscript. Many of the ideas contained in this manuscript were stimulated by discussion and research conducted while the author was on sabbatical at Haskins Laboratories. That research was supported, in part, by BRS Grant RR–05596 to Haskins Laboratories, and NINCDS Grant NS 10995 to the author.

REFERENCES

Ades, A. How phonetic is selective adaptation? Experiments on syllable position and vowel environment. *Perception & Psychophysics*, 1974, *16*, 61–67.

Bailey, P. J., Summerfield, Q., & Dorman, M. F. On the identification of sine-wave analogues of certain speech sounds (SR–51/52). *Status Report on Speech Research*, Haskins Laboratories, New Haven, Conn., 1977.

Berliner, J. E., & Durlach, N. I. Intensity perception, IV: Resolution in roving-level discrimination. *Journal of the Acoustical Society of America*, 1973, *53*, 1270–1287.

Berliner, J. E., Durlach, N. I., & Braida, L. D. Intensity perception, VII: Further data on roving-level discrimination and the resolution discrimination and bias edge effects. *Journal of the Acoustical Society of America*, 1977, *61*, 1577–1585.

Blodgett, H. C., Jeffress, L. A., & Taylor, R. W. Relation of masked threshold to signal-duration for various interaural phase-combinations. *American Journal of Psychology*, 1958, *71*, 283–290.

Blumstein, S. E., & Stevens, K. N. Perceptual invariance and onset spectra for stop consonants in different vowel environments. *Journal of the Acoustical Society of America*, 1977, *60*, S90. (Abstract)

Blumstein, S. E., & Stevens, K. N. Acoustic invariance for place of articulation in stops and nasals across syllabic context. *Journal of the Acoustical Society of America*, 1978, *62*, S26. (Abstract)

Brady, P. T., House, A. S., & Stevens, K. N. Perception of sounds characterized by a rapidly changing resonance frequency. *Journal of the Acoustical Society of America*, 1961, *33*, 1357–1362.

Braida, L. D., & Durlach, N. I. Intensity perception, II: Resolution in one-interval paradigms. *Journal of the Acoustical Society of America*, 1972, *51*, 483–502.

Campbell, R., & Counter, S. A. Temporal integration and periodicity pitch. *Journal of the Acoustical Society of America*, 1968, *45*, 691–693.

Carney, A. E., Widin, B., & Viemeister, N. Noncategorical perception of stop consonants differing in VOT. *Journal of the Acoustical Society of America*, 1977, *62*, 961–970.

Cole, R. A., & Cooper, W. E. Three models of perceptual adaptation to speech. *Journal of the Acoustical Society of America*, 1976, *59*, S26. (Abstract)

Cole, R. A., & Scott, B. Toward a theory of speech perception. *Psychological Review*, 1974, *81*, 348–374.

Collins, M. J., & Cullen, J. K., Jr. Temporal integration of tone glides. *Journal of the Acoustical Society of America*, 1978, *63*, 469–473.

Cooper, W. E. Selective adaptation to speech. In R. Restle, R. M. Shiffrin, N. J. Castellan, H. Lindman, & D. B. Pisoni (Eds.), *Cognitive theory*, (Vol. 1). Potomac, Maryland: Lawrence Erlbaum Associates, 1975.

Cooper, W. E., & Blumstein, S. E. A labial feature analyzer in speech. *Perception & Psychophysics*, 1974, *15*, 591–600.

Creelman, C. D., & Macmillan, N. A. Auditory phase and frequency discrimination: A comparison of nine procedures. *Journal of Experimental Psychology: Human Perception and Performance*, 1978, *4*, 691–701.

Cudahy, E., & Leshowitz, B. Effects of a contralateral interference tone on auditory recognition. *Perception & Psychophysics*, 1974, *15*, 16–20.

Cullen, J. K., Jr., & Collins, M. J. Temporal integration of two component tone-glides. *Journal of the Acoustical Society of America*, 1978, *63*, S32. (Abstract)

Cutting, J. E., & Dorman, M. F. Discrimination of intensity differences carried on formant transitions varying in extent and duration. *Perception & Psychophysics*, 1976, *20*, 101–107.

Cutting, J. E., & Rosner, B. S. Categories and boundaries in speech and music. *Perception & Psychophysics*, 1974, *16*, 564–570.

Delattre, P. C., Liberman, A. M., & Cooper, F. S. Acoustic loci and transitional cues for consonants. *Journal of the Acoustical Society of America*, 1955, *27*, 769–773.

Diehl, R. L., Lang, M., & Parker, E. M. A further parallel between selective adaptation and response contrast. *Journal of the Acoustical Society of America*, 1978, *64*, S19. (Abstract)

Dorman, M. F. Discrimination of intensity differences in formant transitions in and out of syllable context. *Perception and Psychophysics*, 1974, *16*, 84–86.

Dorman, M. F., Raphael, L., & Liberman, A. M. Some experiments on the sound of silence in phonetic perception. *Journal of the Acoustical Society of America*, 1979, *65*, 1518–1532.

Dorman, M. F., Raphael, L., Liberman, A. M., & Repp, B. H. Some masking like phenomena in speech perception (SR–42/43). *Status Report on Speech Research*, Haskins Laboratories, New Haven, Conn., 1975.

Durlach, N., & Braida, L. D. Intensity Perception, I: Preliminary theory of intensity resolution. *Journal of the Acoustical Society of America*, 1969, *46*, 372–383.

Egan, J. P., & Clarke, F. R. Psychophysics and signal detection. In J. B. Sidowski (Eds.), *Experimental Methods and Instrumentation in Psychology*. New York: McGraw-Hill, 1966.

Eimas, P. D. Auditory and phonetic coding of the cues for speech: Discrimination of the [r−l] distinction by young infants. *Perception & Psychophysics*, 1975, *18*, 341–347.

Eimas, P. D., Cooper, W. E., & Corbit, J. D. Some properties of linguistic feature detectors. *Perception & Psychophysics*, 1973, *13*, 247–252.

Eimas, P. D., & Corbit, J. D. Selective adaptation of linguistic feature detectors. *Cognitive Psychology*, 1973, *4*, 99–109.

Elliott, L. L. Changes in the simultaneous masked threshold of brief tones. *Journal of the Acoustical Society of America*, 1965, *38*, 738–746.

Elliott, L. L. Backward and forward masking. *Audiology*, 1971, *10*, 65–76.

Erickson, D., Fitch, H. L., Halwes, T. G., & Liberman, A. M. A trading relation in perception between silence and spectrum. *Journal of the Acoustical Society of America*, 1977, *61*, S46–S47. (Abstract)

Fletcher, H. Auditory patterns. *Review of Modern Physics*, 1940, *12*, 47–65.

Fujisaki, H., & Kawashima, T. On the modes and mechanisms of speech perception. *Annual Report of the Engineering Research Institute* (Vol. 28). Faculty of Engineering, University of Tokyo, Tokyo, 1969, 67–73.

Ganong, W. F. III. Effect of selective adaptation on the discrimination of small differences in voice onset time (VOT). *Journal of the Acoustical Society of America*, 1977, *62*, S77. (Abstract)

Green, D. M. Masking with continuous and pulsed sinusoids. *Journal of the Acoustical Society of America*, 1969, *46*, 939–946.

Green, D. M. Temporal auditory acuity. *Psychological Review* , 1971, *78*, 540–551.

Green, D. M., Birdsall, T. G., & Tanner, W. P., Jr. Signal detection as a function of signal intensity and duration. *Journal of the Acoustical Society of America*, 1957, *29*, 523–531.

Green, D. M., & Sewall, S. T. Effects of background noise on auditory detection of noise bursts. *Journal of the Acoustical Society of America*, 1962, *34*, 1207–1216.

Green, D. M., & Swets, J. A. *Signal detection theory and psychophysics*, New York: John Wiley & Sons, 1966.

Hawkins, J. E., & Stevens, S. S. The masking of pure tones and of speech by white noise. *Journal of the Acoustical Society of America*, 1950, *22*, 6–13.

Hirsh, I. J. Auditory perception of temporal order. *Journal of the Acoustical Society of America*, 1959, *31*, 759–767.

Jeffress, L. A. A stimulus-oriented approach to detection theory. *Journal of the Acoustical Society of America*, 1964, *36*, 766–774.

Jeffress, L. A. Stimulus-oriented approach to detection re-examined. *Journal of the Acoustical Society of America*, 1967, *41*, 480–488.

Jeffress, L. A. Binaural signal detection: Vector theory. In J. V. Tobias (Ed.), *Foundations of modern auditory theory* (Vol. 1). New York: Academic Press, 1972.

Julesz, B., & Hirsh, I. J. Visual and auditory perception—An essay. In E. E. David, & P. B. Denes (Eds.), *Human communication: A unified view*. New York: McGraw-Hill, 1972.

Kallman, H. J., & Massaro, D. W. Similarity effects in backward recognition masking. *Wisconsin Human Information Processing Program* (Report No. 4), Madison, Wisc., 1978.

Kaplan, H. L., Macmillan, N. A., & Creelman, C. D. Tables of d′ for variable-standard discrimination paradigms. *Behavior Research Methods and Instruction*, 1978, *10*, 796–813.

Liberman, A. M. Delattre, P. C., & Cooper, F. S. Some cues for the distinction between voiced and voiceless stops in initial position. *Language and Speech*, 1958, *1*, 153–167.

Liberman, A. M., Harris, K. S., Eimas, P. D., Lisker, L., & Bastian, J. An effect of learning on speech perception: The discrimination of durations of silence with and without phonetic significance. *Language and Speech*, 1961, *4*, 175–195.

Liberman, A. M., Harris, K. S., Hoffman, H. S., & Griffith, B. C. The discrimination of speech sounds within and across phoneme boundaries. *Journal of Experimental Psychology*, 1957, *54*, 358–368.

Liberman, A. M., Harris, K. S., Kinney, L. A., & Lane, H. The discrimination of relative onset-time of the components of certain speech and nonspeech patterns. *Journal of Experimental Psychology*, 1961, *61*, 379-388.

Lisker, L. Closure duration and the intervocalic voiced-voiceless distinction in English. *Language*, 1957, *33*, 42-49.

Lisker, L., Liberman, A. M., Erickson, D. M., Dechovitz, D., & Mandler, R. On pushing the voice-onset-time (VOT) boundary about. *Language and Speech*, 1978, *20*, 209-216.

Luce, R. D. Detection and recognition. In R. D. Luce, R. R. Bush, & E. Galanter (Eds.), *Handbook of mathematical psychology*. New York: John Wiley & Sons, 1963.

Macmillan, N. A., Kaplan, H. L., & Creelman, C. D. Psychophysics of categorial perception. *Psychological Review*, 1977, *84*, 452-471.

Marcus, S. M. Distinguishing "slit" and "split"—an invariant timing cue in speech perception. *Perception & Psychophysics*, 1978, *23*, 58-60.

Massaro, D. W. A comparison of forward versus backward recognition masking. *Journal of Experimental Psychology*, 1973, *100*, 434-436.

Massaro, D. W. Preperceptual images, processing time, and perceptual units in speech perception. In D. W. Massaro (Ed.), *Understanding language*. New York: Academic Press, 1975.

Massaro, D. W. Auditory information processing. In W. K. Estes (Ed.), *Handbook of learning and cognitive processes*. Hillsdale, N.J.: Lawrence Erlbaum Associates, 1976.

Mattingly, I. G. Speech cues and sign stimuli. *American Scientist*, 1972, *60*, 327-337.

Mattingly, I. G., Liberman, A. M., Syrdal, A. K., & Halwes, T. Discrimination in speech and nonspeech modes. *Cognitive Psychology*, 1971, *2*, 131-157.

Miller, J. D., Wier, C. C., Pastore, R. E., Kelly, W. J., & Dooling, R. J. Discrimination and labeling of noise-buzz sequences with varying noise lead times. *Journal of the Acoustical Society of America*, 1976, *60*, 410-417.

Nàbělek, I. V. Masking of tone slides. In S. K. Hirsh, E. H. Eldridge, I. J. Hirsh, & S. R. Silverman (Eds.), *Hearing and Davis: Essays honoring Hallowell Davis*. St. Louis: Washington University Press, 1976.

Nàbělek, I. V. Temporal summation of constant and sliding tones at masked auditory threshold. *Journal of the Acoustical Society of America*, 1978, *64*, 751-763.

Nàbělek, I. V., & Hirsh, I. J. On the discrimination of frequency transitions. *Journal of the Acoustical Society of America*, 1969, *45*, 1510-1519.

Pastore, R. E. Detection of periodically and randomly interrupted noise signals, *Perception & Psychophysics*, 1973, *14*, 581-584.

Pastore, R. E. Categorical perception: A critical re-evaluation. In S. K. Hirsh, D. H. Eldgredge, I. J. Hirsh., & S. R. Silverman (Eds.), *Hearing and Davis: Essays honoring Hallowell Davis*. St. Louis: Washington University Press, 1976.

Pastore, R. E. Contralateral cueing effects in the perception of aspirated stop consonants. *Journal of the Acoustical Society of America*, 1978, *64*, S17. (Abstract) (a)

Pastore, R. E. Phonemes and alphanumeric character: Possible components of parallel human communication systems. *Visible Language*, 1978, *12*, 27-42. (b)

Pastore, R. E., Ahroon, W. A., Baffuto, K. J., Friedman, D., Puleo, J. S., & Fink, E. A. Common-factor model of categorical perception. *Journal of Experimental Psychology: Human Perception and Performance*, 1977, *3*, 686-696.

Pastore, R. E., Ahroon, W. A., Wolz, J., Puleo, J. S., & Berger, R. S. Discrimination of intensity differences on formant-like transitions. *Perception & Psychophysics*, 1975, *18*, 244-246.

Pastore, R. E., Freda, J. S., & Barnett, M. L. Contralateral cueing effects in forward masking. *Journal of the Acoustical Society of America*, 1977, *62*, S96-S97. (Abstract)

Pastore, R. E., Friedman, C. J., & Baffuto, K. J. Comparative evaluation of the AX and two ABX procedures. *Journal of the Acoustical Society of America*, 1976, *60*, S120. (Abstract)

Pastore, R. E., Friedman, C. J., & Barnett, M. L. Backward and simultaneous context effects on frequency discrimination with sinusoidal stimuli. *Journal of the Acoustical Society of America,* 1978, *63,* S51. (Abstract)

Pastore, R. E., & MacLatchy, C. S. Signal detection: Post-stimulus change effects. *Journal of the Acoustical Society of America,* 1974, *56,* S45. (Abstract)

Pastore, R. E., & MacLatchy, C. S. Some nonmasking auditory postsignal effects. *Perception & Psychophysics,* 1975, *16,* 455-459.

Pastore, R. E., & Scheirer, C. J. Signal detection theory: Considerations for general application. *Psychological Bulletin,* 1974, *81,* 945-958.

Penner, M. J. Effect of masker duration and masker level on forward and backward masking. *Journal of the Acoustical Society of America,* 1974, *56,* 179-182.

Pisoni, D. B. Auditory short-term memory and vowel perception. *Memory and Cognition,* 1975, *3,* 7-18.

Pisoni, D. B. Identification and discrimination of the relative onset time of two-component tones: Implications for voicing perception in stops. *Journal of the Acoustical Society of America,* 1977, *61,* 1352-1361.

Pisoni, D. B., & Lazarus, J. H. Categorical and noncategorical modes of speech perception along the voicing continuum. *Journal of the Acoustical Society of America,* 1974, *55,* 328-333.

Pisoni, D. B., & Tash, J. Auditory property detectors and processing place features in stop consonants. *Perception & Psychophysics,* 1975, *18,* 401-408.

Pollack, I. Detection of rate of change of auditory frequency. *Journal of Experimental Psychology,* 1968, *77,* 535-541.

Puleo, J. S., & Pastore, R. E. Reducing backward masking through temporal contralateral cueing. *Journal of the Acoustical Society of America,* 1977, *62,* S25. (Abstract)

Pynn, C. T., Braida, L. D., & Durlach, N. I. Intensity perception, III: Resolution in small-range identification. *Journal of the Acoustical Society of America,* 1972, *51,* 559-565.

Repp, B. H. Relative amplitude of aspiration noise as a cue for syllable initial stop consonants. *Language and Speech,* 1979, *22,* 173-189.

Repp, B. H., Liberman, A. M., Eccardt, T., & Pesetsky, D. Perceptual integration of temporal cues for stop, fricative, and affricative manner. *Journal of Experimental Psychology: Human Perception and Performance,* 1978, *4,* 621-637.

Ronken, D. A. Masking produced by sinusoids of slowly changing frequency. *Journal of the Acoustical Society of America,* 1973, *54,* 905-915.

Samoilova, I. K. Masking of short tone signals as a function of the time interval between masked and masking sounds. *Biofizika,* 1959, *4,* 550-558.

Samuel, A. G. The effect of discrimination training on speech perception: Noncategorical perception. *Perception & Psychophysics,* 1977, *22,* 321-330.

Sawusch, J. R., & Pisoni, D. B. On the identification of place and voicing features in synthetic stop consonants. *Journal of Phonetics,* 1974, *2,* 181-194.

Sergeant, R. L., & Harris, J. D. Sensitivity to unidirectional frequency modulation. *Journal of the Acoustical Society of America,* 1962, *34,* 1625-1628.

Sheeley, E. C., & Bilger, R. C. Temporal integration as a function of frequency. *Journal of the Acoustical Society of America,* 1964, *36,* 1850-1857.

Sparks, D. W. Temporal recognition masking—or interference? *Journal of the Acoustical Society of America,* 1976, *60,* 680-686.

Stevens, K. N., & Blumstein, S. E. Invariant cues for place of articulation in stop consonants. *Journal of the Acoustical Society of America,* 1978, *64,* 1358-1368.

Stevens, K. N., & Klatt, D. H. Role of formant transitions in the voiced-voiceless distinction for stops. *Journal of the Acoustical Society of America,* 1974, *55,* 653-659.

Steigel, M. S., & Bilger, R. C. Temporal summation as a function of signal definition and psychophysical method. *Journal of the Acoustical Society of America,* 1975, *57,* S6. (Abstract)

Studdert-Kennedy, M., Liberman, A. M., Harris, K. S., & Cooper, F. S. Motor theory of speech perception: A reply to Lane's critical review. *Psychological Review*, 1970, *77*, 234–249.

Tartter, V., & Eimas, P. D. The role of auditory and phonetic feature detectors in the perception of speech. *Perception & Psychophysics*, 1975, *18*, 293–298.

Thomas, I. G., Hill, P. D., Carroll, F. J., & Garcia, B. Temporal order in the perception of vowels. *Journal of the Acoustical Society of America*, 1970, *48*, 1010–1013.

Tucker, A., Williams, P. I., & Jeffress, L. A. Effect of signal duration and detection for gated and for continuous noise. *Journal of the Acoustical Society of America*, 1968, *44*, 813–816.

Tsumura, T., Sone, T., & Numura, T. Auditory detection of frequency transition. *Journal of the Acoustical Society of America*, 1973, *53*, 17–25.

Wallach, H., Newman, E. B., & Rosenzweig, M. R. The precedence effect in sound localization. *American Journal of Psychology*, 1949, *62*, 315–336.

Warren, R. N. Verbal transformation effect and auditory perceptual mechanisms, *Psychological Bulletin*, 1968, *70*, 261–270.

Warren, R. N., & Ackroff, J. M. Two types of auditory sequence perception. *Perception & Psychophysics*, 1976, *20*, 387–394.

Watson, C. S. Factors in the discrimination of word length auditory patterns. In S. K. Hirsh, D. H. Eldredge, I. J. Hirsh, & S. R. Silverman (Eds.), *Hearing and Davis: Essays honoring Hallowell Davis*. St. Louis: Washington University Press, 1976.

Weber, D. L. Suppression of backward and forward masking. *Journal of the Acoustical Society of America*, 1978, *63*, S2. (Abstract) (a)

Weber, D. L. Suppression and critical bands in band-limited experiments. *Journal of the Acoustical Society of America*, 1978, *64*, 141–150. (b)

Wegel, R. L., & Lane, C. F. The auditory masking of one pure tone by another and its probable relation to the dynamics of the inner ear. *Physical Review*, 1924, *23*, 267–285.

Whittaker, R. G. Pitch-matching of tone glides with a pure tone. *Journal of the Acoustical Society of America*, 1978, *63*, S51. (Abstract)

Wood, C. C. Discriminability, response bias, and phoneme categories in speech discrimination: II. Place of articulation. *Journal of the Acoustical Society of America*, 1976, *59*, S26–27. (Abstract)

Zwicker, E., Flottorp, G., & Stevens, S. S. Critical band width in loudness summation. *Journal of the Acoustical Society of America*, 1957, *29*, 548–557.

Zwicker, E., & Wright, H. N. Temporal summation for tones in narrow-band noise. *Journal of the Acoustical Society of America*, 1963, *35*, 691–695.

Zwislocki, J. Theory of temporal auditory summation. *Journal of the Acoustical Society of America*, 1960, *32*, 1046–1060.

Zwislocki, J. Temporal summation of loudness: An analysis. *Journal of the Acoustical Society of America*, 1969, *46*, 431–441.

6

Temporal Variables in the Perception and Production of Spoken and Sign Languages

François Grosjean
Harlan Lane
Northeastern University

Editors' Comments

As we have noted previously, a recurrent theme in the study of speech is the extent to which the nature of speech, including its acquisition and use, reflects the constraints of a system that has evolved specifically for those purposes. Grosjean and Lane have addressed this issue by comparing the processing of spoken language with the processing of language in a different modality, that is, with the visual language of sign.

In an extensive series of studies that are described in their chapter, Grosjean and Lane compared the two types of language with respect to two issues. The first is the way in which speakers and signers produce changes in rate of production and the way in which listeners and observers perceive these changes in rate. We learn that although there are some interesting differences in the way rate changes occur and are perceived in speech and sign, there is considerable similarity in the processes involved in the two languages. The second is the way in which processing of language, whether speech or sign, depends both on the syntactic structure of the utterance and on certain performance variables (the tendency to bisect). Again, the similarities in processing between speech and sign far outweigh the differences. Findings such as these lead to the conclusion that if there are specialized systems constraining the nature of language and its processing, then these are quite abstract, and apply to both spoken languages and signed languages. Of course, the possibility exists that the processing patterns observed reflect not the operation of specialized language processes, but rather the operation of more general perceptual and cognitive structures.

INTRODUCTION

In the following chapter, we review a number of studies pertaining to rate of utterance and pausing in the perception and production of two spoken languages (English and French) and one sign language (American Sign Language). These studies were carried out in France (University of Paris) and in the United States (Northeastern University) by the two authors and by the first author alone, or in collaboration with other researchers. Before beginning our review, we should present a brief introduction to American Sign Language.

The Sign Language used by deaf communities in the United States since the 19th century, known as American Sign Language (ASL), has only recently become the object of intensive research by linguists and psychologists (Battison, 1978; Bellugi & Fischer, 1972; Frishberg, 1975; Grosjean & Lane, 1977; Lane, Boyes-Braem, & Bellugi, 1976; Stokoe, 1960; Woodward, 1974). They have shown that ASL is a systematic natural form of symbolic communication among a stable community of users and that it has the degree of regularity and structure required of a fully developed language. ASL is not some form of English on the hands; it is a different language with different structural principles. For example, a sign in ASL seems to be composed of at least four distinct parameters: shape of the hand, location of the hand, orientation of the palm, and movement of the hand. To illustrate: The sign for the concept GIRL is made with the hand in a fist, the thumb tip brushing down the lower cheek. Experimental evidence that these parameters are perceptually real for signers was obtained, for example, in a short-term memory study for signs by Bellugi, Klima, and Siple (1975); they found that most errors were formational rather than semantic confusions. The study of sign language is intriguing to researchers interested in the perception and production of language; they hope to isolate those aspects of language specific to the modality (visual or oral) and those common to language in general, irrespective of the mode of communication.

PERCEPTION

In this section, we review the research conducted on subjective scales of rate of utterance. We discuss first the nature of these scales and their invariance across tasks and language; we then account for the role played by the component variables of rate (articulation rate, number, and length of the pauses) in the make-up of these scales.

Perception of Reading Rate by Speakers and Listeners

Lane (1962) reported that the autophonic function for voice level is steeper than the corresponding extraphonic function. He noted that when a speaker judges the characteristics of his or her own speech, the autophonic task, the cues available include tactile and proprioceptive feedback, as well as bone- and air-conducted sidetone. When the speaker stops speaking and judges someone else's speech, the extraphonic task, he or she is deprived of all these cues save the last and, as a listener, must found judgments differently. Because the characteristics of speaking and listening are so different structurally, it was not surprising to find that they are quite different functionally.

The aim of a first study (Lane & Grosjean, 1973) was to confirm, using reading rate, that the speaker's perception of the properties of his or her own speech grows more rapidly than the corresponding physical magnitude and more rapidly than the speaker's perception of these properties in the speech of another. Does apparent rate, like apparent level, grow as a power of physical rate and, if so, with what exponent? Does this autophonic scale have a slope greater than one (log-scale coordinates)? Is it steeper than the corresponding extraphonic scale? And how do the component variables of rate (articulation rate, number, and length of pauses) contribute to the speaker's change of rate?

The method of magnitude production was used to determine the autophonic scale (Lane, Catania, & Stevens, 1961). The listener was asked to read the experimental passage at normal rate. To the apparent rate of this reading, the experimenter signed the numerical value 10. A series of values (2.5, 5, 10, 20, 30) was then named in irregular order and the speaker responded to each value by reading the passage with a proportional apparent rate. The method of magnitude estimation was used to measure extraphonic perception of speech rate. The experimenter played a recording of the experimental passage read at moderate rate (162 wpm); to this standard he assigned the numerical value 10. Next, he played 40 recordings of the passage and the listener assigned to each a number proportional to its apparent rate. In all, five rates of reading by the same speaker were presented eight times in irregular order: 92, 131, 162, 255, and 360 wpm.

The relation between perceived rate and actual rate for the speaker proved to be a power function with a slope of 2.6. Thus autophonic rate joined the other autophonic scales indicating that the sensory mechanisms mediating the speaker's perception of his or her own speech amplify constant stimulus ratios into much larger constant subjective ratios. The relation between perceived rate and actual rate for the listener was also found to be a power function whose slope was 1.5. The disparity between the slopes of the autophonic and extraphonic functions means that when a speaker doubles reading rate, he or she perceives a sixfold increase whereas a listener perceives less than a threefold increase. The generalization that sensation grows more rapidly for the speaker than for the listener was thus borne out, indicating that the speaker does not rely exclusively on hearing in judging his or her rate.

What is the relative contribution of the component variables of rate (articulation rate, number, and length of the pauses) to the autophonic perception of rate? First, it was found that the speaker changes articulation time much less than his or her pause time to achieve a given increase in apparent rate. When autophonic judgments were plotted against these two variables in log–log coordinates, the slopes of the straight lines of best fit were −3.4 and −0.9, respectively. Thus, the speaker who wishes to double his or her apparent rate simply spends half as much time pausing. Does the speaker do this by pausing half as often, or by cutting the durations of his or her pauses in half, or both? The former is correct. On the average, twice the apparent rate was associated with about half the number of pauses but 85% of the average pause duration. The slopes of the straight lines of best fit in log–log coordinates were respectively, −1.1 and −4.3. The nearly linear reduction in pause frequency with autophonic rate is not accomplished, of course, by indiscriminate suppression of pauses. As the speaker moves from slow to fast reading rates, the speaker takes out pauses within constituents, then between constituents, then between clauses and finally, at the fastest rate, even between sentences.

This first study of the perception of reading rate by speakers and listeners raised several questions that we attempted to answer in later studies. How invariant are the autophonic and extraphonic scales of rate? How does the listener integrate the component variables of speaking rate? What is the role of breathing in the change of rate? Do users of American Sign Language and speakers modify the component variables of rate to the same extent when changing rate? And when subjects read or sign slowly, can the patterns of their pausing be predicted largely from the constituent structure of the sentence (as the preliminary results cited in the foregoing imply), or are other variables involved appreciably?

The Autophonic and Extraphonic Scales of Rate and Their Invariance

Grosjean (1977) repeated the Lane and Grosjean (1973) study on the autophonic perception of speech rate with a different passage (''Goldilocks'') and a different group of subjects but the same paradigm. The slope he obtained was 2.5, thus replicating the Lane and Grosjean (1973) result of 2.6. What is of greater interest, however, is that the autophonic scale of rate obtained from speakers was identical to that obtained from signers, as can be seen in Fig. 6.1. The slopes for speech (Mn = 2.5; S.D. = 1.3) were not significantly different from those obtained by signers producing the Goldilocks passage in sign (Mn = 2.7, S.D. = 1.1). Signers covered identical range of rates when going from slow to fast production: 2.6:1 for sign and 2.7:1 for speech. Thus, when either a speaker or signer doubles production rate, he or she will perceive about a sixfold increase. These results suggest that a common mechanism, possibly involving proprioception, may mediate both types of autophonic rate judgments. Whether the movable articulators are, for example, the tongue, the lips and the jaw, or the hands and arms, similar autophonic sensations will guide signers and speakers to produce similar changes in production rate.

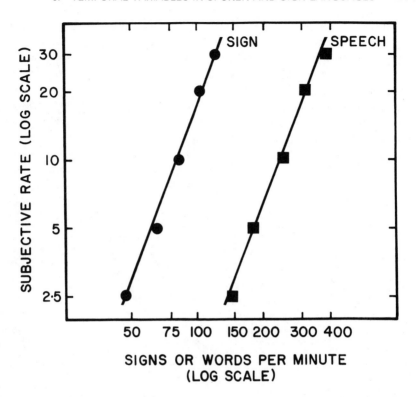

FIG. 6.1. Autophonic scales of signing and speaking rates. Each circle is the geometric mean of 88 signing productions, 4 by each of 22 signers. Each square is the geometric mean of 44 speech productions, 4 by each of 11 speakers. (From Grosjean, 1977. Copyright 1977 by The Psychonomic Society. Reprinted by permission.)

Considerably more research has been conducted on the invariance of the extraphonic scale of rate. Grosjean and Lass (1977) showed that the scale remains invariant across spoken languages (exponent of 2.0 in English and 1.9 in French), texts (the Pop Fan passage and the Rainbow passage yielded exponents of 2.0 and 1.9, respectively), and methods of altering rate (naturally and by means of a speech compressor: exponents of 2.0 and 1.9 respectively for the Pop Fan passage; 1.9 and 2.1 for the Rainbow passage; 1.9 and 1.8 for the Pop Fan passage in French). A strong intramodal range effect was found, however. Both Poulton (1968) and Teghtsoonian (1973) have shown that intramodal range variation affects the exponent of the power law: As the stimulus range increases, the exponent of the Stevens' power law decreases. Teghtsoonian (1973) gives evidence of this for loudness, apparent distance, and apparent length. An examination of the effect in Grosjean and Lass (1977), Lane and Grosjean (1973), and

Grosjean and Lane (1974) revealed that the intramodal range law is also applicable to the speech rate continuum: Reading rates covered a 3.9:1 range in Lane and Grosjean (1973) and resulted in an exponent of 1.5; they covered a 2.7:1 range in Grosjean and Lane (1974) with an exponent of 1.7 and only a 2.4:1 range in Grosjean and Lass (1977) for a slope of 2.0. This intramodal range effect was confirmed in Grosjean and Lass (1977) by cross-modality matching in which subjects matched apparent force of handgrip to apparent speech rate, so it is probably not dependent on habits in using numbers.

Grosjean and Lass (1977) showed that the extraphonic scale of rate is invariant across spoken languages. Is it also invariant across different language modalities? Will listeners of speech and observers of sign perceive changes in rate in an identical fashion, as do signers and speakers? Figure 6.2 gives a

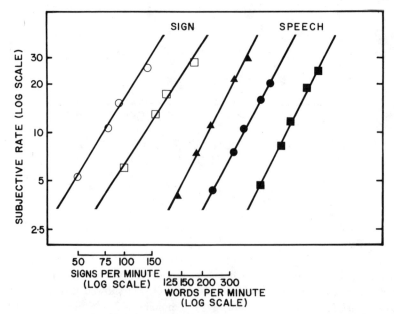

FIG. 6.2.   Extraphonic scales of signing and speaking rates. Each unfilled circle is the geometric mean of 40 magnitude estimations of signing rate, 4 by each of 10 native signers and each unfilled square is the geometric mean of 40 magnitude estimations of signing rate, 4 by each of 10 observers with no knowledge of Sign. For clarity, the two sign functions are separated by a 50-spm interval. Each filled triangle is the geometric mean of 40 magnitude estimations of English-speaking rate, 4 by each of 10 native speakers of English. Each filled circle is the geometric mean of 88 magnitude estimations of French-speaking rate, 4 by each of 22 native speakers of French, and each filled square is the geometric mean of 48 magnitude estimations of French speaking rate, 4 by each of 12 listeners with no knowledge of French. For clarity, the three speech functions are separated by a 100-wpm interval. (From Grosjean, 1977. Copyright 1977 by The Psychonomic Society. Reprinted by permission.)

negative answer. Grosjean (1977) found that estimates of rate in sign are well fit by a straight line in log–log coordinates and that extraphonic rate in sign grows more slowly than autophonic rate (exponents of 1.6 and 2.7, respectively), thus confirming in another modality the disparity reported by Lane and Grosjean (1973) for speech, but that with an identical range of rates in English and sign (2.8:1), the exponent obtained with speech (1.9) was significantly different from the exponent obtained for sign (1.6). Thus, when a speaker doubles his or her rate, a listener perceives almost a fourfold increase whereas when a signer doubles his or her rate, an observer perceives a threefold increase. This difference in the extraphonic perception of rate in speech and sign was confirmed by listeners who knew no French (1.9) and observers who knew no sign language (1.5). We take this to mean that linguistic decoding does not seem to be involved in judgments of changes in signing and speaking rate. Grosjean (1977) ascribed this difference in perception of rate by listeners and observers to the different perceptual modalities involved—auditory on the one hand and visual on the other. This difference in perceptual modalities in its impact on language decoding by listeners and observers is currently the subject of several studies—for example, Grosjean, Teuber, and Lane (1978).

The various studies that have obtained scales of extraphonic rate (Grosjean, 1977; Grosjean & Lane, 1974; 1976; Grosjean & Lass, 1977; Lane & Grosjean, 1973) have all done so without explicitly requiring the listener to process the passages fully: The same passage is used repeatedly and there is no check on comprehension. Would varying the sentences judged affect the listener's perception of rate and would the scale of extraphonic rate be invariant across different processing tasks? These were the questions that motivated a study by Grosjean (1978b) using 12 sentences constructed with the same syntactic structure (Art/Ajd/N/Vb/Art/N), the same number of syllables (13) and the same word frequency (all adjectives, nouns, and verbs were taken from Thorndike & Lorge's [1944] Part II word list). The sentences were recorded at four different rates (80% of normal rate, normal rate [145 wpm], 120% and 140% of normal rate). The 48 rate presentations (12 sentences and 4 rates) were then played to three groups of 14 listeners, who were involved in processing tasks of increasing complexity. The first group was given no comprehension task (Task 0) and was only asked to give magnitude estimations of the rates presented, following the procedure used in previous studies (Grosjean, 1977, for example). The second group (Task 1) was asked to estimate the rate of each sentence, to mark on a 7-cm scale how good their comprehension of that sentence had been, and then to recall one of the words of the sentence as prompted by an answer sheet. A third group (Task 2) first gave an estimate of rate of each sentence and then wrote a continuation sentence to follow the one they had just heard.

The results obtained in the experiment are shown in Fig. 6.3. No significant difference in slopes was found between the three groups. The mean exponents for the three tasks were 1.9 (S.D. = 0.46), 2.2 (0.77) and 2.1 (0.47), respectively.

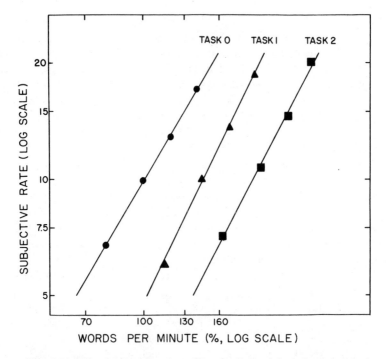

FIG. 6.3.   Extraphonic scales of speaking rate obtained from three groups of subjects involved in different tasks: estimation of rate only (Task 0); estimation of rate, estimation of comprehension, and recall of a word in the sentence (Task 1); estimation of rate and writing a continuation sentence (Task 2). Each point (circle, triangle, or square) is the geometric mean of 168 magnitude estimations, 12 by each of 14 observers. For clarity, the functions are separated by a 30% interval. (From Grosjean, 1978b).

The mean exponent across the three groups was 2.1 (S.D. = 0.60). It would appear from these results that perception of rate is independent of linguistic processing: Listeners who are not asked to process the sentences perceive changes of rate in similar fashion to those who do have to process the utterances. It might be argued that all three groups processed to the deepest level, although not instructed to do so specifically, and then made rate judgements. Grosjean (1977) showed, however, that observers who had no knowledge of sign and listeners who knew no French behaved, on this task, exactly like native speakers of the two languages. The rate judgments of the former group could not interact with sentence analysis. In short, because the task variable and subject sophistication have no effect on rate judgments, they appear to be more a phonetic than a linguistic judgment. Grosjean (1976) found, moreover, that students of French who belonged to four levels of proficiency (Elementary, Intermediate, Advanced, and Advanced Conversation) could not be differentiated on scales of reading rate (the mean exponents were 1.9, 2.0, 2.1, and 2.1, respectively). We can conclude therefore that the perception of rate does not interact with linguistic processing and that listeners and observers base their responses solely on the auditory or visual stimuli when asked to judge change of rate in language production; such factors as how fast the hands and arms are moving and how often and for how long they stop will be of primary importance to the observer, whereas how many syllable peaks occur per second and what the duration and frequency of pauses are will be the bases of the listener's judgment (as we see in the following section).

To conclude, the autophonic scale of rate is invariant across passages and language modality; and the extraphonic scale of rate across passages, spoken languages, method of altering rate, knowledge of the language and processing tasks. This scale is affected, however, by the range of stimuli presented and the language modality of the stimuli: visual or oral.

How the Listener Integrates the Components of Speaking Rate

Although investigators have long been aware that global rate is made up of several variables, specifically, articulation rate and the duration and frequency of pauses (Cotton, 1936; Kelly & Steer, 1949), few researchers have attempted to describe the relative contribution of these component variables to the listener's perception of rate. Kelly and Steer (1949) asked judges to give category estimates of overall rate and of "sentence rate" (i.e., articulation rate) and concluded that the sentence rate method of describing extemporaneous speech is more highly related to audience judgment of global rate than is overall rate of speaking. The trouble with that conclusion, as Clevenger and Clark (1963) point out, is that Kelly and Steer did not study the effects of pausing. Articulation rate, pause time, and overall rate may interact in some way to produce the listener's perception of speech rate. Grosjean and Lane (1976) were interested in determining how the listener combines articulation rate and the number and length of pauses to produce a global impression of speech rate. Taking their cue from functional measurement (Anderson, 1973), they varied each component of speech rate separately in a factorial design. Twenty-seven reading rates of the Pop Fan passage ranging from 97 to 224 wpm were obtained by selection and tape splicing. Each rate corresponded to a combination of one of three levels of articulation rate (4.0, 4.9, and 5.8 syllables/sec), of number of pauses (17, 6, and 3), and of mean length of pauses (.29, .53, and .76 sec). These values were chosen on the basis of three prior studies (Grosjean, 1972; Grosjean & Deschamps, 1975; Lane & Grosjean, 1973) that analyzed the temporal variables in read out and spontaneous speech. The mid value of each variable corresponded to the mean obtained across these studies, whereas the lower and upper values matched levels ±2 standard deviations from that mean. The method of magnitude estimation was used to measure the perception of speech rate and listeners were presented with 81 recordings of the passage, each of the 27 rates presented three times in random order. Averaging over listeners and replications, 27 mean rate estimates were obtained and arranged in a $3 \times 3 \times 3$ matrix.

An analysis of variance on estimates of speech rate showed significant main effects for all three variables, articulation rate, number of pauses, and length of pauses. There was a significant Number of Pauses × Length of Pauses interaction (N.L), but articulation rate did not interact significantly with either of the other two variables in determining estimates of reading rate. A multilinear model (Anderson, 1973) was chosen to describe how listeners integrated the three kinds of information in order to arrive at an overall impression of reading rate. Specifically,

1) $E = W_1 A^m + W_2 (N.\bar{L})^n$

where A = the average phonation time per word, and $N.\bar{L}.$ = the average pause time per word (P). Equation 1 states that rate estimates are the sum of the weighted subjective scale values of articulation rate and pause rate (neglecting constants representing response variability and the intercept). The simple multiplicative interaction of pause number and length was an approximation to the results, because only 31% of their interaction sum of squares was associated with the bilinear component. Once articulation rate and pause rate were converted to their subjective scale values (articulation rate had a slope of -2 and pause rate a slope of $-.2$), the fit of the model was computed by means of multiple regression. The prediction equation obtained was as follows:

2) $E' = A^{-2} + 6P^{-.2} - 10$

Where A and P are given in sec/word. The linear relation between predicted and obtained estimates (least square slope .96) testified that the model well fit the data on which it was based. Of greater interest was the finding that the model predicted well the outcome of the studies of apparent rate, which used a variety of stimulus arrays, languages, and procedures (Grosjean & Lane, 1974; Grosjean & Lass, 1977; Lane & Grosjean, 1973).

Equation 2 describes a trading relation in controlling the listener's impression of speech rate between the time spent articulating and the time spent pausing. The factorial design, in which these two components were decoupled from their natural covariation, allowed us to determine iso-rate contours empirically; they are plotted in Fig. 6.4. As was already apparent from equation 2, a much larger change in pause rate is required to offset a change in articulation rate. This undoubtedly reflects the considerable difference in operating ranges of these two parameters of speech rate. When articulation rate spans four standard deviations (from the low to the high values in this experiment), the physical increase is only 1.5-fold, whereas the comparable standardized range for pause rate corresponds to a 15-fold increase in sec/word. The difference in physical range of the two

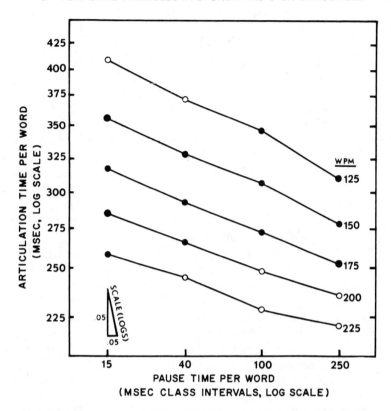

FIG. 6.4.   Iso-rate contours. (The unfilled points were obtained by extrapolation from families of curves obtained in the experiment; WPM = words per minute). (From Grosjean & Lane, 1976. Copyright 1976 by The American Psychological Association. Reprinted by permission.)

variables is reduced somewhat by the perceptual process: According to equation 2, corresponding ranges in rate perceived by the listener are 1.7:1 and 1.4:1, respectively; nevertheless, articulation rate remains the more influential variable.

PRODUCTION

In the following section, we describe how speakers and signers modulate the component variables of rate (articulation rate, number and length of pauses) when changing their global production rate. We isolate some of the factors that influence the duration of both signs and words and study the role of breathing in speech and sign production. Finally, we show how the study of pauses at slow rate can help us analyze the performance structures of sentences in both speech and sign.

Timing in the Production of Speech and Sign

Bellugi and Fischer (1972) and Grosjean (1979) have shown that speakers spend relatively less time articulating than do signers: The articulation time ratio, i.e. the articulation time divided by the total production time, is 78% in speech and 88% in sign. Also, speakers have a faster production rate than do signers: A speaker can produce 2.77 words in the time it takes a signer to produce one sign. (The global physical rates obtained by Grosjean [1979] are respectively 224 wpm and 81 spm for renditions of the Goldilocks story.) Bellugi and Fischer (1972) have shown, however, that speakers and signers produce the same number of propositions per minute in the two languages. Furthermore, speech has a higher pause time ratio than sign (about 16% as compared to 10%). The greater articulation time ratio in sign is due mainly to shorter pauses: Pauses are 59% longer in speech than in sign (0.46 sec and 0.29 sec respectively).

Despite these differences between speech and sign, Grosjean (1977), as reported earlier, found that both speakers and signers cover the same range of rate when progressing from a slow to a fast production rate (speakers covered a 2.7:1 range and signers a 2.6:1 range). The question now becomes: Do they cover identical ranges of rates by using similar strategies? In other words, how do signers and speakers alter the component variables of rate (articulation rate, number and length of pauses) when they change their global production rate (signs or words per minute)? Do signers, like speakers, primarily change the number of pauses and hardly alter the articulation rate and the length of pauses, or do they use a different strategy? And in the latter case, how can we account for this difference in approach? These are the questions posed by Grosjean (1979) in a study of timing in sign and speech.

The Goldilocks passage (Grosjean & Lane, 1977) was used to obtain five different rates of signing from each of five native signers. The idiomatic English translation of the passage was then given to five hearing subjects and similar reading rates were obtained in English. Figure 6.5 gives an indication of the strategies used by speakers and signers. Signers scarcely change their global physical rate by modifying the amount of pausing they put into their signing stream; even at the slowest rate, only 17% of the total signing stream is made up of pauses, as compared with 37% in English. Instead, signers prefer to change their signing rate by altering their articulation rate. Figure 6.5 shows that articulation time in sign covers a much wider range than in speech: 51 sec versus 32 sec. And, inversely, the pause range in sign is only 15 sec whereas it is 20 sec in speech. The figure also shows that signers and speakers diverge in their strategies, especially at slow rate; here, a signer will decrease his or her physical rate by articulating more slowly whereas a speaker will pause more often. At fast rates, however, the two will follow similar tactics, in that both will alter their articulation time more than their pause time.

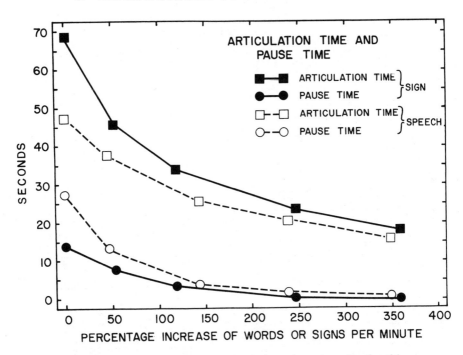

FIG. 6.5.   Articulation time and pause time in sign and speech as a function of the percentage increase in words or signs per minute. Each point (filled for sign, unfilled for speech) is the mean of 5 values, 1 by each of 5 subjects. (From Grosjean, 1979. Copyright 1979 by Plenum Publishing Company. Reprinted by permission.)

When a signer alters his pause time, however little he does so when modifiy-ing his physical rate, does he alter both the number and length of pauses to the same extent or does he prefer, as for speech, to alter the number of pauses much more? Figure 6.6 gives the answer to this question, by displaying the changes in pause length (left axis) and frequency (right axis) that occur as the speaker or signer increases his overall rate. As physical rate is increased from 93 to 416 wpm (a 350% increase in words or signs per minute), the mean length of pauses in speech changes only slightly: from 0.60 sec to 0.26 sec, a range of 0.34 sec. But the number of pauses is altered considerably; from one pause every 2.5 words at the slowest rate (40% of the pause slots filled) to one pause every 60.4 words at the highest rate (2% of pause slots filled). In sign, however, both variables appear to decrease concurrently and regularly as physical rate is in-creased.

Thus both speakers and signers modify the articulation time and pause time in their productions when asked to speed up or slow down. The relative importance

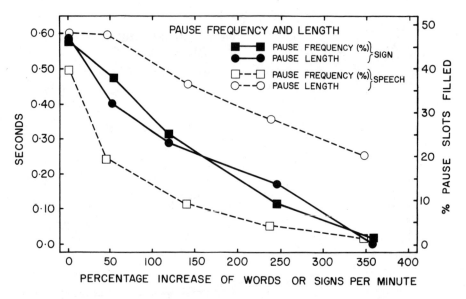

FIG. 6.6.   Pause length and number of pauses (expressed as the percentage of the pause slots in the passage that are filled) in sign and speech as a function of the percentage increase in words or signs per minute. Each point (filled for sign, unfilled for speech) is the mean of 5 values, 1 by each of 5 subjects. (From Grosjean, 1979. Copyright 1979 by Plenum Publishing Company. Reprinted by permission.)

of these two variables will differ, however, in the two modalities: Speakers primarily modify the pause time (by inserting or extracting pauses) and hardly alter their articulation time, whereas signers will alter their rate by mainly changing the time they spend articulating. How can we account for these different strategies? The answer probably lies in the role played by breathing in speech and sign.

In Fig. 6.7, taken from Grosjean (1979), we present the first sentence of the Goldilocks passage produced at normal rate in both English and Sign and the accompanying breathing patterns of the signer and speaker. As can be seen, the signer's respiratory cycle is very regular throughout the sentence: The signer spends 36% of his breathing cycle inhaling during quiet breathing and continues with this same inhalation pattern when signing. The speaker, on the other hand, spends about the same amount of time inhaling during quiet breathing (43% of the breathing cycle) but changes tactics during speech. The speaker now inhales rapidly at the beginning of the sentence (15% of the breathing cycle is spent inhaling), adjusts expiration to serve the needs of speech production (85% of the breathing cycle is spent speaking), and inhales again rapidly during the pause at the end of the sentence. Thus the respiratory cycle during signing remains very regular (it contracts slightly as rate is increased) whereas in speech the breathing pattern is totally reorganized to accommodate the needs of the speaker. We should note also that inhalation in signing can take place during a sign, a pause, or during both. In speech, on the other hand, inhalation can of course only take place during the pauses and must be of minimum duration.

How does this affect the strategies used by signers and speakers when modifiying production rate? As signing is an activity that is independent of breathing, a signer may alter rate mainly by changing the time spent articulating whereas a speaker is compelled by breathing demands to put numerous pauses into his speech, especially at a slow rate, where the speaker has only enough air in reserve to articulate a few words. When this reserve is used up, the speaker must stop articulating and inhale if he or she is to continue articulating. This interaction between breathing and speech may also explain why the speaker increases and decreases pause time by altering the number of pauses, leaving the pause durations relatively constant. Inhalation can only take place during the pauses and must be of a minimum duration. As pause durations cannot be compressed beyond a certain point, a speaker will compensate by pausing less often. This results in the two distinct slopes in Fig. 6.6 relating number and length of pauses to rate for speech. A signer is not faced with the same constraints and can therefore increase or decrease pause time, however little he or she does so, by altering the number and the length of the pauses equally. Were breathing not linked to speech in such a way, we would expect speakers to follow the same strategy as signers when altering their production rate. But given this

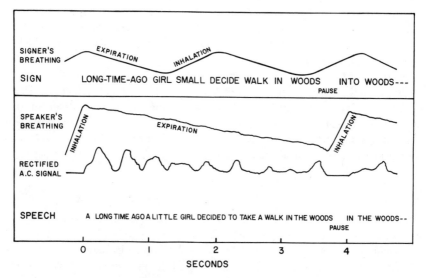

FIG. 6.7. Breathing patterns in signing and speaking at normal rate. The A.C. signal for speech has been full wave rectified and filtered. (From Grosjean, 1979. Copyright 1979 by Plenum Publishing Company. Reprinted by permission.)

linkage, it is not surprising, as Grosjean (1979) showed, that speakers and signers differ in the amount of pausing they put into their productions and that they adopt different strategies when increasing and decreasing rate: Speakers change the time they spend pausing, whereas signers modify the time they spend articulating.

Let us now turn to the factors influencing the articulation time of words and signs. Klatt (1976) lists a number of factors that influence the durational structure of units in speech: the psychological and physical state of the speaker, speaking rate, position of the element within a paragraph, emphasis and semantic novelty, phrase structure lengthening, word-final lengthening, inherent phonological duration of a segment, effect of linguistic stress, and effect of postvocalic consonant and segmental interactions (e.g., consonant clusters). Grosjean (1979) found evidence that a number of these factors, restated in terms of a visual–manual language as necessary, also influenced the duration of signs. The first is signing rate. As rate was increased, the duration of signs decreased. At a rate of 176 signs per minute (spm) the mean was 0.16 sec with a range extending from 0.07 sec (REALLY) to 0.33 sec (CHAIRS). Conversely, as signing rate was decreased, signs were increased in duration. The mean duration of signs at 35 spm was 0.69 sec with values ranging from 0.28 (HARD) to 1.90 sec (LONG-TIME-AGO). The second is semantic novelty. Signs that occur twice in the same syntactic position are on the average 10% shorter on the second occurrence. (Similar findings have been reported for speech by Umeda [1975]). The third is phrase structure lengthening. Signs at the end of a sentence (as defined empirically by Grosjean & Lane [1977]) are about 12% longer than within sentences. (Klatt [1975] reports a 30% increase in vowel duration at phrase boundaries.)

In sum, signers and speakers cover an equal range of rates when asked to speed up or slow down and they do this by varying the articulation time and the pause time (although in different degree); the durations of both signs and words are influenced by rate, semantic novelty, and phrase structure lengthening. These findings led Grosjean (1978a) to postulate some common mechanism that mediates, at least in part, both sign and speech production. This hypothesis will find further support when we examine the distribution of pauses in sign and speech and the hierarchical organization of the speaker's and signer's output.

Breathing, Pausing, and Reading

The results obtained by Grosjean (1979) in comparing breathing patterns in sign and speech encouraged Grosjean and Collins (1979) to investigate further the role of breathing in speech production. They examined breathing pauses in a variable rate reading task and attempted to answer the following questions: What is the relation between linguistic structure and breathing? Do breathing pauses follow the same pattern as nonbreathing pauses when speakers are asked to read at varying rates of speech? For example, as rate is increased, do breathing pauses become shorter and less frequent, disappearing totally within minor constituents and only remaining at sentence breaks? Grosjean (1972) and Lane and Grosjean (1973) showed that this was the case for pauses in general, but they did not separate out breathing from nonbreathing pauses. How much time in a breathing pause is actually devoted to breathing (inspiration) and how is this modified with change of rate? In addition to answering these questions, Grosjean and Collins (1979) attempted, throughout their study, to address the question of whether inhalation controls or, on the contrary, is subservient to pausing.

Speakers were asked to read the Goldilocks passage at five different rates. Their breathing was measured by monitoring rib-cage contraction and expansion with a pneumograph. Breathing pauses (BPs) and nonbreathing pauses (NBPs) were located by means of the oscillographic tracing of the speaker's breathing and their durations were measured (pauses whose durations were less than 200 msec were not included in the analysis). In the linguistic analysis of the pause locations, seven linguistic boundaries were examined: the sentence boundary (END S); the break between two conjoined sentences (END S CONJ); the break between an adverbial or prepositional phrase and the preceding or following NP or VP (PP-ADV); the NP-VP break (NP-VP); the breaks inside the NP subject or object (INS NP); the breaks inside the VP (INS VP); and finally, the breaks within the adverbial or prepositional phrases (INS[PP-ADV]).

Figure 6.8 presents the percentage of pause slots (or word boundaries) filled by a pause as a function of reading rate (as the passage contains 116 words, the maximum number of slots is 115). As rate increases, the number of pauses (Ps) decreases rapidly; from one pause every 2.3 words at the slowest rate (75 wpm) to one pause every 33 words at the highest rate (391 wpm). Both the breathing pause (BP) and nonbreathing pause (NBP) functions follow the same trend, but at somewhat different rates. The steepest of the two functions is that of the NBP; at the slowest rate, there are slightly more NBPs than BPs (23% as opposed to 21%) but then NBPs fall off rapidly so that at normal rate (201 wpm) they account for only 22% of all pauses (3% of the slots) and at the fastest rate they have practically disappeared. The function for the BP falls off more slowly and merges into the function for all pauses (P) at the highest rate, signifying that at fast rates all the pauses inserted into one's speech are in fact breathing pauses. This is not suprising. When asked to read or speak at very fast rates, speakers attempt to delete all pauses (these slow down the overall rate and interfere with the smoothness of the articulation) but are stopped from doing so by the need to breathe; they will therefore pause only when their air reserve has been spent and will then inhale as quickly as possible. It is interesting to note that in Sign Language, where, as we have seen, breathing and signing are unrelated, fast signing rates are completely devoid of pauses (Grosjean, 1978b). Were breathing not linked to speech production in such an absolute way, one would expect speakers to adopt similar tactics when asked to increase their rate of speaking: i.e., to articulate quickly and continuously.

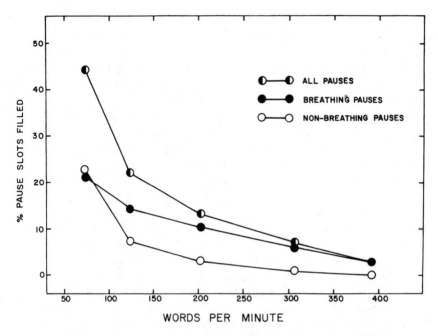

FIG. 6.8.   Number of pauses in the Goldilocks passage (all pauses, breathing and nonbreathing pauses) as a function of wpm. The ordinate is expressed as the percentage of the pause slots in the passage that are filled. Each point is the mean of 12 values, 2 by each of 6 subjects. (From Grosjean & Collins, 1979. Copyright 1979 by S. Karger A. G. Reprinted by permission.)

These results, then, are a first indication that pausing is not directly determined by the need to breathe: at slow rate there are just as many NBPs as BPs, and at normal rate, one-fifth of all pauses are NBPs. It is only at rates faster than normal that the physiological need to breathe takes over and now controls the occurrence of pauses.

Grosjean and Collins (1979) also found that as rate increases, the durations of both pause types decrease. The BPs have the longest durations across all rates; they remain nearly twice as long as NBPs in four of the five reading rates. This is probably because the action of inhaling (in BPs) requires more time than only stopping phonation (NBPs). This seems reasonable considering the complex physiological operations demanded of the inspiratory and expiratory muscles when a breath is taken. It was also found that the component that takes up the most time during the BP is the actual inspiration. Much of the BP, however, especially at slower rates, is *not* taken up with actual breathing, contrary to what might have been expected had breathing constraints been controlling pause duration. About 36% of the BP at slow rate is made up of pre-inspiration time and 14% of post-inspiration time. As speakers increase their speaking rate, they shorten their BPs mainly by decreasing the pre-inspiration component.

Figure 6.9 presents the percentage of pause slots filled by BPs and NBPs at each of seven linguistic locations at five reading rates. As can be seen from the five histograms, the number of BPs at a particular pause slot is not only a function of the rate of reading of the passage but also of the linguistic status of that pause location. BPs occur mainly at major constituent breaks (for example, 78 % of all BPs at 75 wpm are placed either at the End S or End S Conj breaks) but can also occur at minor breaks (inside VPs, NPs, prepositional phrases, etc.). However, as rate is increased, BPs very quickly disappear from these minor constituent breaks and at rates greater than normal, they are confined to the two major breaks, and finally only to the End S location. It is also at these very high rates that speakers no longer take a breath at every sentence break (End S): Only 58% of these pause slots at 305 wpm and 29% at 391 wpm are filled by BPs. When a speaker does pause, however, despite the high rate, the speaker almost invariably breathes during the pause.

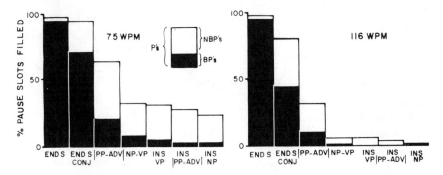

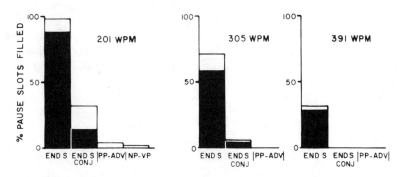

FIG. 6.9.   The percentage of pause slots filled by breathing and nonbreathing pauses at each of seven linguistic locations at five different rates. (From Grosjean & Collins, 1979. Copyright 1979 by S. Karger A. G. Reprinted by permission.)

The frequency of NBPs at a particular pause slot, like that of the breath pauses we have just examined, is also determined by rate and the linguistic status of the pause location. However, very few NBPs ever occur at the END S break (this location is utilized mainly by BPs) and most are inserted at less important breaks. As was seen in Fig. 6.8, the absolute number of NBPs diminishes considerably as rate is increased and at rates faster than normal (305 and 391 wpm), the few NBPs that remain occur mainly at the End S break.

Thus speakers will prefer to take a breath at major linguistic breaks (although they may also take one at less important breaks if the rate is quite slow) and they prefer to pause without breathing at minor breaks. When rate is increased, the minor breaks no longer receive a pause and, consequently, NBPs are the first to disappear. The mean duration of BPs and NBPs was also found to be a function of speaking rate and syntax. Both types of pause were longer at the End S location than at any other location, and as the linguistic importance of the break diminished, so did the duration of BPs and NBPs.

Grosjean and Collins (1979) concluded from these findings that both the duration and frequency of occurrence of BPs depend greatly on rate of speaking *and* on the syntactic nature of the pause location. The higher the order of a syntactic break (End S, End S Conj), the longer and more frequent will be the BPs. The absolute frequency and duration of BPs, at any given location, will also depend on the speaking rate: As rate is increased, BPs will become shorter and fewer. NBPs follow the same pattern but are always shorter than BPs and tend to occur primarily at minor constituent breaks.

This study revealed, then, that breathing in speech depends to a large extent on the speaker's preplanned pause patterns. Pauses, in turn, are controlled by such variables as rate of speaking, the syntactic importance of the boundaries and to a lesser extent by emphatic stress, sentence length, and the tendency to bisect segments (Grosjean, Grosjean, & Lane, 1979). If all of these factors determine that a pause in an utterance will be long, and the speaker needs to take a breath, then inhalation will take place during the pauses. However, if they determine that the pause will be short, then no breathing will occur within that pause and the speaker will have to wait for the next important pause. This subservience of breathing to pausing is reversed only in the case of very fast rates; the physiological need to breathe forces the speaker to stop to inhale—but the speaker does so as rarely and as quickly as possible.

Linguistic Structures and Performance Structures in English and American Sign Language: Studies in Pause Distributions

Considerable research in the 1960s and early 1970s was aimed at demonstrating the psychological reality of surface structures of sentences as they are defined by transformational-generative grammar. Experiments in recall, perception, direct scaling of relatedness and pausing, among others, were used to authenticate the role of syntactic units in processing spoken languages. Some studies were most interested, on the one hand, in showing that clauses are functional units in speech processing. For example, Jarvella (1971) found that words from immediate clauses and sentences were recalled better than corresponding words from previous clauses and sentences, and, in the numerous click studies, researchers found that clicks were displaced perceptually toward clause boundaries (Fodor & Bever, 1965; Holmes & Forster, 1970). In other studies researchers were more interested, on the other hand, in showing that lower order surface constituents are also functional units in speech processing. Levelt (1969) for example, used a method of direct scaling of relatedness, and found that the degree of relatedness between words was inversely related to the number of phrase boundaries separating one word from the other. Johnson (1965, 1968), using a recall task to study the psychological reality of phrase structure rules, found high rank-order correlations between the rank of the constituent break and the transitional error probability at that break. He concluded that the surface constituents of sentences are functional units.

Studies of pausing in reading and spontaneous speech have also shown that sentences are made up of functional units: to a hierarchy of pause frequency and duration corresponds a hierarchy of constituents. There will be, at any given rate of speech, more and longer pauses at the ends of sentences than within them and more and longer pauses at the breaks between major constituents than within them. Goldman-Eisler (1972), in an analysis of nine samples of spontaneous speech, noted that 78% of sentences were divided from each other by pauses longer than 50 csec and that 66% of transitions between clauses and almost all transitions between words (93%) had a pause duration less than 50 csec. In studies of English and French interviews and descriptions, Grosjean and Deschamps (1972, 1973, 1975) obtained quite similar results. In both languages more pauses were present at the end of the sentences than within them, and these pauses were systematically shorter within clauses and sentences. As we have seen in the previous section, Grosjean and Collins (1979) likewise found that linguistic categories were good predictors of the frequency and length of breathing and nonbreathing pauses in an oral reading task.

In sum, all these psycholinguistic studies, involving such diverse tasks as recall, perception, direct scaling of relatedness, and pausing, have shown that a relation exists between the listener's and speaker's segmentation of the stream of speech on the one hand, and a structural description of the sentences comprising that stream, on the other. Thus it is possible, to some extent at least, to delineate from the behavioral data processing units that correspond to structural units—to sentences and constituents within sentences.

However, there are ripples on this calm surface that reflect underlying currents. First of all, the studies have not always found a perfect correspondence between the experimental data and the formal linguistic structure. Levelt (1970) reports that the minor constituents were not always reflected in the hierarchical structure obtained from errors made in a perception in noise study, Johnson

(1965) found that transitional error probabilities were not always predicted by the linguistic structure, and Grosjean and Deschamps (1975) found more and longer pauses inside the verb phrase than between the noun phrase and the verb phrase. Second, most studies concerned with constituents within sentences used very simple structures, providing a weak or at least restricted test of the general hypothesis that phrase structure constituents are processing units. Third, most studies used sentences that were restricted in another sense: They were balanced so that their major constituents had about the same length.

In fact, there is a growing literature that shows that the performance structures of sentences (obtained from experimental data) do not always correspond to the formally motivated phrase markers. Martin (1970), for example, asked subjects to parse sentences by arranging the words of the sentences into "natural groups." The data thus obtained were then hierarchically structured with Johnson's (1967) clustering program. The results showed that subjects did not automatically group the verb with the NP object, as linguistic models would predict, but that in many cases (SV)O clusterings were obtained.

Grosjean et al. (1979) set out to determine whether the sentence structures obtained from silent pausing at reduced reading rate reflect these performance structures and, if so, what the nature of the relation is between the linguistic surface structure and these performance structures. They wanted to arrive at a simple model, presumably taking into account the surface structure of the sentence and certain performance variables that would account for most of the variance in the pause durations when reading sentences.

In a first experiment, they asked six speakers to read 14 sentences embedded in three paragraphs. These sentences were taken from the Bever, Lackner, and Kirk (1969) study of perceptual location of clicks. The method of magnitude production was used to obtain the readings at various rates. The silent pauses produced by the speakers were measured on oscillographic tracings of the readings. The minumum duration for a silence to be counted as a pause was set at 25 csec. The pauses at each word boundary, in each of the 14 experimental sentences, were then pooled across the six speakers and the mean duration computed and expressed as a percent of the total pause duration in that sentence. These pause durations were then used to make hierarchical clusters of the words within the sentences, according to an iterative procedure used by Grosjean and Lane (1977).

The same procedure was used in a second experiment to obtain hierarchical structures from nonbreathing pauses only; in this task, speakers were told not to inhale during their production of the sentences. The two conditions (breathing and nonbreathing) produced structures that were practically indentical. Over the 14 sentences, the mean coefficient of correlation between the two sets of percent pause duration was .87. Furthermore, identical hierarchical structures were obtained by asking native speakers to parse the experimental sentences. For all sentences, the mean coefficient of correlation between pausing and parsing was .92.

Thus pause durations produced reliable performance sentence structures that are not paradigm specific. Similar structures were obtained in the parsing task, and in experiments on short-term memory (Dommergues & Grosjean, 1978) using transitional error probability as a measure (Johnson, 1968). The question now became: What variables determine the performance structure of a sentence?

The predictor variable that should account for most of the total variance in percentage of pause duration, if we base ourselves on preceding studies of pausing, is the surface structure of the sentences. Grosjean et al. (1979) therefore drew a surface structure tree of each experimental sentence, using as a guide the bracketings assigned by Bever, Lackner, and Kirk (1969). The next step was to give every word boundary an index of the complexity of the syntactic relations between words in the sentence. They adopted the following measure: The complexity index (CI) at a particular boundary is the number of nodes dominated by the boundary node, including the boundary node itself. To illustrate, the major surface break in the top sentence of Fig. 6.10 has a CI of nine, because it dominates three nodes on the left and five on the right.

The 14 linguistic trees were indexed in this way; the complexity values at each word boundary were correlated with the percent pause duration at that boundary. The mean coefficient of correlation for the 14 sentences was .76. Thus the surface structure of a sentence is a good predictor of the percent pause duration, not only at major constituent breaks, as shown by previous studies, but at all breaks in the sentence. In Figure 6.10, we illustrate how surface structure and the corresponding pause structure can be quite congruent (the correlation between the two is .92). Most linguistic breaks are respected in pause structure (after *book,* after *expert,* etc.), although some slight variation exists at lower levels (for instance, inside *Closing his client's book* and *the young expert*).

Although the complexity index is on the whole a good predictor of percent pause duration, it fails at times to account for the pause structure of entire sentences or constituents. In the sentence, *John asked the strange young man to be quick on the task,* the main surface structure break is after the noun phrase (*John*), whereas the longest pause is situated after the noun phrase object (*the strange young man*)—the NP–VP break receives only the fourth longest pause, 10%. Furthermore, the third linguistic break is after *quick* but it is given the second longest pause, 19%. These differences are reflected in the coefficient of correlation between complexity index and percent pause duration, which is .60. It would seem from these results that pausing is affected both by the relative importance of constituent breaks, reflected by the complexity index, and the relative length of the constituents. When these are of unequal length, as in this case (the NP contains one word and the VP eleven), speakers will attempt to displace the pause to a point midway between the beginning of the first constituent (for example, an NP) to the end of the second constituent (for example, a VP)- if at that point there occurs a syntactic boundary important enough. It would seem that a compromise takes place between this bisection tendency and the linguistic structure of the sentence.

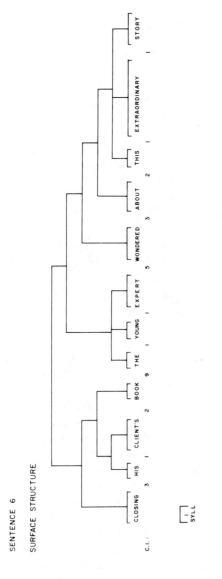

SENTENCE 6

SURFACE STRUCTURE

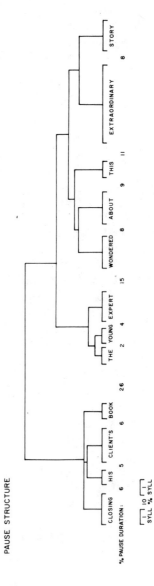

PAUSE STRUCTURE

FIG. 6.10. The surface structure and pause structure of a sentence. (From Grosjean, Grosjean & Lane, 1979. Copyright 1979 by Academic Press. Reprinted by permission.)

Performance pause structures can therefore be characterized as the product of two (sometimes conflicting) demands on the speaker: the need to respect the linguistic structure of the sentence and the need to balance the length of the constituents in the output. A model that predicts these pause structures will have to take these two demands into account.

To assign to each word boundary a predicted share of the total pause duration in light of its structural complexity and distance from the bisection point, Grosjean et al. (1979) used an iterative procedure as follows. They start with the largest constituent, the entire sentence, and assign to each word boundary a complexity index, as described earlier, and a percentage that is its relative proximity to the bisection point computed as follows: the number of words from the start (or end) of the constituent up to the word boundary (whichever is less) divided by half the number of words in the constituent. The boundary with the largest product of complexity index and proximity to the bisection point is the major performance break. The second order breaks and (a linear transformation of) their predicted pause durations are obtained by repeating the procedure on the two segments just obtained. And so on, iteratively, until the lowest order segments (single words) have been delimited and assigned a (linear transformation of) predicted percent pause duration.

In Fig. 6.11, we present the surface structure, the pause structure, and the predicted pause structure of sentence 8 used by Grosjean et al. (1979). The match between surface structure and pausing is relatively good, but several mismatches do occur. The NP–VP break (between *he* and *brought*) is not respected by the pause data and the prepositonal phrase (*By making his plans known*) is organized quite differently in the two structures. Consequently, the coefficient of correlation between the complexity index and the percent pause duration is only .75. The structure that is produced by the model, however, fits the pause data almost perfectly. Because the relative proximity to the bisection point is taken into account, the second main break in the model structure is no longer situated after *he*, as is predicted by the surface structure, but after *out* (a major surface break that is situated near the middle of the sentence), and the third main break is no longer after *by* but after *By making*. In addition, the NP in the prepositional phrase (*the objections of everyone*) is produced in two distinct clusters by the model (*the objections* and *of everyone*), in complete accord with the pause data. The only difference, a small one, between the pause and model structures is in the organization of *he brought out*. In the case of this sentence, therefore, the model values predict the pause data almost perfectly (r = .96).

The mean correlation between the obtained percent pause duration and the model percent pause duration for all 14 sentences was .87. This is significantly different from the mean correlation between percent pause duration and the complexity index (.76) at the .01 level. Thus the model accounted for 73% of the total variance in pause time as compared to 56% accounted for by the complexity index alone.

The variance that the model did not account for could be due to such factors as

SURFACE STRUCTURE

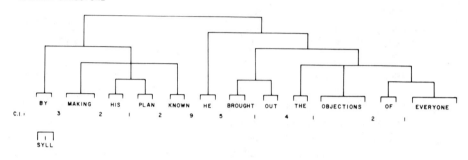

PAUSE STRUCTURE

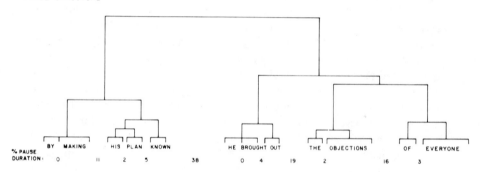

PREDICTED PAUSE STRUCTURE

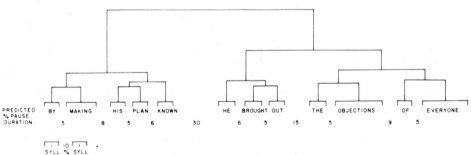

FIG. 6.11. The surface structure, pause structure, and predicted pause structure of a sentence. (From Grosjean, Grosjean, & Lane, 1979. Copyright 1979 by Academic Press. Reprinted by permission.)

the linguistic model itself, the impact that the length of the word has on the preceding and following pause, the stress pattern of the sentence and semantic variables. Grosjean et al. (1979) found, for example, that the percent pause duration of the break preceding a one-, two-, or three-syllable word (at a constant complexity index of 1) is constant (about 4%) but then rises to 9% before a four-syllable word and to 11% before a five-syllable word. Nevertheless, the present model not only accounts for most of the variance of the 14 experimental sentences but is also a good predictor of the pause data obtained in other experiments (Grosjean & Collins, 1979, for example).

Can this model also predict the durations of a language in another modality, American Sign Language? If breaths occur where pauses are predetermined to occur, as we have argued earlier, and if we are now in a position to predict pausing, then there is no reason why the absence of breathing itself in a non-oral language should detract from the predictive accuracy of the pausing model. Grosjean and Lane (1977) asked native users of ASL to sign the Goldilocks passage at five different rates in order to obtain pauses not only between sentences but also between every sign in the sentence. As can be seen from Fig. 6.12, this tactic was, on the whole, quite successful (as it is for speech), and almost every sign is separated from the next by a pause. At the highest rate (173 spm), no holds (pauses in sign) occur between the three sentences: EAT ALL-GONE/THEN SIT THREE DIFFERENT CHAIRS/SAME THING HAPPEN. At the next two rates (130 and 82 spm), the between sentence breaks appear. Then, as the speakers sign the text at rates slower than normal, breaks start emerging between and within major constituents. At 59 spm, the first sentence is already divided up into Conj-Vb-VP2, and at the slowest rate (39 spm), the other two sentences are also partitioned by holds.

In general, Grosjean and Lane (1977) found that long pauses marked the breaks between sentences; somewhat shorter pauses, those between conjoined sentences; and shorter pauses still, those between major constituents. The grand mean duration of pauses between sentences was 229 msec; between conjoined sentences, 134 msec; between NP and VP, 106 msec; within NP, 6 msec., and within VP, 11 msec. The higher the syntactic order of the break, the longer the hold that occurred at the break.

It is particularly interesting that when the data are not averaged across sentences (as was the case in the Grosjean & Lane [1977] study), a number of mismatches are found (as in speech) between the constituent structure of the sentence and the pause durations. Grosjean, Grosjean, and Lane (1979) took all sentences five signs or longer and correlated their pause durations with the complexity indices of a hypothesized surface structure and with values predicted by the performance model. The model was a better predictor than the complexity indices by themselves: $r = 0.85$, as opposed to $r = 0.78$. Thus, signers, like speakers, need to make a compromise between two sometimes conflicting demand: the need to respect the linguistic structure of the sentence and the need to balance the length of the constituents in the output.

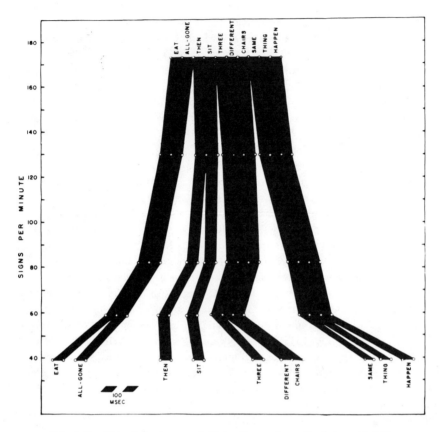

FIG. 6.12.   The relation between hold durations and overall rate in an excerpt from a passage in ASL. As overall rate decreases, the syntactic structure of the sentences emerge in the pattern of hold durations (white spaces). Each hold is the mean of five productions, one by each of five subjects. (From Grosjean & Lane, 1977. Copyright 1977 by Elsevier Sequoia S.A. Reprinted by permission.)

We are currently investigating the nature of performance structures obtained from different experimental paradigms. In our current work on sign (Battison, Lane, & Grosjean, 1978; Grosjean, Battison, Teuber, & Lane, 1978), we are using probe latency, relatedness judgments, parsing, and pausing. The results obtained so far confirm that signers, like speakers, are influenced by the syntactic structure of the sentence and the tendency to process and output constituents of equal length. When sentences are balanced, the syntactic structure predicts the experimental data as well as the performance model, but when the sentences are unbalanced, the syntactic structure is a very poor predictor of pause durations, parsing values, relatedness judgments, and probe latency. These are well predicted by the model, however.

We conclude from this that, for both speakers and signers, performance structures, obtained from a variety of tasks, are the product of at least two conflicting demands, namely, the need to respect the linguistic structure of the sentence and the need to balance the length of the constituents. Performance structures are therefore founded in the decoding and encoding of language (be it visual or oral) and not in the properties of any particular communication modality.

FINAL REMARKS

A listener judging the rate of speech and an observer judging the rate of sign are guided quite differently by comparable changes in rate, as the differing slopes of the two extraphonic scales testify. Inasmuch as it appears that these rate judgments are unaffected by comprehension variables, and hence are based on rather peripheral kinds of evidence, it is not surprising that the different modalities of speech and sign make a difference here.

When we change our focus from the receiver to the sender, however, quite a different state of affairs seems to emerge. At the highest level, proposition rate, we have Bellugi and Fischer's intriguing finding that, despite gross differences in average word duration in the two languages (by a factor of 2), speakers and signers tell stories at about the same proposition rate. Next, the distribution of pausing is tightly constrained by phrase structure in both languages, which suggests that recitation, like shadowing, cannot short-circuit higher order processes that subserve the comprehension and production of novel utterances. Likewise, in both languages, word duration is affected by phrase structure, semantic novelty, and overall rate. The temporal parameters of production in the two languages are comparable even down to the level of the increment in physical rate required for the sender to perceive any given increment in apparent rate. What all these commonalities suggest, of course, is a common path in assembling and sending messages in speech and sign that is longer than we had imagined. At the end of this path, neural messages must be recoded differently for manual or oral articulation. We are tempted to speculate, however, that this recoding is of a rather low and invariant order, much like universal rules of phonetic detail in grammar. One of those details is the awkward need to breathe in the one case, which accounts for some superficial dissimilarities in timing.

ACKNOWLEDGMENTS

The preparation of this chapter was supported in part by Grant 768 2530, National Science Foundation, and Grant 5 RR 07143 NS 14923–01A2, Department of Health, Education, and Welfare.

REFERENCES

Anderson, N. Algebraic models in perception. In E. C. Carterette & M. P. Friedman (Eds.), *Handbook of perception*. New York: Academic Press, 1973.

Battison, R. *Lexical borrowing in American Sign Language*. Silver Spring, Md: Linstok Press, 1978.

Battison, R., Lane, H., & Grosjean, F. *Probed recall latencies reflect both within-clause and across-clause boundaries in American Sign Language*. Unpublished manuscript, Northeastern University, 1978.

Bellugi, U., & Fischer, S. A comparison of Sign Language and spoken language: Rate and grammatical mechanisms. *Cognition*, 1972, *1*, 173-200.

Bellugi, U., Klima, E., & Siple, P. Remembering in signs. *Cognition*, 1975, *3*, 93-125.

Bever, T., Lackner, J., & Kirk, R. The underlying structures of sentences are the primary units of immediate speech processing. *Perception & Psychophysics*, 1969, *5*(4), 225-234.

Clevenger, T., & Clark, M. Coincidental variation as a source of confusion in the experimental study of rate. *Language and Speech*, 1963, *6*, 144-149.

Cotton, J. Syllabic rate: A new concept in the study of speech rate variation. *Speech Monographs*, 1936, *2*, 112-117.

Dommergues, J. Y., & Grosjean, F. *Performance structure in the recall of sentences*. Unpublished manuscript, University of Paris VIII, 1978.

Fodor, J., & Bever, T. The psychological reality of linguistic segments. *Journal of Verbal Learning and Verbal Behavior*, 1965, *4*, 414-420.

Frishberg, N. Arbitrariness and iconicity: Historical change in American Sign Language. *Language*, 1975, *51*, 696-719.

Goldman-Eisler, F. Pauses, clauses, sentences. *Language and Speech*, 1972, *15*, 103-113.

Grosjean, F. *Le rôle joué par trois variables temporelles dans le compréhension orale de l'anglais étudié comme second langue et perception de la vitesse de parole par des lecteurs et des auditeurs*. Thèse de Doctorat de 3° Cycle, Université de Paris VII, 1972.

Grosjean, F. *The perception of rate by second language learners*. Unpublished manuscript, Northeastern University, 1976.

Grosjean, F. The perception of rate in spoken and sign languages. *Perception & Psychophysics*, 1977, *22*(4), 408-413.

Grosjean, F. *Cross-linguistic research in the perception and production of English and American Sign Language*. Paper presented at the National Symposium on Sign Language Research and Teaching, Coronado, Calif., October 1978. (a)

Grosjean, F. *Perception of rate and processing of sentences*. Unpublished manuscript, Northeastern University, 1978. (b)

Grosjean, F. A study of timing in a manual and a spoken language: American Sign Language and English. *Journal of Psycholinguistic Research*, 1979, *8*, 379-405.

Grosjean, F., Battison, R., Teuber, H., & Lane, H. *Performance structures in American Sign Language*. Unpublished manuscript, Northeastern University, 1978.

Grosjean, F., & Collins, M. Breathing, pausing, and reading. *Phonetica*, 1979, *36*(2), 98-114.

Grosjean, F., & Deschamps, A. Analyse des variables temporelles du français spontané. *Phonetica*, 1972, *26*(3), 129-157.

Grosjean, F., & Deschamps, A. Analyse des variables temporelles du français spontané II. Comparaison du français oral dans la description avec l'anglais (description) et avec le français (interview radiophonique). *Phonetica*, 1973, *28*, 191-226.

Grosjean, F., & Deschamps, A. Analyse contrastive des variables temporelles de l'anglais et du français: Vitesse de parole et variables composantes, phènoménes d'hesitation. *Phonetica*, 1975, *31*, 144-184.

Grosjean, F., Grosjean, L., & Lane, H. The patterns of silence: Performance structure in sentence production. *Cognitive Psychology*, 1979, *11*, 58-81.

Grosjean, F., & Lane, H. Effects of two temporal variables on the listener's perception of reading rate. *Journal of Experimental Psychology*, 1974, *102*(5), 893–896.

Grosjean, F., & Lane, H. How the listener integrates the components of speaking rate. *Journal of Experimental Psychology: Human Perception and Performance*, 1976, *2*(4), 538–543.

Grosjean, F., & Lane, H. Pauses and syntax in American Sign Language. *Cognition*, 1977, *5*, 101–117.

Grosjean, F., & Lass, N. Some factors affecting the listener's perception of reading rate in English and French. *Language and Speech*, 1977, *20*(3), 198–208.

Grosjean, F., Teuber, H., & Lane, H. *When is a sign a sign? The on-line processing of gated signs in American Sign Language*. Unpublished manuscript, Northeastern University, 1978.

Holmes, V., & Forster, K. Detection of extraneous signals during sentence recognition. *Perception & Psychophysics*, 1970, *7*, 297–301.

Jarvella, R. Syntactic processing of connected speech. *Journal of Verbal Learning and Verbal Behavior*, 1971, *10*, 409–416.

Johnson, N. The psychological reality of phrase structure rules. *Journal of Verbal Learning and Verbal Behavior*, 1965, *4*, 469–475.

Johnson, N. Sequential verbal behavior. In T. Dixon & D. Horton (Eds.), *Verbal behavior and general behavior theory*. Englewood Cliff, N.J.: Prentice-Hall, 1968.

Johnson, S. Hierarchical clustering schemes. *Psychometrika*, 1967, *32*, 241–254.

Kelly, J., & Steer, M. Revised concept of rate. *Journal of Speech and Hearing Disorders*, 1949, *14*(3), 222–227.

Klatt, D. Vowel lengthening is syntactically determined in a connected discourse. *Journal of Phonetics*, 1975, *3*, 129–140.

Klatt, D. Linguistic uses of segmental duration in English: Acoustic and perceptual evidence. *Journal of the Acoustical Society of America*, 1976, *59*, 1208–1221.

Lane, H. Psychophysical parameters of vowel perception. *Psychological Monographs*, 1962, *76* (44, Whole No. 563).

Lane, H., Boyes-Braem, P., & Bellugi, U. Preliminaries to a distinctive feature analysis of hand-shapes in American Sign Language. *Cognitive Psychology*, 1976, *8*, 263–289.

Lane, H., Catania, A., & Stevens, S. Voice level: Autophonic scale, perceived loudness and effects of sidetone. *Journal of the Acoustical Society of America*, 1961, *33*, 160–167.

Lane, H., & Grosjean, F. Perception of reading rate by listeners and speakers. *Journal of Experimental Psychology*, 1973, *97*, 141–147.

Levelt, W. *The perception of syntactic structures*. Heymans Bulletin No. HB-69-31EX. Groningen University, Department of Psychology, Groningen, Netherlands, 1969.

Levelt, W. Hierarchical chunking in sentence processing. *Perception & Psychophysics*, 1970, *8*(2), 99–103.

Martin, E. Toward an analysis of subjective phrase structure. *Psychological Bulletin*, 1970, *74*, 153–166.

Poulton, E. The new psychophysics: Six models for magnitude estimation. *Psychological Bulletin*, 1968, *69*, 1–19.

Stokoe, W. Sign Language Structure: An outline of the visual communication system of the American deaf. *Studies in Linguistics: Occasional Papers*, 1960 (Ms. No. 8).

Teghtsoonian, R. Range effects in psychological scaling and a revision of Stevens' law. *American Journal of Psychology*, 1973, *86*, 3–27.

Thorndike, E., & Lorge, I. *The teacher's word book of 30,000 words*. New York: Bureau of Publications, Teachers College, Columbia University, 1944.

Umeda, N. Vowel duration in American English. *Journal of the Acoustical Society of America*, 1975, *58*, 434–445.

Woodward, J. Implication variation in American Sign Language: Negative incorporation. *Sign Language Studies*, 1974, *5*, 20–30.

7 Word Recognition in Speech and Reading: Toward a Single Theory of Language Processing

Kathryn T. Spoehr
Brown University

Editors' Comments

Research in the domain of speech perception has tended to focus on the processes that extract the intended phonetic message from the acoustic signal. However, it is known that, at least in normal connected speech, the processes yielding phonetic percepts utilize information not only from the acoustic signal, but also from syntactic, semantic, and cognitive sources.

One of the more important sources of higher order or top-down influences on phonetic perception is the lexical characteristics of target words and surrounding items. Given this, plus the obvious importance of lexical considerations in sentence comprehension, it is somewhat surprising that investigations of word recognition and lexical access have not been more central to the study of speech. Studies of this nature have, of course, long been carried out by investigators concerned with the analysis and understanding of reading. Of particular interest for speech researchers are findings from studies of visual word recognition and lexical access that indicate involvement of processes that are integral to speech perception, that is, processes that occur at the phonetic and phonological levels during perception of spoken language. Spoehr has summarized much of the research on word perception and has provided us with the beginnings of a processing model that incorporates principles derived from the study of speech and printed material. Her view of word processing has considerable appeal both for its generality and for its ability to generate interesting research on how listeners derive higher order linguistic information.

INTRODUCTION

The two most common ways in which people receive linguistic input are through the auditory and visual modalities. Consequently, humans have two language processing mechanisms, one for speech understanding and one for reading, which allow them to derive meaning from language and respond appropriately to it. Needless to say, there are tremendous differences between the operations each of these two language understanding systems must employ to accomplish the same goal. Many of these differences are imposed by the nature of the two information-bearing signals: In speech it is continuous and sequential, whereas in printed material the code elements are discrete and presented simultaneously within each eye fixation. Still other differences arise from the physiological and neurological characteristics of the auditory and visual systems. Nevertheless, the fact that both speech perception and reading are used to understand language carries with it the likelihood that there may be points of commonality, or at least analogy, between the two systems, and that these intersection points are more likely to lie at levels of processing where the derivation of meaning is carried out.

One of the underlying presuppositions of this chapter is that word recognition represents an important step in deriving meaning in both reading and fluent speech recognition, and that it is at the point in processing where the two systems can begin to be compared and contrasted. The importance of word recognition has been recognized by investigators in both speech (e.g., Cole & Jakimik, 1978) and reading (e.g., Laberge & Samuels, 1974). Moreover, there is consensus that at levels of processing prior to word identification, speech perception and reading are independent systems with different types of sensory coding problems. However, at the point at which a word is recognized, its meaning must be accessed and that meaning must be combined with the meanings of other lexical items to produce comprehension. Thus, although the two systems arrive at the point of lexical access by quite different routes, they make use of the same semantic memory store, face the same problems of locating information in that store, and must both integrate individual word meanings. The problem of word recognition therefore provides an initial and potentially informative focal point for comparing the language processing systems of speech recognition and reading.

The purpose of this chapter is to examine word recognition in both speech and reading. Throughout the discussion we are interested in seeing how the two modalities use the same or analogous processing mechanisms to carry out the task of understanding linguistic input. We are also looking for instances in which research in these two areas is converging on a single theory of how the internal lexicon is organized and accessed, and of how the meanings of individual words are combined. The first section examines the similarities and differences between speech and reading from a logical and operational standpoint, and introduces a general information-processing framework within which we may analyze word recognition. The next sections deal with the way in which semantic memory is accessed in speech and reading. First, we examine whether reading involves a recoding of visual input into a phonological form, which then provides access to the internal lexicon. Next, we focus attention on the issues of the size of the unit by which semantic memory is accessed, and its implications for the structure of semantic memory. Finally, the chapter considers in some detail the problems of word recognition in context. In addition to presenting general issues related to how the word recognition process changes when semantic and syntactic context are added, the discussion focuses on perceptual versus decisional influences of context, the separate contributions of syntax and semantic relatedness of context, the role of predictability in recognizing words, and several theoretical approaches from both the speech and reading literature that seem to be converging on a theory of word recognition in connected text.

A FRAMEWORK FOR STUDYING WORD RECOGNITION

Some Comparisons Between Speech and Reading

It is a common observation that speech is the primary form of language process-ing. Mattingly (1972), for example, notes that speech perception is a more natural way of processing language than reading. This is based on the fact that althouth every natural language exists in a spoken form, fewer have written forms. In addition, languages that do have written forms developed the writing system long after the spoken form came into use. Finally, as far as language processing is concerned, "listening is easy and reading is hard" (Liberman, 1968). That is, whereas every normal human child spontaneously learns and masters the spoken language in the child's society, specialized instruction is necessary to learn to read. The child's ability to learn to read depends, among other things, on sensitivity to the sound patterns in his or her language and an ability to segment auditory input into phoneme segments (I. Y. Liberman & Shankweiler, 1979). Moreover, children who lack adequate speech background, such as the congenitally deaf, have difficulty learning to read (Blackwell, Engen, Fischgrund, & Zarcadoolas, 1978). In short, there is a close relationship between reading and speech processing that suggests that the development of mechanisms for the former is dependent upon the mechanisms for the latter.

A second way in which reading depends on speech is in the writing system. Because English is an alphabetic language, orthographic patterns depend heavily on corresponding phonemic patterns. Although the correspondence between let-ters and phonemes is not completely one-to-one, a relatively small set of spelling-to-sound correspondence rules (Venezky, 1967) can define the relation-ship between English spelling and pronunciation. Although estimates of the number of "regularly" spelled words that could be generated from a set of such rules does vary from 80% (Hanna & Hanna, 1959) to 95% (Wijk, 1966), the number is large enough to make the alphabetic characteristics of English important in reading it. As we shall see, although not all readers make use of the alphabetic properties of English in all situations, the relationship is particularly important for learning to read (Frederiksen, 1976), and as a strategy for processing difficult and unfamiliar material (Hardyck & Petrinovich, 1970).

The final way in which speech and reading are related comes from consideration of the necessity to store information for relatively short periods of time so that meanings can be integrated across words in sentences and phrases. Many investigators have noted that this requires the use of short-term memory in both speech (A.M. Liberman, Mattingly, & Turvey, 1972) and reading (Baron, 1977; I. Y. Liberman & Shankweiler, 1979). An important component of the ability to maintain information in temporary working memory, or short-term store, is an articulatory encoding of the information to be maintained here. Studies of memory for visually presented linguistic material to be remembered for short periods of time indicate that memory errors are primarily acoustic/articulatory in nature (Conrad, 1964; Hintzman, 1967; Wickelgren, 1965). Thus, although speech input can be stored relatively directly in STM, visual input must be recoded into a form more suitable for storage in STM. Whether the recoding operation takes place before or after lexical access in reading has been a matter of debate, and one which is discussed in detail in subsequent sections. For the present, however, it is sufficient to note that the necessity for storing information in working memory provides yet an additional link between the visual and auditory language processing systems.

A Stage Model for Word Recognition

Word recognition in both the auditory and visual modalities requires that sensory input be decoded so that the meaning of the input can be retrieved and responded to appropriately. Recent experimental work in both fields has attempted to specify the types of operations that must be performed in order for word recognition to occur, and to incorporate these operations into a valid model of word recognition. Figure 7.1 outlines the major processes involved in word recognition for speech and reading, and illustrates some relationships between these processes and the principal storage mechanisms in the human information-processing system. The processing operations are denoted by circles; information stores are shown as rectangles. The connecting single lines denote lines of information flow and access to information stored in the various memory systems, whereas the double-lined arrows suggest points at which various operations transform or influence information in the system.

The model in Fig. 7.1 illustrates many of the obvious commonalities between word recognition in speech and reading. First, it is likely that the two modalities use the same long-term and short-term memory systems (Massaro, 1977; Neisser, 1967). Thus, access to these common systems must be provided for each

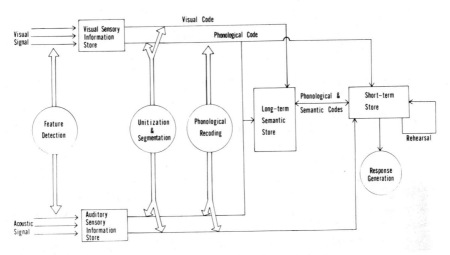

FIG. 7.1.   A model for word recognition in reading and speech.

modality. At more sensory levels, however, speech and reading use analogous, though not identical, processes and memory stores. In the visual system, sensory input is gathered by the visual receptors and is analyzed by a feature detection system. There is now a great deal of evidence that suggests that features such as horizontal, vertical, or diagonal lines, and curves describe visual confusions between characters in both upper- and lower-case typeface (Bouma, 1971; Lindsay & Norman, 1977), and that the English alphabet can adequately be described by approximately six to eight visual features (Gibson, 1969). This featural information is stored in a temporary visual sensory store, which lasts on the order of 150–300 msec. (Sperling, 1960), and is then read out into a more permanent form.

The sensory processing in the auditory system acts in an analogous fashion. The acoustic wave form is analyzed for the presence of linguistic features such as voicing, manner of articulation, or place of articulation (Eimas & Miller, 1978). Massaro (1977) has pointed out that acoustic features could well be continuous such that they indicate the degree to which a certain feature is present in the stimulus. An important aspect of the auditory processing system at this level, then, is that although the features do not uniquely determine phonemic distinctions for individual speech segments, they may be interpreted by subsequent decoding of larger units such as the syllable (Oden & Massaro, 1977). A second important aspect of the sensory processing system for speech is that information in the auditory sensory store, although precategorical in nature, may well last longer than information in the analogous visual store. Estimates of its duration range up to several seconds (Darwin, Turvey, & Crowder, 1972).

The conversion of information in the two sensory information stores to a more permanent form requires that it be entered into a form that can be stored in either short- or long-term memory. Storage in short-term store, as we have already seen, requires that information be coded in a phonological form regardless of whether the meaning of the stimulus is encoded or not. That meaning need not be encoded in short-term memory is obvious from the capacity to store nonsense information. The conversion of visual information to a phonological form can be accomplished either by the application of spelling-to-sound correspondence rules applied to individual or groups of graphemes (Spoehr, 1978) or by rules based on pronunciation by analogy (Glushko & Rumelhart, 1977). Depending upon the type of rule used, the visual input will have to be decomposed into graphemic units of a size to which the rules can be applied, and this process requires the prior operation of unitization or segmentation rules. Thus, in Fig. 7.1 we see a unitization operation operating on visual input prior to its conversion by the phonological coding operation. In speech the recoding operation must combine featural information across several phonemic segments in order to produce a memory code (Klatt, 1980).

As Fig. 7.1 makes clear, it is equally possible for both systems to access semantic information in long-term memory via a phonological code. This means that once a speech-related code has been formed for a given visual input, information in long-term memory may be accessed by the same routines used to find that information during speech processing. An alternate route for visual input does exist, however, and that is the direct visual access route whereby printed words are matched directly to long-term memory representations by their visual featural composition (Green & Shallice, 1976; F. Smith, 1971). Such an access route circumvents the intervening operations of phonological recoding, but may require some segmentation of the visual input depending upon the organization of long-term memory. Once information about a visual input has been located in this way, phonological information about its pronunciation may then be entered into short-term working memory along with any relevant semantic information.

Lines of communication between the short-term and long-term stores in Fig. 7.1 have been included to capture several relationships. First, they provide the means for a phonological representation of a word to be read out of long-term memory for storage in short-term memory. Second, because short-term memory is assumed to be the location where individual words are held until information can be integrated over a phrase or sentence, there must be some path by which the accumulating evidence in short-term memory influences lexical access.

One of the difficulties with any stage model, including that shown in Fig. 7.1, is that it assumes bottom-up processing in which information generated as output from one processing operation serves as the input to the next operation. Clearly the operations must receive information from long- and short-term memory, in order to operate. Such channels of communication between levels are implicit in the type of model shown in Fig. 7.1 although they are not explicitly shown. However, a strictly bottom-up scheme has a more basic problem, which is that processing at all levels in both reading and speech processing seems to be dependent on context. In reading, for example, the interpretation of an ambiguous letter in a word context may be determined by the surrounding letters (Neisser, 1967) as in TʌE CʌT, or by the surrounding words (Massaro, 1977). Similarly, in speech, the identification of an individual phoneme may depend on adjacent acoustic input (A. M. Liberman, Cooper, Shankweiler & Studdert-Kennedy, 1967) within a syllable, on information from subsequent syllables (Rudnicky & Cole, 1978), or by surrounding words (Marslen-Wilson & Welsh, 1978). This has led several theorists to propose parallel models of language processing in which processing is carried out at various levels simultaneously (e.g., Reddy, 1976; Rumelhart, 1977) or that contain serially ordered processes that sometimes overlap in time (McClelland, 1978; Taylor, 1977). The most important characteristic of such systems is that decisions at lower levels of processing may be postponed until higher levels of processing have begun to generate information. Thus the results of hypotheses generated by the lexical access operations, for example, may have a top-down influence upon the process of feature extraction or unitization.

A decision as to whether processing is bottom-up or top-down in either speech or reading can be left until more information has been presented about lexical access and the effects of semantic and syntactic context. The critical points of agreement between the bottom-up and top-down theories consist of the types of operations that are necessary for language processing rather than the order in which they occur. Fortunately, there is sufficient agreement about the components of the system that we are now in a position to examine some of the points of comparison between the word recognition mechanisms in speech perception and reading.

DEFINING THE UNIT OF LEXICAL ACCESS

Because word recognition is designed to yield word meanings that can be effectively combined with other word meanings, an important point of comparison between speech and reading is whether access to those word meanings can take place in the same or even analogous fashion in the two modalities. There are two aspects of this issue that are particularly important. First, is there really a method of long-term memory access for the visual system that is based upon the pronunciational equivalents of the printed words? If so, this would provide support for the access pathway in Fig. 7.1 shared by speech and reading. If such a route can be shown to exist, then it will be necessary to ask how important this option is in natural, fluent reading. The second aspect has to do with the size of the unit that is used to access the lexicon in both speech and reading. To the extent to which the two systems share access pathways, the size of the unit used as input to the lexical access mechanism must be similar. Moreover, even if it can be demonstrated that speech and reading do not always share the same access pathway, it may still be the case that long-term memory is indexed by the same subunits of words so that information can be retrieved regardless of whether it arrives as a phonological or nonphonological code. Let us consider these two aspects of the lexical access problem in turn.

Speech Related Codes in Reading

One of the clearest examples of the role of speech-related coding in reading is in the analysis of the performance of beginning readers. The typical child begins to learn to read after having acquired a considerable vocabulary and many syntactic production and decoding skills from experience with speech processing (I. Y. Liberman, Shankweiler, Liberman, Fowler, & Fischer, 1977): "If the beginning reader is to take greatest advantage of an alphabet and of the language processes he already has, he must convert print to speech or, more covertly, to the phonetic structure that in some neurological form must be presumed to underlie and control overt speech articulation. [p. 20]." Logically, the simplest way for the beginning reader to access word meanings is to transform the visual code into a speech code for which he or she already knows the meaning.

There is considerable evidence that skill in decoding phonetic structure and the ability to recode printed text into a phonological form are important determinants of reading ability in beginning readers. Helfgott (1976) and Zifcak (1976) have both found highly significant correlations between phoneme segmentation ability and reading achievement scores on the word recognition section of the *Wide Range Achievement Test* (WRAT). Such "linguistic awareness" is not the only speech-related phenomenon that distinguishes good from poor readers, however. I. Y. Liberman et al. (1977) have demonstrated that better readers are more likely to form phonological codes for visually presented material than are poor readers. In these experiments the subjects were second graders who were separated into three skill groups according to reading attainment score on the WRAT, and they were asked to memorize five-letter strings of uppercase letters for either immediate or delayed recall. Some of the strings were phonemically confusable such that all of the letters to be remembered were drawn from a class of rhyming consonants, whereas other strings were nonconfusable. The good readers were found to be better than the poorer readers at remembering the nonconfusable strings, but the groups were very nearly the same at remembering the confusable arrays. Moreover, the good readers made no more errors on the nonconfusable strings if recall was delayed by 15 msec, but were significantly worse on delayed recall of confusable strings. The difference between immediate and delayed recall of confusable arrays for less skilled readers was much smaller. Thus, the good readers were much more likely to form a phonological memory code that could be interfered with by rehearsal when confusable letter strings were retained over an extended period of time.

Frederiksen (1976) has demonstrated that skilled readers are distinguishable from less skilled readers by the decoding skills through which visual material is recoded into phonological form. Subjects in these experiments were high-school-age students who were divided into four skill groups based on their performance on the Nelson–Denny reading test. The task was simply to say aloud letter string stimuli as quickly and as accurately as possible. The stimuli were words and matched pronounceable nonwords generated by changing a vowel in each word, and represented a range of orthographic forms that varied in letter length, syllable length, type of vowel, presence or absence of silent -e, and lengths of consonant clusters.

It is clear that the recognition of the nonwords in Frederiksen's experiment could only have been accomplished by phonological recoding, because the correct pronunciation for these items cannot be generated by accessing a lexical entry on the basis of a visual code and reading off the corresponding pronunciation. The naming latency for the nonwords is therefore expected to be a function of orthographic complexity because different orthographic structures will necessitate different recoding procedures. Recognition of the words, on the other hand, could be accomplished by either the recoding or the visual access mechanism. However, the extent to which recoding is used for words can be measured by determining whether naming latency for each word is correlated to the corresponding latency for the matched nonword. The higher the correlation, the more likely it is that the individual is using the same recoding route to recognize both words and nonwords. For the two lower reading skill groups, word latencies are highly predictable by nonword latencies for low-frequency words (61% and 72% variance accounted for in the two groups) but not for high-frequency words (11% and 28%). For the two groups of good readers predictability was 39% and 46% for low-frequency words and 40% in both groups for high-frequency words. Apparently, the low-skill readers use a visual access strategy for words that are well known to them but not for less accessible material. More highly skilled readers appear to have better recoding skills; they can recognize words of all frequencies faster than can less skilled readers and use the recoding strategy even for high-frequency words.

Aside from the differences we observed between good and poor readers, there is considerable other evidence that phonological recoding provides a viable route to word recognition in reading. Evidence comes primarily from three tasks: the pronunciation task, the lexical decision task, and the tachistoscopic report task. Baron (1977) and Brooks (1977) have shown that the existence of orthographic regularity, with its correlative spelling-to-sound correspondences, significantly speeds pronunciation times for letter strings written in an artificial alphabet. In this experiment all subjects learned English word responses to four-character strings in the artificial language. For one group of subjects, those in the Ortho-graphic Condition, each artificial character was in one-to-one correspondence with a letter from the English alphabet and the stimuli could thus be pronounced using spelling-to-sound correspondence rules. In the Paired-Associate Condition the English words were paired with the artificial strings such that no orthographic regularity existed. Subjects in each group read aloud six-item lists of these four-character strings, and their reading time was measured as a function of practice. Initially the Orthographic lists were more difficult and subjects took longer to read them aloud. However, after practice the Orthographic lists became significantly easier than the Paired-Associate lists.

Similar results for English words have been obtained by Baron and Strawson (1976). The task was to read aloud lists of ten letter strings. Lists were classified according to whether the items were "regular" and followed common English orthography and spelling-to-sound correspondences (e.g., glue, chant), were "exception" words that are not pronounced according to orthographic rules (e.g., tongue, chute), or were pronounceable nonwords. The mean time to read the lists of regular words was 4.3 seconds; times for exception and pronounceable nonwords were 5.9 and 7.8 seconds, respectively. It appears that the presence of spelling-to-sound correspondences in the regular words aided subjects in reading them aloud.

Reaction time measures that involve lexical decisions have provided additional evidence that phonological recoding is used in the recognition of words. Rubenstein, Lewis, and Rubenstein (1971) compared nonword lexical decision times for pronounceable strings that were homophonic with high-frequency words, homophonic with low-frequency words, or not homophonic with any word. It was expected that if memory access is carried out on the basis of a phonological code, nonwords that sound like English words may be matched incorrectly with the entries for actual words. Not only would subjects be likely to make more mistakes on such homophonic nonwords, but they would also take longer to make their correct decisions because they would be sidetracked in their lexical search by false matches. The reaction times confirmed these predictions, showing that the nonhomophonic nonwords were by far the fastest items to judge, whereas homophonic items took significantly longer.

In another experiment, Rubenstein et al. (1971) assessed the effect of homophony on decision times for words. The stimuli of interest in this experiment were English words that were of either high or low frequency and were either homophonous with or not homophonous with another English word. Again it was expected that homophones would be more difficult to classify because they would generate more false matches to incorrect same-sounding lexical entries. Homophones did, in fact, take longer to process and resulted in more classification errors than did nonhomophonous words.

Meyer, Schvaneveldt, and Ruddy (1974) have also used the lexical decision task to show that spelling-to-sound correspondence rules can be employed in lexical access. Meyer et al. used a variant of the simple lexical decision task in which two letter strings are presented, and the subject must respond "yes" if both strings are words and "no" otherwise. In these experiments, the graphemic and phonemic relationships between pairs of stimulus words were varied by presenting pairs that were both phonemically and graphemically similar (e.g.,

BRIBE–TRIBE), graphemically similar and phonemically dissimilar (COUCH–TOUCH), or graphemically and phonemically dissimilar (e.g., COUCH–BREAK). Word–nonword and nonword–nonword pairs having these relationships were also used in order to equate the number of positive and negative trials. Meyer et al. found that whereas phonemic similarity paired with graphemic similarity facilitated recognition slightly and nonsignificantly, graphemic similarity alone inhibited recognition and increased decision times relative to the control pairs.

If the words in this experiment were being recognized directly from their visual features alone, with no intermediate phonological encoding step, then the results would be entirely unexpected. However, Meyer et al. can explain them using the concept of "encoding bias." Processing of the first string is carried out through phonological recoding, and if that string is found to be a word, processing is begun on the second string. However, the encoding of the second string is influenced by the encoding operations used for the first, especially when the two strings contain the same final letters. In such cases there may be a tendency to apply the same spelling-to-sound correspondence rules to the second string as were applied to the first because of the graphemic similarities. This tendency will be beneficial if the two words do, in fact, rhyme because the resulting code for the second string will be correct. However, if the two strings are phonemically dissimilar although possessing graphemic similarity, the strategy will lead to an incorrect phonological code and the lexical decision will be delayed.

Some of my own research, plus additional work I have done in collaboration with Edward E. Smith, has used a tachistoscopic report procedure to examine how the phonological recoding process might operate. The experimental task requires the subject to view a letter string that is presented at a near-threshold duration followed by a masking pattern. Immediately after the presentation, the subject is probed for recognition of one of the letter positions by being given two, single-letter alternatives from which the subject must pick the correct letter. The experimental conditions make it unlikely that the subject will be able to correctly recognize every letter in every string, so that differences in report accuracy between different types of letter strings will arise because some types of letter strings are easier to process than others.

The original experiments examined tachistoscopic report accuracy for strings that differed with respect to how easily they might be phonologically recoded (Spoehr & Smith, 1975). The underlying assumption is that if word recognition is mediated by a recoding operation then those strings that are easily recodable should be easy to process and should exhibit higher report accuracy than less recodable strings. Word and nonword letter strings fall at various points along a recodability continuum based on the number of steps necessary to perform the recoding. At the top end of the scale are English words and completely pronounceable nonwords such as RUST and ROST. An intermediate variety of letter string is represented by the string BLST. In this case the missing vowel makes the string's pronunciation an articulatory impossibility unless some type of vo-calic element is inserted either between the B and the L or between the L and the S. Note, however, that with the exception of a single missing vowel, the conso-nant strings that are present are recodable. The string RNOT presents an inter-mediate case of a slightly different type. Although a vowel is present, it is not sufficient to make the string completely recodable because the initial consonant string is an unacceptable beginning for an English word. Thus, despite the vowel, an additional vowel insertion step needs to be carried out in order to make the string recodable. The least recodable type of letter string is one in which no vowels are present and none of the consonant clusters are acceptable for recoding because of positional restrictions. As an example, LSTB would require a minimum of two extra vowels in order for recoding to occur, one either at the beginning or between the L and the S, and the other either at the end or between the T and the B. When strings such as these are presented tachistoscopically the accuracy scores, as shown in Table 7.1, follow the predictions of a recodability hypothesis. The easier it is for a string to be recoded, the more easily it is recognized.

In developing a model of how a string of graphemes can be recoded into a phonological form, Spoehr and Smith (1975) propose that the code for a single syllable is produced in much the same manner as the code for a syllable spoken aloud (MacKay, 1972). When an individual syllable is to be given a phonological representation, it must be decomposed into letter units that can be rendered phonemically by a single speech sound through the application of spelling-to-sound correspondence rules. In addition, sufficient vocalic elements must be added to allow the resulting phonemic segments to be combined into a phonologi-cally legal sequence. Figure 7.2 illustrates the way in which letter strings of various types would be decomposed and vocalic elements added. The syllable is first segregated into the initial consonant or consonant cluster plus the vocalic element and its following consonant(s). If the initial consonant(s) can be ren-dered by a single speech sound (e.g., CH or TH), it is not decomposed further, but is instead given its phonological representation. If the initial consonant(s) cannot be represented in this way, they are further separated until letters or clusters are obtained that are recodable. The vowel with its following conso-nant(s) is decomposed in a similar fashion, first into vowel plus consonant cluster.

TABLE 7.1.
Accuracy of Report From a Tachistoscopic Presentation
as a Function of Recodability

	Word	Pronounceable Nonword	Unpronounceable/ Vowel Present	Unpronounceable/ Vowel Absent	Unrelated
Example	RUST	ROST	RNOT	BLST	LSTB
P (C)	.80	.81	.73	.70	.65

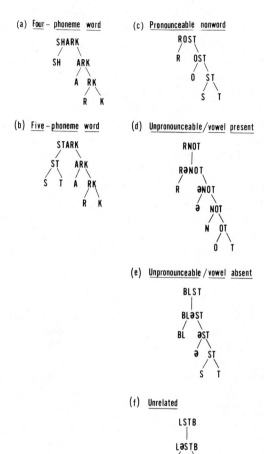

FIG. 7.2. Example recoding decomposition trees for: (a) four-phoneme words; (b) five-phoneme words; (c) pronounceable nonwords; (d) unpronounceable nonwords with vowel present; (e) unpronounceable words with vowel absent; and (f) unrelated letter strings.

The vowel is then given its phonological representation and the final consonant cluster is treated in the same way as the initial cluster.

Because the entire process can be diagrammed in terms of a tree structure, the length and difficulty of the entire translation process can be defined by either the number of levels in the tree or the number of units to be given phonological representations. In cases where a subject must recode a letter string that is unpronounceable, one or more vowel insertion steps are necessary. Evidence suggests that subjects will make the vowel insertion at the first point where the orthographic rules of English are violated when the letter string is scanned from left to right (Spoehr & Smith, 1975). Naturally, each vowel insertion step requires extra processing time, and strings which require such additional steps will be difficult to process and report in the tachistoscopic task.

These rules of syllabic decomposition lead to another interesting prediction by the model. In general, any changes in the stimulus string that shorten the recoding process should result in increased report accuracy. In terms of Fig. 7.2, letter strings that generate fewer nodes and/or less depth to the recoding tree will be easier to report. One way to reduce the size of the recoding tree is to use stimulus strings in which the consonant clusters do not need to be decomposed into individual letter units before receiving their phonemic encodings. In a recent experiment (Spoehr, 1978), I compared performance on letter strings such as SHARK and STARK, whose decomposition trees are illustrated in sections (a) and (b) of Fig. 7.2. The major difference between these two strings is their phoneme length, which is reflected in differences in the number of nodes in their recoding trees. The experiment used both word and pronounceable nonword stimuli (e.g., SHERK and STERK), and the critical cluster could appear at the end of the string as well as at the beginning (e.g., CRUSH, CRUST, CROSH, and CROST). Table 7.2 shows that items containing fewer phonemes were better recognized and that this statistically reliable phoneme length effect was obtained for all stimulus types.

Evidence Against Speech Recoding

Unfortunately, the role of phonological recoding in reading is not as clear as the evidence presented so far would suggest. There are numerous studies that fail to

TABLE 7.2
Probability of a Correct Letter Recognition
as a Function of Phoneme Length

Position of Critical Cluster	Words		Nonwords	
	4 Phonemes	5 Phonemes	4 Phonemes	5 Phonemes
Beginning	.82	.79	.77	.73
End	.80	.76	.74	.67

find evidence for such recoding, or that indicate that recoding is accomplished by reading off the pronunciation of a word already located in long-term memory through a visual code. Bower (1970) presents evidence that recoding is not normally used by skilled readers. In his experiment, Greek-speaking subjects read through normal passages written in Greek, or through passages altered by replacing some letters with others that map into the same sound as the original letters. The speed of reading aloud was found to be one and one-half times as long for the altered passage as for the normal passage. When bilingual subjects were asked to translate the two types of passages into English, fluency was much greater for the normal passages. It appears that for both normal reading and translation, subjects were slowed in their processing by having to convert the altered passages into their phonological form in order to access meanings. This suggests that such recoding is not the normal means of performing these two tasks.

Baron (1973) has also examined the effects of making phonologically consistent changes in reading material. Two of Baron's stimulus phrase types are critical: (1) those that are phonologically sensible but orthographically incorrect; and (2) those that are both orthographically and phonologically sensible. In one task, subjects had to judge each phrase for orthographic sense (i.e., did the words make sense as they were spelled?); and in a second task, subjects judged the phrases as to whether they sounded as if they made sense. Baron supposed that if subjects use a phonological code as the basis of their normal reading, then the orthographic judgments of the phrases of the first type would require an extra orthographic check and thus lead to more errors and slow reaction times relative to type two items. The results of this task showed that although subjects did make significantly more errors on the first type of item, the reaction times for item types one and two did not significantly differ. The results are therefore ambiguous, because the error data suggest phonological recoding is used, whereas the reaction time data suggest that it is not used. In the phonological task, the first type of item should not take any longer than those of the second type, because their phonological codes are identical and meaningful under an auditory criterion. However, subjects did take significantly longer and made significantly more errors on the first type than on the second type, suggesting that the phonological code is either not formed during normal reading or that such a code does not provide an effective means for deriving the meaning of a phrase.

Two studies of naming latency and lexical decision time also argue against the phonological recoding hypothesis. Frederiksen and Kroll (1976) reasoned that if phonological recoding is a necessary step in word recognition then the orthographic variables that affect pronunciation time should also influence lexical decision time in the same way. However, they found that the variables that do affect naming latency (e.g., number of letters, size of consonant clusters) did not seem to affect lexical decision time. Forster and Chambers (1973) also compared naming latencies and lexical decision times, and used high- and low-frequency words, unfamiliar words, and pronounceable nonwords as stimuli. If phonological recoding precedes lexical access, then naming times for all types of words and nonwords should be the same. On the other hand, if pronunciations of words can be read directly from memory, then coding via spelling-to-sound correspondence rules can be eliminated by making an immediate visually based lexical search. Under these conditions, words should have faster naming times than unfamiliar words and nonwords. Also naming times for the known words should be ordered according to the frequency because subjects will be able to look up the pronunciations of more familiar words faster. The results supported the visual access view because naming times were shortest for high-frequency words, next shortest for low-frequency words, and slowest for nonwords and unfamiliar words. Moreover, there was a significant correlation between naming latency and lexical decision times for known words but not for unfamiliar words or nonwords. This suggests that the same, and presumably visually based, access procedure was used for words in both the naming and lexical decision tasks, but that different procedures were used for items that did not appear in memory.

A final set of evidence showing that phonological recoding is not obligatory prior to lexical access, but may develop afterwards, comes from the work of Kleiman (1975) and Stanovich and Bauer (1978). Stanovich and Bauer found a reliable superiority of words with regular spelling-to-sound correspondence rules over words with irregular correspondences in both a naming and a lexical decision task. However, when these investigators imposed a reaction time deadline on responses in the lexical decision task, the advantage for the regular words was eliminated. Because subjects could apparently still perform the task with a good degree of accuracy (upward of 80% correct) even when they are forced to perform it much faster than normal, Stanovich and Bauer conclude that orthographic regularity cannot affect the lexical access stage itself, but affects a stage subsequent to lexical access such as short-term memory encoding. Kleiman (1975) examined the role of recoding in word recognition by having subjects perform an auditory shadowing task during various visual word recognition tasks. Their ability to make decisions about synonymy, graphemic similarity, and category inclusion was much less impaired by shadowing than was their ability to make phonemic similarity and syntactic acceptability decisions. Kleiman argues that a phonological code is "looked up" after visual access to semantic memory, and is used to maintain information in short-term memory. The shadowing task impedes only those tasks that make use of the short-term memory code, namely rhyming and syntax where short-term memory is used to hold task–relevant information.

Strategies and Individual Differences in Recoding

The obvious resolution to the mass of conflicting data on whether phonological recoding or visual access is used during word recognition is to assume that access takes place both ways, as shown in Fig. 7.1. The two routes could be competing processes (e.g., Meyer, Schvaneveldt, & Ruddy, 1974) or cooperating processes (Coltheart, Davelaar, Jonasson, & Besner, 1977). The route that will be operable in any given situation will depend on the processing strategy that is selected by or is characteristic of the subject. Let us examine, in detail, a few experiments that demonstrate such strategy variations.

Davelaar, Coltheart, Besner, and Jonasson (1978) have shown that in a lexical decision task subjects will tend to use a phonological recoding strategy *unless* the experimental conditions are such that it becomes impractical. Subjects were shown pairs of letter strings and responded "yes" if both were words and "no" otherwise. Davelaar et al. compared reaction times for pairs of homophones (GROAN/GROWN) with pairs of nonhomophones (e.g., EARN/GROWN) in situations where the nonwords were either homophonous (e.g., BRANE) or not homophonous (e.g., SLINT) with English words. In the former case, the homophony variation in the words had no effect on lexical decision times, but in the latter case it did. Subjects in these experiments were apparently able to tell within the first few trials whether a phonological recoding strategy would be effective or not; when such a strategy would allow them to differentiate between words and nonwords (as in the SLINT case) they continued to use it as their preferred strategy, but when this strategy led to errors (as in the case of nonwords such as GRONE) it was abandoned in favor of a more useful visual strategy.

Hawkins, Reicher, Rogers, and Peterson (1976) have demonstrated a flexible coding approach to the recognition of homophones in a tachistoscopic task. The Hawkins et al. experiment builds upon a result obtained by Baron and Thurston (1973) that showed that when subjects are presented a word such as BEAR tachistoscopically and asked to choose between the homophonous alternatives BEAR and BARE, performance is no worse than if they are shown a word such as DEAR and given nonhomophonous alternatives (DEAR and DARE). If subjects had been phonologically recoding in order to process the stimuli in this experiment, many phonemically based errors would be expected in the first case because the access code would not allow the subject to distinguish between the two alternatives. Hawkins et al. provide evidence that Baron and Thurston's failure to find a homophony effect is produced by a strategy shift away from phonological recoding because subjects realize that such a strategy is counterproductive when many of the stimuli have homophonous alternatives. Hawkins et al. report that if the stimulus set contains many homophonous alternative pairs, subjects do not recode and accuracy on homophone and nonhomophone pairs is equal (66.5% and 67.8% respectively). However, if there are relatively few homophonous alternatives in the set, subjects continue to use a recoding strategy that leads them to produce many more errors on the few homophonous stimuli included (58.3% vs. 72.5% correct).

Carr, Davidson, and Hawkins (1978) have used the tachistoscopic report task to determine: (1) the extent to which processing strategy differs as a function of task requirements; and (2) the extent to which strategy shifts are automatic as opposed to being controlled by the subjects. Carr et al. used report accuracy on words, pronounceable pseudowords, and unpronounceable nonsense strings using several different stimulus set compositions to examine these questions. The comparison between performance on pseudowords and words is particularly critical. Subjects must surely recognize pseudowords using an orthographic recoding scheme, because there are no lexical entries for these items from which to read off complete pronunciations, although words could be recognized in either way. However, if words are processed using recoding, it is expected that performance on them should be the same as on pseudowords, all other conditions being equal. The data of interest come from blocks of test trials containing words, pseudowords, and nonsense strings that were embedded in much larger stimulus sets of one of three types: those that led subjects to strongly expect words, pseudowords, or nonsense. If subjects expect words, accuracy on both pseudowords and nonsense is low (72.9% and 69.8% respectively) relative to words (84.5%), indicating that pseudowords are processed more like unrelated letter strings when they are unexpected. A similar result is obtained if nonsense strings are expected (85.4%, 66.7%, and 69.0% correct on words, pseudowords, and nonsense). Apparently, even when words are unexpected, there is a benefit of lexicality resulting from automatic access via a visual code, a benefit that is not shared by pseudowords. However, when pseudowords *are* expected, accuracy on both words and pseudowords is high, whereas performance on nonsense is still poor (78.6%, 74.2%, and 63.5%, respectively). Subjects apparently switch into a recoding strategy for both words and pseudowords if the frequency of pseudowords is high enough to warrant the strategy. Carr et al. (1978) conclude that "utilizing orthographic structure in the computation of internal codes that will survive masking and support recognition performance is not automatic but is under some degree of strategic control [p. 686]."

In my own work using the tachistoscopic report task (Spoehr, 1978), I have studied variables other than stimulus set composition that might affect the type of processing strategy employed by subjects in word recognition. One variable that should determine whether phonological recoding is necessary is the presence of a visual mask following the stimulus presentation. A visual mask disturbs any visual code that a subject might be trying to maintain and use in recognizing a stimulus, so that a more productive strategy would be to try to recode the string phonologically to prevent its disruption by a mask. A second factor that could influence the importance of forming a phonological code is the introduction of a delay between the presentation of a stimulus and the time at which a report of it is made. With increasing delay intervals, it becomes more and more necessary to have a phonological code that can be stored and maintained in short-term memory.

My experiment (Spoehr, 1978) used the presence of the phoneme-length effect as an indicator of whether phonological recoding was taking place under differing masking and delay-of-report conditions. One group of subjects saw

English words that differed in phoneme length under masked presentation conditions, whereas another group of subjects saw them under unmasked conditions. The exposure duration was set at threshold for each subject, and subjects made their responses by picking one of two single-letter alternatives that probed one of the stimulus letter positions after the stimulus had disappeared. A delay was introduced between stimulus presentation and response selection by presenting the two probe alternatives after some delay measured from the offset of the stimulus (subjects in the masked condition viewed the mask during this interval), and the delay could be 0, 100, 250, 500, 1000, or 2000 msec.

Table 7.3 summarizes the results of the experiment. Clearly, with no mask, subjects did not use recoding at any delay because it was possible to keep the stimulus information in a visual form for later comparison with the probes. However, with a mask, verbal recoding was necessary at longer delays in order to keep the stimulus in short-term memory until the alternatives appeared, and the subjects showed a phoneme length effect. At shorter delay intervals the subjects could still apparently answer on the basis of a visual code and recoding was unnecessary. Thus there was no phoneme-length effect at these short delays. Although the data do not reveal whether recoding is an optional or obligatory process, they do indicate considerable processing flexibility on the part of the subjects.

Although experimental conditions may greatly influence the reliance subjects place on phonological recoding, some of the recoding and visual access effects we observe must clearly be due to individual differences in preferred word recognition strategy. Although as Frederiksen's (1976) work points out, some of these differences may be correlated with reading skill, even among highly skilled readers it is possible to distinguish individuals who generally recode and those who generally do not. Baron and Strawson (1976), for example, selected two groups of subjects who differ on their reliance on orthographic recoding

TABLE 7.3
Probability of a Correct Letter Report as a Function of
Masking Conditions, Delay of Report and Phoneme Length.

Delay (msec)	Masked Presentation		Unmasked Presentation	
	4 Phonemes	5 Phonemes	4 Phonemes	5 Phonemes
0	.70	.71	.52	.54
100	.74	.77	.59	.64
250	.78	.76	.71	.73
500	.81	.75	.72	.72
1000	.82	.72	.73	.72
2000	.83	.73	.72	.72

mechanisms versus whole-word visual mechanisms. The "Chinese" were subjects who were good at whole-word mechanisms but were poor on spelling-to-sound correspondences. The "Phonecians," on the other hand, were good at decoding spelling-to-sound, but poor at whole-word recognition mechanisms. The subjects for each group were chosen on the basis of their performance on detecting nonword homophones of English words (Phonecians are good at this, Chinese are not), and their ability to spell better if they must verify a spelling already written than if they generate it themselves (this is characteristic of Chinese and much less so of Phonecians).

Baron and Strawson then had these two groups of subjects read aloud lists of orthographically regular or exception words that were printed in upper-, lower-, or alternating mixed-case type. Exception words were overall higher in frequency than regular words. Phonecians tended to read regular words faster than exception words when the items were printed entirely in one case, whereas the Chinese were faster on the exception words. Mixing the case of the type slowed down reading times for both groups of subjects, but made the exception words vastly more difficult for the Phonecians. Apparently a preference for recoding helps in reading regular words, hurts exception words, and makes lexical access on the basis of a visual code particularly cumbersome if this route is necessitated by unfamiliar visual patterns in mixed case. When one relies on the whole-word visual method to find a pronunciation, pronunciations for more frequent words will be easiest to find.

In summary, there are several conclusions to be drawn about phonological recoding in reading. First, it appears that the recognition processes in speech and reading can access semantic memory through a common pathway; visual material can be recoded into a speech-related form. Second, we have seen at least one mechanism by which such recoding might be accomplished (Spoehr, 1978; Spoehr & Smith, 1975). Finally, evidence shows that recoding of visually presented material is not an obligatory process, and so multiple access routes must exist between the visual sensory system and long-term memory. The extent to which the speech-related route is used depends upon the skill and inclination of the individual, and upon experimenter-imposed conditions.

Lexical Access

As was noted earlier, word recognition requires finding the meaning of the word in lexical memory. It is of critical importance, therefore, to understand how long-term memory is organized, and more important, how the matching operation responsible for the Höffding step (Neisser, 1967) takes place. The storage of semantic information in long-term memory has been variously characterized as hierarchical (Collins & Quillian, 1969), as a featurally based semantic space (Smith, Shoben, & Rips, 1974), or as an associative network (Anderson & Bower, 1973; Collins & Loftus, 1975). Although it is obviously important to have semantic relationships represented in such a lexicon, it is just as important that the information be easily retrievable. Because it is clear that skilled readers and listeners can locate meanings extraordinarily rapidly, and that access is not always based upon the same type of code for the two modalities, it is likely that there is a directory system through which input could be matched to its appropriate lexical entry. The organization of the lexical directory would surely be different for phonological and visual access codes, and the organization of each directory should be such that it would optimize the location of needed information. Collins and Loftus (1975) and Forster (1976) have each proposed networks or directories parallel to the semantic lexicon that facilitate the location of material in long-term memory.

Forster's (1976) proposal is particularly relevant because he suggests a system that contains orthographic, phonological, and semantic/syntactic directories or access files; each file contains appropriately coded entries paired with pointers leading to the associated semantic and lexical information in a single Master File. He further assumes that entries in each access file are grouped together in bins according to file-appropriate commonalities, and that within each bin the access codes are ordered with respect to frequency of usage. The latter assumption is used to account for the fact that high-frequency words are typically recognized faster than low-frequency words (e.g., Forster & Chambers, 1973; Frederiksen & Kroll, 1976). According to the bin model, the first step in the lexical access process is to compute the bin location of the required access code, and then the appropriate bin is searched for the pointer leading to the Master File. The bin approach to the organization of lexical access provides a convenient framework within which to examine a second commonality between word recognition in reading and speech: There is now a good deal of evidence to suggest that the syllable provides an excellent way of organizing bins in both the orthographic and phonological access files, and that regardless of whether speech and reading share a common access code, lexical access in both systems is based on the syllabic unit.

Syllables in Visual Word Recognition

The visual word recognition literature is full of conflicting evidence regarding the size of the basic unit of processing. The smallest unit for which evidence has accumulated, aside from the individual feature, is the individual letter (McClelland, 1976). On the other hand, several investigators have shown that words could be recognized as units without prior identification of letters or other subunits (Johnson, 1975; Rumelhart & Siple, 1974; F. Smith, 1971). In between these extremes there is evidence for word subunits of various sizes including the spelling pattern (Gibson, 1965) and, of course, the syllable (Spoehr & Smith, 1973). The purpose of the present discussion is not to evaluate the relative merits of each of these proposals, because these arguments have been reviewed elsewhere (Smith & Spoehr, 1974). Instead, it examines how the syllable can be used as a perceptual unit in visual word recognition, and reviews the evidence that shows that the orthographic access file is organized syllabically.

Two experiments done by myself and Edward E. Smith (Spoehr & Smith, 1973) demonstrate that subjects make use of syllabic structure in processing tachistoscopically presented words. Subjects were presented with five-letter English words that were either one or two syllables long, and that were matched in pairs for other variables such as frequency and number of vowels. Report accuracy was higher for one- than for two-syllable words (70% vs. 64% with a full report procedure, and 80% vs. 71% with a forced-choice procedure), indicating that it was easier for subjects to process the one-syllable items. In a later paper (Spoehr, 1978), I demonstrated that the syllable effect could not be attributed to simple phoneme length.

The theoretical explanation for this result is that processing in this task proceeds syllable by syllable. Subjects first identify the letters and then use this information to divide the stimulus into syllables. In order for the word to be completely recognized, each syllable must be coded into a phonological form that could not be destroyed by the visual mask we used. In our original explanation of the results of these experiments, we suggested that this phonological code was achieved by applying the spelling-to-sound correspondence rules of English to each syllable prior to lexical access. However, it is equally possible that the same data could have resulted if the subjects had used the syllabic information to access the lexical entry via a syllabically organized orthographic access file, and then read off the pronunciation into short-term memory. The point is that the more syllables there are in a stimulus, the less likely it is that the recognition procedure will be completed before the mask appears, and the less likely it is that the subject will report the item correctly.

In order for this scheme to work, it was necessary for us to show that it is possible to divide a letter string into syllabic units purely on the basis of orthographic information. We found that some very simple parsing rules devised by Hansen and Rodgers (1965) provide an adequate means of dividing words into syllable-sized units called Vocalic Center Groups (VCGs), and that this parsing procedure could be carried out knowing only which letters in a string were vowels and which were consonants. Moreover, the unit boundaries defined by the VCG parsing rules provided a more adequate description of the perceptual boundaries evidenced in our data than did boundaries defined by the conventional syllabification rules of English based on morphemic considerations.

Taft and Forster (1975, 1976) have run a series of experiments that suggest that lexical access in visual word recognition is based upon syllable-sized units. Taft and Forster (1975) initially demonstrated that recognition of prefixed words is carried out by first removing the prefix, and then searching the lexicon for the stem morpheme. In Experiment 1, they compared lexical decision times for nonwords of two types: "real stem" items such as *juvenate,* which are derived by removing a prefix morpheme from an English word (in this case, *rejuvenate*), and matched "pseudo stem" nonwords such as *pertoire*, which are derived by removing the same letters from a word in which they do not constitute a morphemic prefix (*repertoire*). The real stem nonwords took over 40 msec. longer to classify than did the pseudo stem nonwords, apparently because the real stem nonwords match lexical entries used in the recognition of prefixed English words, and an extra search had to be carried out to determine whether an appropriate prefix had also been presented.

The hypothesis that syllable prefixes are typically separated during word recognition is further confirmed by Taft and Forster's (1975) Experiment 3, in which lexical decision times were compared for nonwords that were composed of real stems and an illegal prefix (e.g., *dejuvenate*), and nonwords that were composed of pseudo-stems with a prefix (e.g., *depertoire*). The result that the real stem nonwords took nearly 90 msec. longer to reject is explained by supposing that for both types of items the intial prefix is removed and a search made for the remaining morpheme. For the pseudo-stem nonwords no such morphemic entry is found and a subsequent search for the entire string as a nonprefixed word yields negative results. For the real stem nonwords, a morphemic entry is found for the second part of the string and a check is made to see whether a legal prefix had been presented with it. After this additional prefix checking step has yielded a negative result, the system makes the search for the entire string with negative results in the same way it does for pseudo-stem strings. The difference in reaction time between the two types of items results from the extra prefix checking step.

In their second paper, Taft and Forster (1976) provide more direct evidence on the syllabic organization of lexical access. In Experiment 1, lexical decision times were compared for two-syllable nonwords that were composed either of two words (e.g., *dustworth*), a word and a nonword (e.g., *footmilge*), a nonword and a word (*trowbreak*), or two nonwords (e.g., *mowd flisk*). Decision times were substantially longer when the first syllable of the string was an English word, suggesting that subjects look up lexical entries on the basis of the first syllable. When the first syllable of a nonword causes a spurious match to the first syllable of a real word, interference is caused and a delay in decision time results. Experiment 2 examines decision times for nonwords such as *plat*, which is the first syllable of an English word, *brot*, which is not the first syllable of a word but which is a beginning letter sequence for a word, and *pren*, which is neither a syllabic or letter sequence beginning of a word. It was predicted that if words were accessed by their first syllable, it would take longer to reject items such as *plat*, which would match the access file entry for a word (e.g., *platter*). Using similar reasoning it was predicted that decisions for actual words such as *neigh*, which is the first syllable of another lexical entry *neighbor*, would take longer than for words such as *shrew* and *scoff*, which are not parts of other words. These predictions were confirmed by the decision latencies. Additional data reported by Taft and Forster confirm that the nonword interference effects discussed earlier do not occur if the nonword is the last, rather than the first, syllable of an English word (Experiment 3), that the interference effects can be obtained even when the syllable boundary is not signaled by an unlikely sequence of consonants (Experiment 4), and that the frequency of occurrence of the first syllable as an individual lexical entry will determine the magnitude of the interference effect for both words and nonwords (Experiment 5).

Syllables in Speech Processing

The literature on lexical access in fluent speech processing also suggests a syllable based access route, though the data is qualitatively different in at least one important respect. The data presented thus far for visual word recognition is based on processing of individual items, whereas word recognition in speech has been studied in the context of connected discourse. As becomes apparent, the visual word recognition literature is just beginning to consider contextual influences on recognition skills, so that experiments analogous to the ones in speech have simply not been carried out. Also, because the word to be recognized in reading is a physically distinct entity, whereas the word in fluent speech clearly is not, it is more difficult to talk about word recognition in speech without reference to contextual influences. The evidence showing the importance of the syllable in recognizing words in speech should be viewed with these points in mind.

The two most common speech tasks showing syllabic influences are the target detection and the shadowing tasks. In target detection, the subject is instructed to listen for the occurrence of a specified sound, either an individual phoneme, a syllable, a word, or perhaps a phrase, or the subject may be asked to listen for mispronunciations of an unspecified type. Both accuracy and speed of detection are used to assess processing mechanisms. In the shadowing task, subjects repeat verbatim an auditory message, and are instructed to include any mispronunciations that might occur in the message. The dependent variables in this type of task include shadowing latency between the presentation of a particular word in the passage and the subjects' articulation of it, the frequency of fluent restorations where the subject produces a correctly pronounced word instead of the mispronounced version actually presented, and the frequency of exact repetitions of mispronunciations.

Savin and Bever (1970) used a target detection task to see how quickly subjects could respond to the presence of either an initial consonant phoneme or an entire syllable target in a series of consonant–vowel–consonant syllables. Because subjects took longer to respond to the individual phonemes, they apparently processed the stimuli as entire syllables first, and then decomposed those syllables in order to discriminate the component phonemes. Although this superiority for syllables over individual phonemes has been replicated using sentences rather than CVC syllables as background materials (Warren, 1971),

Savin and Bever's conclusions have been criticized by Foss and Swinney (1973) and McNeill and Lindig (1973). Foss and Swinney (1973), for example, found that detection times in two-syllable words were faster for entire word targets than for first syllables, which were, in turn, faster than times for individual phonemes. McNeill and Lindig (1973) showed that detection times for targets of different sizes, either phonemes, syllables, words, or sentences, depended upon the type of material being searched: Syllables were most easy to detect when the search lists were composed of syllables, words were easiest when the materials were words, and so forth.

Massaro (1977) has recently suggested that the results of Foss and Swinney (1973) and McNeill and Lindig (1973) do not necessarily argue against the syllable-processing hypothesis. Foss and Swinney, for example, constructed their stimulus materials such that a subject could detect a target word merely on the basis of its first syllable, and also reject a nontarget word on the basis of its first syllable. Thus it is not clear that subjects completely processed word targets. Massaro also points out that subjects in the McNeill and Lindig (1973) study generally responded in less than ⅓ of a second, meaning that they had detected a target long before they could have heard an entire word or sentence. Thus initial syllable information was very important in this experiment as well. Massaro's conclusion is reinforced by Marslen-Wilson's (1973) shadowing data, which show that some subjects are capable of shadowing a prose passage within a 250 msec lag. The fact that the errors that were made by these ''close'' shadowers were semantically and syntactically congruous with the text, indicates that subjects were actually recognizing the words within one syllable of the presentation.

The importance of the first syllable in recognizing words in fluent speech has been demonstrated by Cole (1973) using a mispronunciation detection task. Subjects listened to a prose passage in which mispronunciations had been introduced into either the first, second, or third syllable of three-syllable words. Each mispronunciation was created by changing a single consonant phoneme in the correct version by either one, two, or four distinctive features according to the feature classification system of Keyser and Halle (1968). The changes were in the syllable-initial position in the first syllable, and in the syllable-final position in the second and third syllables. The more features that were changed in the pronunciation, the more likely the subjects were to detect the change, regardless of the syllable in which it occurred. However, when a sound was changed by only one feature, subjects were much less likely to detect the error if it occurred in the second or third syllable. In addition, the detection times in this experiment showed that subjects were much faster at detecting errors in the second and third syllables than in the first syllable for all three types of feature changes.

This data can be accounted for by assuming that subjects detect the mispronunciations by recognizing the entire word, and that the word is accessed on the basis of its first syllable. If a mispronunciation occurs in the first syllable, detection takes a long time because the subject must search through an erroneous section of his or her lexicon consistent with the mispronounced syllable until it is clear that there is no lexical entry with that pronunciation. Even for slight pronunciational errors, the subject will eventually realize that the word has been mispronounced. When the error occurs in either the second or third syllable it is likely that the subject will have already identified the word on the basis of its first syllable by the time the last two syllables are presented. Because information about the last two syllables is not necessary for making the recognition, those syllables might be ignored altogether, and slight mispronunciation in them would go undetected. However, if information from the second and third syllables is necessary to complete lexical access, it will become quickly apparent that a mispronunciation has occurred in one of these two syllables, and the detection time will be fast.

Marslen-Wilson (1975) has obtained a similar result using shadowing. Subjects almost never restored mispronounced phonemes when they occurred in the first syllable of a word but did restore mispronunciations in the second and third syllables of words. Here the subjects are clearly shadowing by recognizing each word as quickly as possible, and producing the pronunciation on the basis of their stored representation of it. If the mispronunciation occurs before the word has been completely identified, the mispronunciation will be produced, otherwise it will not.

The speech results thus suggest that the initial syllable of a word plays an important role in its recognition. By accessing word meanings on a syllabic basis, the system can reduce the amount of effort expended in processing subsequent syllables that often contain redundant information, and can integrate individual word meanings quickly enough to influence processing of subsequent material. This data also reinforces the conclusions drawn in the previous section on visual word recognition that a syllabically organized directory provides access to semantic information stored in long-term memory.

THE INFLUENCE OF CONTEXT
ON WORD RECOGNITION

Thus far, we have looked at word recognition as a problem of how an individual lexical item is processed, and have seen several commonalities between the way in which that is accomplished in speech and reading. However, because word recognition in everyday experience rarely involves understanding isolated lexical entities, it is important to understand how the processing of words affects the processing of other words. The remainder of this chapter deals with contextual effects and how different aspects of context influence word processing in each of the language understanding systems.

General Influences of Context on Word Recognition

The presence of semantic and syntactic context has long been known to have a facilitory effect on the recognition of spoken words. Miller, Heise, and Lichten (1951) required subjects to identify individual words in the presence of auditory noise. They found that recognition could be made at lower signal-to-noise ratios if the items were presented within the framework of a sentence rather than as part of a series of scrambled words from a restricted vocabulary. Miller and Isard (1963) showed further that word identification in noise was best when words appeared in grammatical and semantically sensible sentences, next best when they appeared in grammatical but meaningless sentences, and worst when they appeared in ungrammatical word strings.

A similar set of findings has been obtained with visual presentation of word stimuli. Tulving and Gold (1963) measured visual threshold durations for the identification of words following differing amounts and types of context. In the "congruous" contextual conditions, the target word was preceded by part or all of a nine-word sentence in which the target fitted appropriately as the last word (e.g., "Three people were killed in a terrible highway *collision.*"). In the "incongruous" condition, the targets were preceded by all or part of a sentence for which the target was not a suitable completion (e.g., "She likes red fruit and jams of strawberry and *collision.*"). The amount of context could be either the eight, four, two, or one word preceding the target in the sentence, or the target could be presented alone. Visual threshold durations were found to decrease with increasing amounts of congruous context, but rose significantly with increasing amounts of incongruous context.

A more recent visual study by Schuberth and Eimas (1977) replicates the congruity effect with a lexical decision task. In this experiment, subjects were asked to decide if a letter string was a word or nonword, and made their decisions after having received no context, or a sentence frame of the type used by Tulving and Gold. Decision times were faster relative to the no context trials for the items appearing after the sentence frames with which they were congruous, and were slower after frames with which they were incongruous. Apparently, context influences lexical access as well as simple naming.

Effects of Predictability on Word Recognition

One of the most obvious hypotheses that can be made about the contextual facilitation effects described in the foregoing is that facilitation occurs whenever contextual cues allow the subject to make reasonable predictions about the item to be recognized next. Being able to restrict the set of possibilities lessens the amount of work a subject needs to do in order to uniquely identify an item. Moreover, it is clearly the case that not all words are as tightly constrained by their contexts as others. Thus it should be true that word recognition performance ought to be a function of contextual constraint, and that the preceding hypothesis about the mechanism by which context facilitates word recognition can be tested by manipulating amount of contextual constraint.

Data from word recognition in speech bears out the hypothesis that word recognition improves as context restricts the number of possibilities for a particular item. Morton and Long (1976) used a phoneme detection task in which subjects monitored sentences for the occurrence of plosive or nonplosive initial consonants. The words in which these target sounds occurred were either high-transition probability or low-transition probability as determined by how often they were produced as completions by a different group of subjects for the sentences in which they occurred. Detections were made approximately seventy milliseconds faster when the target sound was in a high-transition probability word, and the effect was consistent across target types.

Cole and Jakimik (1978) used Morton and Long's materials to determine the effect of differing amounts of constraint on detection of mispronunciation. The initial phonemes of the high- and low-transition probability words that had served as targets in the Morton and Long study were mispronounced in the Cole and Jakimik study, and the sentences in which they appeared were embedded in short paragraphs in which other mispronunciations were inserted. The results showed that subjects were just as likely to detect mispronunciations in the two types of words, but they did so 150 msec faster in high-transition probability words. A second experiment showed that constraint could be provided by as little as a single word preceding the mispronounced word in a sentence. Subjects detected mispronunciations almost 100 msec faster when the immediately preceding word constrained the target highly (e.g., mink coat) than when it constrained the target word very little (e.g., pink coat).

Along similar lines, Marslen-Wilson and Welsh (1978) have shown that constraint also affects performance in the shadowing task. Subjects were much more likely to make a fluent restoration of a mispronounced phoneme in a word that was highly constrained by the previous sentence context (57.0%) than when it was in a word that was less constrained (41.1%). It should be noted, in line with the earlier discussion of syllables, that regardless of the amount of contextual constraint, fluent restorations were still more likely in the third syllable than in the first syllable of the mispronounced word.

The pattern of results for contextual constraint in visual word recognition is analogous. Tulving and Gold (1963) noted that the visual threshold durations in their experiment could be affected by different amounts of context simply because longer contexts made the target word more predictable. They therefore measured both the transition probability for and amount of information transmitted by each of their target words and found that both measures increased as the number of prior context words increased. However, only transition probability significantly predicted the threshold durations.

Several lexical decision experiments have confirmed that transition probability is a significant predictor of word recognition in context. Schuberth and Eimas (1977) used English words of high- and low-frequency and either high- or low-transition probability as completions to their sentence context frames and found that the high-transition probability words were recognized about 50 msec faster than their matched low-transition probability counterparts regardless of frequency. It should be noted, however, that the Schuberth and Eimas (1977) incongruous items were not only unpredictable in their sentence frames, but also semantically anomolous (e.g., The puppy chewed the *hour*.). It is possible to manipulate constraint in the form of transition probability without using semantically anomolous items. Richard Schuberth and I (Scuberth & Spoehr, in preparation) have recently done this experiment, factorially varying frequency of the completion word (either high or low) and its transition probability (either high or low). Table 7.4 shows the lexical decision latencies for words in the four target classes. There are significant effects of both variables on lexical retrieval time, and the two factors are additive. Applying the logic of the additive factors method (Sternberg, 1969), it appears that frequency and degree of congruity influence different stages of word recognition.

Syntactic Versus Semantic Contextual Factors

The amount of constraint imposed upon a lexical item by its preceding context depends on two criteria for item selection (Chomsky, 1965): strict subcategorization and selectional rules. Strict subcategorization refers to the constraints required to make a word grammatical in the context of the other words in the sentence. Thus the sentence, "The puppy chewed the give" is ungrammatical because the final word, *give,* violates strict subcategorization rules that require a noun to complete the direct object noun phrase. Selectional rules determine the semantic relationships that govern a word's co-occurrence in a sentence. Thus the sentence, "The flower chewed the bone" violates a selectional rule that requires an animate noun that has the property of teeth as the subject of the sentence. The fact that constraint results from the joint contributions of strict subcategorization and selectional rules raises the question of how much of the contextual effect we observe in word recognition are contributed by the syntactic component and how much by the semantic component. That is, will context

TABLE 7.4
Mean Decision Latency (msec)

HiTP-HiF	HiTP-LoF	LoTP-HiF	LoTP-LoF	PN	NPN
661	718	677	758	814	734

improve word recognition if we provide a grammatically correct context even when the meaning is anomalous?

Miller and Isard's (1963) result shows that both syntax and semantics contribute to the constraint-induced facilitation in an auditory word recognition task. These results have recently been extended to the shadowing task and to the detection task by Marslen-Wilson (Marslen-Wilson, 1975; Marslen-Wilson & Tyler, 1975). In the first of these two studies, subjects shadowed prose that was either normal, contained target words that were semantically anomalous (i.e., violated selectional rules), or were syntactically as well as semantically anomalous (i.e., violated strict subcategorization rules). The target words in each of these three context conditions were pronounced normally or were mispronounced in either the first, second, or third syllable. In normal text the number of fluent restorations was an increasing function of the syllable in which the error occurred. Fewer restorations were made in the semantically anomalous text, and fewer still in the syntactically altered text, but for all types of material fewer restorations were made if the first one or two syllables had been correctly pronounced. Marslen-Wilson and Tyler (1975) had subjects monitor passages for a target word. Detection times were much faster in normal prose than in syntactically correct prose where the semantic information was absent, and both of these were faster than detection in lists of randomly ordered words. The auditory data are thus in close agreement that even when selectional rule constraint is missing, syntactic constraint still facilitates word recognition.

The directly analogous experiments in visual word recognition have not been carried out, although there are several results that suggest that similar conclusions can be drawn for reading. Klein and Klein (1973) have used a visual word boundary task to test for the effects of constraint. Subjects placed boundaries between words in printed text in which the spaces and punctuation had been omitted, and did so more accurately if the words formed normal prose, than if they formed semantically irregular prose, and even less accurately if the words appeared in random order. Forster (1970) used rapid, successive visual presentation of words in a sentence and obtained better recognition when the words formed a syntactically correct sentence than when they did not.

Unfortunately, neither of these studies looks at the recognition process for an individual lexical item in a situation remotely resembling reading. One study that has examined the contributions of semantic and syntactic context in a reading-related task that is comparable to other word recognition tasks is one carried out by Fischler and Bloom (1979). Although these investigators did not vary the constraint characteristics of the entire sentence in the same way as in auditory studies, they do have data on the differences between single word completions to normal sentences that are either: (1) syntactically correct and highly constrained by selectional rules; (2) syntactically correct and constrained little by selectional rules; or (3) syntactically correct but semantically inappropriate. Subjects made lexical decisions on these items under conditions where they received a previous context prime, or under conditions when no context prime had been presented. The presence of context plus high semantic constraint facilitated lexical decisions by about 20 msec relative to the unprimed condition. Latencies to unlikely words were about 30 msec slower and latencies to anomolous words about 90 msec. slower than decisions made in the absence of syntactic constraint in the no context conditions. Thus, the facilitation contributed by selectional rules seems to operate only for a few highly likely word choices, whereas the serious violation of these rules can even negate the benefits produced by the presence of syntactic cues.

Is Context a Perceptual or a Decisional Variable?

Thus far, we have seen that a word's context improves recognition performance primarily by constraining the set of possibilities through the operation of strict subcategorization and selectional rules. One important question not answered by these data, however, is whether the constraining effect operates at early perceptual levels of processing or at later decision-making points. That is, are top-down processing constraints evident from the very moment a subject begins the task of identifying a word?

Investigators of word recognition in fluent speech seem to be in general agreement that context exerts an immediate perceptual influence on the recognition of input. These conclusions are based on several empirical findings. First, the fact that Marslen-Wilson's (1973) shadowers showed clear evidence of being sensitive to semantic and syntactic constraints when they were shadowing at latencies of 250 msec suggests that contextual cues are important at even these very short processing intervals. Second, Garnes and Bond (1976) have shown that semantic constraint interacts with acoustic information in the disambiguation of phonetic features. Subjects identified synthesized words that began with stop consonant sounds taken from the /b/-/d/-/g/ continuum. Their identification of phonemes that were good examples of each of these three categories was not affected by surrounding sentence context, but in the boundary regions between phonemes it was found that context did influence the subject's report in the direction of the phoneme that made the contextually appropriate word.

Finally, data reported by Marslen-Wilson and Welsh (1978) also support our earlier conclusion. They argue that fluent restorations in shadowing "reflect immediate perceptual processing" rather than a "deliberate process of adjustment" after an initial perception of the incorrect pronunciations. In order to support this conclusion, they examine the shadowing latencies for time intervals immediately preceding and following the presentation of a mispronounced word and its subsequent repetition aloud. They find that shadowing latency is not disrupted at any point immediately surrounding the presentation or fluent restoration of a mispronounced word, indicating that the context has had the immediate and direct effect of causing the subject to fail to notice the mispronunciation. On the other hand, in those instances where subjects do notice the mispronunciation and make an exact repetition of it, there is a sizeable disruption of the shadowing latency. Marslen-Wilson and Welsh (1978) conclude that in the case of fluent restorations "the shadower/listener does behave as if his immediate percept of a particular word does not always require a full analysis of the phonetic input corresponding to that word [p. 38]."

A series of demonstrations of the immediate effects of context on word recognition in fluent speech comes from the work of Cole and his associates. Two experiments reported by Cole and Jakimik (1978) and Cole, Jakimik, and Cooper (in press) show that context affects the segmentation of acoustic input into syllabic units, and thus affects the interpretation given to a particular acoustic sequence. In one experiment mispronunciations are introduced into English words appearing in the middle of prose passages. The critical items are those of the type *cargo* and *car go,* which are altered by replacing an interior stop consonant in the one-word version or the corresponding first phoneme of the second word of the two-word version with another stop consonant (e.g., car*k*o or car *k*o). Although the identical acoustic sequence is presented for both segmentations, for some subjects that sequence is embedded in a prose passage that suggests the one-word segmentation, whereas for other subjects the context suggests the two-word segmentation. When presented without context, the critical stimuli favor each of their two interpretations approximately equally. The argument is made that because detection of a mispronunciation is slower when it occurs in the first syllable of a word than when it is in a later syllable (Cole, 1973), the context should have a significant effect on the speed of detection of the mispronunciation. Specifically, detection of the mispronunciation should take longer when the context favors a two-word segmentation than when it favors a one-word segmentation. The data reveal that, in fact, decisions are several hundred milliseconds faster when the context favors the one-word segmentation.

A second experiment by Cole and Jakimik show that even a few previous words of context can have a significant effect on segmentation decisions and thus on word recognition. Following the same logic as in the previous experiment, mispronunciations were inserted either on the first phoneme of the second word of a two-word sequence, or on the first phoneme of the second syllable of an acoustically identical one-word sequence. The segmentation of the sequence was biased only by the first few words of a sentence context that preceded the critical phoneme (e.g., "He was noted for *g*etting the right number." vs. "He just hated for*g*etting the right number."). Again it was found that detection of mispronunciations was much faster when contextual cues forced a segmentation that put those errors in the second syllable of a word rather than in the first syllable of a new word.

One advantage of auditory presentation is that words are, by necessity, presented in a strictly serial fashion, and it is possible to know exactly when a subject begins to process any given word. With visual presentation, however, processing of several items can take place in parallel, and it is often impossible to know, even with the use of an eye tracking apparatus, when the subject begins to process an individual item. Thus, there are no data on processing times for every word in a continuous reading task as there are for shadowing in speech, for example. Therefore, the visual data that suggest a top-down, perceptual influence of context on word recognition are more indirect in nature.

Most of the data that support the conclusion that context influences perceptual encoding mechanisms in visual word recognition make use of the additive factors logic, and assume a sequential stage model (Sternberg, 1969). Meyer, Schvaneveldt, and Ruddy (1975) separate the word recognition process into roughly three operations; graphemic encoding, lexical memory retrieval, and response execution. Graphemic encoding is a perceptual operation that operates on the visual feature input, and its duration can be expected to be affected by any experimental manipulation that affects the rate at which featural information can be processed. In their own experiment, Meyer et al. used stimulus quality to affect the processing time at this stage. Lexical access, on the other hand, will be affected by manipulations that determine how fast a word can be located in memory. Although Meyer et al. did not use this particular variable in their study, word frequency is clearly such a variable (Schuberth & Eimas, 1977). One way to determine whether context affects perceptual encoding, lexical access, or even response execution is to vary semantic context factorially with another variable known to affect processing at one of these stages. By the logic of the additive factors method, if context interacts with an encoding variable such as stimulus quality it can be said that the two factors influence the same stage of processing, whereas if the two factors are additive they must affect different stages.

Meyer et al. (1975) used single words to provide context for their target items. The context words could be either semantically related to the target word (e.g., bread-butter) or semantically unrelated to the target (e.g., nurse-butter), and stimuli could appear either in their intact form or degraded by the superimposition of a dot pattern. Lexical decisions were significantly faster for intact than for degraded stimuli, and for semantically related than for unrelated targets. Moreover, the interaction between stimulus quality and context was significant. These results have been confirmed by Becker and Killion (1977), using stimulus intensity as the determinant of quality. Thus it appears that context does affect the same stage of processing that quality does: the perceptual encoding stage.

Stanners, Jastrzembski, and Westbrook (1975) have shown that frequency and quality, although having significant individual effects on lexical decision times with single word contexts, do not interact, and Schuberth and Eimas (1977) have shown that frequency and contextual effects do not interact in a sentence context experiment. Taken together, these results suggest that quality and context affect perceptual encoding, whereas frequency affects a later lexical access stage.

Unfortunately, the picture is not as clear cut as we would like it. Most of the evidence supporting the interpretation we have proposed so far for visual word recognition comes from experiments where the context is provided through the semantic associations between the target string and a single other word. At least one study using sentence frames as contextual cues has shown results that contradict those obtained in the single-word context studies. To briefly review the situation, recall that Schuberth and Eimas (1977) varied contextual congruity and word frequency using sentence frame contexts and found no interaction between the two. Schuberth and I (Schuberth & Spoehr, in preparation) have replicated this finding in a lexical decision experiment using sentence frame contexts, and manipulating the congruity and frequency of the target words. Targets were presented in either an intact or degraded form. We obtained significant main effects of all three factors on the decision times but did not obtain any interactions; that is, contextual congruity did not interact with stimulus quality the way it does with single-word contexts. The reasons why this discrepancy should occur between single-word and sentence contexts remain to be found. Forster (1976) has pointed to an important difference between the two types of context. Single-word contexts operate by virtue of semantic associations between lexical entries in the long-term memory master file. Sentences, on the other hand, are less likely to include words that are direct semantic associates of one another. Thus, sentences make considerably less use of associative relations as a means of providing context.

One final approach to the question of whether context affects perceptual operations or decisional operations has been taken by Schuberth (1978) In this experiment, a signal detection approach was taken to separate out contextual influences in perceptability of stimulus strings versus response bias and decisional aspects of the task. Subjects received a sentence frame context on each trial of the experiment followed by a briefly exposed congruous word, incongruous word, or nonword. Subjects made a word/nonword classification of the stimulus string and a confidence rating on their decision. The nonparametric measure, A', was used to determine subjects' sensitivities to congruous and incongruous words relative to nonwords, and it was found that contextual congruity exerted a significant effect on this measure. Subjects detected congruous words better than incongruous words. Thus it appears that at least part of the influence of context is at the perceptual level.

Massaro (1977) has recently strongly argued that higher order context and featural encoding mechanisms have independent and temporally separated influences on word recognition in both speech and reading. To see how the argument works, consider how a subject might encode the ambiguous character c. If this featural information is presented in the word context -oin, the subject will likely use the other orthographic information to interpret the character as the letter c, whereas the context -dit would favor an interpretation of e. The contexts -tsa and -ast favor both letters equally. Massaro presented ambiguous characters that ranged from good examples of c to good examples of e along a continuum described by the length of the crossbar in the character, and embedded them in orthographic contexts of the four types just described. Subjects were much more likely to report an *e* when it was contextually favored, and a *c* when it was contextually favored, at all points along the *e/c* continuum, though these effects were greater for ambiguous intermediate characters than for the good examples of *e* and *c*. A parallel result for speech stimuli has recently been obtained by Ganong (1978), who has shown that the interpretation of acoustic information from ambiguous stimuli along stop consonant continua (e.g., a /b/-/p/ continuum) is influenced by lexical context information.

The data from this experiment are fit well by Massaro's model, which assumes stochastic independence between the information contributed by the visual stimulus and the information contributed by the context. That is, the "amount of e-ness" is the product of the amount of e-ness indicated by the visual features of the stimulus multiplied by the amount of e-ness suggested by the context. The probability that a subject will report an *e* is computed according to Luce's Choice Axiom. Under this formulation, context provides a type of "perceptual" information that would influence the amount of e-ness detected by the subject, but would not influence the criterion value that would determine whether that amount of e-ness was sufficient for an *e* response. Thus, context would show up as a perceptual variable in an experiment such as Schuberth's.

Massaro extends the model to account for the data of Marslen-Wilson and Welsh (1978). The critical assumptions for this application are that feature detection and the evaluation of featural information are not dependent on the amount of constraint placed upon a word by its context. Thus, acoustic information is one independent source about the identity of a word. A second source is the lexical information available at each syllable boundary; the amount of lexical information increases from the first to the third syllable of a word, but is not dependent upon sentence context either. Finally, sentence context provides a third independent source of information in recognizing a word. The probability that a subject will fail to detect a mispronunciation is a multiplicative function of these three sources of information.

Massaro's independence model may not be as radically different from the proposals of Marslen-Wilson and Cole as it might seem. Certainly neither of the latter two investigators have proposed that context affects perception by directing the feature extraction process such that some features would be extracted in some contexts and not in others. Rather, contextual information for them appears to influence the interpretation of that featural information. Massaro's independence model provides a mechanism for quantifying how contextual cues have their influence on the word recognition process. It also has the potential of explaining why single words and sentence contexts have different effects on word recognition in reading, because it may well be that the amount and type of contextual information in the two situations is different.

Theoretical Explanations of Context Effects

The Logogen Model.   The most commonly known model of word recognition that provides for the effect of context is the Logogen Model proposed
by Morton (Morton, 1969, 1970). Morton assumes that each lexical item in
memory is represented by a memory location, or logogen, that contains relevant semantic, lexical, and phonemic information about it. Each logogen
has a counter associated with it, and during speech recognition or reading
the counter may be incremented when it receives either stimulus or contextual
information that is consistent with the logogen. As more and more consistent
information is found, the logogen counter will continue to increment until it
reaches a threshold level. At this point the logogen is activated and the word is
recognized by sending its pronunciation to the response output system. It is
assumed that the first logogen to reach threshold generates the response and that
the count levels of unactivated logogens are not available to any other processing
mechanisms in the system. A final assumption is that high-frequency words are
recognized more quickly than low-frequency words because the thresholds for
the former are lower than those for the latter. Because the effects of context and
stimulus input are assumed to be independent sources of information in the
logogen system, the model is similar to Massaro's in that the combined influence
of the two sources of information is computed by multiplying the strengths of the
two types of information. Finally, note that although the original Logogen Model
assumes that phonemic information about a visual stimulus is generated only
after recognition of the item has taken place, the model does not preclude identification of written words by accumulation of phonemic features generated by a
phonological recoding process.

The Logogen Model is capable of accounting for many of the empirical
findings discussed so far in both modalities. For example, it accounts for the
frequency effects found in word recognition in both modalities, for the facilitation provided by congruous sentence contexts, and for the inhibitory effects of
incongruous semantic context. Because of the contributions of context in the
model's recognition process, moreover, it will also predict that fluent restorations will be more likely in highly constrained conditions than in less constrained
conditions because it is more likely that context in the former situation will push
a logogen over threshold in the presence of erroneous acoustic information.

Marslen-Wilson and Welsh (1978) make three additional assumptions that
allow the Logogen Model to account for even more of their data. First, it is
necessary that the only logogen information of which the subject is aware be the
output from the logogen that reaches threshold. This makes it possible for subjects to be unaware of partial excitation of incorrect logogens consistent with the
acoustic input, so that many of the mispronunciations in the shadowing task go
undetected. Second, it must be assumed that "the acoustic-phonetic analysis of
the input should normally only be available to other parts of the system via its

effects on the logogen system" (Marslen-Wilson & Welsh, 1978, p. 46). This makes it possible for subjects to carry out the detection task in which subjects clearly must be sensitive to mispronunciations only within a specific lexical environment. Finally, in order to account for the syllable effects in their data and Cole's data, Marslen-Wilson and Welsh postulate that stimulus information from the first syllable has relatively more incremental influence on the counter than does information from later syllables.

The major difficulty with the Logogen Model for both the visual and auditory data seems to be in its inability to account for "nonword" effects. In visual recognition, for example, it is not clear how a subject could ever read aloud a pronounceable nonword if he or she were dependent upon a logogen system—there are simply no logogens in the system containing stored pronunciations for nonwords. Marslen-Wilson and Welsh (1978) point out the analogous problem for speech by noting that subjects are, in fact, "recognizing" nonwords both when they make exact repetitions of mispronounced syllables in shadowing and when they detect errors in a detection task. Although adding a direct path from the input to the Response Buffer (which would certainly require phonological recoding in the visual case) would allow subjects to identify nonwords, this mechanism makes incorrect predictions of Cole's (1973) results on the speed with which detections of one-, two- or four-feature mispronunciations can be made. Moreover, even with the addition of this direct path mechanism, the Logogen Model cannot account for the surprising finding obtained by Schuberth and Eimas (1977) that the recognition of nonwords, as well as of congruous words, is facilitated by a sentence context.

Active Direct Access.   Because the logogen system seems to be inadequate to handle all of the data in both the visual and auditory modalities, other schemes need to be considered. Marslen-Wilson and Welsh (1978) propose what they call an Active Direct Access recognition system that builds on the strengths of the Logogen Model but that avoids several of its failures. The basic elements of memory are assumed to be individual units corresponding to individual lexical items, and the initiation of stimulus information activates a set of these units that are consistent with the input. Because each memory element is a "computationally active processing entity," the elements can actively respond to information that yields mismatches. In the Logogen Model, inconsistent information would simply fail to activate a logogen further, whereas in the Active Direct Access Model inconsistent information will cause an element to be removed from the set of potential candidates. Word recognition occurs when the set of consistent memory elements is reduced to a single member.

This model successfully predicts many of the auditory results. Small deviations such as one-feature mispronunciations will not always cause an element to be deactivated, so that fluent restorations and detection misses will sometimes occur. The fact that mispronunciations in the late syllables of a word are less likely to be detected is predicted if acoustic input ceases to be fully analyzed after the word has been successfully recognized on the basis of its beginning. Thus, the speech syllable effect is not caused by syllables per se, but simply because third syllable information enters the system too late to be of use. Finally, lexical elements can drop out of consideration whenever syntactic and semantic constraint requirements mismatch the possibilities allowed by a particular acoustic input. High constraint conditions will thus eliminate lexical candidates at a faster rate than low constraint conditions, and recognition will be faster with high constraint.

The Active Direct Access Model can also be applied to visual data. Its ability to account for the effects of congruity and incongruity is straightforward. It would further predict the additive relationship between congruity and stimulus quality because with degraded stimuli, inconsistent sensory evidence that would rule out possible alternative identifications would enter the system at a slower rate but would combine with contextual information in the same way as sensory evidence from an intact stimulus.

The Active Direct Model does have its share of difficulties, however. The effects of word frequency are difficult to cope with under this scheme. If it is assumed that higher frequency words require more disconfirming evidence than lower frequency words in order to be dropped from the set of possible identifications, then an interaction between frequency and severity of mispronunciation is predicted for auditory shadowing and detection performance. This prediction has been neither confirmed nor disconfirmed because none of the existing data address the question. However, such a frequency assumption would predict additive effects of stimulus quality, frequency, and congruity in the visual word recognition data, a result that is not consistently obtained. Another major difficulty posed by visual word recognition to the Active Direct Access Model is in its assumption that letters are processed in serial order. The simultaneous presentation of letters in a printed word makes it likely that processing of these elements will occur in parallel (Travers, 1973). Therefore recognition time will not necessarily be predicted, as it is in the auditory case, by the point at which the letters in left-to-right order distinguish the correct entry from all other possibilities.

The Bin Model.   Interestingly enough, the Active Direct Access Model is not extremely different from Forster's (1976) bin approach that was discussed earlier in this chapter. A principal objection to Forster's account is that context cannot have an influence on word recognition until after an appropriate entry in the Master File has been accessed on the basis of bottom-up information alone (Marslen-Wilson & Welsh, 1978). The problem seems to be that the Bin Model, as proposed, provides no mechanism for the stimulus information and contextual information to *jointly* determine an entry in the Master File. The obvious modification is that stimulus information need not accrue until only one access code in the orthographic or phonological access file is left. Using the mechanism proposed by Marslen-Wilson and Welsh, it is possible that several access codes, each pointing to a different Master File entry, are activated by early input. With increasing stimulus input some of the access codes are deactivated. Simultaneously, codes in the semantic/syntactic access file that are contextually congruous are also activated, and some of these will point to the same Master File entries as pointers from the orthographic or phonological access files do. Recognition will be made when the set of Master File entries being pointed to by both the orthographic and/or phonological access file codes *and* the semantic/syntactic access file codes is reduced to a single entry. Organization of the orthographic access file into bins by syllables or initial letter sequences, and of the phonological access file into bins by syllables or initial phoneme sequences would facilitate location of the entires. Organization of codes within a bin by frequency would facilitate recognition of high-frequency words assuming that a word is recognized any time a semantic/syntactic pointer leads to the same Master File entry as a pointer from an activated entry near the top of an orthographic or phonological access bin.

SUMMARY AND CONCLUSIONS

In this chapter, we have attempted to compare and contrast the word recognition process in reading and fluent speech understanding. Although there are obvious and important differences at sensory and perceptual levels between the two systems, it appears that at higher levels the two modalities reflect the operation of more general mechanisms that have been developed for language understanding. We have seen that phonological recoding of visually presented words offers subjects a processing strategy that allows them to make use of the same lexical access pathways used during speech processing. We have also seen a correspondence between the two systems in the type of unit by which access is made to lexical information stored in long-term memory. That is, the syllable provides a convenient unit of analysis for both language understanding systems. Finally, we have seen that contextual information has very similar effects on the word recognition process in the two modalities and that several theoretical accounts of word recognition are equally applicable to the two systems. On the whole, the similarities between the two systems give promise that as data accumulate on how the recognition of words takes place in speech and reading, we may be able to converge on a single account of how humans understand language.

ACKNOWLEDGEMENT

The preparation of this chapter and several of the experiments reported in it were supported by National Science Foundation grant BNS76-82337 to the author.

REFERENCES

Anderson, J. R., & Bower, G. C. *Human associative memory*. Washington, D.C.: Winston & Sons, 1973.

Baron, J. Phonemic stage not necessary for reading. *Quarterly Journal of Experimental Psychology*, 1973, *25*, 241–246.

Baron, J. Mechanisms for pronouncing printed words: Use and acquisition. In D. LaBerge & S. J. Samuels (Eds.), *Basic Processes in reading: Perception and comprehension*. Hillsdale, N.J.: Lawrence Erlbaum Associates, 1977.

Baron, J., & Strawson, C. Use of orthographic and word-specific knowledge in reading words aloud. *Journal of Experimental Psychology: Human Perception and Performance*, 1976, *2*, 386–393.

Baron, J., & Thurston, I. An analysis of the word superiority effect. *Cognitive Psychology*, 1973, *4*, 207–228.

Becker, C. A., & Killion, T. H. Interaction of visual and cognitive effects in word recognition. *Journal of Experimental Psychology: Human Perception and Performance*, 1977, *3*, 389–401.

Blackwell, P. M., Engen, E., Fischgrund, J. E., & Zarcadoolas, C. *Sentences and other systems*. Washington, D.C.: Alexander Graham Bell Foundation for the Deaf, 1978.

Bouma, H. Visual recognition of isolated lower-case letters. *Vision Research*, 1971, *11*, 459–474.

Bower, T. G. R. Reading by eye. In H. Levin & J. P. Williams (Eds.), *Basic studies on reading*. New York: Basic Books, 1970.

Brooks, L. Visual pattern in fluent word identification. In A. S. Reber & D. L. Scarborough (Eds.), *Toward a psychology of reading*. Hillsdale, N.J.: Lawrence Erlbaum Associates, 1977.

Carr, T. H., Davidson, B. J., & Hawkins, H. L. Perceptual flexibility in word recognition: Strategies affect orthographic computation but not lexical access. *Journal of Experimental Psychology: Human Perception and Performance*, 1978, *4*, 674–690.

Chomsky, N. *Aspects of the theory of syntax*. Cambridge, Mass.: MIT Press, 1965.

Cole, R. A. Listening for mispronunciations: A measure of what we hear during speech. *Perception & Psychophysics*, 1973, *11*, 153–156.

Cole, R. A., & Jakimik, J. Understanding speech: How words are heard. In G. Underwood (Ed.), *Strategies of information processing*. New York: Academic Press, 1978.

Cole, R. A., Jakimik, J., & Cooper, W. E. A model of word recognition from fluent speech. In R. A. Cole (Ed.), *Perception and production of fluent speech*. Hillsdale, N.J.: Lawrence Erlbaum Associates, in press.

Collins, A. M., & Loftus, E. F. A spreading-activation theory of semantic processing. *Psychological Review*, 1975, *82*, 407–428.

Collins, A. M., & Quillian, M. R. Retrieval time from semantic memory. *Journal of Verbal Learning and Verbal Behavior*, 1969, *8*, 240–247.

Coltheart, M., Davelaar, E., Jonasson, J. T., & Besner, D. Access to the internal lexicon. In S. Dornic (Ed.), *Attention and performance VI*. London: Academic Press, 1977.

Conrad, R. Acoustic confusions in immediate memory. *British Journal of Psychology*, 1964, *55*, 75–78.

Darwin, D. J., Turvey, M. T., & Crowder, R. G. An auditory analogue of the Sperling partial report procedure: Evidence for brief auditory storage. *Cognitive Psychology*, 1972, *3*, 255–267.

Davelaar, E., Coltheart, M., Besner, D., & Jonasson, J. T. Phonological recoding and lexical access. *Memory & Cognition*, 1978, *6*, 403–409.

Eimas, P. D., & Miller, J. L. Effects of selective adaptation on the perception of speech and visual patterns: Evidence for feature detectors. In H. L. Pick & R. Walk (Eds.), *Perception and experience*. New York: Plenum Press, 1978.

Fischler, I., & Bloom, P. A. Automatic and attentional processes in the effects of sentence contexts on word recognition. *Journal of Verbal Learning and Verbal Behavior*, 1979, *18*, 1–20.

Forster, K. I. Visual perception of rapidly presented word sequences of varying complexity. *Perception & Psychophysics*, 1970, *8*, 215–221.

Forster, K. I. Accessing the mental lexicon. In R. J. Wales & E. C. T. Walker (Eds.), *New approaches to language mechanisms*. Amsterdam: North-Holland, 1976.

Forster, K. I., & Chambers, S. M. Lexical access and naming time. *Journal of Verbal Learning and Verbal Behavior*, 1973, *12*, 627–635.

Foss, D. J., & Swinney, D. A. On the psychological reality of the phoneme: Perception, identification, and consciousness. *Journal of Verbal Learning and Verbal Behavior*, 1973, *12*, 246–257.

Frederiksen, J. R. *Decoding skills and lexical retrieval*. Paper presented at the meeting of the Psychonomic Society, St. Louis, November 1976.

Frederiksen, J. R., & Kroll, J. F. Spelling and sound: Approaches to the internal lexicon. *Journal of Experimental Psychology: Human Perception and Performance*, 1976, *2*, 361–379.

Ganong, W. F. *Phonetic categorization in auditory word perception*. Paper presented at the Acoustical Society of America, Providence: RI, May 1978.

Garnes, S., & Bond, Z. S. *The relationship between semantic expectation and acoustic information*. Proceedings of the Third International Phonology Meeting, Vienna, 1976.

Gibson, E. J. Learning to read. *Science*, 1965, *148*, 1066–1072.

Gibson, E. J. *Principles of perceptual learning and development*. New York: Appleton-Century-Crofts, 1969.

Glushko, R. J., & Rumelhart, D. E. *Orthographically regular and irregular words: Pronunciation by analogy*. Paper presented at the annual meeting of the Psychonomic Society, Wash, D.C., November 1977.

Green, D. W., & Schallice, T. Direct visual access in reading for meaning. *Memory & Cognition*, 1976, *4*, 753–758.

Hanna, J. S., & Hanna, P. R. Spelling as a school subject: A brief history. *National Elementary Principal*, 1959, *38*, 8–23.

Hansen, D., & Rodgers, T. S. An exploration of psycholinguistic units in initial reading. In *Proceedings of the Symposium on the Psycholinguistic Nature of the Reading Process*. Detroit: Wayne State University Press, 1965.

Hardyck, C. D., & Petrinovich, L. R. Subvocal speech and comprehension level as a function of the difficulty level of reading material. *Journal of Verbal Learning and Verbal Behavior*, 1970, *9*, 647–652.

Hawkins, H. L., Reicher, G. M., Rogers, M., & Peterson, L. Flexible coding in word recognition. *Journal of Experimental Psychology: Human Perception and Performance*, 1976, *2*, 380–385.

Helfgott, J. Phonemic segmentation and blending skills of kindergarten children: Implications for beginning reading acquisition. *Contemporary Educational Psychology*, 1976, *1*, 157–169.

Hintzman, D. L. Articulatory coding in short-term memory. *Journal of Verbal Learning and Verbal Behavior*, 1967, *6*, 312–316.

Johnson, N. F. On the function of letters in word identification: Some data and a preliminary model. *Journal of Verbal Learning and Verbal Behavior*, 1975, *14*, 17–29.

Keyser, S. J., & Halle, M. What we do when we speak. In P. Kolers & M. Eden (Eds.), *Recognizing patterns*. Cambridge, Mass.: MIT Press, 1968.

Klatt, D. K. A new look at the problem of lexical access. In R. A. Cole (Ed.), *Perception and production of fluent speech*. Hillsdale, N.J.: Lawrence Erlbaum Associates, 1980.

Kleiman, G. M. Speech recoding in reading. *Journal of Verbal Learning and Verbal Behavior*, 1975, *14*, 323–339.

Klein, H. A., & Klein, G. A. Studying the use of context for word identification decisions. In P. L. Macke (Ed.), *Diversity in mature reading: Theory and research*. National Reading Conference 22nd Yearbook, Boon, N.C.: National Reading Conference, 1973.

LaBerge, D., & Samuels, S. J. Toward a theory of automatic information processing in reading. *Cognitive Psychology*, 1974, *6*, 293–323.

Liberman, A. M. Relations between speech and reading. In J. F. Kavanagh (Ed.), *Communicating by language: The reading process*. Bethesda, Md.: National Institute of Child Health and Human Development, 1968.

Liberman, A. M., Cooper, F. S., Shankweiler, D. P., & Studdert-Kennedy, M. Perception of the speech code. *Psychological Review*, 1967, *74*, 431–461.

Liberman, A. M., Mattingly, I. G., & Turvey, M. T. Language codes and memory codes. In A. W. Melton & E. Martin (Eds.), *Coding processes in human memory*. Washington, D.C.: Winston & Sons, 1972.

Liberman, I. Y., & Shankweiler, D. Speech, the alphabet, and teaching to read. In L. Resnick & P. Weaver (Eds.), *Theory and practice of early reading* (Vol. 2). Hillsdale, N.J.: Lawrence Erlbaum Associates, 1979.

Liberman, I. Y., Shankweiler, D., Liberman, A. M., Fowler, C., & Fischer, F. W. Phonetic segmentation and recoding in the beginning reader. In A. S. Reber & D. L. Scarborough (Eds.), *Toward a psychology of reading*. Hillsdale, N.J.: Lawrence Erlbaum Associates, 1977.

Lindsay, P. H., & Norman, D. A. *Human information processing*. New York: Academic Press, 1977.

MacKay, D. G. The structure of words and syllables: Evidence from errors in speech. *Cognitive Psychology*, 1972, *3*, 210–227.

Marslen-Wilson, W. D. Linguistic structure and speech shadowing at very short latencies. *Nature*, 1973, *244*, 522–523.

Marslen-Wilson, W. D. Sentence perception as an interactive parallel process. *Science*, 1975, *189*, 226–228.

Marslen-Wilson, W. D., & Tyler, L. K. Processing structure of sentence perception. *Nature*, 1975, *257*, 784–786.

Marslen-Wilson, W. D., & Welsh, A. Processing interactions and lexical access during word recognition in continuous speech. *Cognitive Psychology*, 1978, *10*, 29–63.

Massaro, D. W. *Reading and Listening* (Tech. Rep. 423). Technical report from the Project on Studies in Reading, Language, and Communication. Wisconsin Research and Development Center for Cognitive Learning. University of Wisconsin, December 1977.

Mattingly, I. G. Reading, the linguistic process, and linguistic awareness. In J. F. Kavanagh & I. G. Mattingly (Eds.), *Language by ear and by eye*. Cambridge, Mass.: MIT Press, 1972.

McClelland, J. L. Preliminary letter identification in the perception of words and nonwords. *Journal of Experimental Psychology: Human Perception and Performance*, 1976, *2*, 80–91.

McClelland, J. L. *On the time relations of cognitive processes: Theoretical explorations of systems of processes in cascade*. Paper presented at the annual meeting of the Psychonomic Society, San Antonio, Tex., November 1978.

McNeill, D., & Lindig, K. The perceptual reality of phoneme, syllables, words, and sentences. *Journal of Verbal Learning and Verbal Behavior*, 1973, *12*, 419–430.

Meyer, D. E., Schvaneveldt, R. W., & Ruddy, M. G. Functions of graphemic and phonemic codes in visual word-recognition. *Memory & Cognition*, 1974, *2*, 309–321.

Meyer, D. E., Schvaneveldt, R. W., & Ruddy, M. G. Loci of contextual effects on visual word-recognition. In P. M. A. Rabbitt & S. Dornic (Eds.), *Attention and performance V*. London: Academic Press, 1975.

Miller, G. A., Heise, G. A., & Lichten, W. The intelligibility of speech as a function of the context of the test materials. *Journal of Experimental Psychology*, 1951, *41*, 329–335.

Miller, G. A., & Isard, S. Some perceptual consequences of linguistic rules. *Journal of Verbal Learning and Verbal Behavior*, 1963, *2*, 217–228.

Morton, J. Interaction of information in word recognition. *Psychological Review*, 1969, *76*, 165–178.

Morton, J. A. A functional model of memory. In D. A. Norman (Ed.), *Models of human memory*. New York: Academic Press, 1970.

Morton, J., & Long, J. Effect of word transitional probability on phoneme identification. *Journal of Verbal Learning and Verbal Behavior*, 1976, *15*, 43–51.

Neisser, U. *Cognitive Psychology*. New York: Appleton-Century-Crofts, 1967.

Oden, G. C., & Massaro, D. W. *Integration of place and voicing information in identifying synthetic stop-consonant syllables* (WHIPP Rep. #1). Wisconsin Human Information Processing Program, July 1977.

Reddy, R. Speech recognition by machine: A review. *Proceedings of the IEEE*, 1976, *64*, 501–531.

Rubenstein, H., Lewis, S. S., & Rubenstein, M. A. Homographic entries in the internal lexicon: Effects of systematicity and relative frequency of meanings. *Journal of Verbal Learning and Verbal Behavior*, 1971, *10*, 645–657.

Rudnicky, A. I., & Cole, R. A. Effect of subsequent context on syllable perception. *Journal of Experimental Psychology: Human Perception and Performance*, 1978, *4*, 638–647.

Rumelhart, D. E. Toward an interactive model of reading. In S. Dornic (Ed.), *Attention and performance VI*. Hillsdale, N.J.: Lawrence Erlbaum Associates, 1977.

Rumelhart, D. E., & Siple, P. The processes of recognizing tachistoscopically presented words. *Psychological Review*, 1974, *81*, 99–118.

Savin, H. B., & Bever, T. G. The nonperceptual reality of the phoneme. *Journal of Verbal Learning and Verbal Behavior*, 1970, *9*, 295–302.

Schuberth, R. E. *Effects of context on the classification of words and nonwords*. Unpublished doctoral dissertation, Brown University, 1978.

Schuberth, R. E., & Eimas, P. D. Effects of context on the classification of words and nonwords. *Journal of Experimental Psychology: Human Perception and Performance*, 1977, *3*, 27–36.

Schuberth, R. E., & Spoehr, K. T. *Interaction of stimulus and contextual information in the lexical decision process*. Manuscript in preparation,

Smith, E. E., Shoben, E. J., & Rips, L. J. Structure and process in semantic memory: A featural model for semantic decisions. *Psychological Review*, 1974, *81*, 214–241.

Smith, E. E., & Spoehr, K. T. The perception of printed English: A theoretical perspective. In B. H. Kantowitz (Ed.), *Human information processing: Tutorials in performance and cognition*. Hillsdale, N.J.: Lawrence Erlbaum Associates, 1974.

Smith, F. *Understanding reading*. New York: Holt, Rinehart & Winston, 1971.

Sperling, G. The information available in brief visual presentations. *Psychological Monographs*, 1960, *74*, (11, Whole No. 498).

Spoehr, K. T. Phonological encoding in visual word recognition. *Journal of Verbal Learning and Verbal Behavior*, 1978, *17*, 127–142.

Spoehr, K. T., & Smith, E. E. The role of syllables in perceptual processing. *Cognitive Psychology*, 1973, *5*, 71–89.

Spoehr, K. T., & Smith, E. E. The role of orthographic and phonotactic rules in perceiving letter patterns. *Journal of Experimental Psychology: Human Perception and Performance*, 1975, *1*, 21–34.

Stanners, R. F., Jastrzembski, J. E., & Westbrook, A. Frequency and visual quality in a word-nonword classification task. *Journal of Verbal Learning and Verbal Behavior*, 1975, *14*, 259–264.

Stanovich, K. E., & Bauer, D. W. Experiments on the spelling-to-sound regularity effect in word recognition. *Memory & Cognition*, 1978, *6*, 410–415.

Sternberg, S. The discovery of processing stages: Extensions of Donders' method. *Acta Psychologica*, 1969, *30*, 276–315.

Taft, M., & Forster, K. I. Lexical storage and retrieval of prefixed words. *Journal of Verbal Learning and Verbal Behavior*, 1975, *14*, 638–647.

Taft, M., & Forster, K. I. Lexical storage and retrieval of polymorphemic and polysyllabic words. *Journal of Verbal Learning and Verbal Behavior*, 1976, *15*, 607–620.

Taylor, D.A. Time course of context effects. *Journal of Experimental Psychology: General,* 1977, *106,* 404–426.

Travers, J. R. The effects of forced serial processing on identification of words and random letter strings. *Cognitive Psychology,* 1973, *5,* 109–137.

Tulving, E., & Gold, C. Stimulus information and contextual information as determinants of tachistoscopic recognition of words. *Journal of Experimental Psychology,* 1963, *66,* 319–327.

Venezky, R. L. English orthography: Its graphical structure and its relation to sound. *Reading Research Quarterly,* 1967, *2,* 75–105.

Warren, R. M. Identification times for phonemic components of graded complexity and for spelling of speech. *Perception & Psychophysics,* 1971, *9,* 345–349.

Wijk, A. *Rules of pronunciation for the english language.* London: Oxford University Press, 1966.

Wickelgren, W. A. Short-term memory for phonemically similar lists. *American Journal of Psychology,* 1965, *78,* 567–574.

Zifcak, M. *Phonological awareness and reading acquisition in first grade children.* Unpublished doctoral dissertation, University of Connecticut, 1976.

8 Dependency Relations During the Processing of Speech

Peter D. Eimas
Brown University

Vivien C. Tartter
Rutgers University at Camden

Joanne L. Miller
Northeastern University

Editors' Comments

A relatively recent innovation in the study of speech perception has been the attempt to employ the methodology and theory of modern cognitive psychology. Although this information-processing view has not been without its critics, it has, nevertheless, extended the experimental approach to the study of speech as well as the theoretical conception of the perceptual process.

This view of pattern recognition usually assumes that processing of complex patterns occurs at a number of different levels and that the pattern is represented or encoded differently at each of these levels. A further assumption that is often made is that at some relatively early stage of processing, the signal is analyzed into a set of elements or feature values that, in combination, define the final percept. In the application of this type of system to speech perception, investigators have centered their research on a variety of quite different problems. Some, for instance, have attempted to provide experimental support for the idea of different levels of processing, whereas others have sought evidence for analytic mechanisms and their operating characteristics. An example of the latter is this research by Eimas, Tartter, and Miller. They investigated whether the processing channels for speech function independently of one another, or whether there exist interactions or dependencies among channels. Of particular interest is that they did not find a single instance of independence among channels, and in addition, the form of the processing interaction varied systematically with the nature of the information to be processed. These findings illustrate, at a relatively low level of analysis, the general interactive nature of speech processing and the rather considerable complexity that theories of speech will ultimately need to explain.

INTRODUCTION

Theoretical descriptions of the processes that are involved in the perception of
speech at the phonetic level of language often include the assumption that at
some level or stage of processing the neural transform of the acoustic signal is
analyzed into a set of distinctive phonetic features (Eimas & Miller, 1978;
Pisoni, 1975b). Inasmuch as listeners actually perceive phonetic segments,
which are defined in terms of distinctive features, models of this nature must also
possess some process of integration that recombines or recodes the distinctive
features into a form that permits segmental perception. In recent years, the
mechanisms by which the speech signal is analyzed into feature information have
been extensively studied and many of the operating and tuning characteristics of
the channels of analysis assumed to underlie the perception of speech have been
explicated (Anderson, 1975; Cooper, 1974; Eimas & Corbit, 1973; Eimas &
Miller, 1978; Ganong, 1977; McNabb, 1975; Miller, 1975, 1977b; Sawusch,
1977; Stevens, 1973; Tartter & Eimas, 1975). Of course, a number of theoretical
issues pertaining to these mechanisms of analysis await resolution. One of these,
namely, whether the channels of analysis responsible for the extraction of feature
information operate independently of one another or whether there exist dependencies among these channels during the course of analysis, is the central theme
of the present chapter.

  The problem of dependent relations during the processing of speech, although
not usually addressed directly in theoretical descriptions of the perception and
processing of speech, has had a relatively long history in the experimental study
of speech perception, dating back at least to the 1955 study of Miller and Nicely.
They examined the perceptual confusions that occur during listeners' attempts to
perceive speech embedded in various noise conditions. From their analyses based
on an information-theory approach, Miller and Nicely concluded that the feature
values that define a single phonetic segment were extracted from the speech
signal independently of one another. This conclusion was supported by Corcoran, Dorfman, and Weening (1968) who, in applying a different model of independence to a selected portion of the Miller–Nicely data, found insufficient
evidence to reject the assumption of independent analyses of phonetic features.
However, more recently, Holloway (1971) and Smith (1973) have both
reanalyzed the Miller–Nicely confusion matrices and have both concluded that
dependencies do in fact exist during the analysis of speech.[1] Indeed, Holloway

---

[1]A number of studies (e.g., Wickelgren, 1966) have reported that feature information is recalled
independently of the feature information with which it was originally presented. However, as was
true for the perceptual data of Miller and Nicely (1955), subsequent analyses (Smith, 1973) have
shown that the recall of feature information is not independent. Whether the dependency relations
found in perceptual processing and those obtained in recall are the same is not, as yet, known.

(1971) has noted that Corcoran et al. (1968) may have arrived at their conclusions as a result of using a restricted sample of the data for their reanalysis rather than as a result of the channels of analysis being truly independent.

Additional evidence for dependency relations in the perception of speech has been reported in several studies that investigated the ability of listeners to assign members of different series of synthetic speech patterns to phonetic categories. These series varied continuously along complex acoustic continua such as voice onset time (VOT) or the starting frequency and direction of the second- and third-formant transitions. The variation in these continua was always sufficient to signal a change in the feature value of one or more phonetic features and hence a change in the final phonetic percept. For example, Lisker and Abramson (1970) found that the location of the phonetic boundary distinguishing voiced from voiceless stops in English varied as a function of the place of articulation of the series. Similar dependency effects were found for speakers of Thai (Lisker & Abramson, 1970) and speakers of Spanish (Abramson & Lisker, 1973). This form of dependency effect is in accord with a model offered by Haggard (1970), who assumed a unidirectional dependency with the processing of voicing information being dependent on the processing of place of articulation information. However, the data certainly do not eliminate the possible existence of a dependency relation in the other direction as well, in that no test was made for a possible dependence of the analysis of place information on the analysis of voicing information. Miller (1977a) directly tested for the possibility of a mutual dependence during the processing of the information for place of articulation and voicing by requiring listeners to categorize the members of six series of synthetic speech patterns. Three of the series varied continuously in VOT and differed from each other in place of articulation (a [b-p], [d-t], and [g-k] series), whereas the remaining three series varied continuously in the starting frequency and direction of the second- and third-formant transitions and differed from each other in voicing and manner (a [b-d], [p-t], and [m-n] series). She found, as did Lisker and Abramson (1970; Abramson & Lisker, 1973), that the voicing boundary varied reliably with changes in place of articulation and similarly that the place of articulation boundary varied as a function of the voicing and manner quality of the stimuli. Evidence for a mutual dependency in the processing of the information for voicing and place of articulation had also been found in a study by Sawusch and Pisoni (1974). They obtained an identification function for a series of synthetic speech patterns that varied simultaneously along two acoustic continua, one of which signaled a change in voicing, and the other a change in place of articulation. In their attempts to predict the identification function obtained from the bidimensionally varying series from identification functions for each of the dimensions presented alone, Sawusch and Pisoni showed that the best fitting function was derived from a model in which the features of voicing and place of articulation were assumed to be processed in a mutually dependent manner.

Dependency effects during the processing of speech have also been demonstrated in a large number of studies that have used a selective adaptation procedure (cf. Eimas & Corbit, 1973). These studies, although primarily intended to assess the effects of selective adaptation (as evidenced by alterations in the locus of the phonetic boundary) on the manner in which speech patterns are classified into phonetic categories, have shown that the magnitude of the adaptation effect is less if the adapting stimulus and identification series differ acoustically or phonetically. Thus, for example, Cooper and Blumstein (1974) found smaller adaptation effects for a series of stimuli that varied with respect to place of articulation when the adapting stimulus differed in manner of articulation or voicing from the identification series than when the adapting and test stimuli shared the same values along these phonetic features. Effects of this nature indicate that the analysis of the information for one feature (place of articulation in the foregoing example) does not occur independently of the information signaling other features (voicing and manner of articulation). In a similar manner, studies that have demonstrated the occurrence of contingent-adaptation effects likewise permit the conclusion that there is a lack of independence in the analysis of phonetic features (Cooper, 1974; Miller & Eimas, 1976). However, it is possible that the dependency relations evidenced by boundary shifts as a result of procedures such as selective adaptation are not the same with regard to either the level at which the dependency occurs or the underlying causal factors as the dependency relations found in the studies described in the present chapter.

As is apparent from our review, there is considerable evidence favoring the existence of dependency efffects or processing interactions (cf. Garner & Morton, 1969) during the analysis of the phonetic feature information defining a single phonetic segment. Of course, speech provides nonphonetic as well as phonetic information, that is, information about suprasegmental aspects as well as segmental units.[2] Although there is substantial evidence that the perception of segmental and suprasegmental information may utilize different processing mechanisms (e.g., Wood, Goff, & Day, 1971), there is relatively little information concerning the possible interactions between these two systems. However, Wood (1974, 1975a) has shown that the analysis of pitch and place of articulation occurs in a dependent manner, although the dependency is asymmetric or unidirectional; pitch is processed independently of place, but the analysis of place is dependent on the prior analysis of pitch.

The experiments reported herein are our initial efforts to specify the particular

---

[2]Linguistic terminology dictates that we should reserve the adjective nonphonetic for descriptions of nonspeech acoustic information. However, inasmuch as the psychological literature has often used the descriptor nonphonetic to signify suprasegmental, we use the two terms interchangeably, as we also use the words phonetic and segmental. Nonspeech acoustic information is described in just these terms.

dependency relations that exist during the processing of various combinations of phonetic features and during the processing of combinations of phonetic and nonphonetic features. More exactly, we are concerned with determining whether a given dependency is asymmetric, mutual, or mutual and asymmetric. An asymmetric dependency is one in which the analysis of one feature occurs independently of a second feature, but the analysis of the second feature requires information from the prior analysis of the first feature. A mutual dependency exists when the analysis of the information for one feature affects the analysis of the information for a second feature and conversely. Furthermore, the magnitude of the processing interaction or dependency is approximately equal in both directions. A mutual and asymmetric dependency is characterized by processing interactions in both directions, but the extent of the interaction is greater in one direction than in the other.

Inasmuch as the nature of the dependency relation may vary with the nature of the features (that is, with whether both are phonetic or one is phonetic and the other nonphonetic), with the particular combinations of features, as well as with the particular feature values, we have investigated the processing of a number of feature combinations, and in some instances with a variety of specific feature values. Thus, when the two features under consideration were both phonetic in nature, we investigated the processing of place and manner of articulation (with a large number of particular feature values), and voicing and place of articulation. When the feature combinations were phonetic and nonphonetic, we examined the processing of place of articulation and loudness, voicing and pitch, vocalic quality and loudness, and finally vocalic quality and pitch.

In all of these studies, we have used a modified two-choice, speeded classification procedure, originally developed by Garner (e.g., Garner, 1974) for the study of dimensional processing in visual patterns, and later adapted by Wood and Day (1975) for the study of feature processing in phonetic segments and syllables. This experimental paradigm seemed ideally suited to our purposes in that it had been shown to be capable of detecting a number of different forms of dependency relations during the processing of auditory information, whether phonetic or nonphonetic. For example, Wood and Day (1975) found a mutual dependency during the processing of consonants and vowels in consonant-vowel syllables. Mutual dependencies have also been obtained with two nonphonetic dimensions (e.g., pitch and intensity [Wood, 1975a]). An asymmetric or unidirectional dependency has been obtained when one dimension signaled a phonetic distinction (place of articulation) and the second dimension signaled a nonphonetic distinction (pitch), with the processing of place of articulation being dependent on the prior analysis of pitch, whereas the analysis of pitch information was independent of the analysis of place information. However, this particular dependency relation is not contingent on one feature being phonetic and the other being nonphonetic, inasmuch as Blechner, Day, and Cutting (1976) found a unidirectional dependency in the analysis of two acoustic features in a nonspeech context (rise time and intensity) as did Pastore, Ahroon, Puleo, Crimmins, Golowner, and Berger (1976) with very different acoustic dimensions. More recently, a mutual asymmetric dependency has been found when two phonetic features are processed, place and manner of articulation (Eimas, Tartter, Miller, & Keuthen, 1978). These last findings are discussed in more detail in the section on phonetic feature processing.

The application of the speeded classification procedure requires that listeners classify stimuli that may assume one of two values along each of two dimensions as quickly as they can without sacrificing accuracy. Of course, when we refer to binary-valued dimensions in the case of the phonetic features that make up the segmental units and syllables of speech, it is with respect to the values along these features within a given experiment, as it is obviously the case that the features of speech may assume more than two values. The speeded classification of these stimuli typically occurs under three conditions: (1) when only the target dimension varies from trial to trial (the control condition); (2) when both the target and nontarget dimensions vary and the variation in the target dimension is orthogonal with respect to the variation in the nontarget or irrelevant dimension (the orthogonal condition); and (3) when both dimensions vary, and the variation in the target dimension is perfectly correlated with the variation in the nontarget dimension (the correlated condition).

Inferences regarding the presence of dependency relations in processing the two dimensions or features come from comparisons of the decision times (i.e., the classification times) in the control condition with the decision times in the orthogonal and correlated conditions. Consider first the comparison of the decision times in the control and orthogonal conditions. Independent processing of both features, that is, the absence of any processing interactions or dependencies, may be assumed if the decision times in these two conditions do not reliably differ. A dependency relation, on the other hand, may be assumed if the decision time for the orthogonal condition is longer than the decision time for the control condition; i.e., a processing dependency is inferred if variation in a second, irrelevant dimension interferes with the processing of the target dimension. In addition to being able to infer a processing dependency from a comparison of the decision times in the control and orthogonal conditions, it is possible to infer whether the dependency is mutual, mutual and asymmetric, or asymmetric. If the increment in decision times for both dimensions is approximately equal, then the dependency relation may be assumed to be equal. Should the increment for one of the dimensions be reliably greater than for the second dimension, then the dependency is mutual and asymmetric. Finally, an asymmetric dependency is evidenced if there is an increment in decision times in the orthogonal condition for only one of the dimensions.

Interpretation of decision-time differences between the control and correlated conditions is more difficult than interpretation of differences between the control and orthogonal conditions (Garner & Morton, 1969). For example, the presence of a redundancy gain, i.e., faster classification times in the correlated condition compared to the control condition, can occur under some conditions if the mechanisms for analysis of both features operate in an independent parallel manner (see Lockhead, 1972, and Wood, 1975b for specific details of this argument). In addition, a redundancy gain can occur if at some level of analysis in the perceptual system the two dimensions are treated (processed) as a unitary event or "blob" (Lockhead, 1972). However, in this situation it is not clear whether the channels that ultimately analyze the stimulus event into dimensional values operate in an independent or dependent manner. It is probably the case that either mode of operation is a reasonable possibility. Finally, the absence of a redundancy gain is compatible with dependency relations among the channels of analysis (cf. Eimas et al., 1978). Thus, the comparison of decision times in the correlated and control conditions provides weak evidence at best concerning the existence of processing interactions and most likely should not be over inter-preted without the presence of corroborating evidence.[3]

EXPERIMENTAL FINDINGS

General Procedure

In each of the experiments reported in this discussion, the subjects were 12 paid volunteers from the Brown University community. All of the listeners were naive with respect to the exact purposes of the experiments and all were native speakers of English with no known hearing impairments. With only a few exceptions, different subjects were recruited for each experiment.

The stimuli were four consonant-vowel or vowel-consonant syllables, and each stimulus represented one of the four possible combinations of dimensional values from two-binary-valued dimensions. The four stimuli can be designated by means of the following notation: $S_{1,1}$, $S_{2,1}$, $S_{1,2}$, and $S_{2,2}$, where the first subscripted number represented the value along the first dimension and the second number represents the value along the second dimension. Table 8.1 illustrates the manner in which the dimensional values were combined to form

---

[3]We have only considered the situation where the decision times in the orthogonal condition are equal or longer than the control time and where the times in the correlated condition are equal or faster than the control times inasmuch as faster orthogonal times and slower correlated times relative to the control times are not plausible outcomes.

TABLE 8.1
Description of the Manner in Which the Dimensional Values
Were Combined to Form the Stimulus Sets

		Dimension 2	
		Value 1	*Value 2*
Dimension 1	Value 1	$S_{1,1}$	$S_{1,2}$
	Value 2	$S_{2,1}$	$S_{2,2}$

the four stimuli. The stimuli were arranged in various ways to form eight experimental tapes: four control tapes, two correlated tapes, and two orthogonal tapes. The stimuli for each of the control tapes differed along the target dimension and had a constant value on the nontarget dimension. There were thus two possible tapes for each target dimension. When Dimension 1 was the target dimension, the stimuli were $S_{1,1}$ and $S_{2,1}$ for one tape and $S_{1,2}$ and $S_{2,2}$ for the second tape. When Dimension 2 was the target dimension, the two stimuli were $S_{1,1}$ and $S_{1,2}$ for the first tape and $S_{2,1}$ and $S_{2,2}$ for the second tape. The two stimuli in each of the correlated tapes differed from each other along both dimensions, with the dimensional values being perfectly correlated. The actual stimulus values were $S_{1,1}$ and $S_{2,2}$ for one tape and $S_{2,1}$ and $S_{1,2}$ for the other tape. All four stimuli were used in the two orthogonal tapes. Each tape consisted of 64 randomly ordered test stimuli, with each of the two or four syllables appearing an equal number of times. The test trials were preceded by 12 practice trials, again with an equal number of instances of each of the two or four syllables.

In most of the experiments, the listeners heard two of the four control tapes and both correlated and orthogonal tapes. In some experiments, the correlated tapes were omitted, inasmuch as they were considered to be tangential to the main purposes of these particular experiments. For all three types of tapes, control, correlated, and orthogonal, one of the two tapes was classified according to the values along Dimension 1 and the second tape was classified according to the values along Dimension 2. Selection of the particular control tapes and the order in which the six tapes were presented were completely counterbalanced across listeners. At the beginning of an experiment, the listeners were given a general description of the purpose of the experiment and the procedures to be used. In addition, the subjects were given careful instructions and pretraining for the purposes of teaching them the manner in which the stimuli were to be classified into feature values, i.e., how the four stimuli could be described in terms of two values along each of two dimensions. Prior to the presentation of each tape, listeners were informed of the target dimension and the manner in which the nontarget dimension varied. Additional procedural details are found in Eimas et al. (1978).

Phonetic Feature Processing

The first two series of experiments describe the processing dependencies that arise when two phonetic features were the basis for classifying the stimuli. In the first series of studies, the two phonetic features were manner of articulation and place of articulation, and in the second series, the two features were place of articulation and voicing.

Manner and Place of Articulation.   The stimuli used in the first experiment of this series (Experiment 1) were synthetically produced consonant-vowel syllables. With respect to place of articulation, the consonants were either labial or alveolar, and with respect to manner of articulation, the consonants were either stop or nasal. The final vowel was [a] in all instances. The stimuli were perceived as [b], [d], [m], or [n] plus the vowel [a]. A complete description of the acoustic characteristics of these stimuli can be found in Eimas et al. (1978). The stimuli of Experiment 2, conducted by Keuthen (1975) in our laboratory, were the naturally produced consonant-vowel syllables, [ba], [da], [va], and [za]. The values on the place of articulation feature were again labial and alveolar, although it should be noted that [b] is actually bilabial and [v] is labiodental. The manner distinction was stop consonant versus fricative. In Experiment 3, the stimuli were the naturally produced syllables, [ba], [ga], [wa], and [ja]. The manner distinction was stop consonant versus glide and the place of articulation distinction was between segmental units produced with the major constriction in the front of the oral cavity and sounds produced with the constriction toward the back of the oral cavity. The consonant [g] is a velar stop and [j] is an alveolarpalatal glide, whereas both [b] and [w] are labial with respect to place of articulation.

Table 8.2 shows the mean reaction times for correct responses that have been

TABLE 8.2
Mean Decision Times (in msec) as a Function of
Target Features and Conditions (Experiments 1, 2, and 3)
(Adapted from Eimas et al., 1978.)

			Condition	
Experiment	Feature	Control	Correlated	Orthogonal
1	Place	493	443	675
	Manner	492	450	544
2	Place	593	568	749
	Manner	602	598	695
3	Place	580	534	738
	Manner	561	544	657

averaged over trials and listeners as a function of target dimension and test condition for each of the three experiments. Initial analyses revealed no effects attributable to the order in which the six tapes were presented. Moreover, the errors, which were approximately 4% in Experiment 1, 2% in Experiment 2, and 1% in Experiment 3, were randomly distributed across conditions in each of the experiments.

Analyses of the decision time data revealed a statistically significant interference effect in each experiment for both target dimensions. Even more important was the finding that, in each experiment, the magnitude of the interference effect was greater when place of articulation was the target dimension than when manner of articulation was the target dimension. Thus, the processing of the information for place and manner of articulation is not achieved by means of independently operating channels of analysis, but rather by channels that show a mutual dependency on each other, with the extent of the dependency being greater for place of articulation than for manner of articulation.

The faster decision times in the correlated conditions were statistically significant in Experiment 1 and very nearly significant in Experiment 3. However, before concluding that these faster classification times actually reflect a true redundancy gain, it is necessary to eliminate the possibility that they can be attributed to a selective serial processing strategy (Wood, 1974). This strategy describes the situation wherein listeners use their more discriminable (and hence faster) dimension to classify the stimuli in the correlated condition, despite experimental instructions to use a particular target dimension. To test for the presence of a selective serial processing strategy, a comparison is made between the listeners' correlated decision times and their faster control time. Should the correlated times and the faster control time differ reliably from each other, then it is possible to infer the presence of a true redundancy gain (Wood, 1974, 1975a). Analyses of this nature of the present data revealed that all of the faster times in the correlated conditions could be ascribed to the operation of a selective serial processing strategy. Thus, although it may be of some interest that listeners were able to use their more discriminable dimensions to classify the redundant stimuli, whether voluntarily or not, evidence of this nature actually provides relatively little information regarding the nature of processing interactions during the perception of speech.

It is important to note that the presence of a mutual, asymmetric interference effect during processing could reflect an asymmetry in the discriminability of the values along the two features rather than an asymmetry in processing, that is, in the dependency relation that occurs during extraction of the particular values for manner and place of articulation.[4] If the values from one dimension were more

---

[4]There is evidence that for at least some naturally produced speech, the features of manner and place of articulation are not equally salient or discriminable. For example, Miller and Nicely (1955) found that listeners were more likely to make errors in place of articulation than in manner of

discriminable than the values from the second dimension, then the first dimension should be easier to process in the orthogonal condition when it is the target dimension and harder to ignore when it is the nontarget dimension compared to the dimension with the less discriminable feature values. Consequently, if in these three experiments the place of articulation values were in fact less discriminable than the manner values, then the expectation would be for longer classification times in the orthogonal condition when place of articulation is the target dimension than when manner of articulation is the target dimension. Of course, this form of asymmetry in discriminability would also be expected to be reflected in the decision times for the two dimensions in the control condition. However, the decision times in the control conditions were neither systematically nor reliably different in the three experiments. Although this finding reduces the possibility that the asymmetric interference effects were simply a reflection of an asymmetry in discriminability, it does not eliminate a discriminability explanation. It is possible that the levels of both dimensions were sufficiently discriminable such that, if floor effects were present, no differences in decision times could be obtained. Consequently, a more adequate test of the discriminability hypothesis would be to reduce the discriminability of the values on the dimension presumed to be more discriminable and then assess the effect of this reduction on the pattern of interference arising from the presence of a variable nontarget dimension.

Experiment 4 tested the discriminability hypothesis by varying the acoustic information underlying the manner distinction in a way that was assumed to decrease the discriminability of the two manner values, while leaving unaltered the discriminability of the two place values. If the discriminability of the two manner values was in fact decreased and the discriminability hypothesis was correct, then the asymmetric interference effects should be eliminated, or at least significantly reduced. However, if the asymmetry was a consequence of the manner in which the information for manner and place of articulation was processed, then the experimental manipulations should leave the asymmetric interference effects unaltered. Of course, the reductions in discriminability cannot be so extreme as to preclude the reliable classification of the manner distinction, inasmuch as an outcome of this nature, although undoubtedly eliminating the asymmetry, would render the experiment meaningless.

---

articulation, and Mohr and Wang (1968) found that listeners judged stimuli to be farther apart if they differed in manner than if they differed in place (but see Singh & Black, 1966, for conflicting data). Mohr and Wang also found a dependency relation in that the judged distance between place values was greater for stop consonants than for nasal consonants, and a similar but smaller dependency was found for the judged distance between manner values; the distance was greater for alveolar than for labial sounds. However, inasmuch as we do not have precise specifications of the acoustic characteristics of these stimuli, it is not possible to state whether the saliency differences and dependency effects are simply a function of the acoustics of the stimuli or whether they reflect some inherent characteristic of the particular phonetic feature.

The stimuli for this experiment were three sets of synthetically produced speech signals, one of which, with only slight modification, was the same set used in the first experiment of this series. The second and third sets were produced by altering the acoustic parameters underlying the manner distinction in a way that was assumed to reduce the discriminability of the nasal-stop distinction. A more complete explication of the acoustic changes is found in Eimas et al. (1978), and a rationale for the specific changes is found in Miller and Eimas (1977). Each of the listeners received all three sets of stimuli for classification in a counterbalanced order. Inasmuch as this experiment was specifically concerned with the effects of discriminability on the pattern of interference effects, the correlated tapes were not presented.

Table 8.3 presents the mean decision times for Experiment 4 as a function of target dimension, test condition (control and orthogonal tapes), and the discriminability of the stimulus patterns. Preliminary analysis again showed no effect of order of presentation of the tapes, and the errors, which never exceeded 3% for any cell in Table 8.3, were greater for manner targets than for place targets, as one might expect. Analysis of the decision times in the control conditions indicated that we were successful in making the nasal–stop distinction less discriminable, while leaving the labial–alveolar distinction unchanged. The increment in the classification times when manner was the target dimension in Sets 2 and 3 was reliable, whereas the changes in times for the place targets did not even approach statistical significance. As examination of Table 8.3 indicates, there was a mutual, asymmetric interference effect for each of the three sets of stimuli, that was confirmed by statistical analysis. Moreover, the magnitude of the asymmetry was independent of the discriminability of the stimuli, being 71, 60, and 67 msec for the three sets of stimuli, respectively. Given that the

TABLE 8.3
Mean Decision Times (in msec) for Each Target Feature and
Condition as a Function of Stimulus Set (Discriminability of Manner
Distinction).[a]

Stimulus Set	Feature	Condition		Difference
		Control	Orthogonal	
1	Place	452	583	131
	Manner	445	505	60
2	Place	467	590	123
	Manner	494	557	63
3	Place	454	577	123
	Manner	494	550	56

[a] Experiment 4 (From Eimas et al., 1978. Copyright 1978 by the Psychonomic Society. Reprinted by permission.)

TABLE 8.4
Mean Decision Times
(in msec)
as a Function of
Target Features
and Conditions
(Experiment 5)

	Condition	
Feature	Control	Orthogonal
Place	518	693
Manner	468	550

presence and, more important, the magnitude of the asymmetry were unrelated to the discriminability of the manner cues, it is extremely unlikely that the asymmetry in the interference effects that was present in the first three experiments was in any way a function of the relative discriminability of the particular manner or place values. It would thus appear that the mechanisms underlying the processing of manner and place information are mutually and asymmetrically dependent, with the analysis of the information for place of articulation being more dependent on the analysis of manner of articulation than the analysis of manner is on place.

The final two experiments in this series were undertaken to extend the generality of this conclusion, and did not include the correlated condition. Our previous experiments had consistently used stop consonants as one pole of the manner distinction, albeit with three other distinctions, nasals, fricatives, and glides. Thus, it is possible, though perhaps unlikely, that this pattern of dependency is restricted to manner distinctions that include a stop consonant contrast. To test this possibility, the manner distinction in Experiment 5 was a nasal-fricative contrast. The place values were labial and alveolar. The stimuli were the naturally produced consonant vowel syllables, [ma], [na], [va], and [za]. The results, shown in Table 8.4, again indicated a mutual and asymmetric pattern of interference that was confirmed by statistical analyses.

It is also possible that this mutual asymmetric dependency relation is restricted to the features of place and manner of articulation when they occur in syllable-initial position. Experiment 6 investigated this possibility by using synthetically produced vowel-consonant syllables [ab], [ad], [am], and [an], that were in effect the mirror images of the first set of stimuli in Experiment 4. As Table 8.5 shows, the results of this experiment were in complete accord with the previous experiment: The pattern of interference was mutual and asymmetric.

The results of this series of six experiments are remarkably consistent; the processing of the information for place and manner of articulation is marked by a

TABLE 8.5
Mean Decision Times
(in msec)
as a Function of
Target Features
and Conditions
(Experiment 6)

	Condition	
Feature	*Control*	*Orthogonal*
Place	584	724
Manner	588	653

mutual asymmetric dependency, with the mechanisms underlying the analysis of place of articulation showing the greater dependency. Moreover, this pattern of dependency is evidenced with: (1) stimulus patterns that are synthetic or natural speech; (2) variations in the discriminability of the manner contrast; (3) variations in the particular combinations of manner and place values; and (4) variation in the syllable position of the target features. As Eimas et al. (1978) have remarked:

> Findings of this nature are in accord with a parallel processing model . . . [in which] the mechanisms of analysis, while functioning in a temporally overlapping and interactive fashion, are, to some extent, hierarchically arranged, in that some processes of analysis require the outputs from other analyzers before their analyses can be completed. To accommodate the present data within this theoretical framework, it is only necessary to assume that, although the mechanisms for the analysis of place and manner information do function to a large extent in a parallel and interactive manner, the analysis of place of articulation requires some form of input from the system that processes manner of articulation [p. 18].

Voicing and Place of Articulation.   The stimuli for the first experiment in this series, Experiment 7, were the synthetically produced consonant-vowel syllables, [ba], [da], [pa], and [ta]. The consonantal segments were voiced ([b] and [d]) or voiceless ([p] and [t]) with respect to the voicing feature and labial ([b] and [p]) or alveolar ([d] and [t]) with respect to the place feature. The two syllables with voiced stop consonants were the same as the two stop consonant patterns used in Experiment 1. The voiceless consonants were created by changing the voice onset time values from 0 msec to +50 msec, a change often shown in the past to be sufficient to signal a change in voicing from voiced to voiceless (e.g., Lisker & Abramson, 1970). Speeded classification times were obtained from listeners for the control, correlated, and orthogonal tapes under two different sets of instructions. In the first instructional condition, listeners were required to classify the stimuli on the basis of a phonetic feature code as was done in the manner-place studies. They were informed of the phonetic distinctions that differentiated these speech patterns and the response buttons were labeled with feature values. The second instructional condition required that listeners classify the stimuli according to the more natural segmental code and the response buttons were labeled with the orthographic symbol representing the phonetic segment, i.e., b, p, d, or t. This variation in procedure was investigated inasmuch as there is considerable evidence that the perceived structure of the stimulus or the manner in which it is encoded (cf. Garner, 1974; Jenkins, 1974) may alter the processing operations. Furthermore, it is conceivable that forcing listeners to use a somewhat artificial classificatory code may in and of itself yield a processing strategy that is different from that which would be found under more natural conditions, i.e., when the classification is based on the immediate percept. Twelve subjects were tested under each of the two sets of instructions.

The mean decision times for each of the two instructional sets as a function of targets and conditions are shown in Table 8.6. The analyses of errors, which averaged less than 5% of the responses, showed them to be randomly distributed across all conditions. Separate analyses of the decision times data revealed an absence of any order effects and, more important, significant interference effects for both features, regardless of the instructions. However, when the classification code was segmental, the pattern of interference was mutual, whereas when the classification code was based on phonetic features, it was mutual and asymmetric; the analysis of the information for place of articulation was interfered with more by voicing information than the analysis of voicing was interfered with by place information. But an analysis of all of the data did not reveal a significant mutual asymmetric interference effect for the phonetic code instructions; i.e., there was not a reliable code by target by condition interaction. Thus, there is at best relatively weak evidence for an alteration in the pattern of dependency as a function of instructions.

TABLE 8.6
Mean Decision Times (in msec) as a Function of Target Features,
Conditions, and Classification Code (Experiment 7)

Code	Feature	Condition		
		Control	Correlated	Orthogonal
Feature	Place	392	378	548
	Voicing	405	373	498
Segment	Place	381	369	495
	Voicing	381	380	490

TABLE 8.7
Mean Decision Times (in msec) as a Function of
Target Features and Conditions (Experiment 8)

Feature	Condition		
	Control	Correlated	Orthogonal
Place	553	507	654
Voicing	543	536	678

We subsequently replicated the feature code condition twice, once with the same synthetic speech patterns and once with naturally produced speech, and we found in both instances that the pattern of interference was mutual. Indeed, if there is any evidence in the dependency relation for an asymmetry it is in the opposite direction from that previously found, as may be seen in the data for the naturally produced syllables of Experiment 8 in Table 8.7 and for the synthetic patterns of Experiment 9 in the upper portion of Table 8.8. It would appear then that the mutual asymmetric interference pattern found in Experiment 7 under the feature code instructions was most likely an error due to sampling and that the actual pattern of interference and dependency for this combination of features is mutual, regardless of instructions.

Experiment 9 also investigated the effects of discriminability on the dependency relation.[5] It will be recalled that changing the discriminability of the less dependent feature in the manner-place studies left the interference pattern unaltered. Whether changes in discriminability of the voicing dimension would leave the pattern of interference for voicing and place of articulation unchanged was a second reason for undertaking Experiment 9. In order to reduce the discriminability of the voicing distinction, the VOT values were changed; voiced stops were created with VOT values of $+20$ msec and voiceless stops were made with VOT values of $+30$ msec. The acoustic cues underlying the place distinction, the formant transitions, were not changed. Twelve listeners heard the two sets of stimuli in a counterbalanced order, but because of experimenter error the data from one listener had to be discarded.

The overall error rate in Experiment 9 was less than 5%, and as might be expected, there were more errors in the low-discriminability condition (Set 2) than in the high-discriminability condition. Analysis of the decision times for the control conditions alone revealed that we were successful in reducing the dis-

---

[5]As was true for place and manner of articulation, there are data indicating differences in the saliency or discriminability of the phonetic features of voicing and place of articulation, although the evidence is less consistent (e.g., Miller & Nicely, 1955; Mohr & Wang, 1968; Singh & Black, 1966; Weiner & Singh, 1974). However, these data are again of limited value in that we do not know the exact acoustic characteristics of the stimuli.

criminability of the voicing distinction without seriously reducing the discriminability of the place distinction; the increment in decision times was statistically reliable for the voicing targets only. As is evident from inspection of Table 8.8, the pattern of interference differs as a function of the discriminability of the voicing distinction. When the voicing distinction was made less discriminable, the pattern of interference tended to be mutual and asymmetric, with the greater interference effect occurring for the less discriminable voicing feature. A number of statistical analyses were performed on these decision time data, two of which showed that the asymmetry just missed the .05 level of significance, whereas a third, more detailed, analysis revealed a significant asymmetry.

Further inspection of the data for Experiments 7, 8, and 9 reveals a number of instances of substantial (and often significant) decrements in the decision times in the correlated conditions (e.g., when place was the target dimension in Experiment 8 and in Experiment 9, Set 1, and when voicing was the target dimension in Experiment 9, Set 2). All of the faster correlated times can be attributed to listeners using a selective serial processing strategy in that in no instance was the faster control time reliably different from the correlated decision times. Given these data and the data from the manner-place studies, it would appear that true redundancy gains are not characteristic of the processing of phonetic feature information.

In the final experiment of this series, which was conducted by Keuthen (1975), we attempted to extend the generality of the conclusion that the processing of place and voicing is marked by a mutual dependency, at least when the values along both features are approximately equally discriminable. The stimuli for Experiment 10 were the naturally produced consonant-vowel syllables [va], [fa], [za], and [sa], and thus the processing of voicing and place of articulation was investigated within the fricative manner class. The results of this study are shown in Table 8.9. Preliminary analyses revealed a random distribution of

TABLE 8.8
Mean Decision Times (in msec) as a Function of
Target Features, Condition, and Stimulus Set,
i.e., Discriminability of Voicing Distinction (Experiment 9)

Stimulus Set	Feature	Condition		
		Control	Correlated	Orthogonal
1	Place	496	459	598
	Voicing	479	451	599
2	Place	527	523	622
	Voicing	614	557	797

TABLE 8.9
Mean Decision Times (in msec) as a Function of
Target Feature and Conditions (Experiment 10)

Feature	Condition		
	Control	Correlated	Orthogonal
Place	613	597	719
Voicing	645	571	786

errors, which were less than 1% of the responses, and no effects due to the order in which the tapes were presented. Further analysis revealed the pattern of interference to be mutual, although there was actually a 35 msec asymmetry in the interference effect, with the larger effect occurring when voicing was the target dimension. However, this asymmetry may be a function of an asymmetry in the discriminability of the feature values. The two control conditions differed by 32 msec, with the voicing control condition having the slower time. If this difference actually represents a difference in discriminability, then, given the results of Experiment 9, a small asymmetry in the interference effect would not be unexpected. The correlated effect for the voicing dimension was once more a result of selective serial processing.

The results of this series of experiments support the contention that the analysis of the information for voicing and place of articulation is marked by a mutual dependency relation, provided only that both distinctions are approximately equal in discriminability (cf. Miller, 1977a; Sawusch & Pisoni, 1974). However, if one of the distinctions is less discriminable than the other, then the pattern of interference is mutual and asymmetric, with the less discriminable distinction yielding the greater interference effect.[6]

It is possible to accommodate these data by assuming a processing model for the analysis of voicing and place of articulation that operated in an interactive and temporally overlapping manner when both distinctions are equally discriminable. However, when one feature distinction is less discriminable than the other, then the channel of analysis for the less discriminable distinction must rely more on information from the second channel for completion of its analysis than it would normally do under conditions of equal discriminability. Which is to say, with an inequality in discriminability there is greater dependency of one channel of analysis on the other and hence, an asymmetry in the mutual interference effect.[7]

---

[6]Keuthen (1975) has explored in our laboratory the dependency relation between manner of articulation and voicing. The stimuli were the naturally produced syllables [da], [ta], [za], and [sa]. She found a mutual dependency relation, but whether this relation is subject to change as a function of such factors as discriminability has not as yet been determined.

[7]If this model is correct, then it might also be expected that the decision times for the more discriminable place dimension would also increase, in that it would take longer to process the voicing

Of course, it remains to determine why a mutual pattern of dependency is affected by discriminability, whereas a mutual asymmetric dependency, found with place and manner of articulation, is not.

Phonetic and Nonphonetic Feature Processing

There is considerable evidence that different processing mechanisms are responsible for the analysis of consonantal feature information and suprasegmental information. The focus of much of this research has been the hemispheric specialization for various aspects of the speech signal. Although there are discrepancies in the literature, the majority of evidence, neurophysiological (e.g., Wood, 1975b; Wood, Goff, & Day, 1971) and behavioral (Blumstein & Cooper, 1974; Haggard & Parkinson, 1971), indicates that phonetic (consonantal) and nonphonetic features of speech are differentially processed by the two hemispheres, thereby implicating different mechanisms. Specifically, the left (or language) hemisphere seems to be primarily responsible for the analysis of consonantal features, whereas suprasegmental features appear to be analyzed by the right hemisphere or jointly by both hemispheres. (For additional evidence indicating differences in processing phonetic and nonphonetic information, see Sawusch, Pisoni, & Cutting, 1974.) Granted that different mechanisms are involved in the extraction of consonantal and suprasegmental information, the issue remains as to whether or not these mechanisms operate independently of one another during the perception of speech.

In a series of studies, Wood (1974, 1975a) used the speeded classification paradigm to investigate the processing of place of articulation (labial and velar) and pitch (high and low). In both studies, the pattern of interference was asymmetric; random variation across trials in pitch significantly slowed the classification of place of articulation, whereas the same form of variation in place of articulation did not alter the classification time for pitch. These findings indicate a unidirectional dependency between the process of analysis of pitch and place, with the analysis of place being dependent on the prior analysis of pitch, which is independent of the analysis of place. In one study (Wood, 1975a), the correlated condition was omitted, but in the other study (Wood, 1974), there was a significant redundancy gain that could not be attributed to selective serial processing. Although a significant redundancy gain may indicate processing interactions, as noted in the introduction, it is not necessary to apply this interpretation (Wood, 1975b). Be that as it may, the validity of the redundancy gain is questionable.

---

information needed by the place analyzers when the voicing distinction is made less discriminable. Table 8.8 shows that this increment did occur, although the effect is small and not statistically significant. In the same vein, this increment in the processing times for place would also be expected when the manner distinction was made less discriminable, an event that did not occur. We have no adequate explanation of this failure.

First, Eimas et al. (1978) have argued that Wood actually did not obtain a true redundancy gain, but that Wood arrived at the conclusion that he did because of a statistical error. Second, Wood's redundancy gain is anomalous in that in none of the other, now numerous, studies in which this procedure has been used with speech has a true redundancy gain been reported.

In order to determine whether the asymmetric pattern of interference found by Wood is unique to the features of pitch and place of articulation or whether it is true of other combinations of consonantal and suprasegmental features, Goldin, in our laboratory, investigated the dependency relation that exists during the analysis of place of articulation and loudness (Experiment 11) and during the analysis of voicing and pitch (Experiment 12). The syllables in the place-loudness study were four synthetically produced syllables, a loud and soft [ba] and a loud and soft [da]. The place distinction was signaled by variation in the second- and third-formant transitions and the loudness difference was cued by a 20 dB intensity difference. For the voicing-pitch study, the four syllables were again synthetic speech patterns, consisting of a high and low [bae] and a high and low [pae]. The voicing difference was cued by a 60 msec difference in VOT and the pitch distinction was cued by a 36 Hz difference in fundamental frequency (F_0). The high-pitched syllables had an F_0 of 140 Hz, and the low-pitched syllables had an F_0 of 104 Hz.

The results of Experiments 11 and 12 are shown in Table 8.10. First, unlike the results of Wood (1974), there was no evidence of a true redundancy gain in either experiment. The reliable decrease in decision times for the pitch targets in the voicing-pitch study can be explained once more on the basis of selective serial processing. Second, as was found by Wood, the results of both studies showed an asymmetric pattern of interference. In each case, random variation in the consonantal feature did not reliably affect the speed of processing the non-phonetic feature, whereas variation in the nonphonetic feature did retard significantly the decision times for processing the consonantal features.[8]

The findings of Wood and Goldin suggest that an asymmetric dependency exists between the mechanisms responsible for the analysis of consonantal information and those responsible for the analysis of suprasegmental information. The question naturally arises as to whether this same form of dependency exists between the processes underlying the analysis of vowel quality and suprasegmental information. If the determining factor for the form of the dependency is the general class of information being analyzed, phonetic and nonphonetic, then the processing of a vowel distinction and either a pitch or loudness distinction should yield a unidirectional dependency relation. However, there is reason to expect

---

[8]In all four Experiments in this series (11, 12, 13, 14) the error rates were quite low, being less than 3% in each study, and the errors were consistently found to be randomly distributed across the experimental conditions. In addition, as in all of the earlier studies that we discussed, there were no effects due to the order in which the classification tapes were presented.

TABLE 8.10
Mean Decision Times (in msec) as a Function of
Target Features and Conditions (Experiments 11 and 12)

Experiment	Feature	Control	Condition Correlated	Orthogonal
11	Place	418	400	476
	Loudness	418	418	438
12	Voicing	437	404	564
	Pitch	456	402	471

that the processing interactions for vocalic and suprasegmental features may be different from the interactions for consonantal and suprasegmental features. A number of experimental paradigms have found different patterns of processing for consonants and vowels. For example, studies concerned with hemispheric specialization for the processing of speech, although typically finding evidence of greater left hemisphere processing for consonantal information, often have found no evidence for specialization by either hemisphere for vowels (e.g., Studdert-Kennedy & Shankweiler, 1970; but see Spellacy & Blumstein, 1970, for an example of the conditions that yield evidence of greater left hemisphere involvement in the processing of vowels). Moreover, the identification of consonants does not seem to be greatly influenced by experimental context, whereas the identification of vowels (and suprasegmental information) has been shown to be markedly influenced by contextual variation (e.g., Eimas, 1963; Simon, 1977). Finally, studies on the categorical perception of speech have shown that within-category distinctions for vowels are typically easier to make and are more influenced by task parameters than is the case for consonants (e.g., Pisoni, 1973, 1975a). It would appear then that vowels and consonants may undergo different forms of processing. Furthermore, it has been argued not only that consonants and vowels are processed differently, but also that they are functionally distinct, serving quite different roles in speech. Specifically, it has been claimed that consonants are the primary carriers of segmental information whereas vowels, although certainly also carriers of segmental information, are the primary conveyers of suprasegmental information, i.e., pitch, loudness, and the like (cf. Studdert-Kennedy, 1974). Thus, it may be the case that the processing of vocalic information not only differs from consonantal processing, but also is more closely tied to the processing of suprasegmental speech information. If this is so, then the processes responsible for the analysis of vocalic information and those responsible for the analysis of suprasegmental information may be mutually dependent, giving rise to a mutual interference effect.

To test this possibility, two studies were undertaken that paired a vowel distinction with a nonphonetic distinction (Miller, 1978). The first experiment (Experiment 13) used two consonant-vowel syllables, [ba] and [bae], at each of two pitch levels. The vowel distinction was cued primarily by differences in the steady-state formant frequencies, but also by differences in the starting frequencies of the formant transitions. The pitch difference was signaled by variation in F_0, being 104 Hz and 140 Hz for the low and high values, respectively. The results of this experiment are shown in the upper portion of Table 8.11. There was no correlated effect, but there was a significant interference effect. Moreover, the magnitude of the interference effect did not differ for the two target dimensions; the dependency relation was mutual.

The second study, Experiment 14, paired a vowel distinction with a distinction in loudness. The four syllables were the low-pitched [ba] and [bae] at each of two loudness levels, 20 dB apart. The results, presented in the lower portion of Table 8.11, show the same pattern of mutual interference and analyses of the data revealed significant and approximately equal interference effects for both features. Thus, regardless of whether the vowel contrast was paired with pitch or loudness, there was evidence for a mutual dependency in processing vocalic and nonphonetic speech information, which contrasts with the asymmetric dependency marking the processing of consonantal and nonphonetic feature combinations. Unfortunately, from the results of the present studies, it is not possible to specify whether the mechanisms for the analysis of vowel quality and pitch (or loudness) are distinct, but mutually dependent, or whether the processing of these two types of speech information actually share at least some of the same processors.[9]

CONCLUDING REMARKS

The present experiments strongly indicate that the processing of acoustic information underlying a particular segmental or suprasegmental feature value does not occur by means of independently operating channels of analysis. The mechanisms that extract the feature values from the speech signal, whether phonetic or nonphonetic, interact with one another. Moreover, and most interesting, there is no single form to the pattern of interaction or dependency. Rather the dependency relation that exists during the processing of any two feature values is a function of the particular combination of features. Thus, for example, the dependency relation in processing the acoustic correlates of place and manner of

---

[9]It is important to note that in our studies the consonantal distinctions were cued primarily by transitional information, whereas the vowel distinctions were cued primarily by steady-state information. Thus, the different pattern of performance found for consonants and vowels may have been due to the difference in stimulus structure rather than to the functional (or phonetic) difference between consonants and vowels.

TABLE 8.11
Mean Decision Times (in msec) as a Function of
Target Features and Conditions.[a]

Experiment	Feature	Condition		
		Control	Correlated	Orthogonal
13	Vowel	561	540	603
	Pitch	558	542	628
14	Vowel	466	460	501
	Loudness	443	438	472

[a] Experiments 13 and 14 (Adapted from Miller, 1978. Copyright 1978 by the Psychonomic Society. Reprinted by permission.)

articulation is mutual and asymmetric, with the determination of place of articulation being more dependent on the determination of manner of articulation than the converse. The analysis of the acoustic properties signaling voicing and place of articulation is, in contrast, marked by a mutual dependency; that is, a dependency that is equal in degree in either direction, provided only that the discriminability of the particular values is approximately equal for both features. This same pattern of dependency characterizes the processing of vocalic and suprasegmental features, whereas an asymmetric dependency has consistently been found for consonantal and suprasegmental features. In the latter case, the analysis of consonantal features (voicing and place of articulation) is dependent on the prior analysis of suprasegmental features (pitch and loudness), which occurs independently of the phonetic analyses.

It is important to note that the various patterns of dependency cannot be classified on the basis of which features are phonetic and which are nonphonetic. Although at times certain patterns of dependency have been assumed to reflect different levels of processing for phonetic and nonphonetic features (e.g., Wood, 1974), more recent evidence makes this assumption questionable at best. For example, as noted earlier, the asymmetric pattern of interference found by Wood (1974) for place of articulation and pitch is not a unique characteristic of processing one phonetic and one nonphonetic feature, as the work of Blechner et al. (1976) and Pastore et al. (1976) indicates. In addition, two of the present studies, the two vowel experiments, have shown that a mutual dependency is obtained when phonetic and nonphonetic features are combined for analysis as well as when two phonetic features are processed. Finally, a mutual asymmetric dependency, characteristic of the processing of manner and place of articulation, has also been obtained with nonphonetic dimensions, albeit with visual and not with acoustic dimensions (Pomerantz & Sager, 1975).

The inability to relate the various patterns of dependency to separate processing systems for phonetic and nonphonetic aspects of speech signals is in agreement with experimental findings indicating that the analysis of complex acoustic signals, whether phonetic or nonphonetic, is mediated by mechanisms that are part of a general auditory system (cf. Cutting & Rosner, 1974; Eimas & Miller, 1978; Kuhl & Miller, 1975). Of course, if this is indeed true, then another classification scheme is necessary to rationalize the many forms of dependency. One such scheme would be to relate the patterns of interference to characteristics of the signal. Although we are able to state that certain patterns of dependency are consistently obtained with particular combinations of features, we are not as yet able to extend this analysis further and describe the specific spectral (or perhaps functional) characteristics that yield a particular dependency relation. However, it is our belief that these descriptions exist and that continued research will yield these lawful specifications.

Research of this nature, although serving to refine our theoretical understanding of the perception of speech by explicating the operating properties of auditory analyzers, has at the same time raised a number of issues that will need clarification before a theory of speech perception can even approximate completeness. For example, a major question left unanswered by our research (although not by our research alone) is the level of processing at which the dependency occurs. Our working assumption has been that the locus of interaction is at the level at which feature information, phonetic or nonphonetic, is extracted from the signal, and not at a response level, to state but one of the possible alternative levels. That is, it is our hypothesis that the interference effects that reflect processing dependencies occur as a result of interactions (or cross-talk) between channels of analysis. Regardless of the locus of this dependency effect, there remains the necessity of rationalizing the various forms of dependency, as we discussed previously, as well as describing the conditions, if any, under which a particular dependency relation may be altered by such factors as discriminability and instructions.

ACKNOWLEDGMENTS

Preparation of this report and the authors' research reported herein was supported in part by Grant HD 05331 from the National Institute of Child Health and Human Development to PDE, by a Predoctoral Fellowship MH5282 from the National Institute of Mental Health to VCT, and by a Postdoctoral Fellowship NS 00143 from the National Institute of Neurological and Communicative Disorders and Stroke to JLM. We would like to express our gratitude to Dr. Alvin M. Liberman for generously making the facilities of the Haskins Laboratories available to us. Our work at the Haskins Laboratories was supported by an NICHHD Contract NIH-71-2420 from the National Institute of Child Health and Human Development to Haskins Laboratories. We would also like to thank Sheila Polofsky, Hilary Walker, Patricia Keegan, Robin D'Alli, and Arlene McAuley for assistance in testing subjects and analyzing data.

REFERENCES

Abramson, A. S., & Lisker, L. Voice-timing perception in Spanish word-initial stops. *Journal of Phonetics*, 1973, *1*, 1–8.

Anderson, F. *Some implications for the operation of feature detectors in speech perception: Use of identification response time as a converging operation.* Unpublished doctoral dissertation, Brown University, 1975.

Blechner, M. J., Day, R. S., & Cutting, J. E. Processing two dimensions of nonspeech stimuli: The auditory-phonetic distinction reconsidered. *Journal of Experimental Psychology: Human Perception and Performance*, 1976, *2*, 257–266.

Blumstein, S. E., & Cooper, W. E. Hemispheric processing of intonation contours. *Cortex*, 1974, *10*, 146–158.

Cooper, W. E. Contingent feature analysis in speech perception. *Perception & Psychophysics*, 1974, *16*, 201–204.

Cooper, W. E., & Blumstein, S. E. A labial feature analyzer in speech perception. *Perception & Psychophysics*, 1974, *15*, 591–600.

Corcoran, D. W. J., Dorfman, D. D., & Weening, D. L. Perceptual independence in the perception of speech. *Quarterly Journal of Experimental Psychology*, 1968, *20*, 336–350.

Cutting, J. E., & Rosner, B. S. Categories and boundaries in speech and music. *Perception & Psychophysics*, 1974, *16*, 564–570.

Eimas, P. D. The relation between identification and discrimination along speech and non-speech continua. *Language and Speech*, 1963, *6*, 206–217.

Eimas, P. D., & Corbit, J. D. Selective adaptation of linguistic feature detectors. *Cognitive Psychology*, 1973, *4*, 99–109.

Eimas, P. D., & Miller, J. L. Effects of selective adaptation on the perception of speech and visual patterns: Evidence for feature detectors. In R. D. Walk & H. L. Pick, Jr. (Eds.), *Perception and experience*. New York: Plenum, 1978.

Eimas, P. D., Tartter, V. C., Miller, J. L., & Keuthen, N. J. Asymmetric dependencies in processing phonetic features. *Perception & Psychophysics*, 1978, *23*, 12–20.

Ganong, W. F., III. *Selective adaptation and speech perception.* Unpublished doctoral dissertation, Massachusetts Institute of Technology, 1977.

Garner, W. R. *The processing of information and structure.* Potomac, Md.: Lawrence Erlbaum Associates, 1974.

Garner, W. R., & Morton, J. Perceptual independence: Definitions, models, and experimental paradigms. *Psychological Bulletin*, 1969, *72*, 233–259.

Haggard, M. P. The use of voicing information. *Speech synthesis and perception* (Vol. 2). Cambridge: Psychological Laboratory, Cambridge University, 1970.

Haggard, M. P., & Parkinson, A. M. Stimulus and task factors as determinants of ear advantages. *Quarterly Journal of Experimental Psychology*, 1971, *23*, 168–177.

Holloway, C. M. A test of the independence of linguistic dimensions. *Language and Speech*, 1971, *14*, 326–340.

Jenkins, J. J. Remember that old theory of memory? Well, forget it! *American Psychologist*, 1974, *29*, 785–795.

Keuthen, N. J. *Studies on the organization of phonetic feature levels.* Unpublished honors thesis, Brown University, 1975.

Kuhl, P. A., & Miller, J. D. Speech perception by the chinchilla: Voiced–voiceless distinction in alveolar plosive consonants. *Science*, 1975, *190*, 69–72.

Lisker, L., & Abramson, A. S. The voicing dimension: Some experiments in comparative phonetics. In *Proceedings of the Sixth International Congress of Phonetic Sciences*, Prague, 1967. Prague: Academia, 1970.

Lockhead, G. R. Processing dimensional stimuli: A note. *Psychological Review*, 1972, *79*, 410-419.

McNabb, S. D. Must the output of the phonetic detector be binary? In *Research on speech perception* (Progress Report, No. 2). Bloomington: Department of Psychology, Indiana University, 1975.

Miller, G. A., & Nicely, P. An analysis of perceptual confusions among some English consonants. *Journal of the Acoustical Society of America*, 1955, *27*, 338-352.

Miller, J. L. Properties of feature detectors for speech: Evidence from the effects of selective adaptation on dichotic listening. *Perception & Psychophysics*, 1975, *18*, 389-397.

Miller, J. L. Nonindependence of feature processing in initial consonants. *Journal of Speech and Hearing Research*, 1977, *20*, 519-528. (a)

Miller, J. L. Properties of feature detectors for VOT: The voiceless channel of analysis. *Journal of the Acoustical Society of America*, 1977, *62*, 641-648. (b)

Miller, J. L. Interactions in processing segmental and suprasegmental features of speech. *Perception & Psychophysics*, 1978, *24*, 175-180.

Miller, J. L., & Eimas, P. D. Studies on the selective tuning of feature detectors for speech. *Journal of Phonetics*, 1976, *4*, 119-127.

Miller, J. L., & Eimas, P. D. Studies on the perception of place and manner of articulation: A comparison of the labial-alveolar and nasal-stop distinctions. *Journal of the Acoustical Society of America*, 1977, *61*, 835-845.

Mohr, B., & Wang, W. S.-Y. Perceptual distance and the specification of phonological features. *Phonetics*, 1968, *18*, 31-45.

Pastore, R. E., Ahroon, W. A., Puleo, J. S., Crimmins, D. B., Golowner, L., & Berger, R. S. Processing interaction between two dimensions of nonphonetic auditory signals. *Journal of Experimental Psychology: Human Perception and Performance*, 1976, *2*, 267-276.

Pisoni, D. B. Auditory and phonetic memory codes in the discrimination of consonants and vowels. *Perception and Psychophysics*, 1973, *13*, 253-260.

Pisoni, D. B. Auditory short-term memory and vowel perception. *Memory and Cognition*, 1975, *3*, 7-18. (a)

Pisoni, D. B. Information processing and speech perception. In G. Fant (Ed.), *Speech communication* (Vol. 3). New York: John Wiley & Sons, 1975. (b)

Pomerantz, J. R., & Sager, L. C. Asymmetric integrality with dimensions of visual pattern. *Perception & Psychophysics*, 1975, *18*, 460-466.

Sawusch, J. R. Peripheral and central processes in selective adaptation of place of articulation in stop consonants. *Journal of the Acoustical Society of America*, 1977, *62*, 738-750.

Sawusch, J. R., & Pisoni, D. B. On the identification of place and voicing features in synthetic stop consonants. *Journal of Phonetics*, 1974, *2*, 181-194.

Sawusch, J. R., Pisoni, D. B., & Cutting, J. E. *Category boundaries of linguistic and nonlinguistic dimensions of the same stimuli*. Paper presented at the 87th meeting of the Acoustical Society of America, New York, 1974.

Simon, H. *Anchoring and selective adaptation of phonetic and nonphonetic categories in speech perception*. Unpublished doctoral dissertation, City University of New York, 1977.

Singh, S., & Black, J. W. Study of twenty-six intervocalic consonants as spoken and recognized by four language groups. *Journal of the Acoustical Society of America*, 1966, *39*, 372-387.

Smith, P. T. Feature-testing models and their application to perception and memory for speech. *Quarterly Journal of Experimental Psychology*, 1973, *25*, 511-534.

Spellacy, F., & Blumstein, S. The influence of language set on ear preference in phoneme recognition. *Cortex*, 1970, *6*, 430-439.

Stevens, K. N. *The potential role of property detectors in the perception of consonants*. Paper presented at Symposium on Auditory Analysis and Perception of Speech, Leningrad, USSR, August 1973.

Studdert-Kennedy, M. The perception of speech. In T. A. Sebeok (Ed.), *Current trends in linguistics*. The Hague: Mouton, 1974.

Studdert-Kennedy, M., & Shankweiler, D. Hemispheric specialization for speech perception. *Journal of the Acoustical Society of America, 1970, 48,* 579-594.

Tartter, V. C., & Eimas, P. D. The role of auditory detectors in the perception of speech. *Perception & Psychophysics, 1975, 18,* 293-298.

Weiner, F. F., & Singh, S. Multidimensional analysis of choice reaction time judgments on pairs of English fricatives. *Journal of Experimental Psychology, 1974, 102,* 615-620.

Wickelgren, W. A. Distinctive features and errors in short-term memory for English consonants. *Journal of the Acoustical Society of America, 1966, 39,* 388-398.

Wood, C. C. Parallel processing of auditory and phonetic information in speech discrimination. *Perception & Psychophysics, 1974, 15,* 501-508.

Wood, C. C. Auditory and phonetic levels of processing in speech perception: Neurophysiological and information-processing analyses. *Journal of Experimental Psychology: Human Perception and Performance, 1975, 1,* 3-20. (a)

Wood, C. C. A normative model for redundancy gains in speeded classification: Application to auditory and phonetic dimensions in speech discrimination. In F. Restle, R. M. Shifrin, N. J. Castellan, H. Landman, & D. B. Pisoni (Eds.), *Cognitive theory* (Vol. 1). Potomac, Md: Lawrence Erlbaum Associates, 1975. (b)

Wood, C. C., & Day, R. S. Failure of selective attention to phonetic segments in consonant-vowel syllables. *Perception & Psychophysics, 1975, 17,* 346-350.

Wood, C. C., Goff, W. P., & Day, R. S. Auditory-evoked potentials during speech perception. *Science, 1971, 173,* 1248-1251.

9 The Processing of Phrase Structures in Speech Production

Jeanne Paccia-Cooper
Boston University

William E. Cooper
Harvard University

Editors' Comments

An interesting development in the study of speech is described in this chapter by Paccia-Cooper and Cooper. As we have noted, much of the current speech research, including that demonstrating higher order, top-down influences on phonetic perception, has been primarily directed toward achieving an understanding of the processes of perception and production at the phonetic level. Paccia-Cooper and Cooper (and see the final section of Chapter 6 by Grosjean and Lane) have, in marked contrast, studied a number of lower level acoustic phenomena, which are readily measurable, to infer the existence of higher order units or structures, as well as strategies, that speakers use in the planning and execution of speech. Thus, for example, by measuring the acoustic characteristics that are associated with phrase-final lengthening, Paccia-Cooper and Cooper were able to infer that the mental plans that underlie the production of speech make use of certain syntactic constituents, as opposed to others. This approach, like that of Grosjean and Lane, constitutes an important advance in our quest to develop performance-based models of language processing, in that it demonstrates how a relatively simple and direct means may be used for discovering the structural units and processing strategies involved in the production and perception of language.

INTRODUCTION

Traditionally, work in psycholinguistics has placed a rather heavy emphasis on determining whether mental representations of the speaker-hearer correspond to structures generated by formal linguistic theory. This aspect of psycholinguistics is often described as the search for the "psychological reality" of linguistic constructs, and much remains to be done along this line. But there exists another important area of psycholinguistic research, less riveted to linguistics proper, which is aimed at understanding how structural representations are processed by the speaker–hearer in real time. To date, progress on issues of processing has been hampered by a lack of experimental paradigms that are sensitive to real-time operations. However, this drawback is being overcome, both in studies of sentence perception (e.g., Cutler & Norris, 1979; Marslen-Wilson & Welch, 1978) and in studies of sentence production, discussed here later.

The complex mental operations that we routinely perform during speech production occur at a number of distinct stages of processing. Viewed generally, these stages include processing sites for semantic, syntactic, and phonological computations. One source of empirical support for distinguishing these stages is derived from analyses of errors committed during spontaneous speech. These errors may involve the exchange, substitution, addition, or deletion of linguistic elements associated with any one of the semantic, syntactic, or phonological types of representation (e.g. Fromkin, 1971; Garrett, 1975).

Because the acoustical output of speech is most closely associated with the phonological level of internal coding, the phonological code of the speaker is better understood than are the syntactic or semantic codes. Yet, properties of the observable acoustic signal can be shown to reflect these higher level coding operations as well.

In this chapter, we confine our focus to syntactic coding operations in speech production and the manner in which these operations may be inferred from the study of speech properties. We review some of the more recent experimental work on this problem and also present a number of new experiments. The studies are devoted to two related questions: How is syntactic information structurally represented in speech production? How is such information processed in real time?

STRUCTURAL REPRESENTATIONS

How are syntactic structures represented in speech? At a glance, there seems to be no issue at all—the speaker simply represents syntactic structures as these are described in a formal grammar. But the literature in linguistic science often reveals high-minded disagreement on the form that a grammar should take. In such cases, we need a way of selecting among the plausible candidates for syntactic representations. The study of acoustical properties of speech provides such a method.

But, before delving into experimentation, let us raise some issues about the coding of phrase structure. These issues are best understood in the context of linguistics proper, so we begin with a brief description of phrase structure rules as these are defined in a formal grammar.

Most generally, the phrase structure system of a language refers to the set of rules that define its syntactic constituents and their hierarchical interrelationships. In addition, this system determines the left-to-right ordering of the constituents (Chomsky, 1957; Jackendoff, 1977). Phrase structure rules are of the form "X → Y" (rewrite constituent "X" as constituents[s] "Y") and are applied in a fixed order. For example, the structural representation of the simple sentence "Harry rode the new pony" involves the application of the rewrite rules in (1) following the top-down, left-to-right order specified in (2).

(1)

     (i) Sentence (S) → Noun Phrase (NP) + Verb Phrase (VP)
    (ii) NP → N
   (iii) VP → Verb (V) + NP
   (iv) NP → Determiner (DET) + Adjective (ADJ) + N
    (v) N → Harry
   (vi) V → rode
  (vii) DET → the
 (viii) ADJ → new
   (ix) N → pony

(2)

     (i) S
    (ii) NP + VP
   (iii) N + VP
   (iv) N + V + NP
    (v) N + V + DET + ADJ + N
   (vi) Harry + V + DET + ADJ + N
  (vii) Harry + rode + DET + ADJ + N
 (viii) Harry + rode + the + ADJ + N
   (ix) Harry + rode + the + new + N
    (x) Harry + rode + the + new + pony

The derived phrase structure can be schematized by the tree diagram in Fig. 9.1.

Given this kind of linguistic description, we may ask whether the speaker computes such a representation during speech coding. This question may be divided into two parts: (a) are syntactic constituents such as Noun Phrase and Verb Phrase processed as units?; (b) are constituents related to one another hierarchically in a manner specified by linguistic theory? (e.g., does the constituent Verb Phrase dominate the constituents Verb and Noun Phrase?). The answers to these questions are complicated by the possibility that syntactic coding may involve more than a single level of representation. In a transformational grammar, we find a familiar distinction between two major levels of syntactic representation—underlying and surface structure. These levels are mediated by a system of transformational rules that operate to add, delete, or move constituents

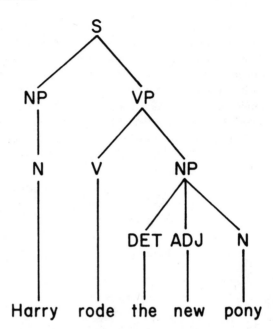

FIG. 9.1.   Structural representation of the sentence "Harry rode the new pony" according to Chomsky's phrase structure rule: S → NP + V + NP.

during the derivation of a sentence. The transformational component of the formal grammar has spurred a great deal of psycholinguistic research aimed at determining whether corresponding mental operations occur during speech production and/or perception (Cooper & Paccia-Cooper, 1980; Fay, 1979; Fodor, Bever, & Garrett, 1974). In this chapter, however, we confine our attention to the phrase structures of sentences whose surface and underlying representations are believed to be isomorphic in all relevant respects. By so doing, we are able to investigate some of the more common phrase structure representations.

From a linguistic standpoint, the representation of phrase structure in formal grammar is no less important and no less controversial than is the representation of transformational rules. The importance of providing a correct description of phrase structure rules has recently been underscored by attempts to diminish the scope and power of the transformational component of the grammar (Chomsky, 1973; Jackendoff, 1977). Psycholinguistically, the description of the speaker's phrase structure code would represent an important advance in our understanding of the mental operations that accompany speech production.

CONSTITUENT STRUCTURES AS UNITS
IN SPEECH PRODUCTION

A number of linguistic constructs appear to serve as units of processing in speech production. In phonological representations, these units correspond to the syllable, phoneme, and distinctive feature. Exchange errors in spontaneous speech can involve any of these units: entire syllables, as in "must*up* and ketch*ard*" for "mustard and ketchup"; phonemes, as in "*t*ay *d*rip" for "day trip," and possibly even distinctive features such as voicing, as in "*g*lear *p*lue" for "clear blue" (Fromkin, 1971). The evidence from exchange errors favoring phonemes and syllables as bona fide units of processing is relatively straightforward, but the role of distinctive features is more difficult to document, because errors that appear to involve feature exchanges may in fact be attributable to phoneme exchanges (see, for example, Shattuck-Hufnagel, 1979).

From a syntactic standpoint, one question of interest concerns the size of the domain over which the speaker programs speech. The study of exchange errors bears on this issue, because such errors imply that the involved segments are represented simultaneously. Phoneme exchanges frequently occur across word boundaries, as the examples in the foregoing paragraph indicate. However, such errors almost never span clause boundaries (Boomer & Laver, 1968; Garrett, 1975). It appears, then, that the speaker does compute a phonemic representation over a domain larger than a single word, but generally not larger than a clause.

Other evidence from speech production also points to the clause as a unit of processing. Clause boundaries are favored locations for breathing (Henderson, Goldman-Eisler, & Skarbeck, 1965; Webb, Williams, & Minifie, 1967). In addition, these boundaries are typically accompanied by systematic changes in the prosodic structure of the speech wave. The changes include pausing, segmental lengthening, fall-rise patterns of fundamental frequency (F_0), and the consequences of blocking phonological rules that normally operate across word boundaries (see Cooper, 1980, for a review).

Unlike speech errors, pausing, segmental lengthening, F_0 patterns, and phonological rule-blocking effects all form an integral part of the speaker's acoustical representation. As such, they provide a means of tapping a number of details about the nature of the speaker's syntactic code. For example, the study of speechwave properties enables us to determine the form of the speaker's internal representation of constituents that are smaller than the clause, yet larger than the single word. This advantage is important because such constituents form the core of a phrase structure grammar.

According to a Chomskyan grammar, a clause is first broken down into two major phrasal constituents, Noun Phrase, and Verb Phrase (as noted earlier in [1]). We may now ask whether these constituents are represented as such during speech production. This question is particularly relevant for the Verb Phrase, because the existence of this constituent remains somewhat controversial on purely linguistic grounds. Whereas Chomsky and his associates have always maintained that the Verb Phrase is essential for capturing certain regularities of the grammar, Keyser and Postal (1976), among others, have argued that a clause is directly elaborated in terms of three constituents—Noun Phrase, Verb, and Noun Phrase, as shown in Fig. 9.2.

Because the initial breakdown of the clause into smaller constituents is a property that must be specified for all sentences generated by the grammar, the

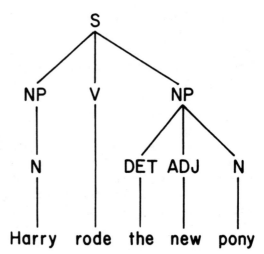

FIG. 9.2. Structural representation of the sentence "Harry rode the new pony" according to Keyser and Postal's phrase structure rule: S → NP + V + NP.

dispute over the existence of a Verb Phrase constituent is pivotal for both linguistic and psycholinguistic theories. One of the experiments in a recent study (Cooper, Paccia, & Lapointe, 1978) bears on this issue. In this study, the phenomena of pausing and segmental lengthening were examined at key locations in different readings of a variety of structurally ambiguous sentences. The relevant experiment involved sentences like (3):

(3) My Uncle Abraham presented his talk naturally.

Here, an ambiguity arises because the adverb *naturally* can modify either the entire sentence or just the verbal constituent (specified as either Verb or Verb Phrase, depending on the speaker's unit of representation). For the reading in which the adverb modifies the entire sentence, (3) can be paraphrased as in (3'):

(3') Of course my Uncle Abraham presented his talk.

The alternative reading of (3), in which *naturally* modifies the verbal material only, can be paraphrased as in (3"):

(3") My Uncle Abraham presented his talk in a natural way.

For present purposes, interest in this type of ambiguous sentence stems from its alternative forms of representation, depending on how the sentence is broken down into smaller constituents. According to a Chomskyan analysis, in which a sentence is immediately elaborated in terms of the two constituents Noun Phrase and Verb Phrase, the alternative readings of (3) are represented structurally as in Fig. 9.3.

The two readings of (3) are represented quite differently according to a theory in which sentences are directly expanded in terms of the three constituents Noun

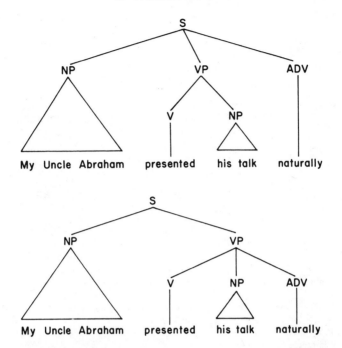

FIG. 9.3. Two structural representations of the ambiguous sentence (3) according to Chomsky's linguistic analysis (S → NP + VP). The upper tree represents the (3′) reading and the lower tree represents the (3″) reading, as designated in the text.

Phrase, Verb, and Noun Phrase, as shown in Fig. 9.4.[1] The alternative structural representations yield different predictions about the duration of the key word *talk* in each reading of (3), based on the following considerations. Previous work has revealed that speech segments are lengthened at the ends of phrases. Other experiments provide independent evidence for the notion that phrase-final lengthening is cumulative when two or more phrase boundaries terminate at a given location (Cooper et al., 1978). According to the Chomskyan account, the duration of *talk* should be longer in the reading given in (3′), because, as shown in Fig. 9.3, this key word marks the end of the entire VP constituent as well as the end of the NP direct object constituent in the (3′) reading, whereas *talk* marks the end of only

---

[1]Keyser and Postal (1976) do not deal specifically with the problem of assigning adverbs in a structural representation. Our structural representations of the alternative readings of Sentence (3), according to Keyser and Postal's rewrite rule "S → NP + V + NP", take into account the modifying relationship between the adverb *naturally* and the constituent it modifies in each reading. Because Reading (3″) expresses a modifying relationship between two constituents that are nonadjacent in a linear string (between the verb *presented* and the adverb *naturally*), its corresponding tree diagram in Fig. 9.4 yields an unorthodox terminal string in which the order of the involved words differs from the order in which they appear in Sentence (3).

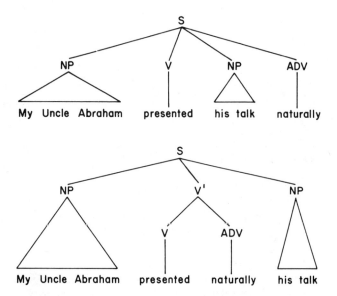

FIG. 9.4.   Two structural representations of the ambiguous sentence (3), according to Keyser and Postal's linguistic analysis (S → NP + V + NP). The upper tree
corresponds to the (3′) reading, whereas the lower tree represents the (3″) reading,
as designated in the text.

the NP direct object in (3′). Alternatively, according to the type of analysis proposed by Keyser and Postal (1976), in which no VP node is employed, *talk* should
be longer in reading (3″). On their account, *talk* occurs at the end of the NP direct
object in both readings, but in reading (3″), *talk* additionally marks the end of
the entire S constituent, according to the structural representation presented in
Fig. 9.4.

Our earlier experiment (Cooper et al., 1978) provided a test of the different
predictions of the two theories. Ten speakers with no formal linguistic training
read the two versions of (3) and two versions of another structurally ambiguous
sentence of the same type. The durations of the key word and of the following
phrase were analyzed with the aid of computerized techniques that permit very
accurate measurements (Huggins, 1969). In this case, the measured word duration included the interval for *talk* beginning with the release burst of the stop
consonant /t/ and ending at the start of the silent interval for the word-final stop
/k/. Measurements of the pause duration included this silent interval, any release
burst of /k/, and an optional interval of silence preceding the word-initial nasal of
naturally.

The results showed that the duration of *talk* was significantly longer in the
(3′) reading, as predicted by the Chomskyan analysis. The lengthening effect
averaged 15% for this particular ambiguous sentence. The duration of the follow-

ing silent interval was also substantially longer for the (3') reading, averaging 40% lengthening.

This experiment suggests, then, that speakers process a phrase unit corresponding to the VP constituent in the grammar. Although evidence cited earlier indicates that speakers process clauses as units, the present experiment suggests that such units are further broken down into major constituents like Noun Phrase and Verb Phrase.

Hierarchical Representation of Constituents

If the foregoing account is correct, then we can infer that the speaker's representation of constituents involves hierarchical coding. In the foregoing case, the VP constituent dominates the direct object NP constituent in the formal grammer (see Fig. 9.3). The coinciding occurrence of the VP and NP phrase boundaries at the end of *talk* in (3') is permitted because of this hierarchical relationship.

Is there a simpler, linear account of the previous results? One plausible alternative was considered and ruled out in our original report (Cooper et al., 1978). This particular linear alternative involved the relative distance between the modifier (in this case, *naturally*) and the first word of the two possible modified constituents. However, there remains a similar candidate to be dealt with. According to this latter alternative, lengthening of *talk* may be due to the fact that the next word, *naturally,* modifies a constituent that begins earlier in the linear string in absolute terms, as in (3') versus (3''). For (3'), the adverb *naturally* modifies the entire sentence, whereas for (3''), the same adverb modifies only the verbal constituent. This sort of account could explain such lengthening in psychological terms as a reflection of extra time needed by the speaker to retrieve a relation involving a modifed constituent uttered earlier in the temporal string. Although this linear alternative can handle each of the sentence structures discussed in our earlier report (Cooper et al., 1978), it falters when we consider question–answer situations like the one following in (4):

(4) *Question:* What is my Uncle Abraham doing?
Answer: Presenting his talk naturally.

In the answer of (4), we have an ambiguity similar to (3). Here, the surface structure contains no subject NP, and so the constituents that *naturally* modifies begin at the same location in surface structure. Yet, informal observation tells us that *talk* would be lengthened for the (3') reading of (4). The linear account cannot handle this fact. However, the hierarchical account does provide an explanation, based on the principle of cumulative phrase-final lengthening. As in (3), the VP in (4) dominates the NP direct object for the (3') reading, but not for the (3'') reading.

Paragraph Contexts

Our experimental task is designed to provide rather tight control over extrasyntactic factors that would otherwise influence the timing of speech segments (see Bierwisch, 1966; Grosjean, Grosjean, & Lane, 1979; Klatt, 1976). This approach stands in contrast to studies that attempt to make inferences about syntactic coding on the basis of examining a large and undifferentiated corpus of real speech (e.g., Goldman-Eisler, 1968). Both approaches can in principle provide valuable information, but the kinds of information they yield are quite different. Whereas our technique enables us to probe the representation of relatively subtle syntactic distinctions, the more naturalistic and global approach allows one to make claims about very general properties of the speaker's code.

In order to begin to bridge the gap between experimental control and naturalistic observation, we embedded sentences like (3) in paragraph contexts that disambiguated the two possible readings in such a way that the speakers were not aware of any ambiguity. Generally, the results were similar to those obtained for sentences spoken in isolation. The magnitudes of effect were smaller in the paragraph contexts, suggesting that, although the presence of lengthening is largely determined by internalized, automatic processing by the speaker, the magnitude of lengthening may also be influenced by whether or not the speaker is consciously seeking to disambiguate a particular string.

PROCESSING ISSUES

Having discussed the speaker's representation of syntactic units, we turn to the consideration of issues concerning the processing of these structures. Three topics are covered. First, we consider whether constituents are planned in a top-down fashion. Next, the question of whether constituents are planned in a left-to-right manner is addressed. Finally, some of the processing details about speech planning and execution are examined with an eye toward determining how the speaker's orchestration of planning and execution of phrases influences speech wave properties. The reader should be forewarned that we raise many questions during the next few subsections that are not yet answered, largely because only now are we in a position to even ask such questions in a rigorous form. On the positive side, we present some new experimental results that provide at least some basis for making inferences about the form of the speaker's on-line processing.

Top-Down Processing

Having obtained evidence in favor of a hierarchical type of syntactic representation in speech, we may ask whether syntactic constituents are processed serially from largest to smallest, following the top-down method of applying rewrite rules in the formal grammar as shown in (2). This question is difficult to deal with, both theoretically and experimentally.

At first glance, top-down coding of constituents seems to be a logical necessity. But this intuition is not well founded. It is possible, for example, that the speaker first plans the subject NP and, by definition, simultaneously begins planning the clause. The same situation holds for other hierarchically related constituents. So the serial versus parallel issue of information processing is a real one. We do not arrive at a resolution here, although a discussion of our efforts seems worthwhile in view of the importance that is usually accorded this issue in attempts to construct a theory of speech processing.

How can this question be put to an experimental test? We present one plausible approach based on real-time speech output, reaching the conclusion that even this test cannot provide the required information. It is instructive to work through this example, because the issue it addresses seems to be unresolvable on general grounds (e.g., Townsend, 1972).

The test for speech involves the phenomenon of phrase-final lengthening discussed previously. We noted that the lengthening effect is cumulative when two hierarchically related phrases end with the same word, such as when a word marks the termination of both an NP direct object and the VP that dominates it. Assuming that lengthening for each constituent involves some percentage increase to the key word's inherent duration, our prediction of the total amount of lengthening produced for a word marking the simultaneous end of more than one phrase will differ depending on whether the effects are applied in series or in parallel.[2] In particular, the word should be lengthened by a greater amount if the effects are programmed serially. To illustrate why this should be so, we consider a hypothetical example involving the duration of the noun-verb homophone *coach*. In order to establish the magnitude of lengthening for a word in phrase-final position, we must first determine its inherent duration. The inherent duration of a word may be construed as the word's duration when it occurs in nonphrase-final position, as in (5):

(5) If Ann and Martha *coach* Andrew's teammates we'll quit.

Let us assume that the duration of *coach* in this environment is 200 msec. Suppose further that *coach* is lengthened by 10% when it occurs at the end of an

---

[2]Although we use the familiar terms *serial* versus *parallel* throughout this discussion, our test applies to only one of two possible types of serial-parallel distinction, in which the serial model includes the condition that the output of one stage provides the input to the next (dependent model) and the parallel model includes the condition that the two stages do not interact (independent model). The serial-dependent versus parallel-independent models appear to be the most plausible processes of applying segmental lengthening in speech production (for further discussion of these general models, see Townsend, 1974).

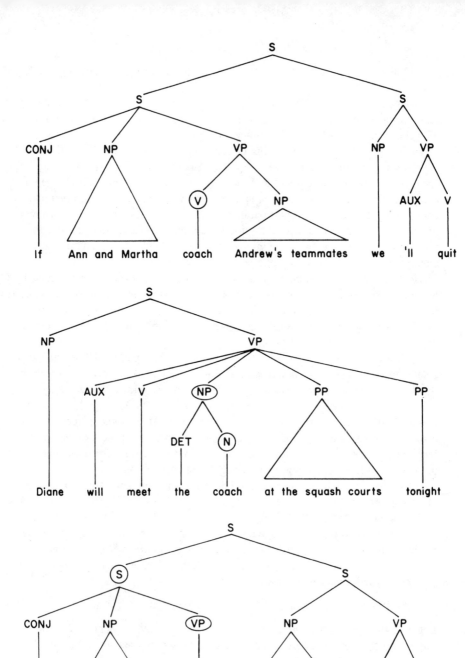

FIG. 9.5. Structural representation of Sentences (5)–(7). In the top diagram, the key word *coach* occurs in nonphrase-final position. In the middle diagram, the same key word occurs at the end of an NP. In the bottom diagram, the key word appears at the end of a VP and S. In each case, the nodes ending with the key word are circled.

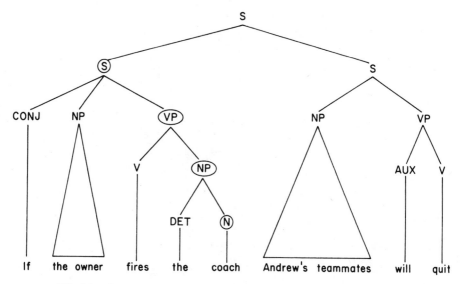

FIG. 9.6.   Structural representation of Sentence (8). Here, the key word *coach* marks the end of four constituents: N, NP, VP, and S, as circled in the tree diagram.

NP, as measured in (6), and that the same word is lengthened by 30% when it occurs at the end of the two constituents VP and S, as in (7). The corresponding tree diagrams for these sentences appear in Fig. 9.5.

(6) Diane will meet the *coach* at the squash courts tonight.

(7) If Ann and Martha *coach* Andrew's teammates will quit.

Given that lengthening effects are cumulative—as we found in our earlier experiment with sentences like (3)—we can predict the total duration of *coach* when it marks the end of all three of the constituents NP, VP, and S, as in (8). The tree diagram for this sentence appears in Fig. 9.6.

(8) If the owner fires the *coach* Andrew's teammates will quit.

If the lengthening effects are applied serially, the total duration of *coach* in (8) should average 286 msec. Assuming a top-down application of the lengthening effects, this total duration is obtained by the calculation in (9).[3]

---

[3]Note that the same result would be obtained by applying the two stages of lengthening in the opposite serial order; that is, bottom-up. Thus, in principle, our test can distinguish between serial versus parallel models, but not between the particular top-down and bottom-up versions of a serial model. However, top-down application is the more justifiable of the two on linguistic grounds, based on the system of rewrite rules discussed earlier.

(9) Total duration of *coach* in (8) assuming top-down serial application of the VP/S and NP lengthening effects:
  (i) 200 msec (inherent word duration)
  (ii) $200 + (200 \times 30\%) = 260$ msec (duration after VP/S lengthening applied)
  (iii) $260 + (260 \times 10\%) = 286$ msec (duration after NP lengthening applied)

On the other hand, the total duration of *coach* should average only 280 msec if the lengthening effects are added in parallel, assuming the additivity is linear. This calculation is shown in (10).

(10) Total duration of *coach* in (8) assuming parallel linear application of the VP/S and NP lengthening effects:
  (i) 200 msec (inherent word duration)
  (ii) $200 + (200 \times 30\%) + (200 \times 10\%) = 280$ msec (duration after VP/S lengthening and NP lengthening applied)

In this case, the predicted difference in total duration for the two models is only 6 msec. Such a small effect could easily be obscured by normal variations in speech rate. This effect could be magnified somewhat by measuring a word with a larger inherent duration, such as a polysyllabic word, but, in any event, the predicted difference would remain relatively small, because the magnitude of the effect critically depends on the percentage difference in lengthening between VP/S and NP, which is probably not more than 20%. But even surmounting this drawback would not permit a conclusive demonstration that lengthening effects are applied either in series or else in parallel. Evidence in favor of a serial model could alternatively be accounted for by a parallel model in which the effects are added in a nonlinear fashion. Conversely, a nonlinear serial model, although less plausible, could handle results otherwise attributable to a linear parallel model. In short, whereas the serial versus parallel models of applying phrase-final lengthening can be distinguished mathematically under the assumption of linear additivity, the models cannot be adequately tested at present because (a) the predicted difference is very small; and (b) any obtainable difference could be attributed to nonlinear additivity, pending an independent test of linearity.

Left-to-Right Processing

In addition to the top-down issue, the examples in (2) exhibit another feature that may be relevant to speech processing. Within each hierarchical level, the rules in phrase structure are applied left-to-right. Thus, for example, when a clause is elaborated into the major constituents NP and VP, the NP is elaborated in turn before the VP during the next application of rewrite rules. As with the issue of top-down processing, intuition runs strong about the question of left-to-right versus right-to-left processing. The output of speech occurs left-to-right by definition; that is, words spoken before or after one another are conventionally described as occurring to the "left" or "right" of one another. However, it is not necessary that words be considered in left-to-right fashion at all computational stages involved in the planning of speech. For example, at an early stage of coding, the speaker may decide on a particular noun phrase without regard to its linear position in the speech output. In reference to phrase structure, we may ask whether there exists a point during the speaker's computation of a syntactic representation of an utterance at which standard left-to-right processing does not occur.

Yngve (1960) proposed an early model of sentence production that included the assumption that the speaker elaborates phrase structures in a top-down, left-to-right manner. His theory embodied a prediction about the processing load incurred by speakers. Specifically, Yngve proposed that the speaker's processing load is directly proportional to the number of nodes yet-to-be-elaborated in an utterance. Forster (1966, 1967) attempted to test this prediction by presenting subjects with sentence fragments such as those that appear in (11):

(11) (a) On his return to the house he found _____.
(b) _____ the woman in a state of great agitation.

The subjects were asked to complete each sentence fragment by adding material on either the right (11a) or left (11b) to compose a grammatical string. Forster reasoned that if syntactic constituents are elaborated from left-to-right in speech production, then subjects in this completion task should be more adept at completing a sentence fragment when its left-hand portion is provided, as in (11a), than when its right-hand portion is given, as in (11b). Not surprisingly, the results showed that subjects were indeed able to complete fragments like (11a) faster than (11b). Forster (1967) went on to argue that the effect was attributable to processing of phrase structures that correspond to a surface level of syntactic analysis.

Forster's results confirm our intuition that speakers are more capable of completing sentence fragments from left-to-right than from right-to-left. However, the experiments do not provide a satisfactory answer to the question of whether left-to-right processing accompanies syntactic stages in *ongoing* speech production. In short, although the phonetic output of speech proceeds in left-to-right fashion by definition, there is no assurance that left-to-right processing accompanies the syntactic stages of coding that occur beforehand.

Speech Planning

Up to this point, our brief discussion of processing issues has dwelt on the negative. Despite our intuitions about top-down, left-to-right processing, we have found experimental evidence to be lacking in support of these directions of information flow during the internalized stages of syntactic processing. Here, we enlarge the scope of our discussion to include a look at planning during speech production. Recent experimental work provides some information about the nature of this important aspect of processing.

It should be pointed out that the term "planning" is distinct from "left-to-right" processing. The former term simply denotes the speaker's consideration of yet-to-be-spoken material. In our experimental studies, this consideration is manifest in the speaker's programming of the duration and fundamental frequency of a currently generated segment. Note that the existence of planning does not indicate a commitment to left-to-right processing of the upcoming material. Our effort here is primarily devoted to the more general issue of which features of upcoming material influence the ongoing execution of speech.

Evidence from Fundamental Frequency

We begin by citing a particularly clear example of the speaker's ability to "look-ahead." In this case, the speaker's consideration of yet-to-be-spoken material influences fundamental frequency (F_o). The F_o contour of an utterance represents the frequency of quasiperiodic vibration of the vocal folds during voiced portions of speech. Perceptually, this frequency information plays a major role in judgements of pitch. Like segment and pause durations, fundamental frequency is an attribute of the speechwave that can provide useful information about the nature of the speaker's internal processing scheme (e.g., Maeda, 1976; Sorenson & Cooper, 1980).

A salient feature of F_o contours in single-clause declarative sentences consists of a general decline in F_o throughout the sentence. Although many local rises in F_o may be superimposed on this falling contour, the presence of the F_o declination occurs with considerable regularity in both oral reading (e.g., Maeda, 1976; O'Shaughnessy, 1976) and in spontaneous speech (M. Liberman, personal communication, May, 1978). This decline in F_o is generally attributed to a decrease in lung pressure and/or intraoral pressure during the utterances (Maeda, 1976). The declination appears in most languages (Bolinger, 1964), although it is not universal. (C. Grimes, [personal communication, May 1978] cites an example of a Brazilian language in which F_o contours of declarative utterances are generally rising). Thus, although declination is a general feature of F_o contours and seems to represent a physiological running-down of the speech system, this effect is at least partially controlled by higher level commands of the speaker.

This latter point is supported by the observation that long utterances are generally accompanied by a higher F_o at the beginning of the utterance than that produced for shorter utterances (O'Shaughnessy, 1976). This observation indicates that speakers must consider the general length of the sentence prior to the initiation of speech, providing a clear example of look-ahead. In order to provide an experimental test of this possibility, Sorenson and Cooper (1980) asked speakers to read pairs of sentences that varied in length but contained the same word at the beginning of the utterance, as in (12):

(12) (a) The *deer* could be seen from the car.
    (b) The *deer* by the canyon could be seen from the window of the car.

The results showed that the peak F_0 of the first key word in the utterance was indeed significantly higher in long versus short utterances, by an average of 13.5 Hz. The effect demonstrates that speakers perform some very general planning for utterance length and that this planning exerts a systematic influence on the F_0 peak of the first key word of the utterance. Because the effect is present at the very beginning of the sentence, there can be no question that we have here a demonstration of an effect that critically depends on the nature of yet-to-be-spoken material.

Although this experiment indicates the existence of speech planning for oral reading, there is no assurance that the effect will also hold for spontaneous speech. In general, there is a greater likelihood of long-range planning in oral reading, especially because speakers have already familiarized themselves with the material to be read. Yet, this familiarization does not render a foregone conclusion about the influence of planning on the execution of F_0. The speakers in this experiment had no conscious awareness of the F_0 effect, and it is plausible that the look-ahead exhibited here is also present in spontaneous speech.

Beyond demonstrating the existence of long-range planning and its effect on F_0, we would like to know why the speaker begins at a higher F_0 when producing longer sentences. One possibility is that speakers start higher in order to allow more of a frequency range for F_0 fall during the longer utterances. This latter requirement may stem from a need to keep the ending values of F_0 above a certain frequency. Our experimental results indicate that speakers tend to produce a relatively fixed value for the F_0 peak of the last stressed syllable in the utterance regardless of sentence length (see Sorensen and Cooper, 1980, for a more detailed presentation of these and other F_0 effects for long versus short utterances). For present purposes, however, the F_0 effect at the beginning of long versus short utterances serves as a demonstration of long-range planning and its role in determining speechwave values.

Further work is needed to determine (a) whether the magnitude of this effect covaries with the length of an utterance; and (b) whether the presence of intervening syntactic boundaries serves to constrain the planning effect for F_0. Lacking this information, we turn to other sources for a more detailed look at the nature of speech planning.

Evidence from Speech Timing

The planning effect noted for F_0 indicates that speakers consider a very general feature of an utterance—its length—as they begin to speak. Speech planning also appears to influence the timing of word segments and pauses. Consider the phenomenon of constituent-final lengthening discussed earlier. This effect can be attributed to either internalized constraints on the speech production system itself or to the speaker's intention to provide perceptual cues to the listener. Here, we examine the role of the former possibility only, since this possibility presents more than enough challenges of its own.

In terms of speech production, lengthening at the ends of constituents may be explained in terms of either the execution or planning of speech. According to an execution-based account, segmental lengthening represents a relaxation response of the speech processing machinery upon completion of executing a given constituent. In an earlier section, we relied on this type of account in our explanation of speech timing effects for structurally ambiguous sentences in terms of the number of phrases which ended at a key boundary. Indeed, there can be no question that execution plays at least some role in segmental lengthening, since the very last word of an utterance is lengthened considerably, despite the fact that no material remains to be planned.

Alternatively, constituent-final lengthening may occur in order to permit an extra fraction of time in which to plan material not yet spoken in an utterance. In essence, an execution-oriented account attributes speech timing effects primarily to the influence of material just spoken, whereas a planning account relies on the influence of material yet to be spoken. These alternative accounts need not be mutually exclusive. Rather, it is possible that execution and planning phases of processing are in simultaneous operation during the production of an utterance. If this view is correct, then any timing effect observed within an utterance could conceivably reflect both planning and execution. An adequate understanding of speech timing effects, then, would include determining the relative contribution of both planning and execution to the occurrence of segmental lengthening and pausing.

We have recently devised a way to assess this important distinction. The relative contributions to a given effect of material already spoken and that yet to be spoken can be isolated by relying on a method of One-Sided Variation. This method involves holding the material on one side of a given boundary constant while systematically varying the material on the other side of the boundary. Under these conditions, the contributions from one source of segmental lengthening at the boundary is controlled for, so that any observed effect may be attributed to the additional influence of the alternative source. In formal terms, let X denote material to the left of a constituent boundary and Y refer to material to the right of that boundary. By holding Y constant while varying the complexity of X, we may determine the extent to which X-final timing effects are attributable to the execution of constituent(s) X. Alternatively, we may evaluate any role that the planning of Y plays in determining the duration of the X-final segment by systematically varying the complexity of Y while holding X constant.

Earlier, we reported experimental findings which indicate that the global feature of utterance length partially controls the starting F_0 value assumed by a speaker. It therefore seemed profitable to begin our investigation of the issue of speech planning vs. execution by establishing whether the magnitude of timing effects occurring at the juncture between two major clauses is affected by overall clause length. We will first consider the results of an experiment designed to investigate the role of planning. Following this, we will discuss the results of an experiment which bears on the execution-based aspect of this issue. For both of these experiments, the method of One-Sided Variation was employed in order to assess the relative contribution of each of the two processing operations, planning and execution, to the occurrence of clause-final lengthening.

Our investigation of the role of speech planning at the boundary between clauses involved determining whether the overall length of an upcoming clause exerts an influence on segmental timing at the end of the preceding clause. The test sentence pair appears in (14) below. In this pair, it can be seen that the first clause for both sentences is identical, while the second clause varies in length. Thus, any differences in the duration of the key material between the two sentences may be directly attributed to the difference in the length of the upcoming clause.

(14) a. Tom and I will reprimand Sue and *Clark* and Jane will talk to Steven.

  b. Tom and I will reprimand Sue and *Clark* and Jane plans to talk to Steven's brother and send Jeffrey to the principal.

The results for twenty speakers showed that the duration of the key word *Clark* was significantly longer in the (b) sentence, which contained the longer second clause ($p < .001$, $t = 3.97$, $df = 19$; two-tailed t-test for matched pairs). The duration of *Clark* averaged 6% longer in this sentence. Speakers did not produce long pauses in either sentence, and there was no significant effect of pause duration. The result obtained for the key word *Clark* indicates that the timing of clause-final speech segments is influenced by the length of upcoming material. This finding provides inferential support for the notion that segmental lengthening may be programmed as an aid to the speaker in planning at least some aspects of an upcoming constituent. The effect observed here cannot, incidentally, be attributed to a more global effect of lengthening all words in longer utterances (Cooper and Paccia-Cooper, 1980).

Having found that the phenomenon of clause-final lengthening is partially controlled by speech planning, at least in terms of the general feature of the length of upcoming material, we turn now to consider the corresponding contribution of execution-based processing operations. More specifically, we would like to know whether the overall length of a clause affects the magnitude of the speech timing effects occurring at the end of that clause. To this end, we designed an experiment involving the sentence pair in (15), following. In this sentence pair, we varied the overall length of the first clause, while holding constant the second clause. Thus, any difference in either the key word *Jake* or the following pause between the two sentences can be directly attributed to the length of material already spoken.

(15) a. Bob went to visit *Jake* while Mary went on a picnic.
b. Bob went to the hospital in Atlanta to visit *Jake* while Mary went on a picnic.

The results for 10 speakers showed no significant effect of lengthening for the segment marking the end of the longer clause [$p > .20$, $t = 0.77$, $df = 9$]. Likewise, there was no significant difference in the duration of the following pause for the two sentences [$p > .20$, $t = -.44$, $df = 9$]. It thus appears that utterance-internal lengthening at a clause boundary is influenced by the overall length of upcoming material but not by the amount of preceding material.

Planning: Clauses Versus Phrases

We have reviewed evidence showing that material yet to be spoken in an utterance exerts an influence on the timing of speech segments and affects fundamental frequency as well. We are now in a position to take a somewhat closer look at the nature of the speaker's planning and its influence on timing. The main question addressed here concerns exactly what it is that the speaker plans at the point in the utterance at which segmental lengthening is applied. Does the speaker simply note that an upcoming clause is to be uttered and consider a general estimate of its length? Or does the speaker look ahead to the next particular phrase and consider its length?

In order to test this latter possibility, we conducted an experiment in which the length of the upcoming NP in a new clause was varied, while holding the total length of the clause constant. An example sentence pair appears in (16):

(16) a. Kim has decided to take the dog that she bought to the *park* and Ed and the boys who work with my nephew went to the racetrack. (upcoming long NP)
b. Kim has decided to take the dog that she bought to the *park* and Erika plans to visit the museum that Amy works at. (upcoming long VP)

If the speaker's planning is in any way limited by phrase boundaries, we would expect that the duration of *park* would be longer in (16a) relative to (b), because the lengthened NP phrase in (a) immediately follows the key segment, whereas the lengthened VP in (b) does not. The results for 10 speakers showed no significant differences, however. These data suggest that, at the time when segmental lengthening at the clause boundary is programmed, the speaker considers the general length of the upcoming clause but not the separate lengths of its component constituents.

It remains to be determined whether the speaker's representation of upcoming material is computed in terms of number of syllables, number of words, number of syntactic constituents, or is simply a visual representation of the general length of the typewritten utterances used in this particular task. If the preceding experiment had revealed significant differences, we could dispose of this latter task-dependent possibility. However, we cannot yet conclude that the effects of planning observed here are representative of speech independent of oral reading.

Evidence from Blocking of Phonological Rules

In the studies of speech planning discussed so far, it was found that speakers program attributes of F_0 and timing partially on the basis of the length of material yet to be spoken. Aside from this global planning effect, we attempted to study short-range aspects of planning by examining the operation of phonological rules across word boundaries. Consider the rule of Alveolar Flapping, which converts an intervocalic alveolar stop (/d/ or /t/ in English, optionally preceded by /r/ or /n/) into a flap /ɾ/ in the environment of an immediately following vowel. This rule may apply both within words (e.g., *party* → parɾi) and across word boundaries (e.g., *eat a* → iɾə). An interesting feature of this phonological rule is that its application critically depends on the existence of a specific type of phonetic segment on each side of the boundary. Thus, in order for the phonological rule to apply across a word boundary, the speaker must have detailed information about the nature of the segments in both words available simultaneously. Here, then, is another demonstration of "look ahead" in speech. As the speaker utters the word-final phoneme of "eat" in the phrase "eat a pie," he or she may apply Alveolar Flapping, provided that the speaker is aware that the next word begins with a vowel.

For our purposes, it is interesting to consider cases in which this kind of short-term planning is blocked. We may infer from such cases that the speaker's domain of processing either does not simultaneously include the words on both sides of the boundary or else includes a boundary marker prohibiting the application of phonological rules across it. Later, we review some converging evidence from speech errors that supports the former interpretation.

One such constraint was demonstrated by Egido and Cooper (1980). Their study included a test of the occurrence of Alveolar Flapping in sentence pairs that contained matched phonetic material at the key word boundary, but that varied in syntactic structure at this site. An example is provided by the ambiguous string in (17), whose alternative meanings appear in (17') and (17'').

(17) For those of you who'd like to *eat early* lunch will be served.
(17') Lunch will be served for those of you who'd like to eat early.
(17'') An early lunch will be served for those of you who'd like to eat.

Whereas no major syntactic boundary occurs at the key site for reading (17') of (17), a major clause boundary intervenes at this location for reading (17''). The results showed that speakers often flapped at the key site in (17) when (17') was the intended meaning, but not reading (17''). This difference was very striking for each of four sentence pairs tested. For 10 speakers, flapping was observed in the (17') versions for 60% of the utterances, whereas no flapping whatsoever occurred in the (17'') versions.

By itself, this effect does not conclusively demonstrate an influence of syntactic structure. Speakers may also insert a breathing pause at the key site for reading (17''), so it is conceivable that this pause serves as the real blocking agent. To investigate this possibility, we measured the pause durations at the key site for this reading of (17). A total of 55% of these utterances, none of which were flapped, contained pause intervals of less than 150 msec. It appears that breathing pauses cannot occur within such a short silent interval (Grosjean & Collins, 1977); the silent intervals for these utterances represented the stop gap for the word-final [t]. Thus, pausing for breath is not a necessary condition for the blocking of Alveolar Flapping. In addition, data for other cross-word phonological rules indicates that no relation occurs between the existence and/or magnitude of nonbreathing pauses and the blocking of phonological rules (Cooper, 1980). It thus seems reasonable to attribute the blocking effect exhibited here to a direct syntactic influence. In particular, it appears that at the stage of coding where phonological rules are applied, the speaker's domain of processing typically does not extend beyond major clause boundaries. Because of this constraint on processing domains, the speakers cannot look ahead to consider the nature of the segment following the key word boundary in the (17'') version of sentences like (17). Hence, Alveolar Flapping cannot be applied.

This area of inquiry is of special interest because it permits us to draw a parallel between observations of spontaneous speech and results obtained with our experimental paradigm. At the outset of this chapter, we mentioned studies of speech errors that involve the exchange of phonemes (e.g., *D*ick and *J*ane → *J*ick and *D*ane). Recall that these studies indicate that phoneme exchange errors almost never occur across a major clause boundary. Similarly, in our experimental study of blocking, we found that the cross-word phonological rule of Alveolar Flapping typically fails to operate across major clauses. The speaker's *simultaneous* representation of phonemic material on either side of a given constituent boundary is critical for both the occurrence of phoneme exchange errors and the application of Alveolar Flapping. Therefore, both the speech error data and the blocking effect observed by Egido and Cooper may be accounted for by the same constraint on the domain over which a detailed phonemic representation is computed during speech production.

As in the case of F_0 contours, further experimental study of the effect of syntax on the blocking of cross-word phonological rules is needed in order to obtain more detailed information about the types of major syntactic boundaries that constrain look-ahead in speech production. At present, we can only state that the juncture between main clauses constitutes one such boundary.

Evidence from Spontaneous Speech

A recent study based on spontaneous speech also provides information concerning the role of planning during ongoing speech production. While interviewing speakers, Ford and Holmes (1978) randomly presented tones as the interviewees talked. The speakers were asked to respond to each tone by pressing a button. Reaction times were measured and analyzed in an attempt to determine whether RT's would vary as a function of the tone's occurrence at various locations within an utterance. Ford and Holmes found that RT's were slower for tones placed at the ends of clauses, compared with RT's for tones placed at the beginnings of clauses. The slower RT's were accounted for in terms of an increase in the speaker's processing load at clause endings. In addition, Ford and Holmes were able to attribute this increase in processing load to planning as opposed to execution, because the effect on RT was restricted to clause boundaries that did not coincide with the ends of entire sentences.

Taken together, the tone monitoring task of Ford and Holmes and our own analysis of F_0 contours, segment durations, and the blocking of phonological rules provide effective means of obtaining information about the planning operations engaged in by the speaker during the ongoing production of speech. Continued use of these methods with both spontaneous speech and practiced reading should enable us to determine whether the speaker's planning operations differ for each of these two types of speech.

CONCLUSION

We have shown here that measurable properties of the speech wave, including segment and pause durations, fundamental frequency, and the effects of phonological rule-blocking, can provide valuable information about the nature of the speaker's internal programming of an utterance. In particular, speech wave properties can serve as a basis for making inferences about the types of syntactic constituents that are coded in speech production as well as about general features of planning and execution. No doubt there exist many aspects of internal processing that are not faithfully reflected by observable variations in speech wave parameters; yet, a large number of syntactic and extrasyntactic attributes are so reflected, and these can now be studied with a relatively high degree of experimental control and precision of measurement, using a task that approximates ordinary speaking.

In this chapter, we began with a discussion of how the acoustic consequences of speech timing can be used as a tool with which to uncover aspects of the speaker's syntactic representation, using as our example the issue of whether this representation contains a node Verb Phrase that dominates nodes like Verb and Noun Phrase. The evidence from speech timing supported the existence of the Verb Phrase as one of the major structures represented in speech production.

In addition to the question of structural representation, we considered some issues of information processing that pertain to the real-time computation of constituent structures. Our discussion showed that the intuitive directions of information flow, left-to-right and top-down, could not yet be established empirically as descriptions of the flow of information at the stage of coding at which speech timing effects are applied.

Finally, we discussed speech planning in order to show how speakers consider yet to be spoken material in determining phonetic parameters of segments that are currently being executed. Evidence from speech properties, including fundamental frequency contours, timing, and the application of phonological rules, was cited to provide documentation of both long-range and short-range speech planning. Experiments in segmental timing were presented, showing that the magnitude of clause-final lengthening depends on the length of upcoming material.

A great deal remains to be understood about the precise nature of speech planning, particularly its temporal characteristics. For example, we know very little about whether the speaker plans continuously during the utterance of phrases or whether planning of the sort described here is restricted to specific syntactic boundary locations. Finally, we need to know much more about precisely what is being planned during the execution of an utterance. The method of One-Sided Variation introduced here provides an experimental framework for pursuing these questions.

ACKNOWLEDGMENTS

This study was supported by NIH Grant NS-13028. Portions of this chapter are adapted with permission from Cooper and Paccia-Cooper (1980), copyrighted by the President and Fellows of Harvard College. The experimental work presented here was conducted while the authors were at the MIT Research Laboratory of Electronics. We thank Professor Kenneth N. Stevens for providing facilities, and Julie Meister for assistance. In addition, thanks go to Steven Pinker and the editors of this volume for their helpful suggestions.

REFERENCES

Bierwisch, M. Regln für die Intonation deutscher Satze. *Studia Grammatica,* 1966, *7,* 99–201.

Bolinger, D. Intonation as a universal. In *Proceedings of Linguistics IX.* The Hague: Mouton, 1964, 833–844.

Boomer, D. S., & Laver, J. D. M. Slips of the tongue. *The British Journal of Disorders of Communication,* 1968, *3,* 2–12.

Chomsky, N. *Syntactic structures.* The Hague: Mouton, 1957.

Chomsky, N. Conditions on transformatjons. In S. R. Anderson & P. Kiparsky (Eds.), *A festschrift for Morris Halle.* New York: Holt, Rinehart & Winston, 1973.

Cooper, W. E. Syntactic-to-phonetic coding. In B. Butterworth (Ed.), *Language production*. New York: Academic Press, 1980.

Cooper, W. E., & Paccia-Cooper, J. *Syntax and speech*. Cambridge, Mass.: Harvard University Press, 1980.

Cooper, W. E., Paccia, J. M., & Lapointe, S. G. Hierarchical coding in speech timing. *Cognitive Psychology*, 1978, *10*, 154–177.

Cutler, A., & Norris, D. Monitoring sentence comprehension. In W. E. Cooper & E. C. T. Walker (Eds.), *Sentence processing: Psycholinguistic studies presented to Merrill Garrett*. Hillsdale, N.J.: Lawrence Erlbaum Associates, 1979.

Egido, C., & Cooper, W. E. Syntactic blocking of alveolar flapping in speech production: The role of syntactic boundaries and deletion sites. *Journal of Phonetics*, 1980, *8*, 175–184.

Fay, D. Performing transformations. In R. A. Cole (Ed.), *Perception and production of fluent speech*. Hillsdale, N.J.: Lawrence Erlbaum Associates, 1979.

Fodor, J. A., Bever, T. G., & Garrett, M. F. *The psychology of language: An introduction to psycholinguistics and generative grammar*. New York: McGraw-Hill, 1974.

Ford, M., & Holmes, V. M. Planning units and syntax in sentence production. *Cognition*, 1978, *6*, 35–53.

Forster, K. I. Left to right processes in the construction of sentences. *Journal of Verbal Learning and Verbal Behavior*, 1966, *5*, 285–291.

Forster, K. I. Sentence completion latencies as a function of constituent structure. *Journal of Verbal Learning and Verbal Behavior*, 1967, *6*, 878–883.

Fromkin, V. A. The non-anomalous nature of anomalous utterances. *Language*, 1971, *47*, 27–52.

Garrett, M. F. The analysis of sentence production. In G. Bower (Ed.), *Advances in learning theory and motivation* (Vol. 9). New York: Academic Press, 1975.

Goldman-Eisler, F. *Psycholinguistics: Experiments in spontaneous speech*. New York: Academic Press, 1968.

Grimes, C. Personal communication, May 18, 1978.

Grosjean, F., & Collins, M. *Breathing, pausing and reading*. Unpublished manuscript, 1977.

Grosjean, F., Grosjean, L., & Lane, H. The patterns of silence: Performance structures in sentence production. *Cognitive Psychology*, 1979, *11*, 58–81.

Henderson, A., Goldman-Eisler, F., & Skarbek, A. The common value of pausing time in spontaneous speech. *Quarterly Journal of Experimental Psychology*, 1965, *17*, 343–345.

Huggins, A. W. F. A facility for studying perception of timing in natural speech. *Quarterly Progress Report of the MIT Research Laboratory of Electronics*, 1969, *95*, 81–84.

Jackendoff, R. S. $\bar{X}$ *syntax: A study of phrase structure*. Cambridge, Mass.: MIT Press, 1977.

Keyser, S. J., & Postal, P. M. *Beginning English grammar*. New York: Harper & Row, 1976.

Klatt, D. Linguistic uses of segmental duration in English: Acoustic and perceptual evidence. *Journal of the Acoustical Society of America*, 1976, *59*, 1208–1221.

Liberman, M. Personal communication, May 18, 1978.

Maeda, S. *A characterization of American English intonation*. Unpublished doctoral dissertation, Massachusetts Institute of Technology, 1976.

Marslen-Wilson, W. D., & Welch, A. Processing interactions and lexical access during word recognition in continuous speech. *Cognitive Psychology*, 1978, *10*, 29–63.

O'Shaughnessy, D. *Modelling fundamental frequency, and its relationship to syntax, semantics, and phonetics*. Unpublished doctoral dissertation, Massachusetts Institute of Technology, 1976.

Shattuck-Hufnagel, S. Speech errors as evidence for a serial-ordering mechanism in sentence production. In W. E. Cooper & E. C. T. Walker (Eds.), *Sentence processing: Psycholinguistic studies presented to Merrill Garrett*. Hillsdale, N.J.: Lawrence Erlbaum Associates, 1979.

Sorensen, J. M., & Cooper, W. E. Syntactic coding of fundamental frequency in speech production. In R. A. Cole (Ed.), *Perception and production of fluent speech*. Hillsdale, N.J.: Lawrence Erlbaum Associates, 1980.

Townsend, J. T. Some results on the identifiability of parallel and serial processes. *British Journal of Mathematical and Statistical Psychology,* 1972, *25,* 168–199.

Townsend, J. T. Issues and models concerning the processing of a finite number of inputs. In B. H. Kantowitz (Ed), *Human information processing: Tutorials in performance and cognition.* Hillsdale, N.J.: Lawrence Erlbaum Associates, 1974.

Webb, R., Williams, F., & Minifie, F. Effects of verbal decision behavior upon respiration during speech production. *Journal of Speech and Hearing Research,* 1967, *10,* 49–56.

Yngve, V.H. A model and a hypothesis for language structure. *Proceedings of the American Philosophical Society,* 1960, *104,* 444–466.

Author Index

Subject Index